BAT MAN

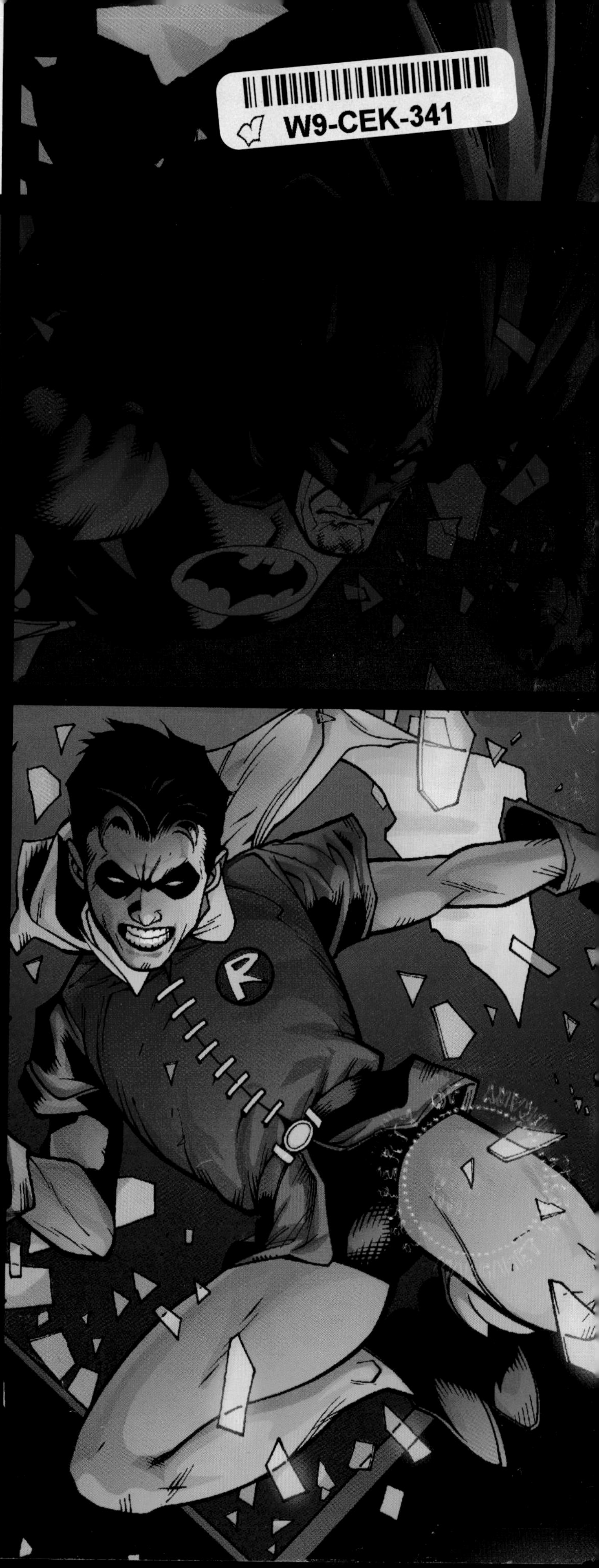

C COMICS
YORK, NEW YORK

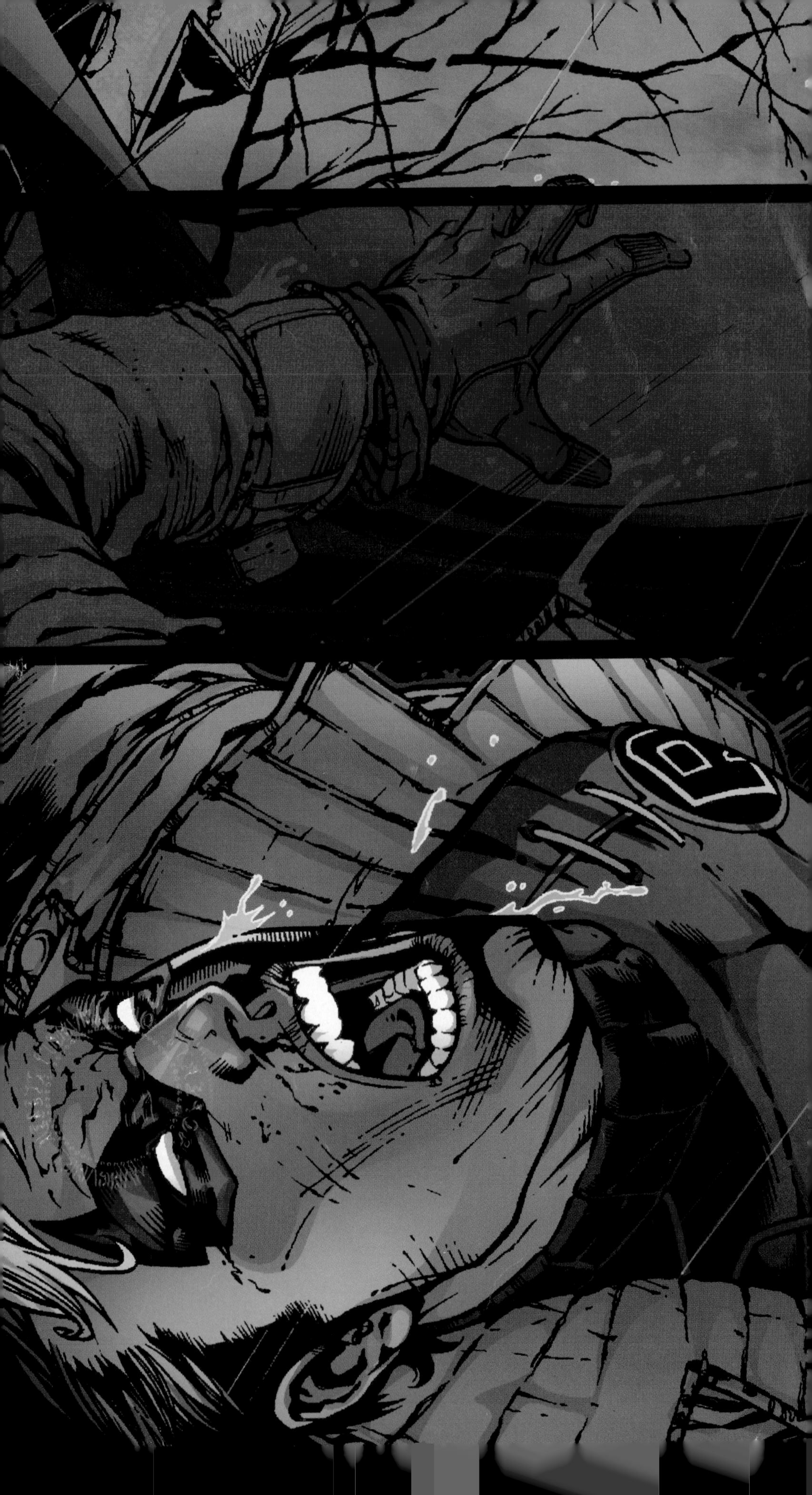

BATMAN

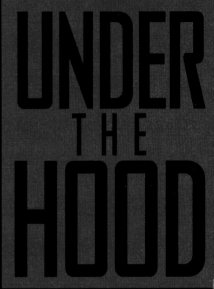

UNDER THE HOOD

JUDD WINICK
WRITER

**DOUG MAHNKE
SHANE DAVIS
ERIC BATTLE**
PENCILLERS

**TOM NGUYEN
RODNEY RAMOS
WAYNE FAUCHER
LARY STUCKER
MARK MORALES**
INKERS

ALEX SINCLAIR
COLORIST

**PAT BROSSEAU
JARED K. FLETCHER
TRAVIS LANHAM**
LETTERERS

**JOCK
SHANE DAVIS**
ORIGINAL COVERS

BATMAN CREATED BY
BOB KANE

DC COMICS

Dan DiDio SENIOR VP-EXECUTIVE EDITOR
Bob Schreck EDITOR-ORIGINAL SERIES
Brandon Montclare ASSISTANT EDITOR-ORIGINAL SERIES
Bob Joy EDITOR-COLLECTED EDITION
Robbin Brosterman SENIOR ART DIRECTOR
Paul Levitz PRESIDENT & PUBLISHER
Georg Brewer VP-DESIGN & DC DIRECT CREATIVE
Richard Bruning SENIOR VP-CREATIVE DIRECTOR
Patrick Caldon EXECUTIVE VP-FINANCE & OPERATIONS
Chris Caramalis VP-FINANCE
John Cunningham VP-MARKETING
Terri Cunningham VP-MANAGING EDITOR
Stephanie Fierman SENIOR VP-SALES & MARKETING
Alison Gill VP-MANUFACTURING
Rich Johnson VP-BOOK TRADE SALES
Hank Kanalz VP-GENERAL MANAGER, WILDSTORM
Lillian Laserson SENIOR VP & GENERAL COUNSEL
Jim Lee EDITORIAL DIRECTOR-WILDSTORM
Paula Lowitt SENIOR VP-BUSINESS & LEGAL AFFAIRS
David McKillips VP-ADVERTISING & CUSTOM PUBLISHING
John Nee VP-BUSINESS DEVELOPMENT
Gregory Noveck SENIOR VP-CREATIVE AFFAIRS
Cheryl Rubin SENIOR VP-BRAND MANAGEMENT
Jeff Trojan VP-BUSINESS DEVELOPMENT, DC DIRECT
Bob Wayne VP-SALES

BATMAN: UNDER THE HOOD, vol. 2

PUBLISHED BY DC COMICS.
COVER, INTRODUCTION AND COMPILATION
COPYRIGHT © 2006 DC COMICS.
ALL RIGHTS RESERVED.

ORIGINALLY PUBLISHED IN SINGLE
MAGAZINE FORM IN BATMAN 645-650,
COPYRIGHT © 2005, 2006 DC COMICS.
BATMAN ANNUAL 25, COPYRIGHT
© 2006 DC COMICS.

DC COMICS,
1700 BROADWAY, NEW YORK, NY 10019
A WARNER BROS. ENTERTAINMENT COMPANY
PRINTED IN CANADA. FIRST PRINTING.
ISBN: 1-4012-0901-7
ISBN 13: 978-1-4012-0901-8

COVER ART BY JOCK

PUBLICATION DESIGN BY
AMIE BROCKWAY-METCALF

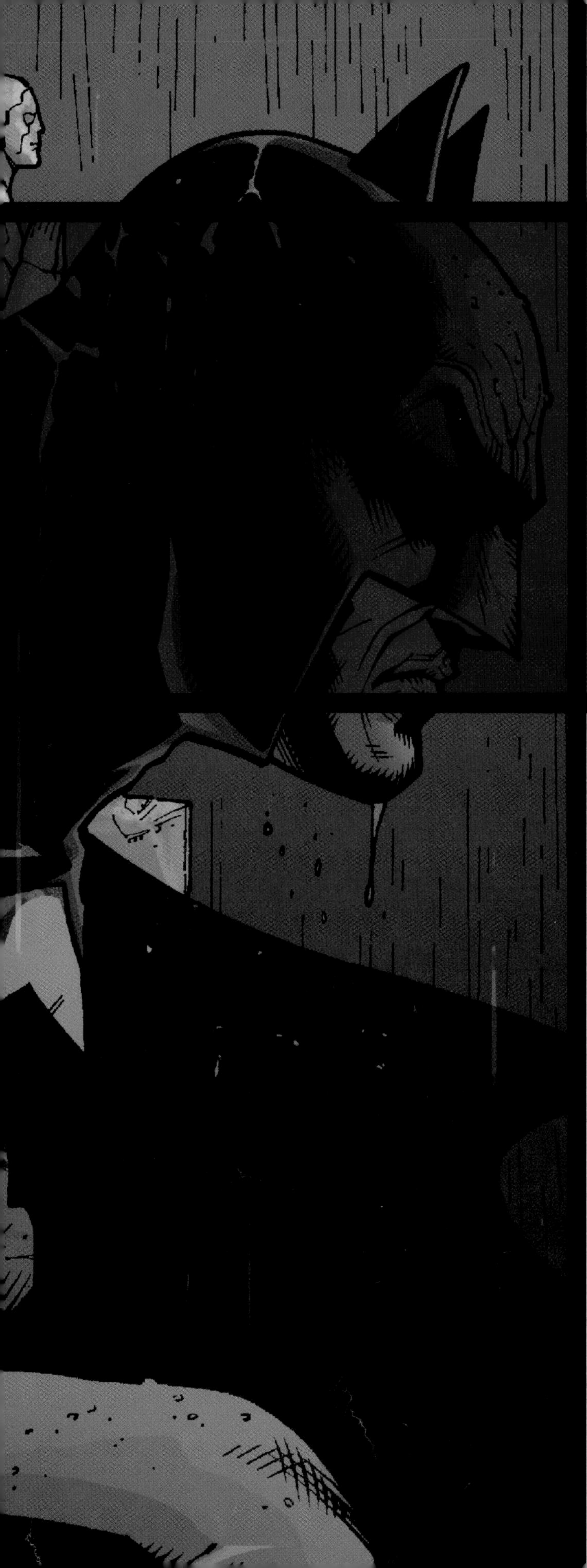

CAST OF CHARACTERS

B A T M A N

Dedicated to ridding the world of crime since the callous murder of his parents, billionaire Bruce Wayne dons the cape and cowl of the Dark Knight to battle evil from the shadows of Gotham City. Over the years, Batman has suffered the loss of two crime-fighting partners: Jason Todd, the second person to take on the mantle of Robin, and Stephanie Brown, formerly the Spoiler and for a brief period of time the fourth Robin, who died due to injuries inflicted by the Black Mask.

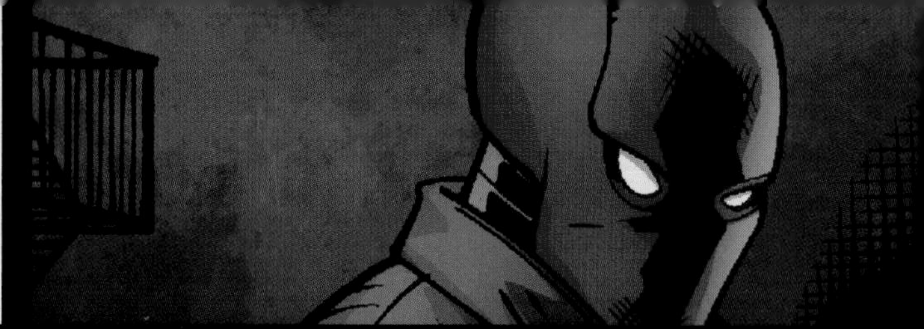

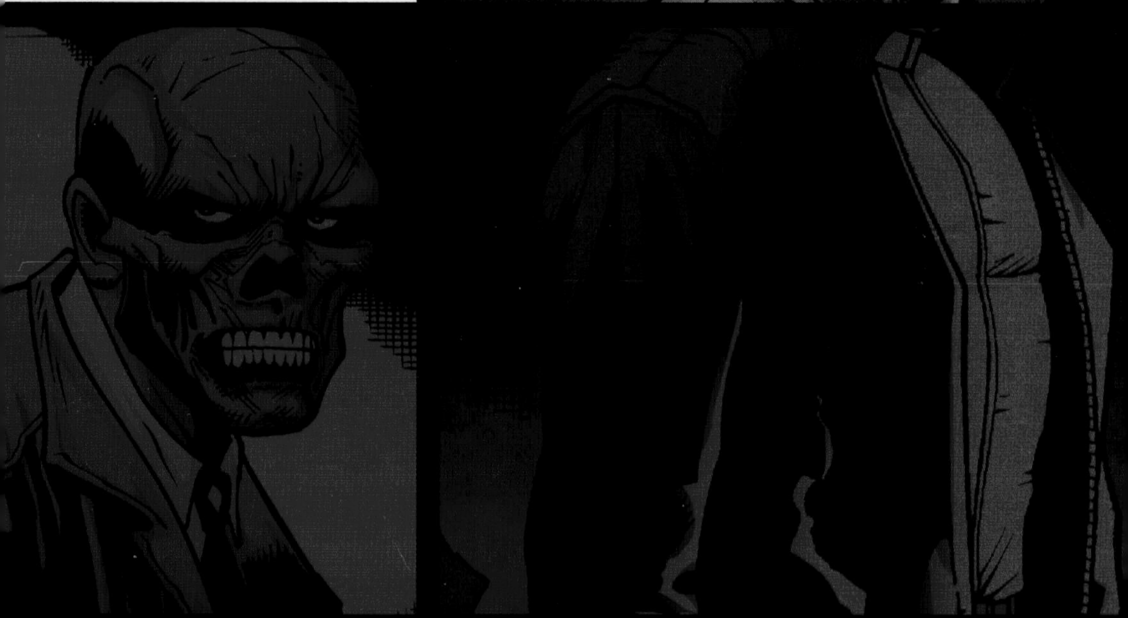

BLACK MASK

Roman Sionis's face was horribly burned in a fire during a fight with the Batman. As the Black Mask, Roman has become one of the most feared and psychotic crime bosses in Gotham's underworld. His preferred form of execution is slow, methodical torture, usually focusing on the face. During Gotham's recent gang war, Black Mask has managed to take control over all crime in the city. All criminals must pledge their allegiance to him, or die.

RED HOOD

Jason Todd was a cocky youth. Living on the mean streets of Gotham, he was forced to steal to survive. One night in the city's infamous Crime Alley, Jason found a very expensive set of tires to steal... what made these tires so special is that they were attached to the Batmobile. Admiring the teen's tenacity, Batman decided to train Jason to be his new partner. When Dick Grayson gave up the identity of Robin, Jason was the natural replacement. The combination of his impetuousness and inexperience as a crime-fighter made Jason a liability to the dynamic duo that Batman needed to correct. Before he could take action, the new Robin was killed by the Batman's oldest nemesis, the Joker.

Years later, a new scourge appeared in Gotham, the Red Hood. He is a menace to the heroes and the villains of this crime-riddled town. The Black Mask, Gotham's new crime boss, wants him dead for all of the operations he's ruined. Batman wants him stopped because of his ruthless methods, and no one fights crime in Gotham without Batman's permission. In a showdown with the Caped Crusader, Red Hood unmasked himself to reveal his identity as a very much alive Jason Todd.

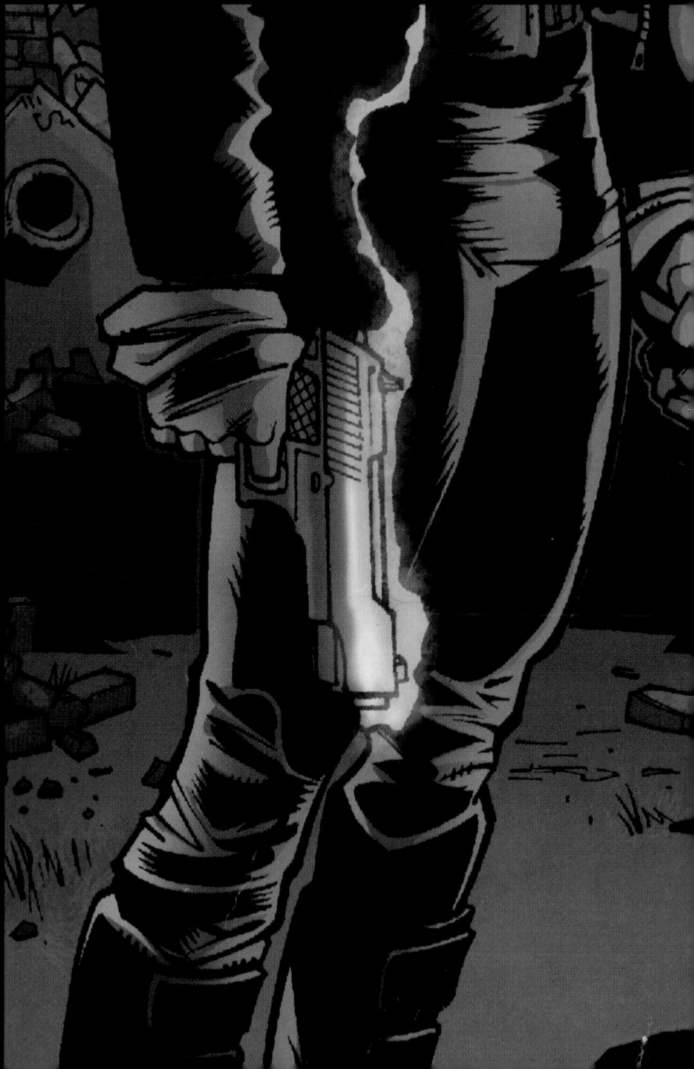

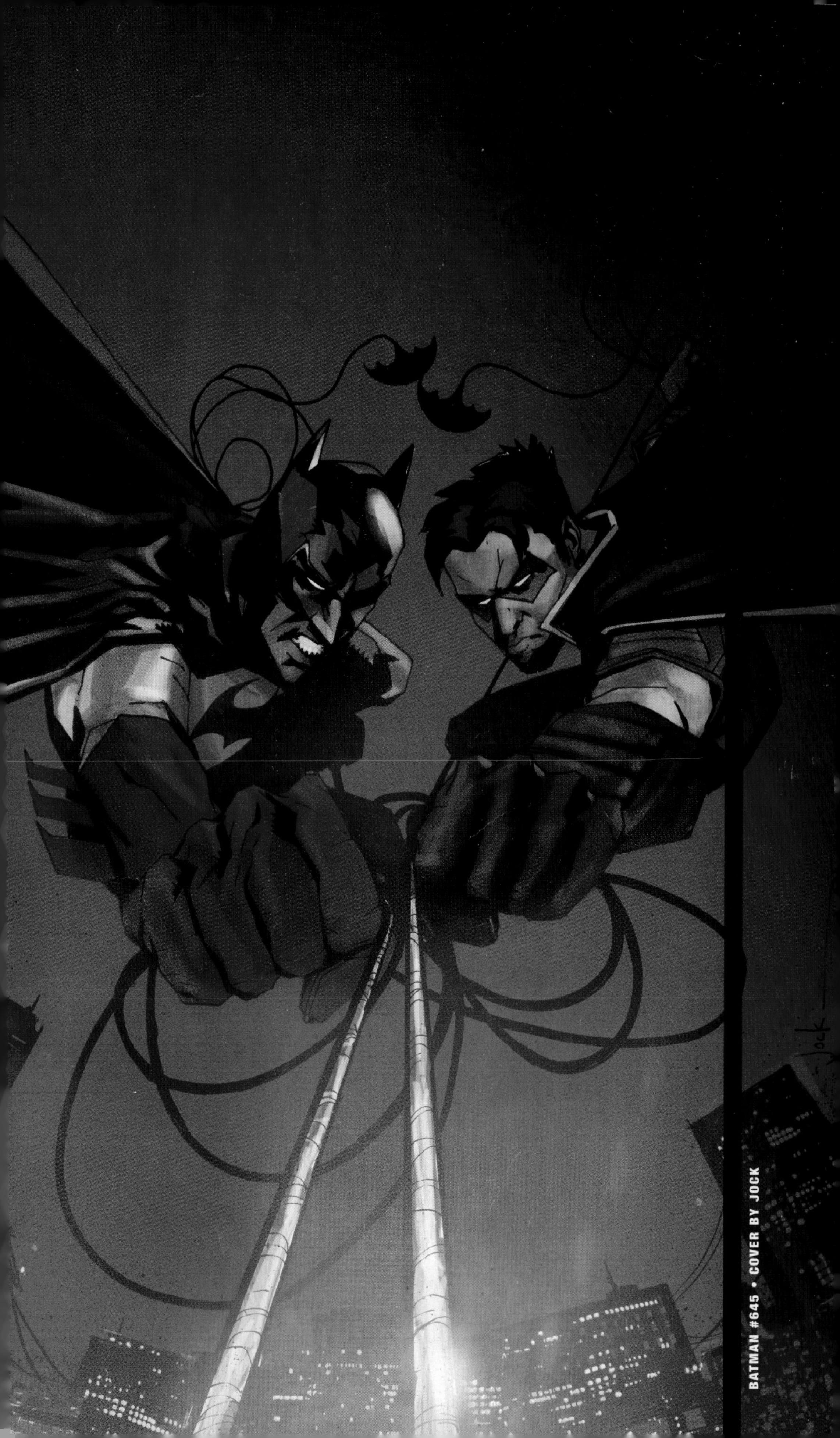

BATMAN #645 • COVER BY JOCK

CHAPTER 1

SHOW ME YESTERDAY, FOR I CAN'T FIND TODAY

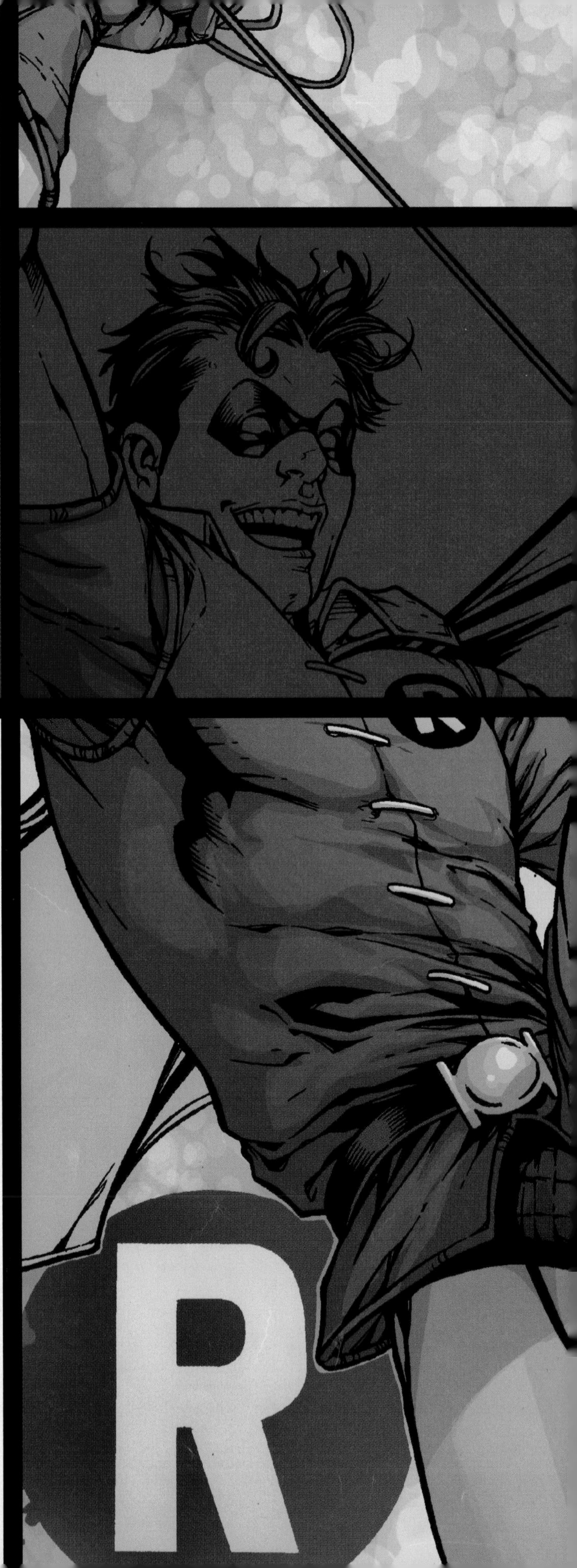

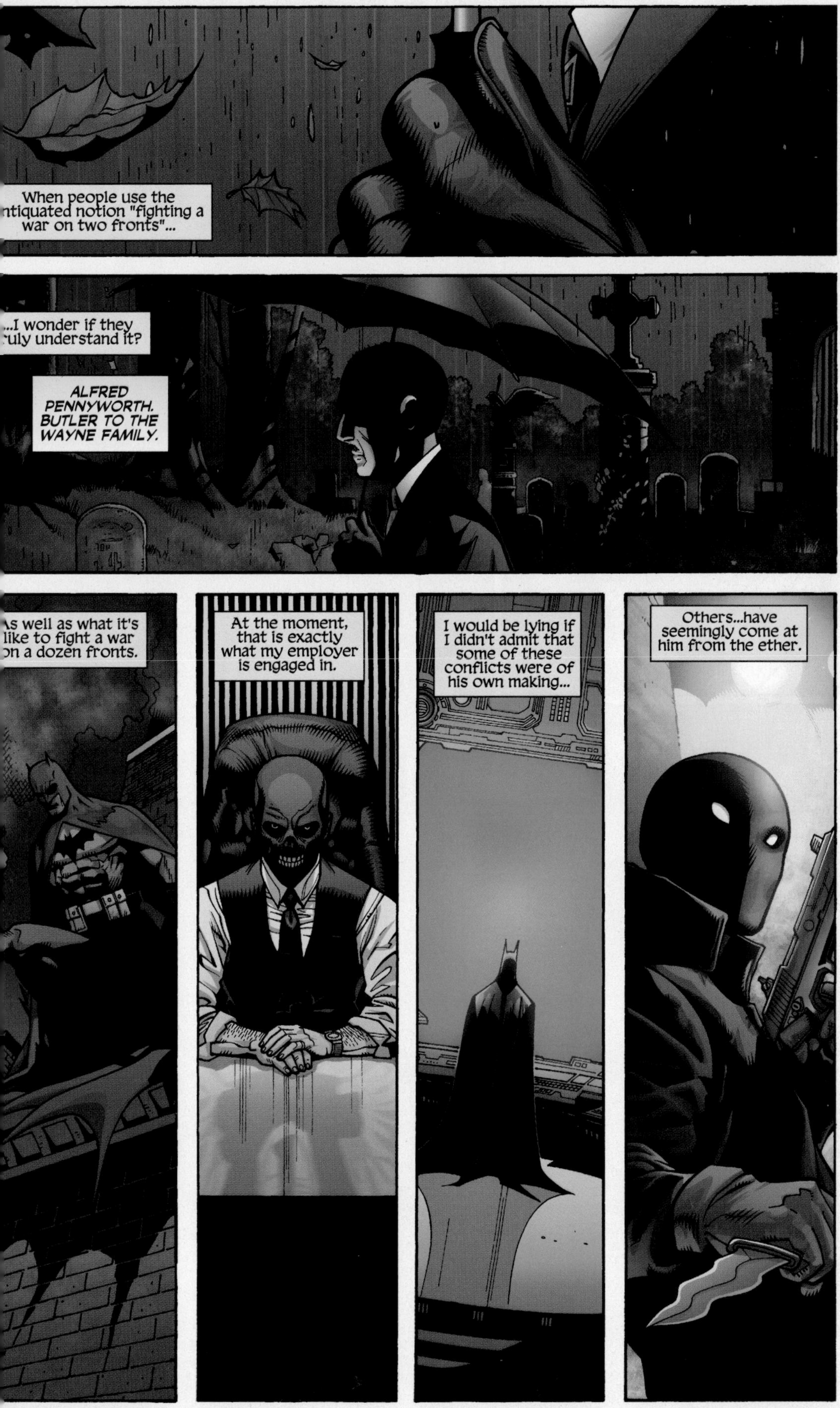
When people use the
ntiquated notion "fighting a
war on two fronts"...
...I wonder if they
ruly understand it?
ALFRED PENNYWORTH. BUTLER TO THE WAYNE FAMILY.
s well as what it's
like to fight a war
n a dozen fronts.
At the moment, that is exactly what my employer is engaged in.
I would be lying if I didn't admit that some of these conflicts were of his own making...
Others...have seemingly come at him from the ether.

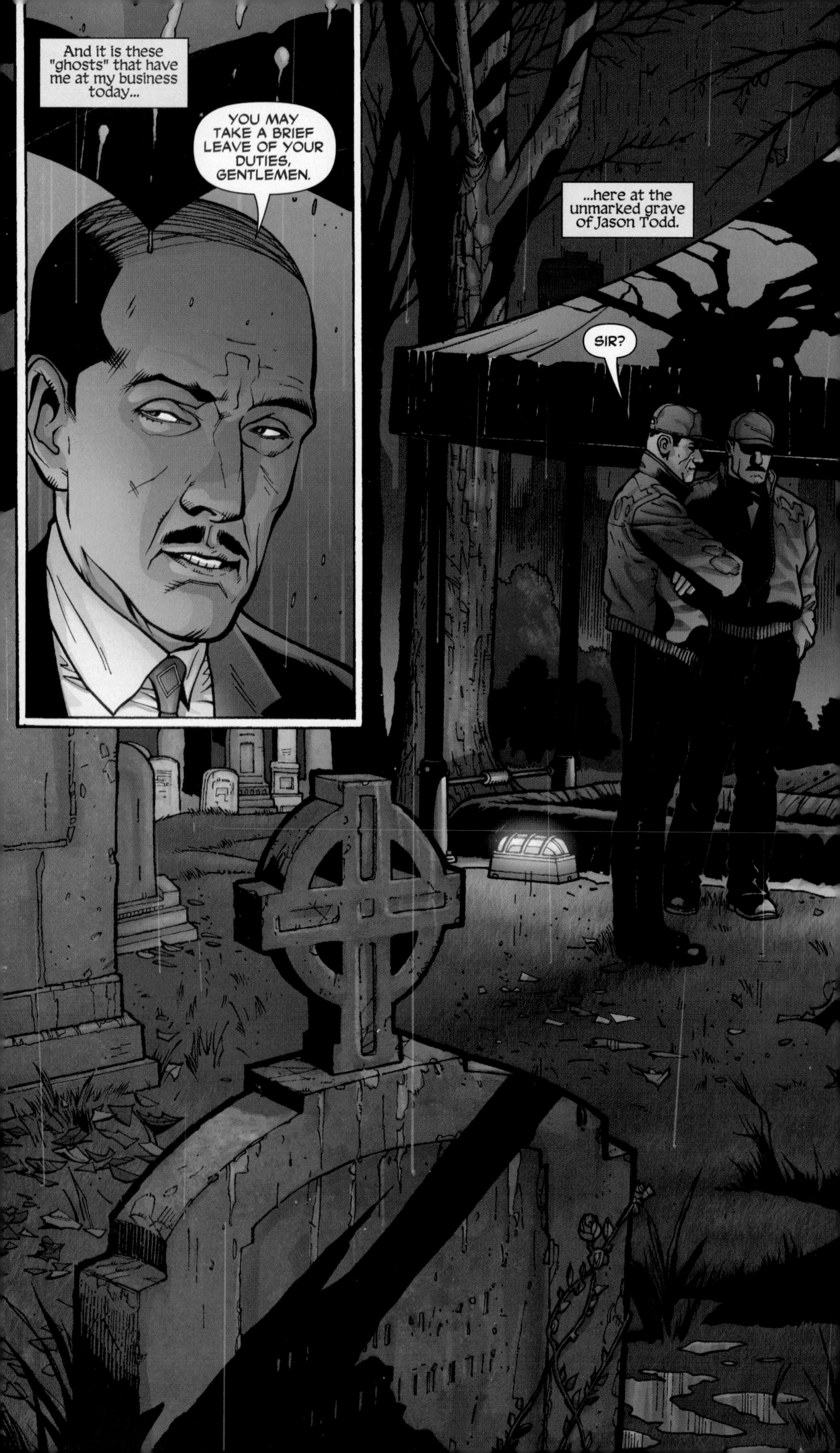
And it is these "ghosts" that have me at my business today...
YOU MAY TAKE A BRIEF LEAVE OF YOUR DUTIES, GENTLEMEN.
...here at the unmarked grave of Jason Todd.
SIR?

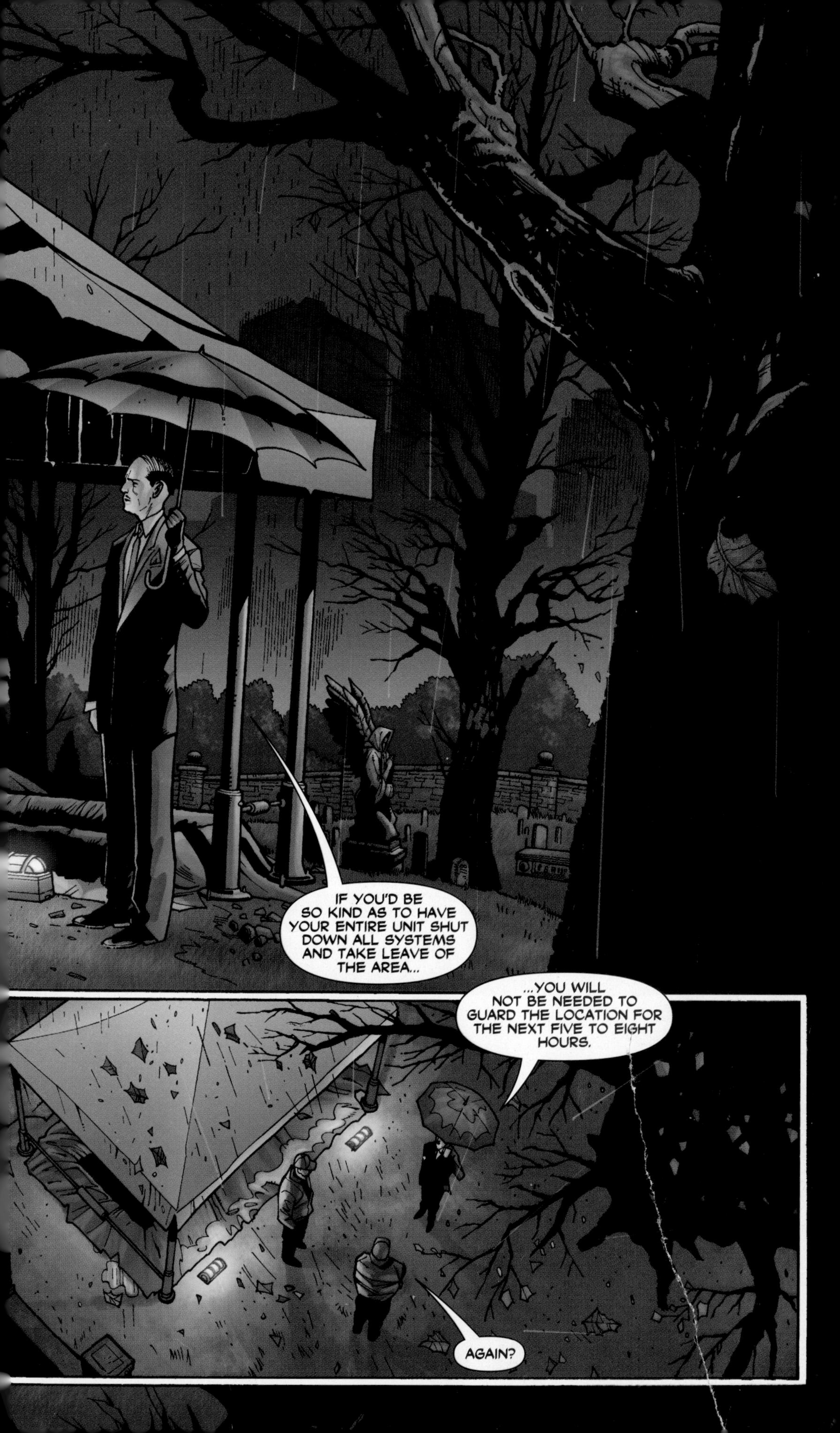
IF YOU'D BE SO KIND AS TO HAVE YOUR ENTIRE UNIT SHUT DOWN ALL SYSTEMS AND TAKE LEAVE OF THE AREA...
...YOU WILL NOT BE NEEDED TO GUARD THE LOCATION FOR THE NEXT FIVE TO EIGHT HOURS.
AGAIN?

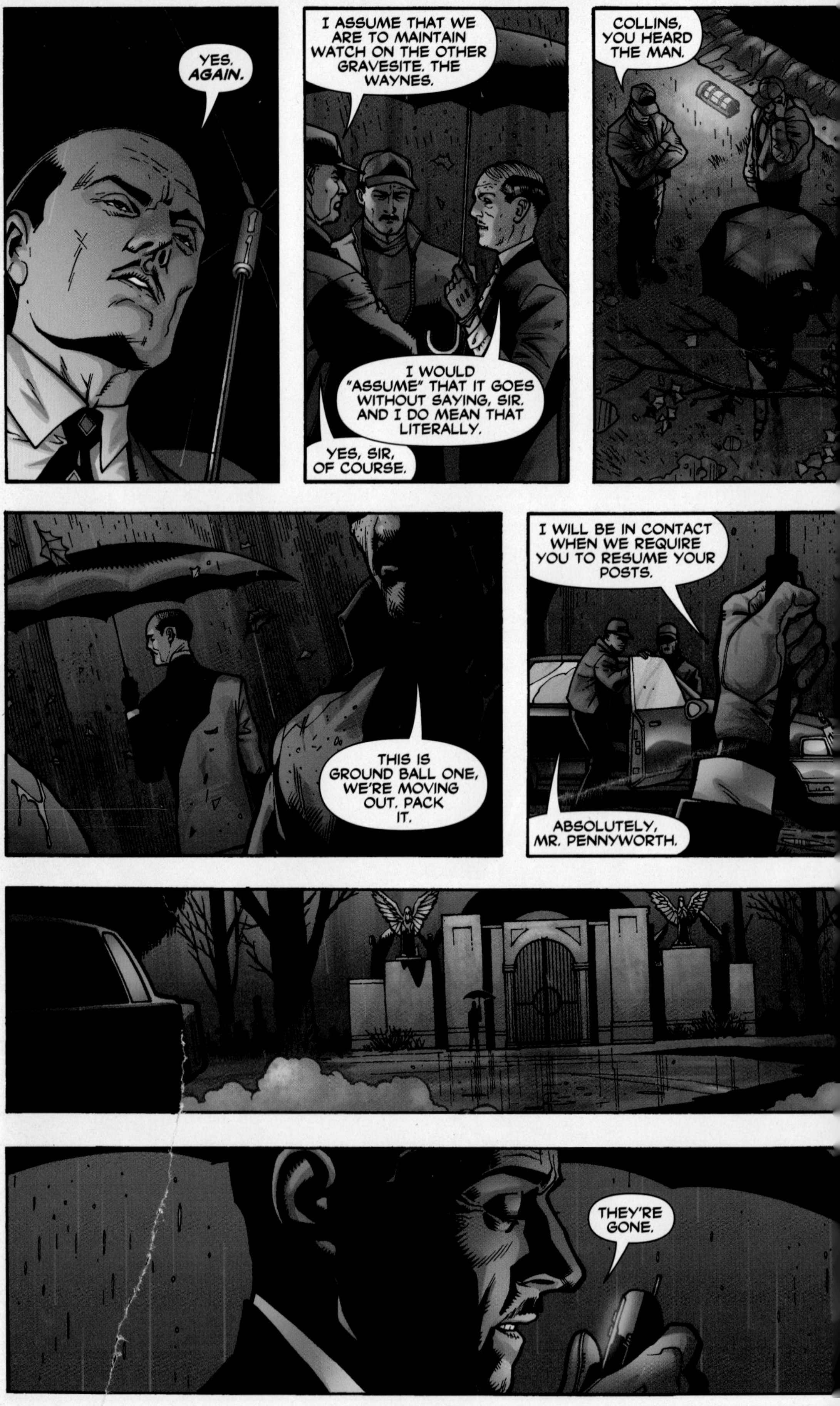
YES. AGAIN.
I ASSUME THAT WE ARE TO MAINTAIN WATCH ON THE OTHER GRAVESITE. THE WAYNES.
I WOULD "ASSUME" THAT IT GOES WITHOUT SAYING, SIR. AND I DO MEAN THAT LITERALLY.
YES, SIR, OF COURSE.
COLLINS, YOU HEARD THE MAN.
THIS IS GROUND BALL ONE, WE'RE MOVING OUT. PACK IT.
I WILL BE IN CONTACT WHEN WE REQUIRE YOU TO RESUME YOUR POSTS.
ABSOLUTELY, MR. PENNYWORTH.
THEY'RE GONE.

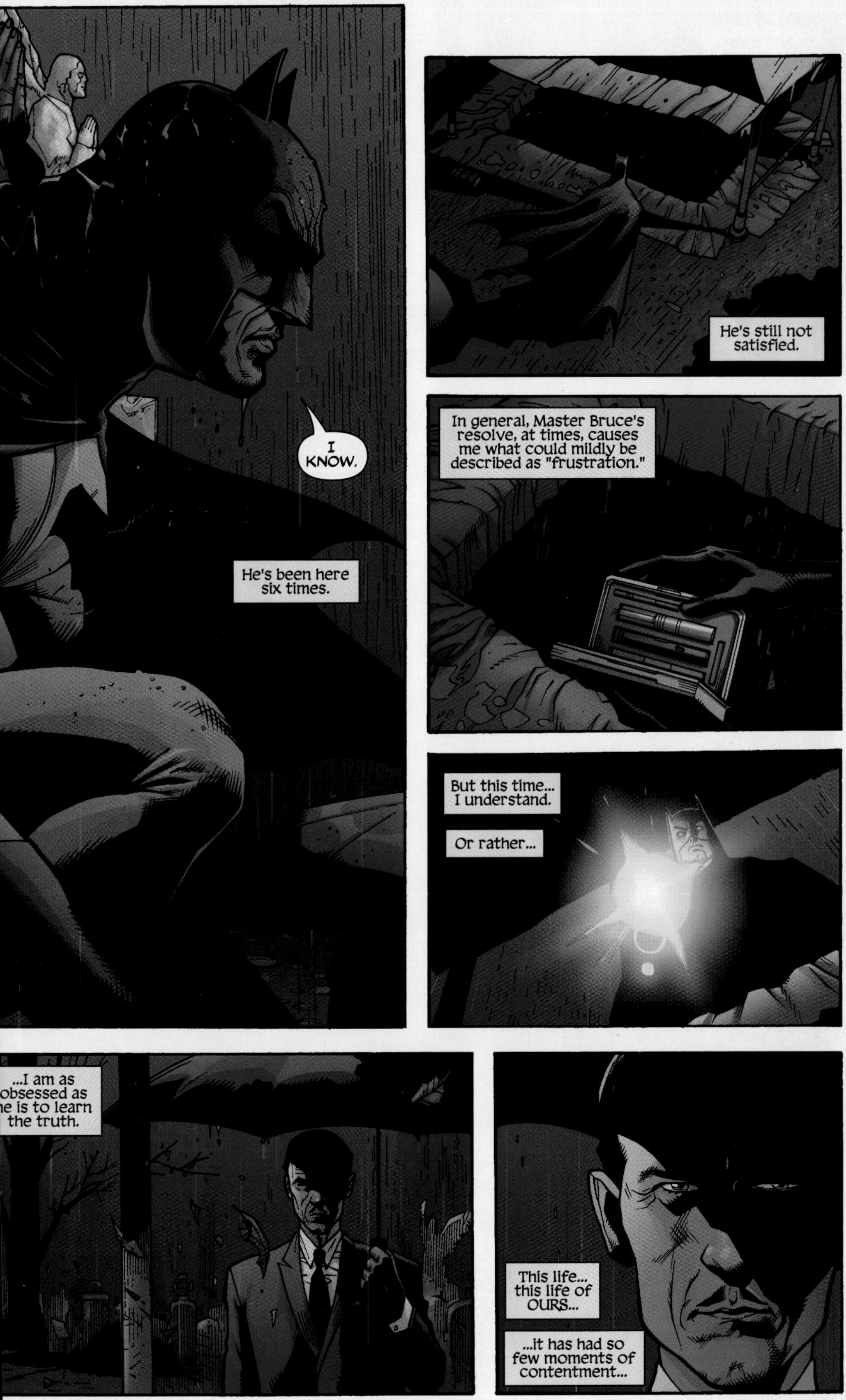
I KNOW.
He's been here six times.
He's still not satisfied.
In general, Master Bruce's resolve, at times, causes me what could mildly be described as "frustration."
But this time... I understand.
Or rather...
...I am as obsessed as he is to learn the truth.
This life... this life of OURS...
...it has had so few moments of contentment...

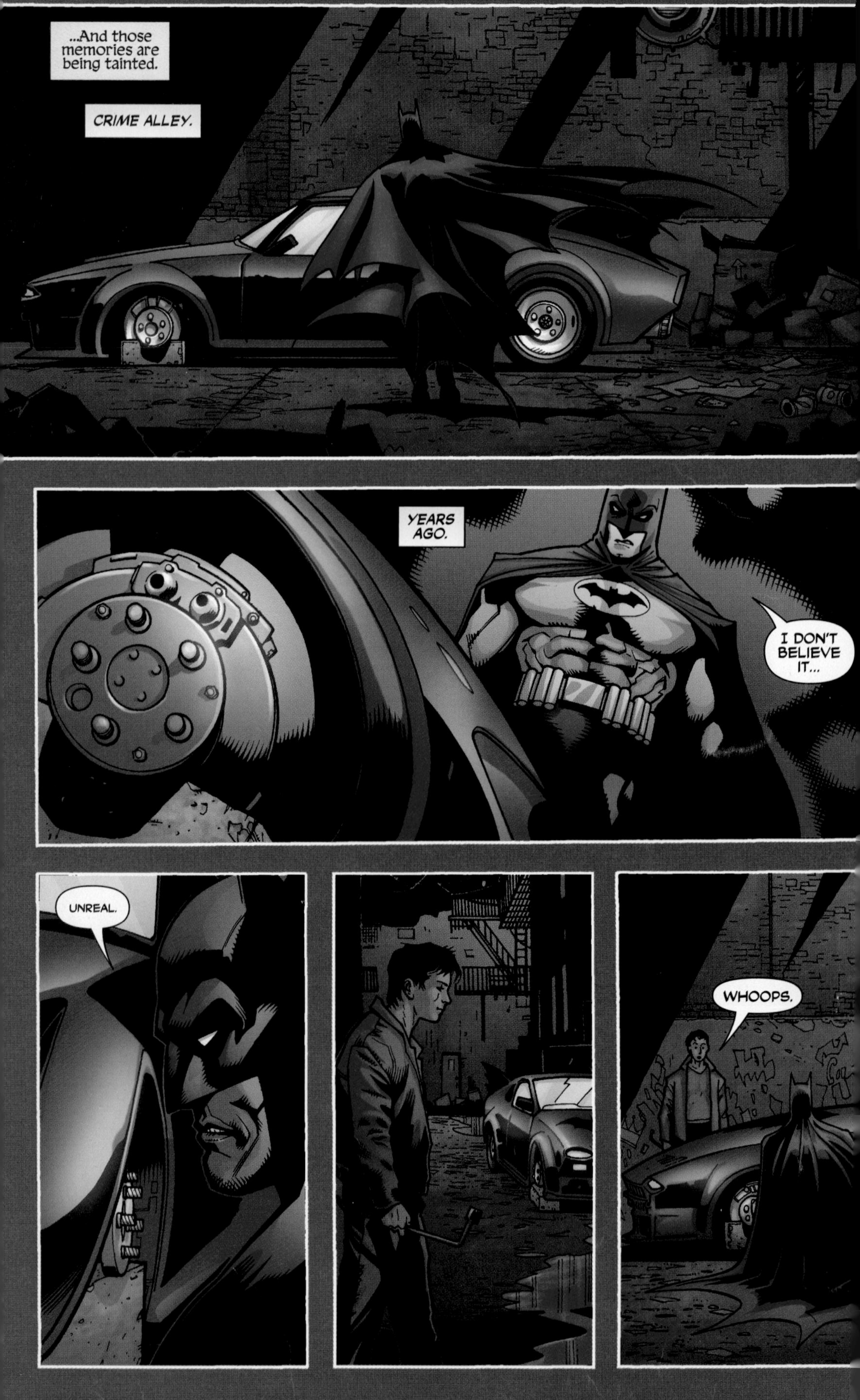
...And those memories are being tainted.
CRIME ALLEY.
YEARS AGO.
I DON'T BELIEVE IT...
UNREAL.
WHOOPS.

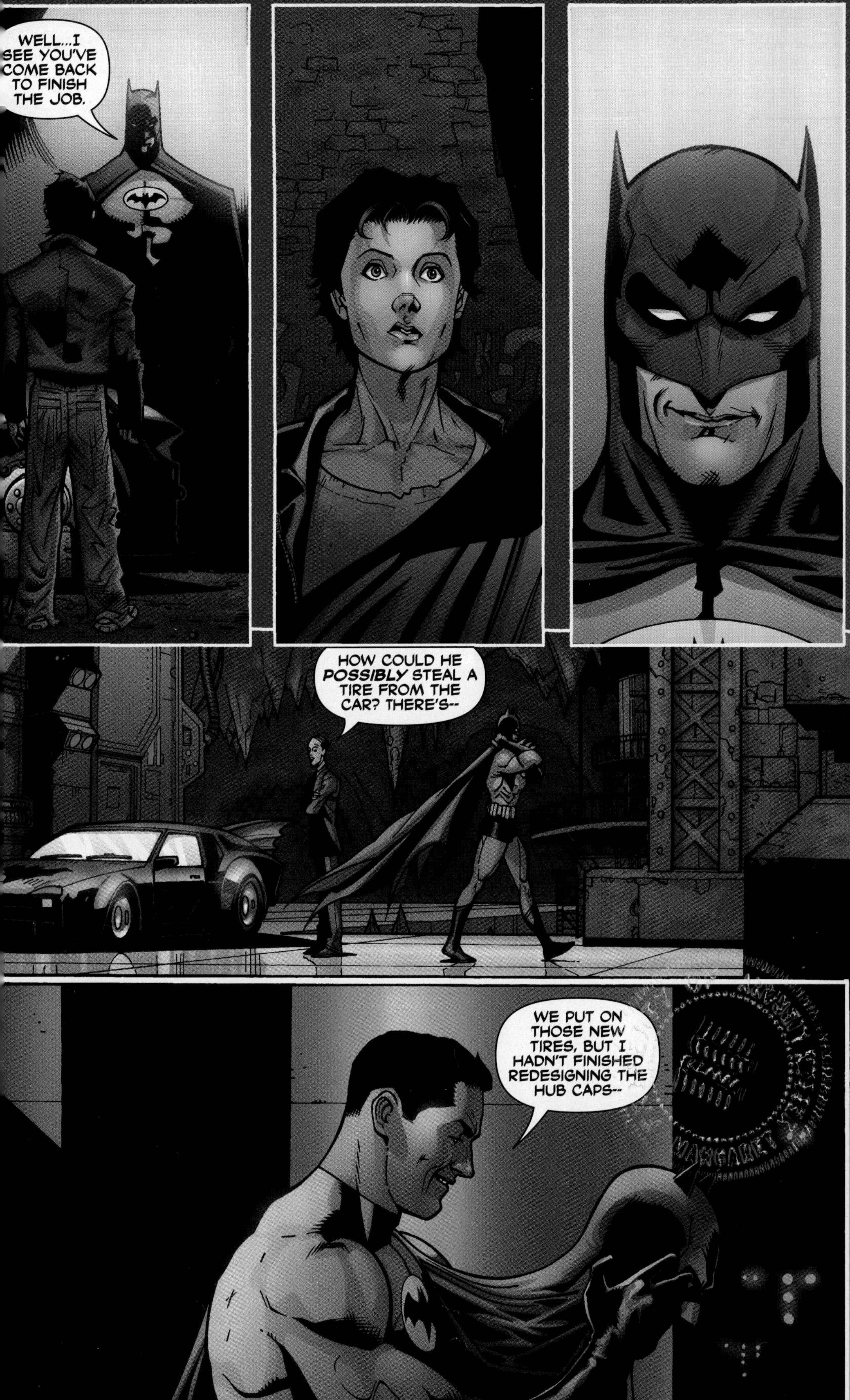
WELL...I SEE YOU'VE COME BACK TO FINISH THE JOB.
HOW COULD HE *POSSIBLY* STEAL A TIRE FROM THE CAR? THERE'S--
WE PUT ON THOSE NEW TIRES, BUT I HADN'T FINISHED REDESIGNING THE HUB CAPS--

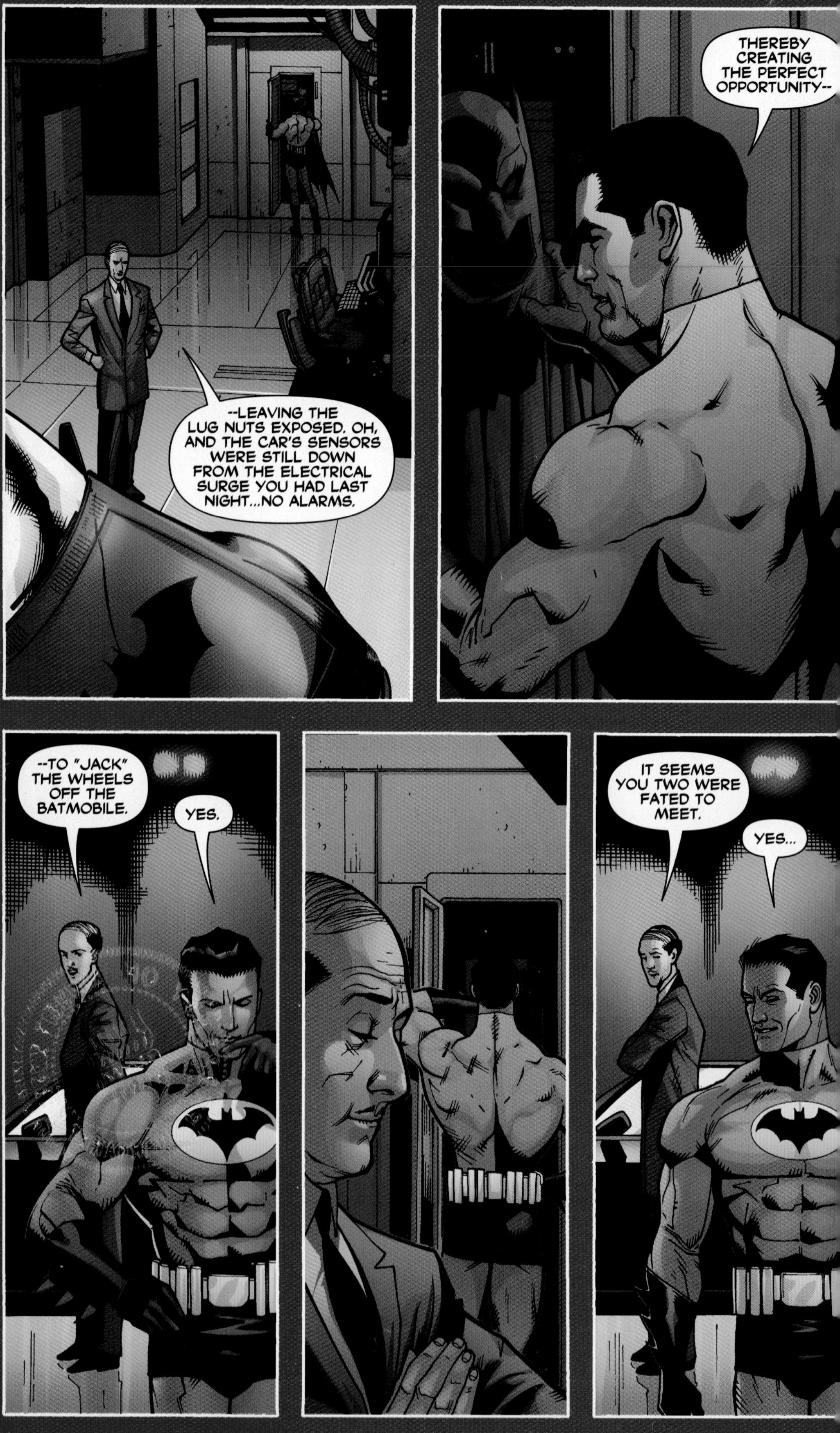
--LEAVING THE LUG NUTS EXPOSED. OH, AND THE CAR'S SENSORS WERE STILL DOWN FROM THE ELECTRICAL SURGE YOU HAD LAST NIGHT...NO ALARMS.
THEREBY CREATING THE PERFECT OPPORTUNITY--
--TO "JACK" THE WHEELS OFF THE BATMOBILE.
YES.
IT SEEMS YOU TWO WERE FATED TO MEET.
YES...

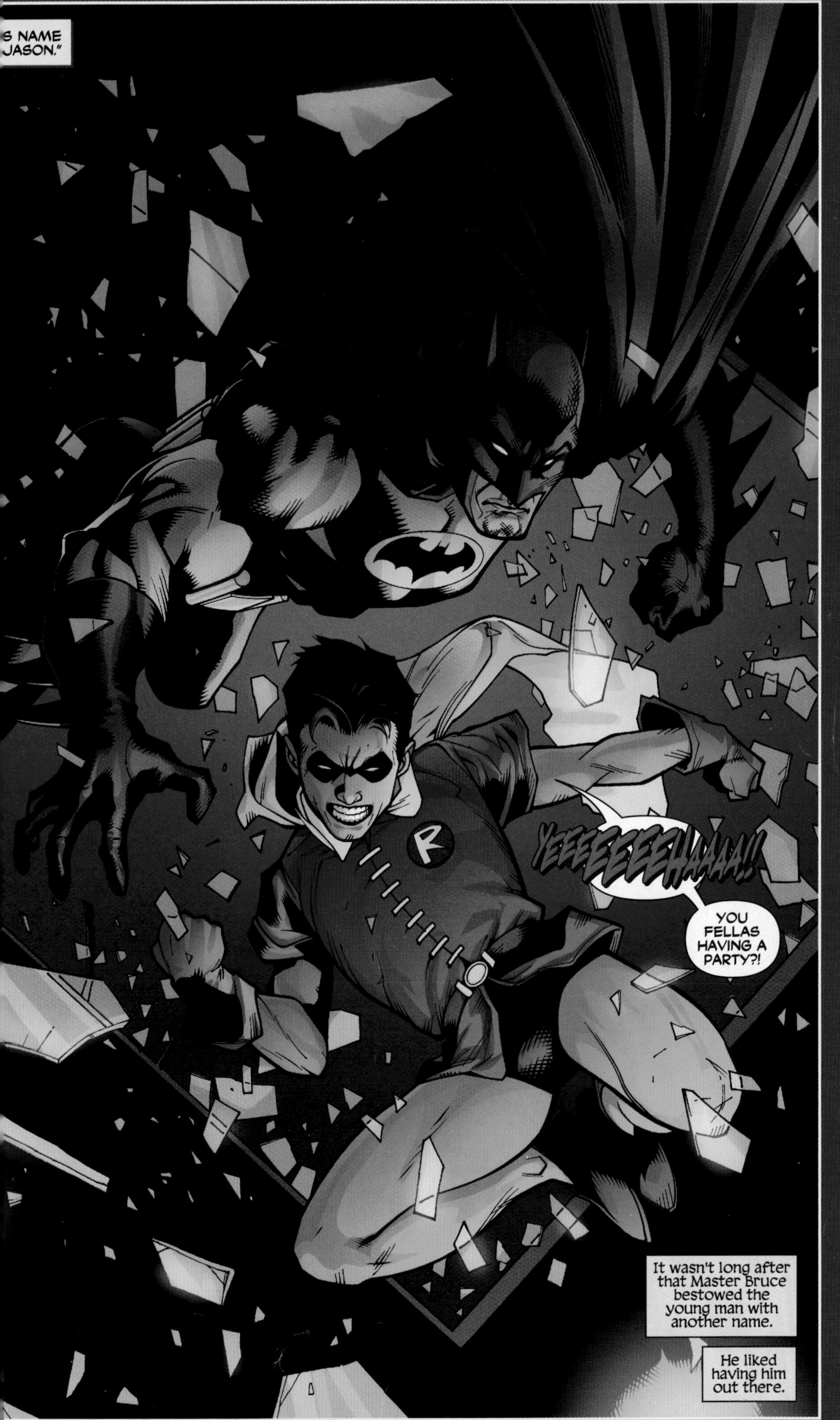

S NAME
JASON."
YEEEEEEEEHAAAA!!
YOU FELLAS HAVING A PARTY?!
It wasn't long after that Master Bruce bestowed the young man with another name.
He liked having him out there.

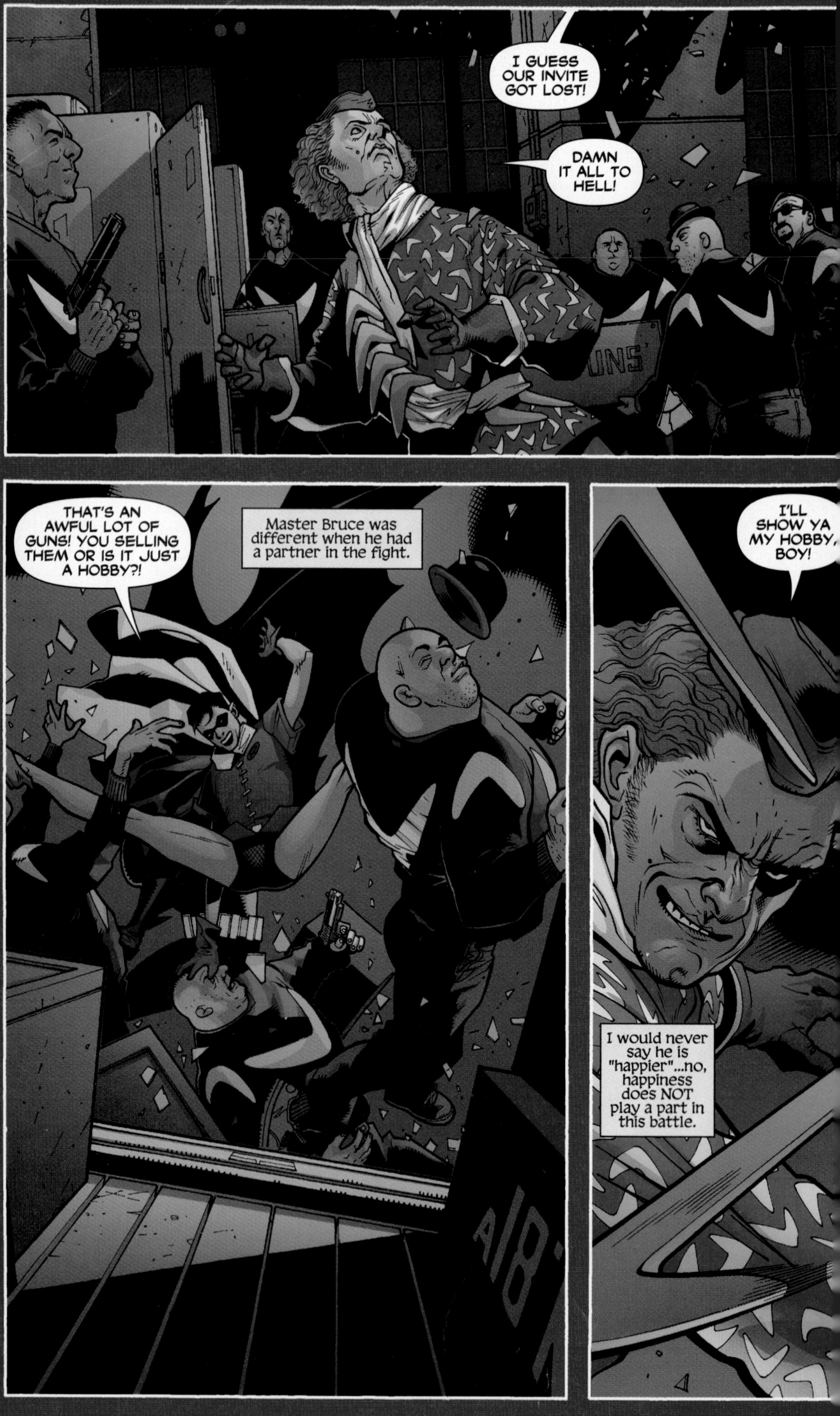
I GUESS OUR INVITE GOT LOST!
DAMN IT ALL TO HELL!
THAT'S AN AWFUL LOT OF GUNS! YOU SELLING THEM OR IS IT JUST A HOBBY?!
Master Bruce was different when he had a partner in the fight.
I'LL SHOW YA MY HOBBY, BOY!
I would never say he is "happier"...no, happiness does NOT play a part in this battle.

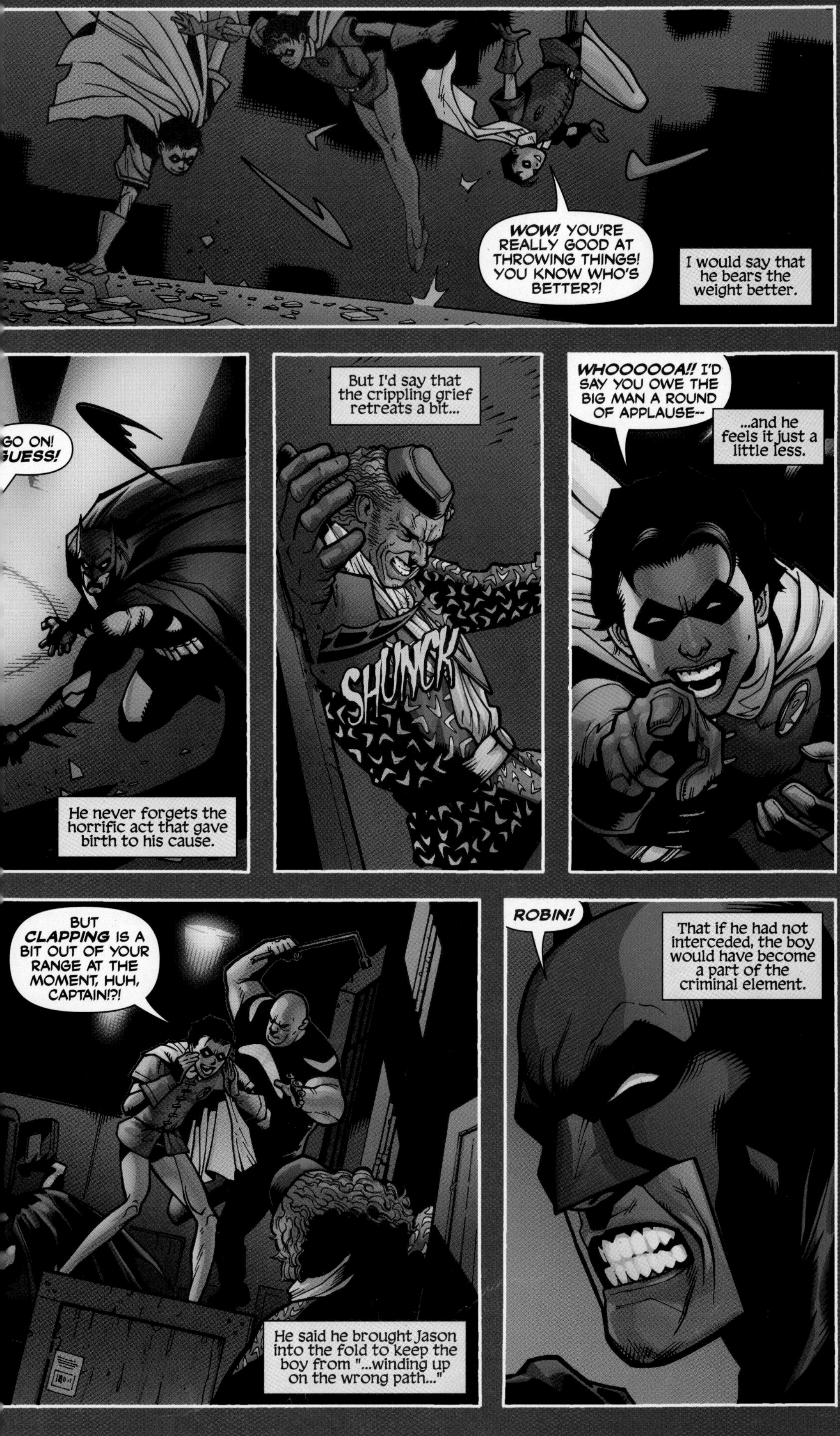

WOW! YOU'RE REALLY GOOD AT THROWING THINGS! YOU KNOW WHO'S BETTER?!
I would say that he bears the weight better.
GO ON! GUESS!
He never forgets the horrific act that gave birth to his cause.
But I'd say that the crippling grief retreats a bit...
SHUNCK
WHOOOOOA!! I'D SAY YOU OWE THE BIG MAN A ROUND OF APPLAUSE--
...and he feels it just a little less.
BUT CLAPPING IS A BIT OUT OF YOUR RANGE AT THE MOMENT, HUH, CAPTAIN!?!
He said he brought Jason into the fold to keep the boy from "...winding up on the wrong path..."
ROBIN!
That if he had not interceded, the boy would have become a part of the criminal element.

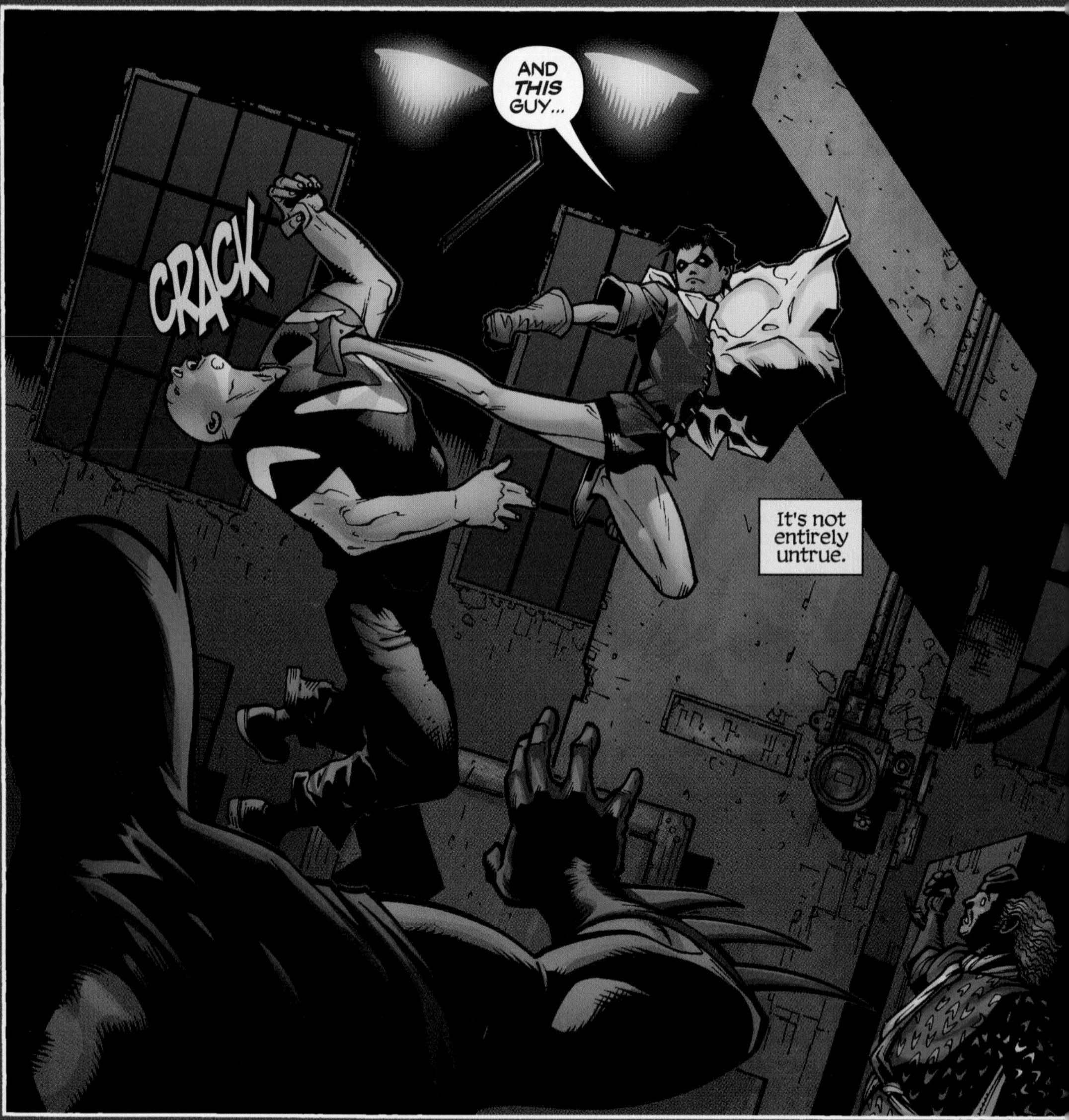
AND THIS GUY...
CRACK
It's not entirely untrue.

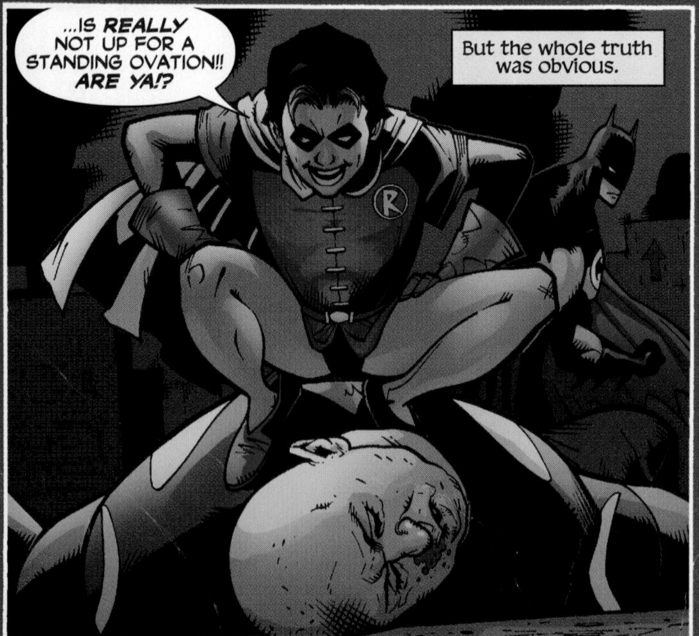
...IS REALLY NOT UP FOR A STANDING OVATION!! ARE YA!?
But the whole truth was obvious.

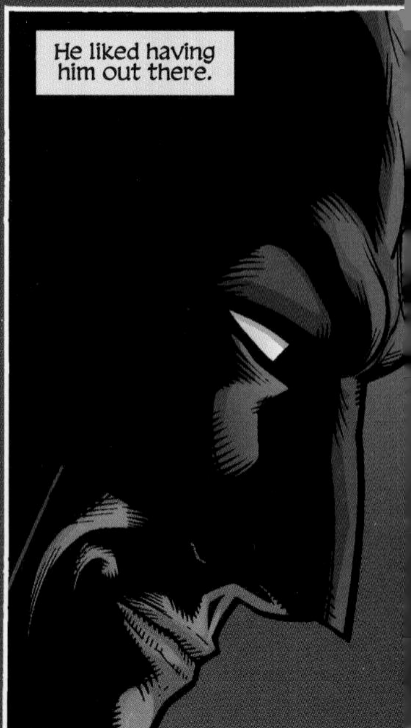
He liked having him out there.

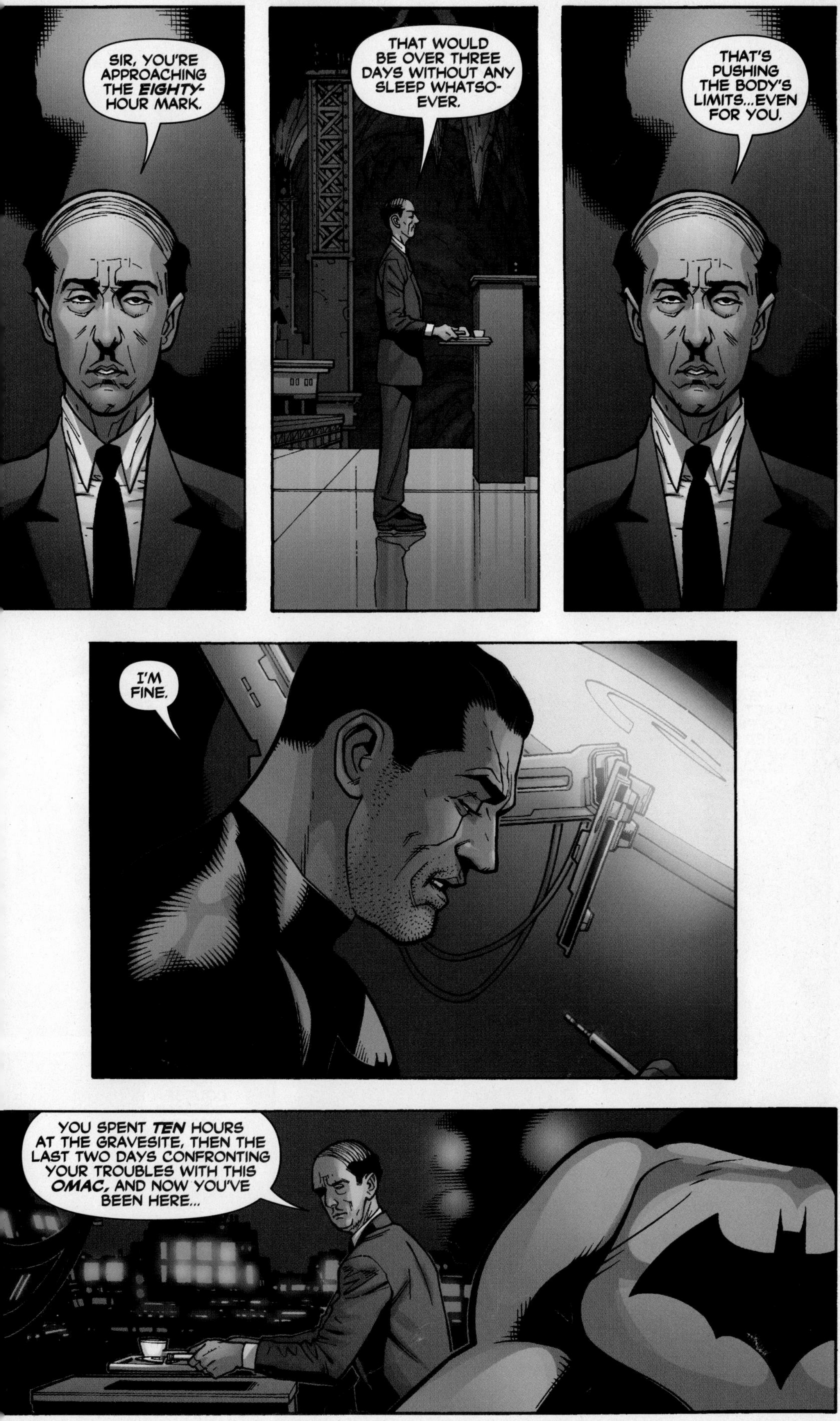
SIR, YOU'RE APPROACHING THE *EIGHTY*-HOUR MARK.
THAT WOULD BE OVER THREE DAYS WITHOUT ANY SLEEP WHATSO-EVER.
THAT'S PUSHING THE BODY'S LIMITS...EVEN FOR YOU.
I'M FINE.
YOU SPENT *TEN* HOURS AT THE GRAVESITE, THEN THE LAST TWO DAYS CONFRONTING YOUR TROUBLES WITH THIS *OMAC*, AND NOW YOU'VE BEEN HERE...

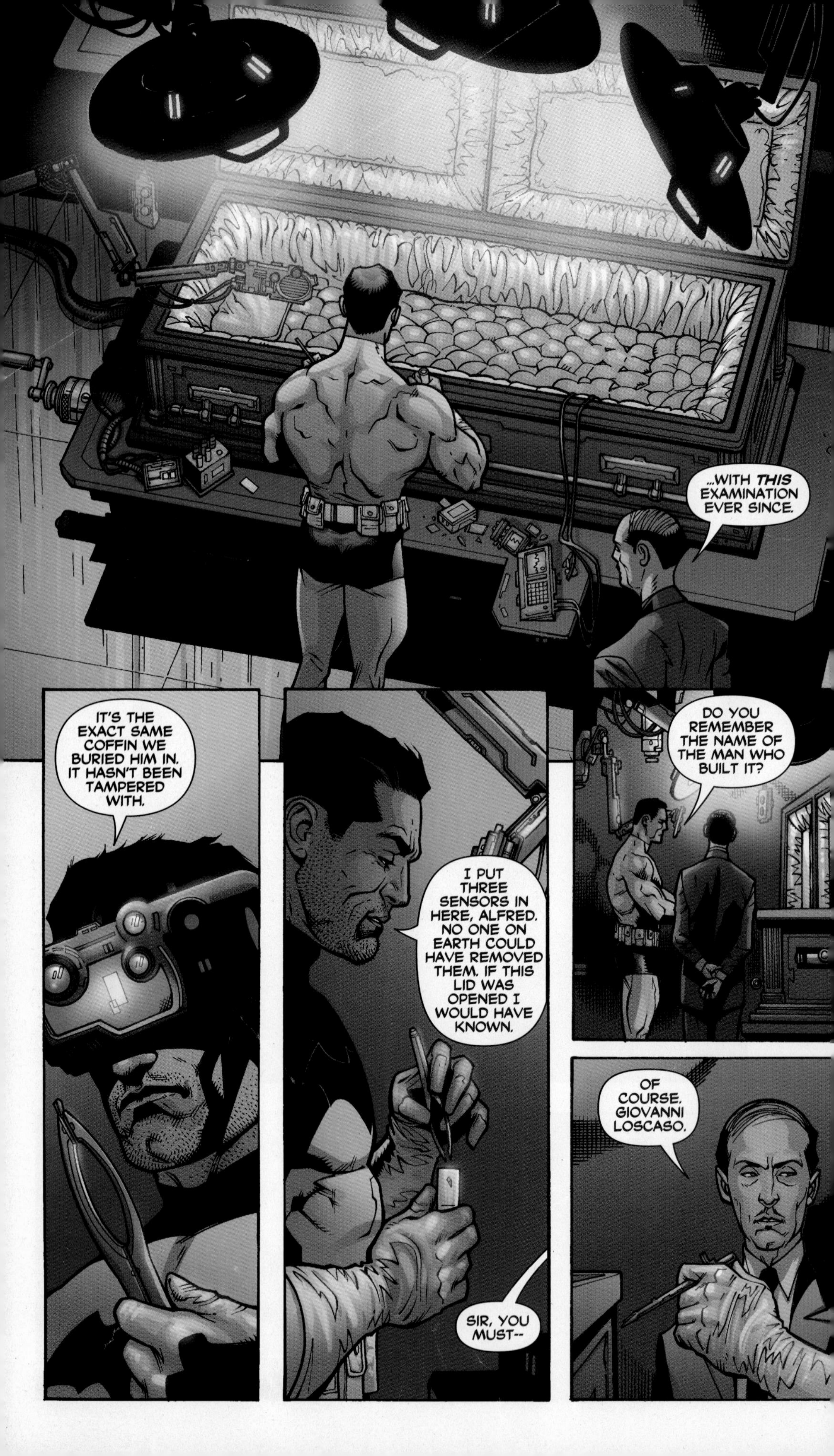
...WITH THIS EXAMINATION EVER SINCE.
IT'S THE EXACT SAME COFFIN WE BURIED HIM IN. IT HASN'T BEEN TAMPERED WITH.
I PUT THREE SENSORS IN HERE, ALFRED. NO ONE ON EARTH COULD HAVE REMOVED THEM. IF THIS LID WAS OPENED I WOULD HAVE KNOWN.
SIR, YOU MUST--
DO YOU REMEMBER THE NAME OF THE MAN WHO BUILT IT?
OF COURSE. GIOVANNI LOSCASO.

THE SAME MAN WHO BUILT MY PARENTS' COFFINS.

YES, PRECISELY. HE *REJECTED* OUR ORIGINAL OFFER, WE THOUGHT IT WAS OVER MONEY.

BUT IT TURNED OUT THAT HE WAS SUFFERING FROM CRIPPLING ARTHRITIS.

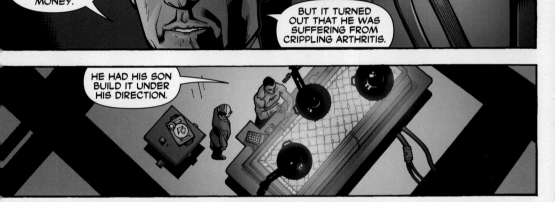

HE HAD HIS SON BUILD IT UNDER HIS DIRECTION.

'ES, AFTER I EXPLAINED HO IT WAS FOR, HIS SON, OT A COFFIN MAKER BUT ONE OF THE GREATEST URNITURE DESIGNERS IN ALL OF EUROPE, COMPLETED THE TASK.

LOSCASO SAID HIS SON DID A BETTER JOB THAN HAD *HE* BUILT IT HIMSELF. THAT HIS SON WAS EASILY A GREATER ARTIST THAN HE HAD EVER BEEN.

"THAT IS A FATHER'S GREATEST TRIUMPH," HE SAID. "TO HAVE A SON SURPASS HIS OWN EXCELLENCE."

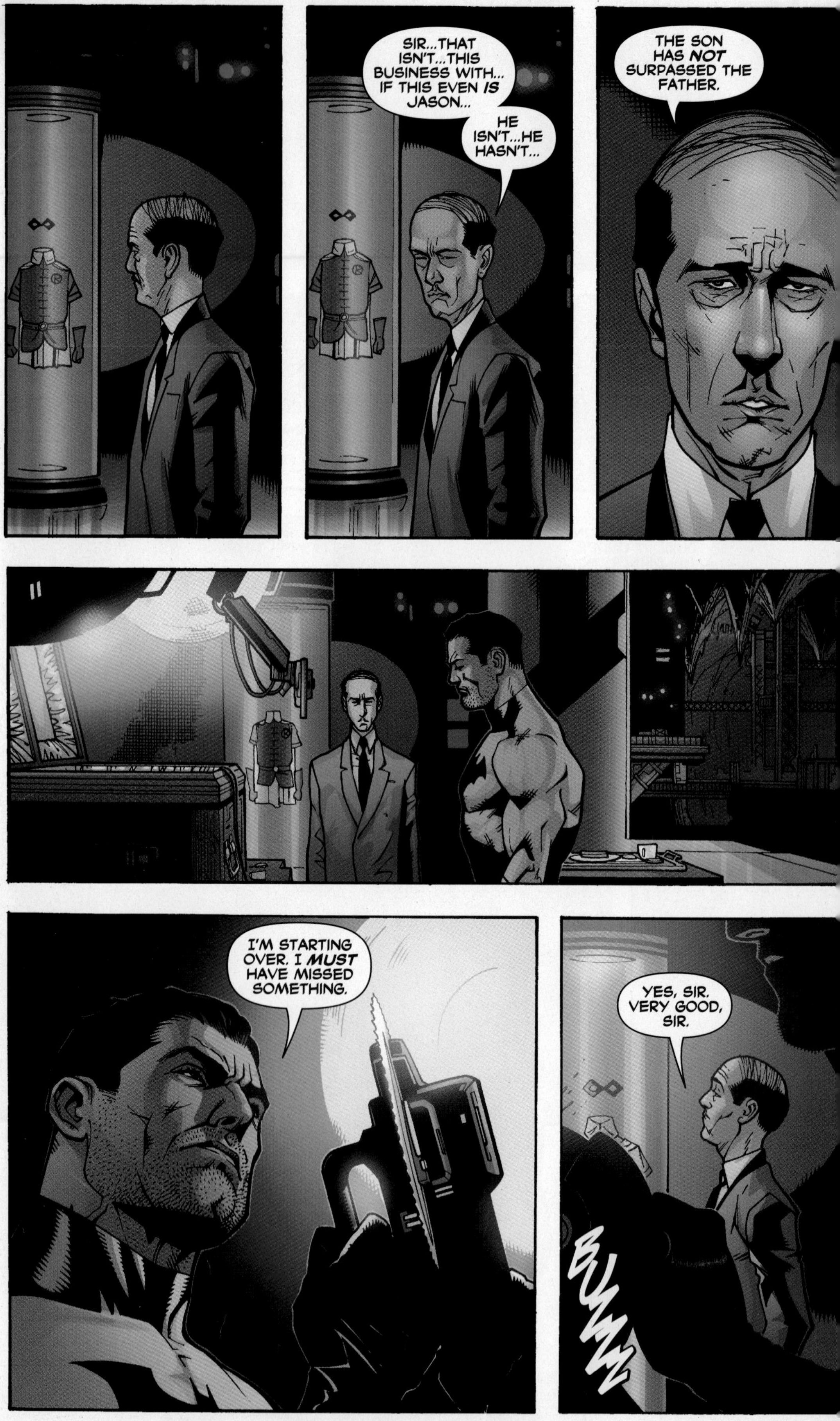
SIR...THAT ISN'T...THIS BUSINESS WITH... IF THIS EVEN IS JASON...
HE ISN'T...HE HASN'T...
THE SON HAS NOT SURPASSED THE FATHER.
I'M STARTING OVER. I MUST HAVE MISSED SOMETHING.
YES, SIR. VERY GOOD, SIR.
BUMMM

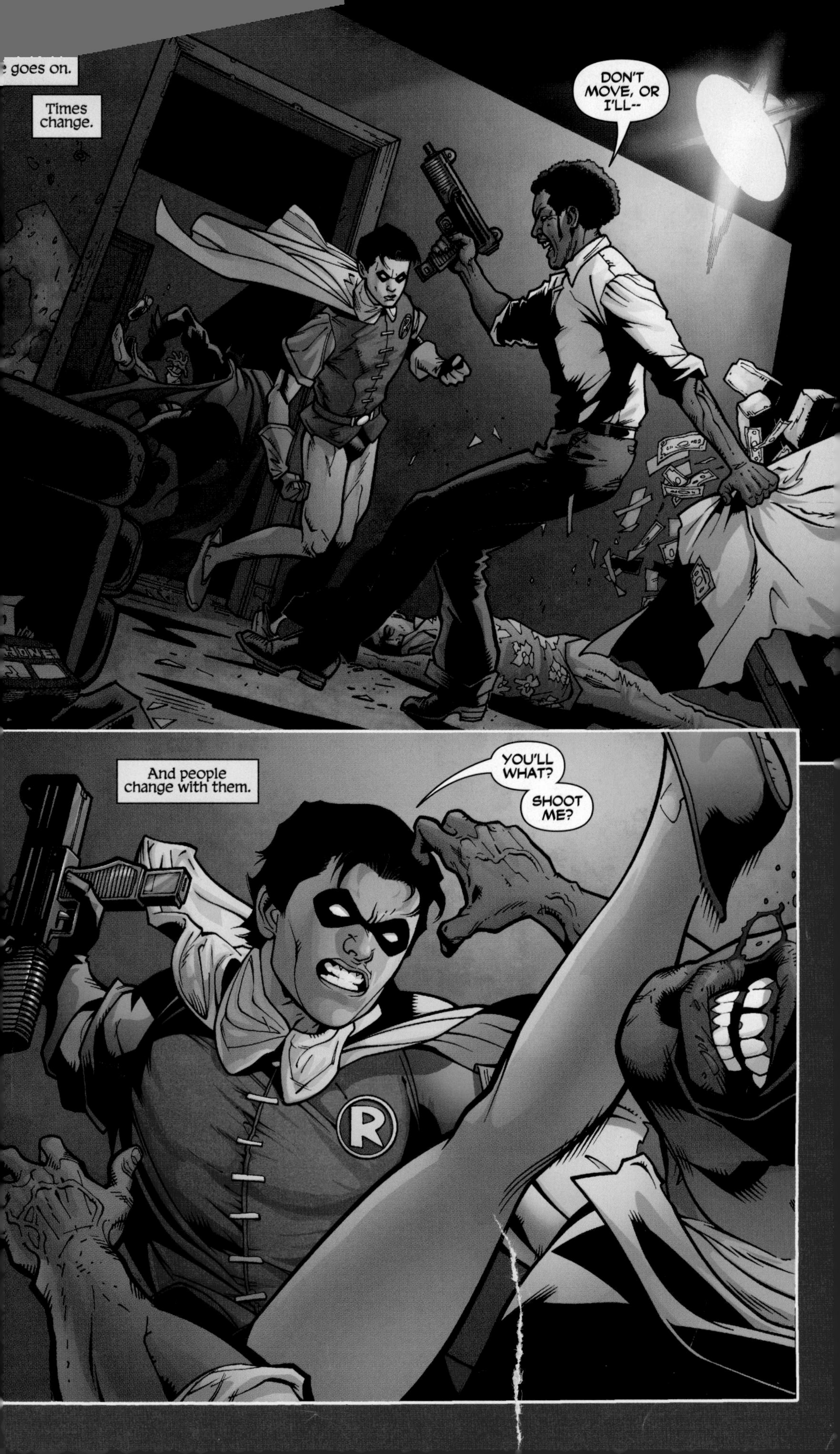
goes on.
Times change.
DON'T MOVE, OR I'LL--
And people change with them.
YOU'LL WHAT?
SHOOT ME?

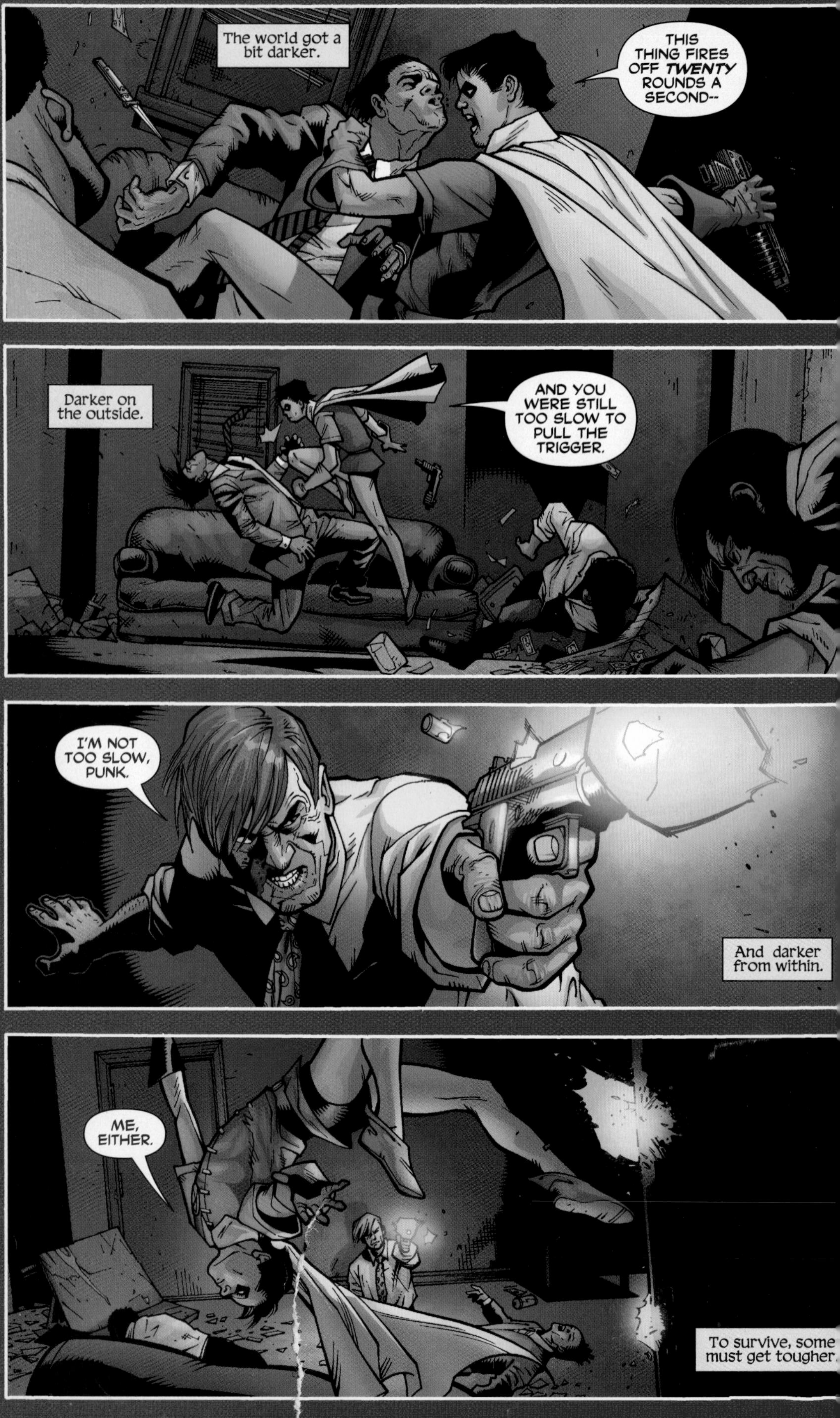
The world got a bit darker.
THIS THING FIRES OFF *TWENTY* ROUNDS A SECOND--
Darker on the outside.
AND YOU WERE STILL TOO SLOW TO PULL THE TRIGGER.
I'M NOT TOO SLOW, PUNK.
And darker from within.
ME, EITHER.
To survive, some must get tougher.

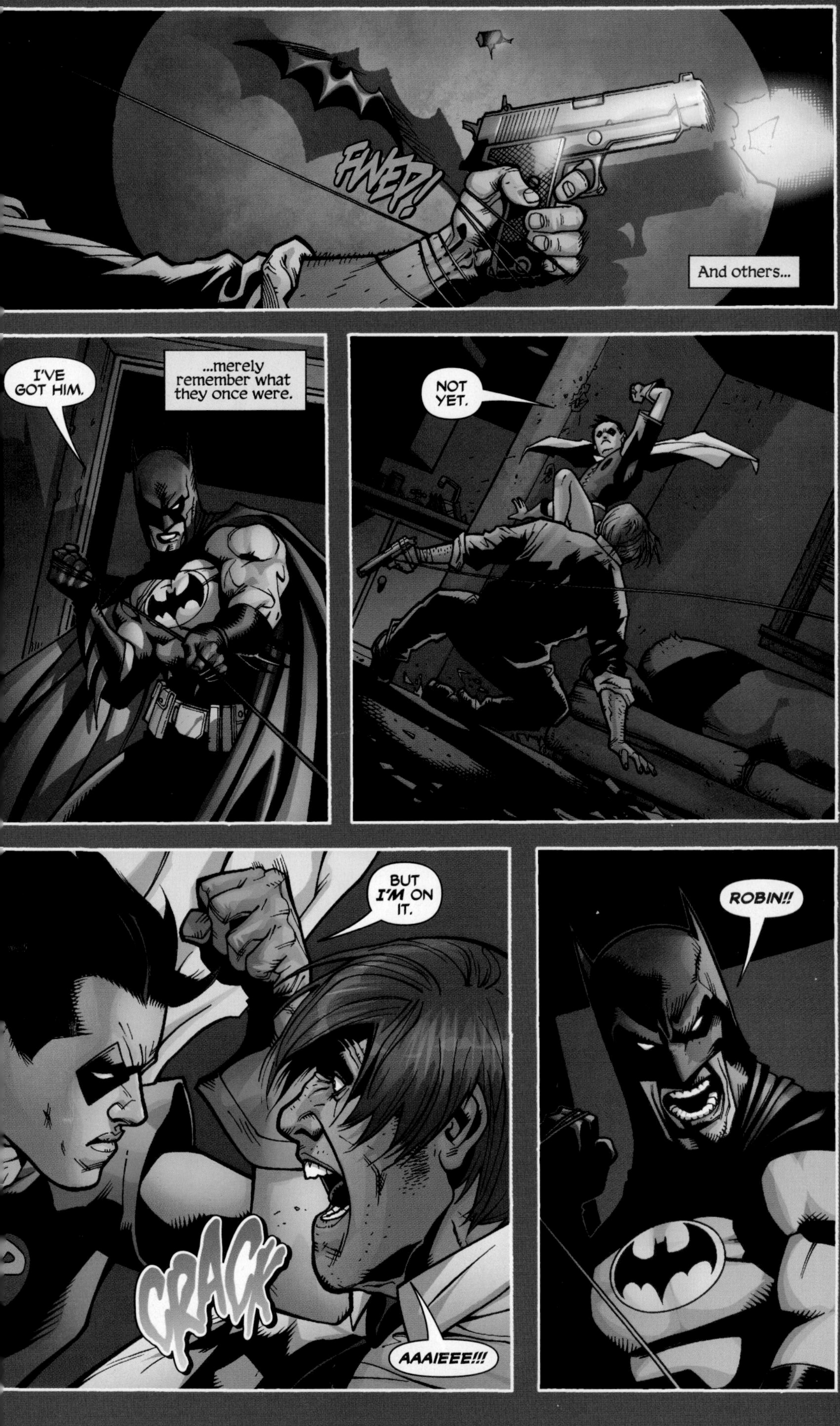
FWED!
And others...
I'VE GOT HIM.
...merely remember what they once were.
NOT YET.
BUT I'M ON IT.
CRACK
AAAIEEE!!!
ROBIN!!

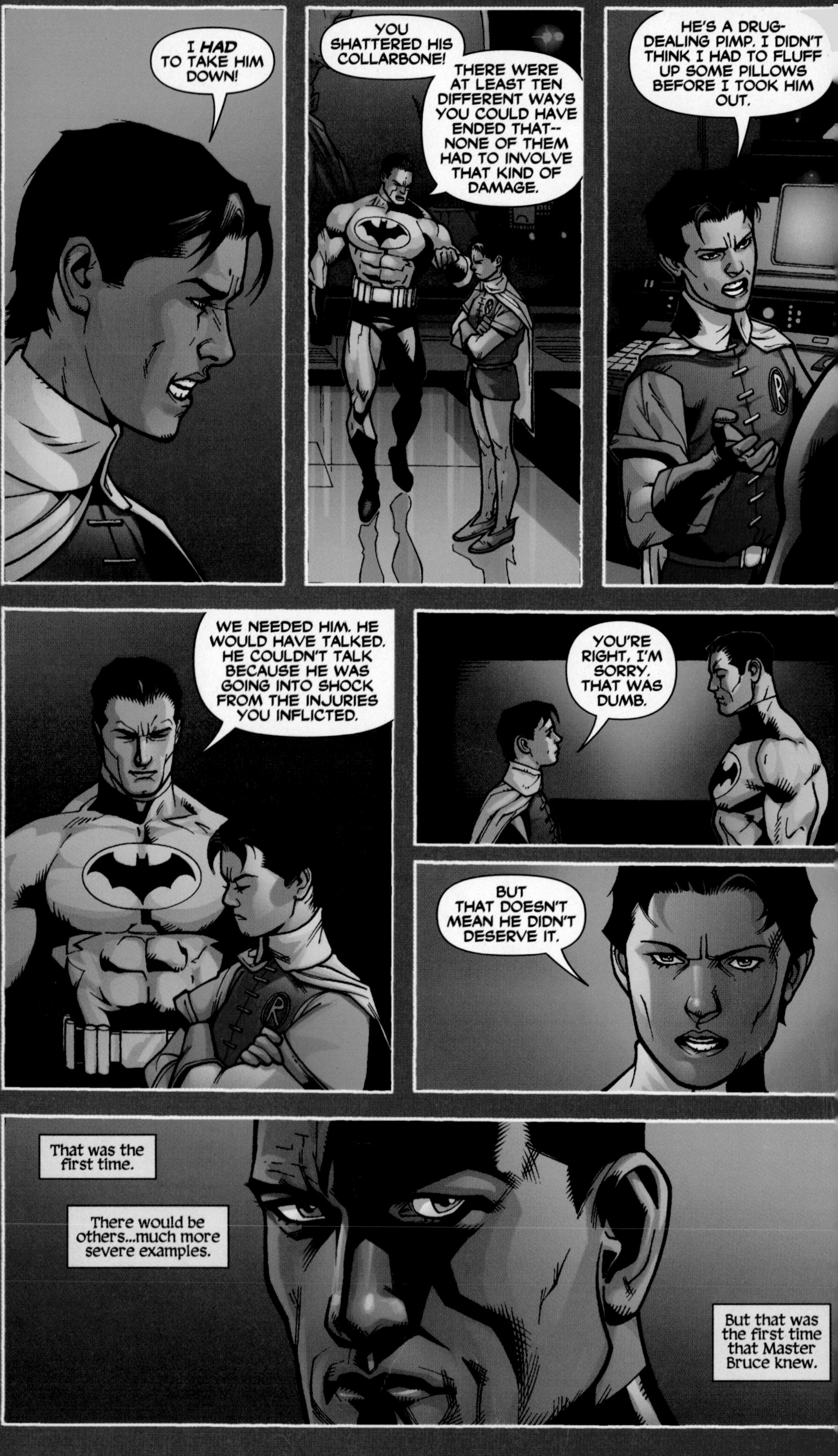
I *HAD* TO TAKE HIM DOWN!
YOU SHATTERED HIS COLLARBONE!
THERE WERE AT LEAST TEN DIFFERENT WAYS YOU COULD HAVE ENDED THAT-- NONE OF THEM HAD TO INVOLVE THAT KIND OF DAMAGE.
HE'S A DRUG-DEALING PIMP. I DIDN'T THINK I HAD TO FLUFF UP SOME PILLOWS BEFORE I TOOK HIM OUT.
WE NEEDED HIM. HE WOULD HAVE TALKED. HE COULDN'T TALK BECAUSE HE WAS GOING INTO SHOCK FROM THE INJURIES YOU INFLICTED.
YOU'RE RIGHT, I'M SORRY. THAT WAS DUMB.
BUT THAT DOESN'T MEAN HE DIDN'T DESERVE IT.
That was the first time.
There would be others...much more severe examples.
But that was the first time that Master Bruce knew.

He knew that Jason Todd was NOT Dick Grayson.

It wasn't about skill, or about endurance, or even their will to succeed.

No. It was that Jason had a "mean streak."

Jason was dangerous.

And as a father... he was at a loss for what to do.

I'VE BEEN STUPID.

SIR?

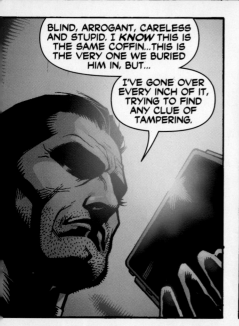

BLIND, ARROGANT, CARELESS AND STUPID. I *KNOW* THIS IS THE SAME COFFIN...THIS IS THE VERY ONE WE BURIED HIM IN, BUT...

I'VE GONE OVER EVERY INCH OF IT, TRYING TO FIND ANY CLUE OF TAMPERING.

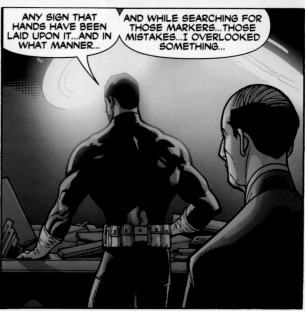

ANY SIGN THAT HANDS HAVE BEEN LAID UPON IT...AND IN WHAT MANNER...

AND WHILE SEARCHING FOR THOSE MARKERS...THOSE MISTAKES...I OVERLOOKED SOMETHING...

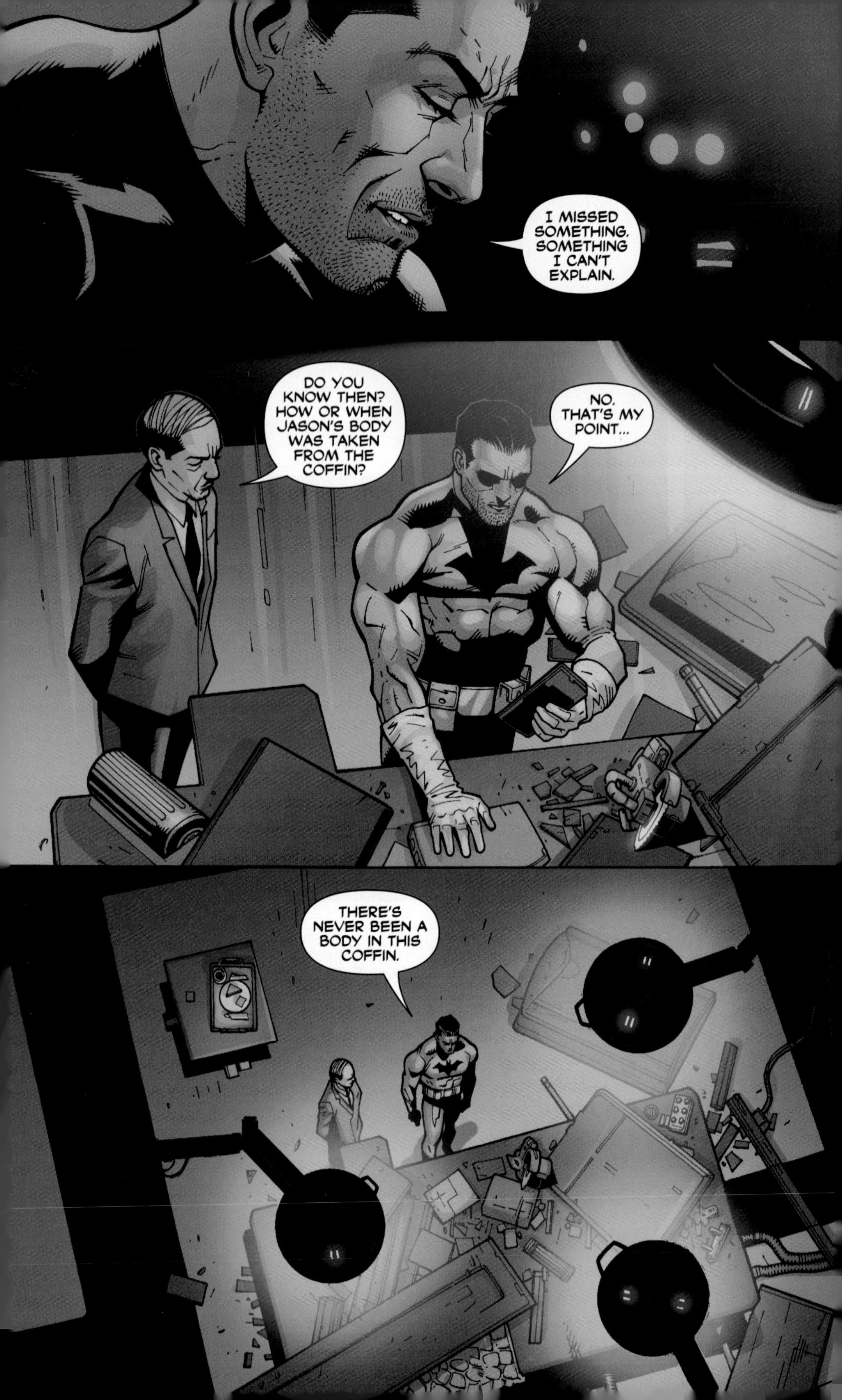
I MISSED SOMETHING. SOMETHING I CAN'T EXPLAIN.
DO YOU KNOW THEN? HOW OR WHEN JASON'S BODY WAS TAKEN FROM THE COFFIN?
NO. THAT'S MY POINT...
THERE'S NEVER BEEN A BODY IN THIS COFFIN.

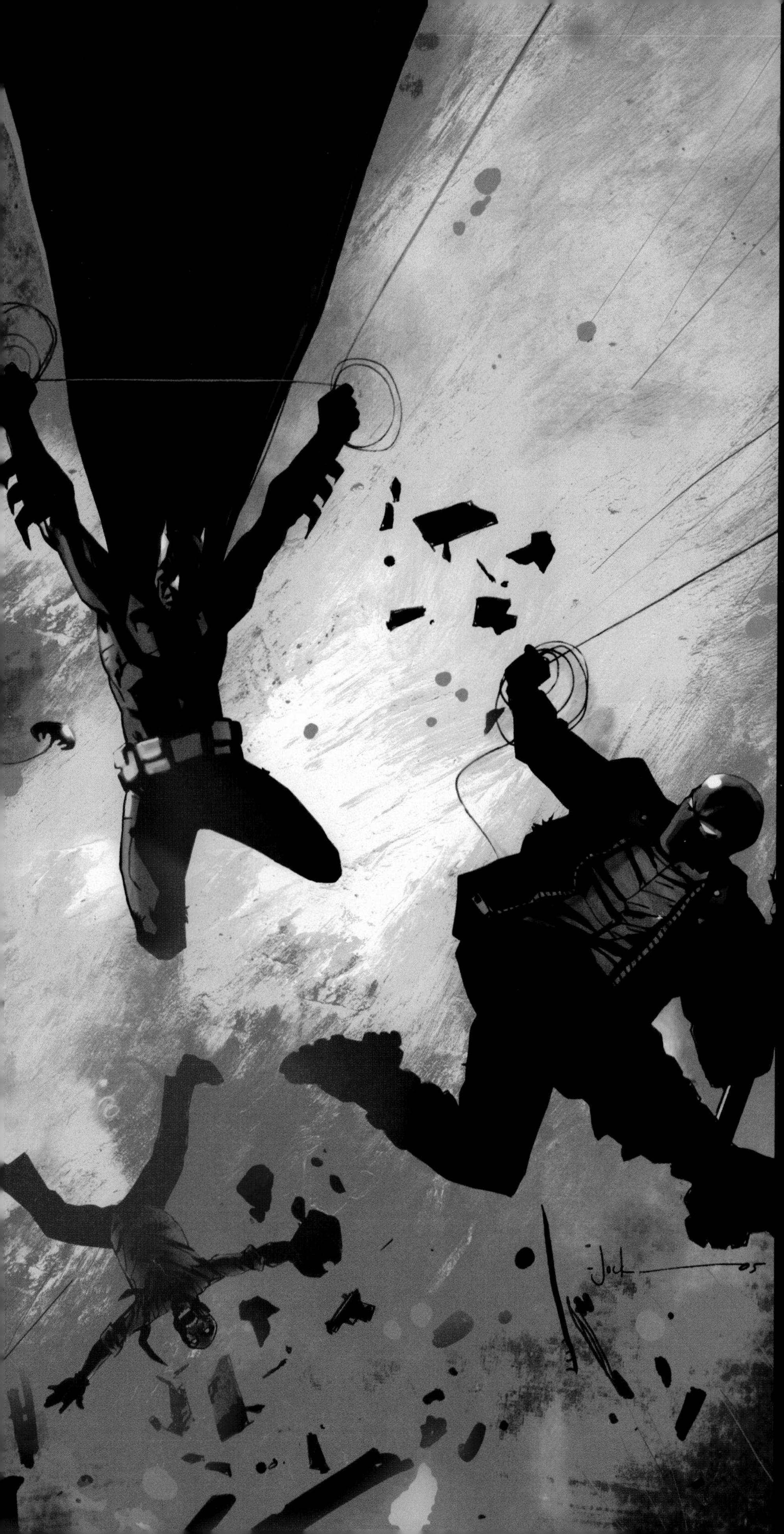

BATMAN #646 • COVER BY JOCK

CHAPTER 2

FRANCHISE
PART 1: SUPPLY SIDE ECONOMICS

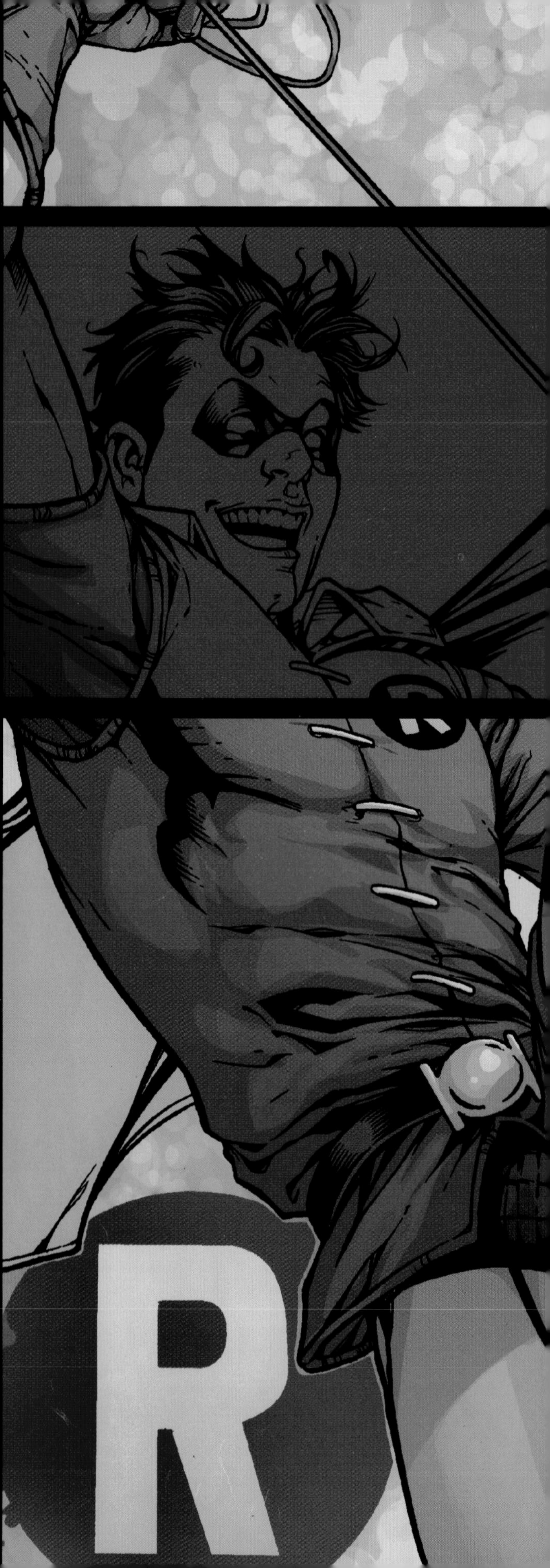
R

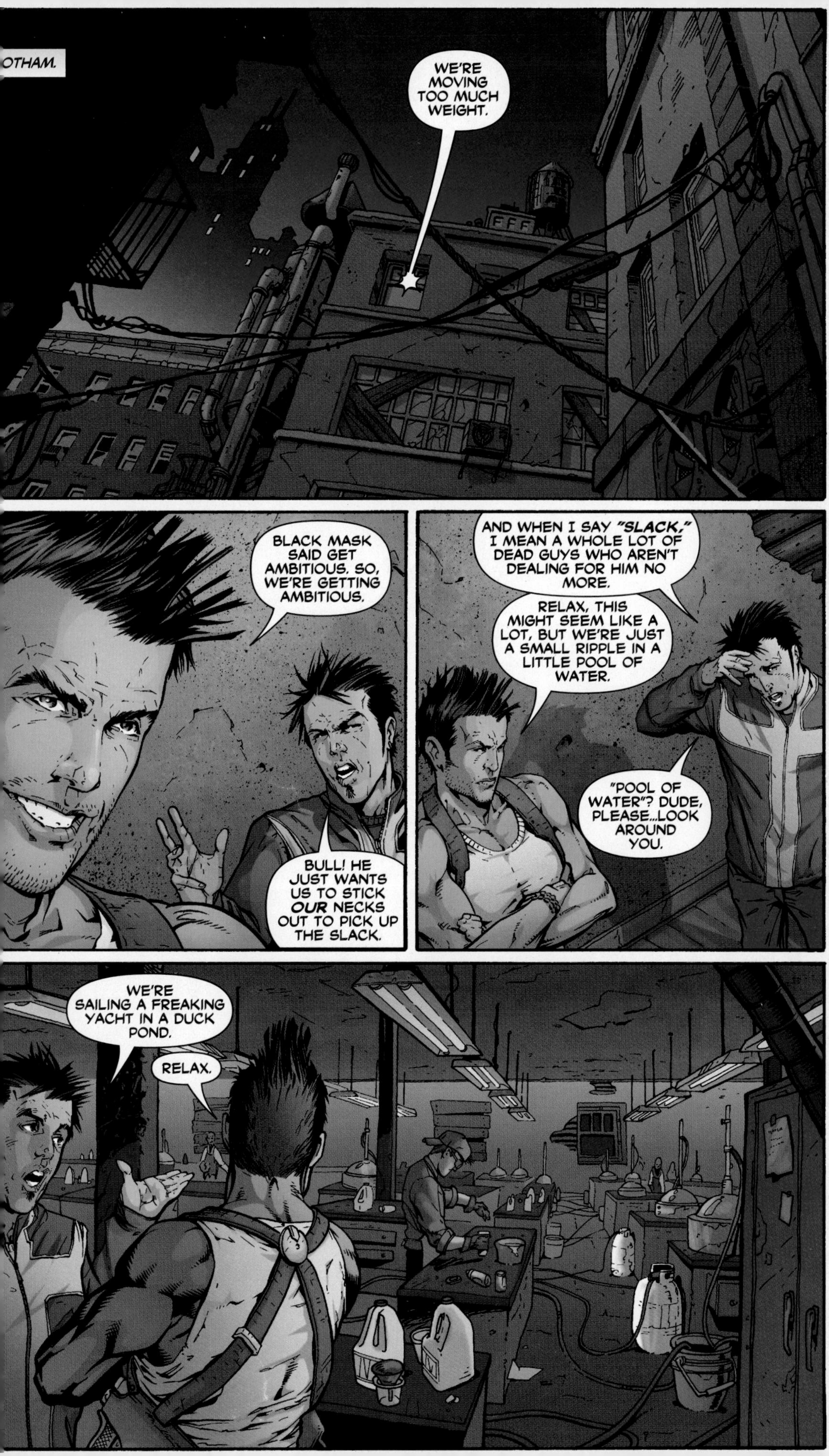
OTHAM.
WE'RE MOVING TOO MUCH WEIGHT.
BLACK MASK SAID GET AMBITIOUS. SO, WE'RE GETTING AMBITIOUS.
BULL! HE JUST WANTS US TO STICK OUR NECKS OUT TO PICK UP THE SLACK.
AND WHEN I SAY "SLACK," I MEAN A WHOLE LOT OF DEAD GUYS WHO AREN'T DEALING FOR HIM NO MORE.
RELAX, THIS MIGHT SEEM LIKE A LOT, BUT WE'RE JUST A SMALL RIPPLE IN A LITTLE POOL OF WATER.
"POOL OF WATER"? DUDE, PLEASE...LOOK AROUND YOU.
WE'RE SAILING A FREAKING YACHT IN A DUCK POND.
RELAX.

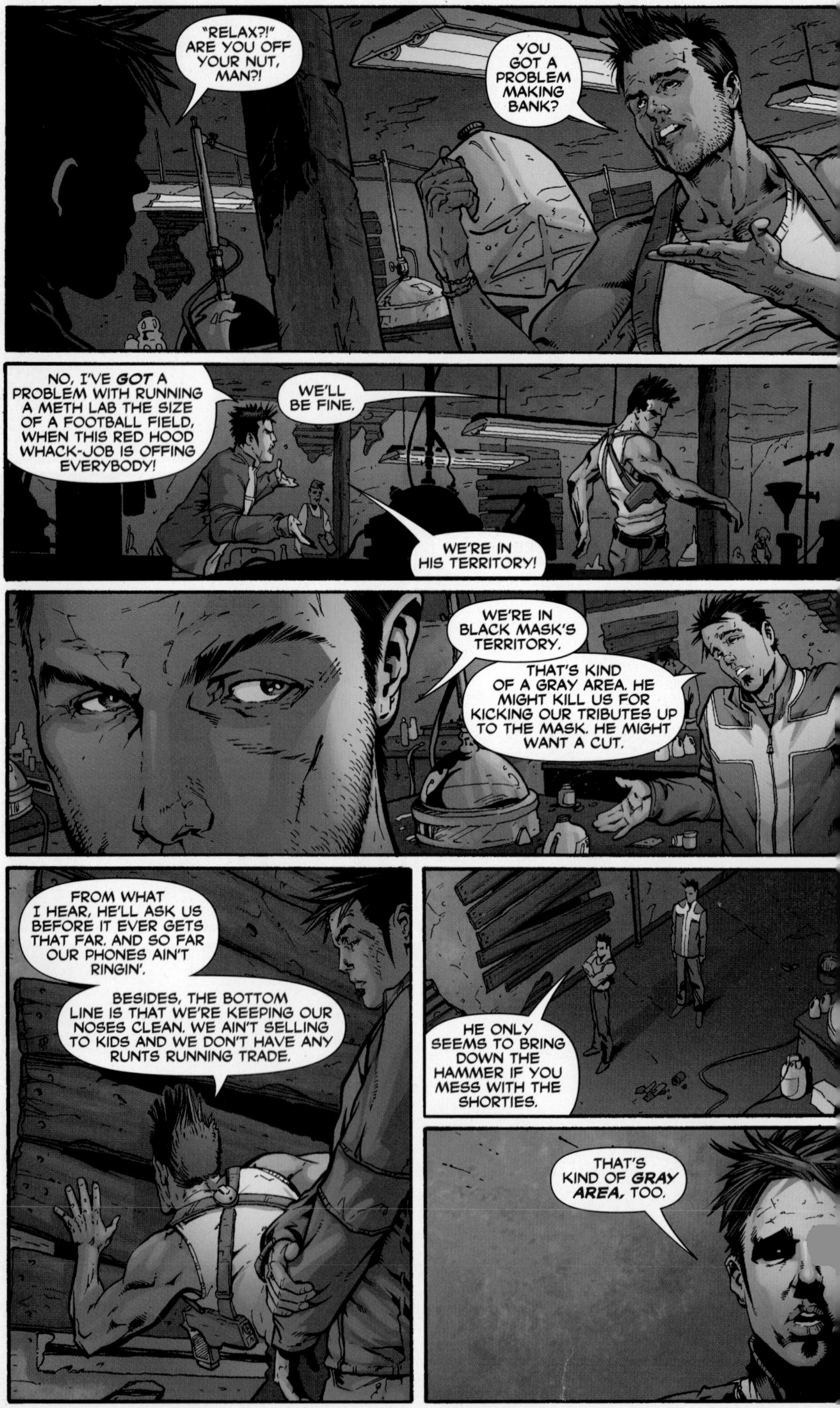
"RELAX?!" ARE YOU OFF YOUR NUT, MAN?!
YOU GOT A PROBLEM MAKING BANK?
NO, I'VE *GOT* A PROBLEM WITH RUNNING A METH LAB THE SIZE OF A FOOTBALL FIELD, WHEN THIS RED HOOD WHACK-JOB IS OFFING EVERYBODY!
WE'LL BE FINE.
WE'RE IN HIS TERRITORY!
WE'RE IN BLACK MASK'S TERRITORY.
THAT'S KIND OF A GRAY AREA. HE MIGHT KILL US FOR KICKING OUR TRIBUTES UP TO THE MASK. HE MIGHT WANT A CUT.
FROM WHAT I HEAR, HE'LL ASK US BEFORE IT EVER GETS THAT FAR. AND SO FAR OUR PHONES AIN'T RINGIN'.
BESIDES, THE BOTTOM LINE IS THAT WE'RE KEEPING OUR NOSES CLEAN. WE AIN'T SELLING TO KIDS AND WE DON'T HAVE ANY RUNTS RUNNING TRADE.
HE ONLY SEEMS TO BRING DOWN THE HAMMER IF YOU MESS WITH THE SHORTIES.
THAT'S KIND OF *GRAY AREA,* TOO.

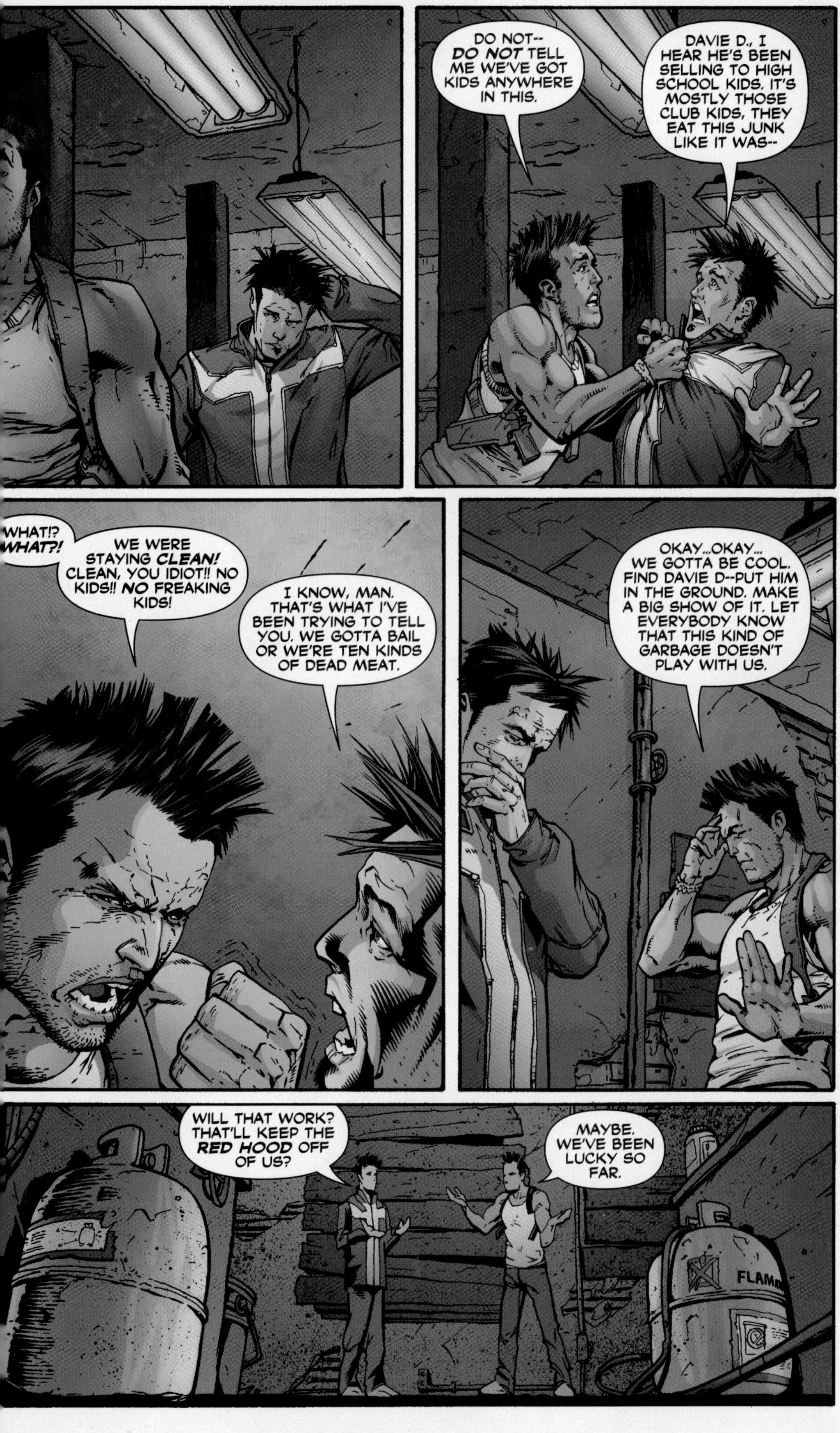
DO NOT--
DO NOT TELL ME WE'VE GOT KIDS ANYWHERE IN THIS.
DAVIE D., I HEAR HE'S BEEN SELLING TO HIGH SCHOOL KIDS. IT'S MOSTLY THOSE CLUB KIDS, THEY EAT THIS JUNK LIKE IT WAS--
WHAT!? WHAT?!
WE WERE STAYING CLEAN! CLEAN, YOU IDIOT!! NO KIDS!! NO FREAKING KIDS!
I KNOW, MAN. THAT'S WHAT I'VE BEEN TRYING TO TELL YOU. WE GOTTA BAIL OR WE'RE TEN KINDS OF DEAD MEAT.
OKAY...OKAY... WE GOTTA BE COOL. FIND DAVIE D--PUT HIM IN THE GROUND. MAKE A BIG SHOW OF IT. LET EVERYBODY KNOW THAT THIS KIND OF GARBAGE DOESN'T PLAY WITH US.
WILL THAT WORK? THAT'LL KEEP THE RED HOOD OFF OF US?
MAYBE. WE'VE BEEN LUCKY SO FAR.
FLAM

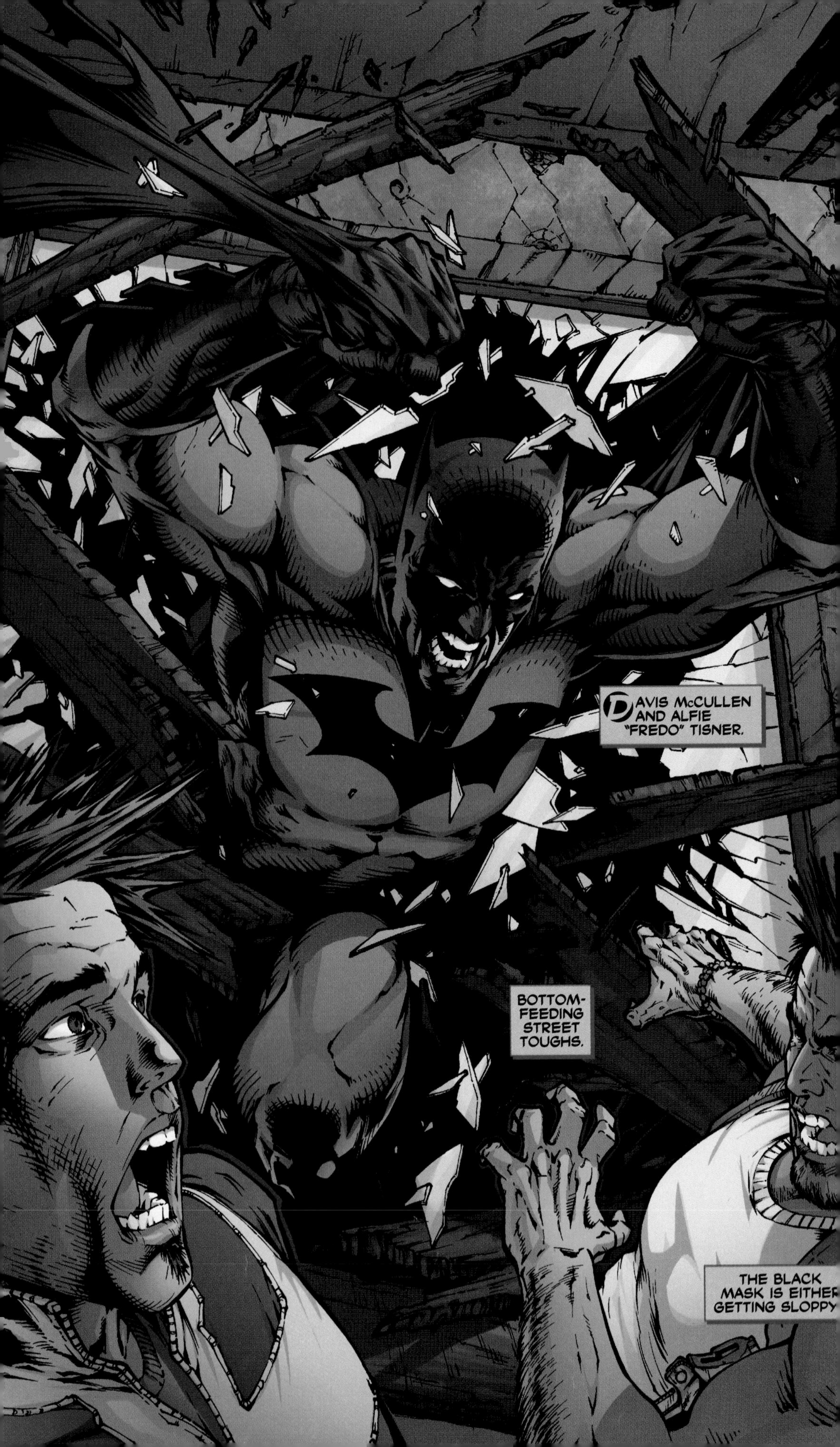
DAVIS McCULLEN AND ALFIE "FREDO" TISNER.
BOTTOM-FEEDING STREET TOUGHS.
THE BLACK MASK IS EITHER GETTING SLOPPY

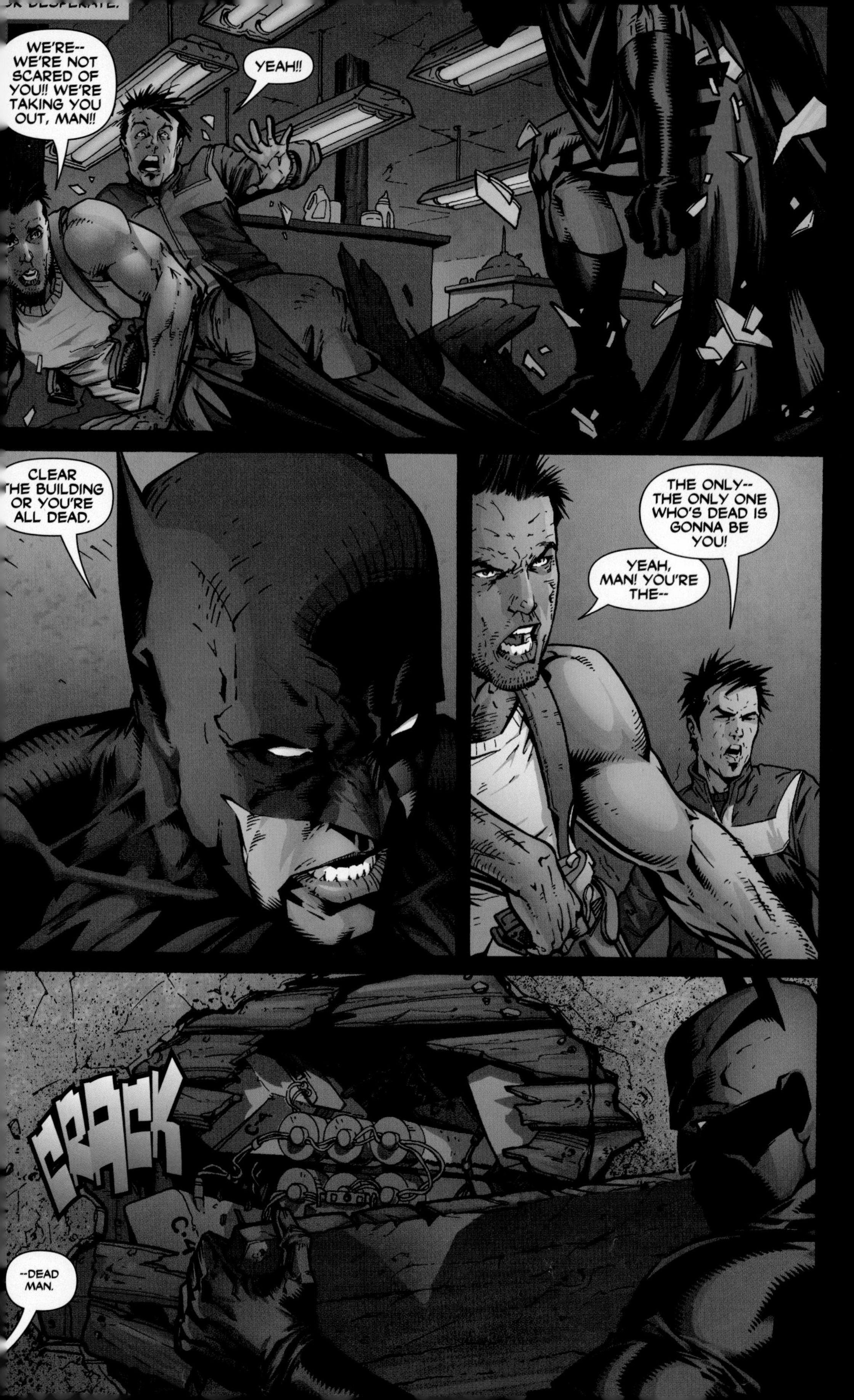

WE'RE-- WE'RE NOT SCARED OF YOU!! WE'RE TAKING YOU OUT, MAN!!
YEAH!!
CLEAR THE BUILDING OR YOU'RE ALL DEAD.
THE ONLY-- THE ONLY ONE WHO'S DEAD IS GONNA BE YOU!
YEAH, MAN! YOU'RE THE--
CRACK
--DEAD MAN.

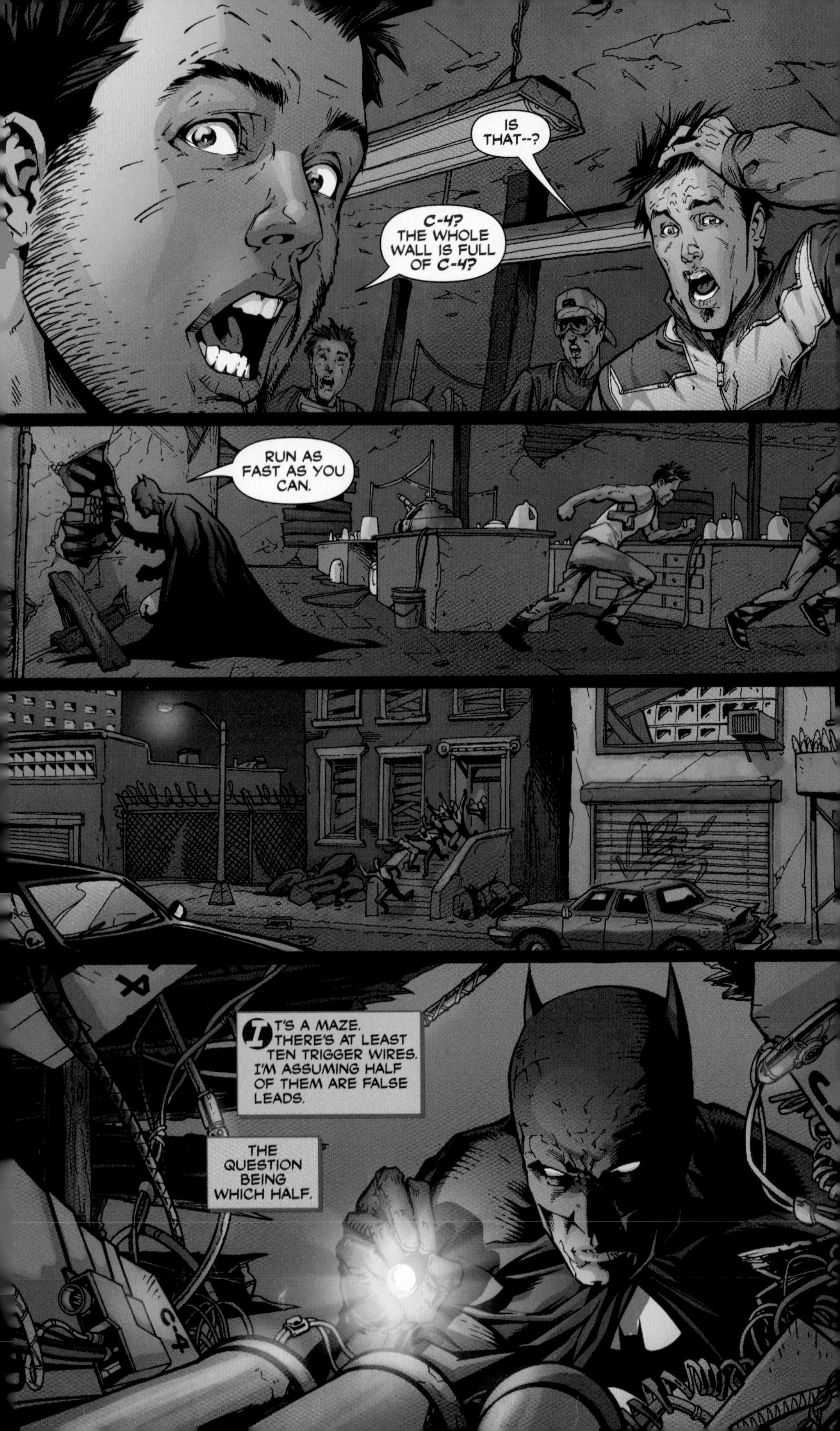
IS THAT--?
C-4? THE WHOLE WALL IS FULL OF C-4?
RUN AS FAST AS YOU CAN.
IT'S A MAZE. THERE'S AT LEAST TEN TRIGGER WIRES. I'M ASSUMING HALF OF THEM ARE FALSE LEADS.
THE QUESTION BEING WHICH HALF.

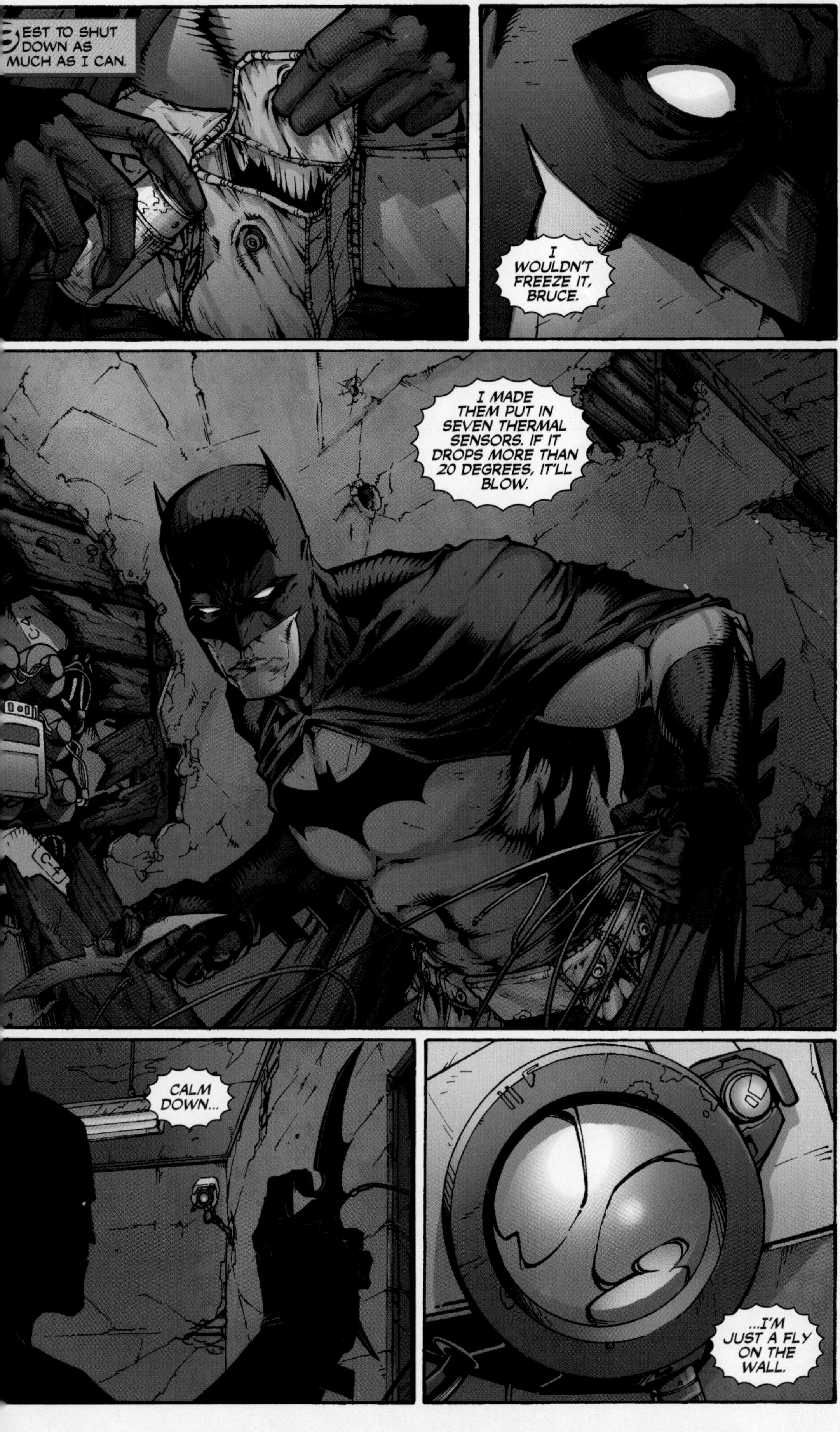
BEST TO SHUT DOWN AS MUCH AS I CAN.
I WOULDN'T FREEZE IT, BRUCE.
I MADE THEM PUT IN SEVEN THERMAL SENSORS. IF IT DROPS MORE THAN 20 DEGREES, IT'LL BLOW.
C-4
CALM DOWN...
...I'M JUST A FLY ON THE WALL.

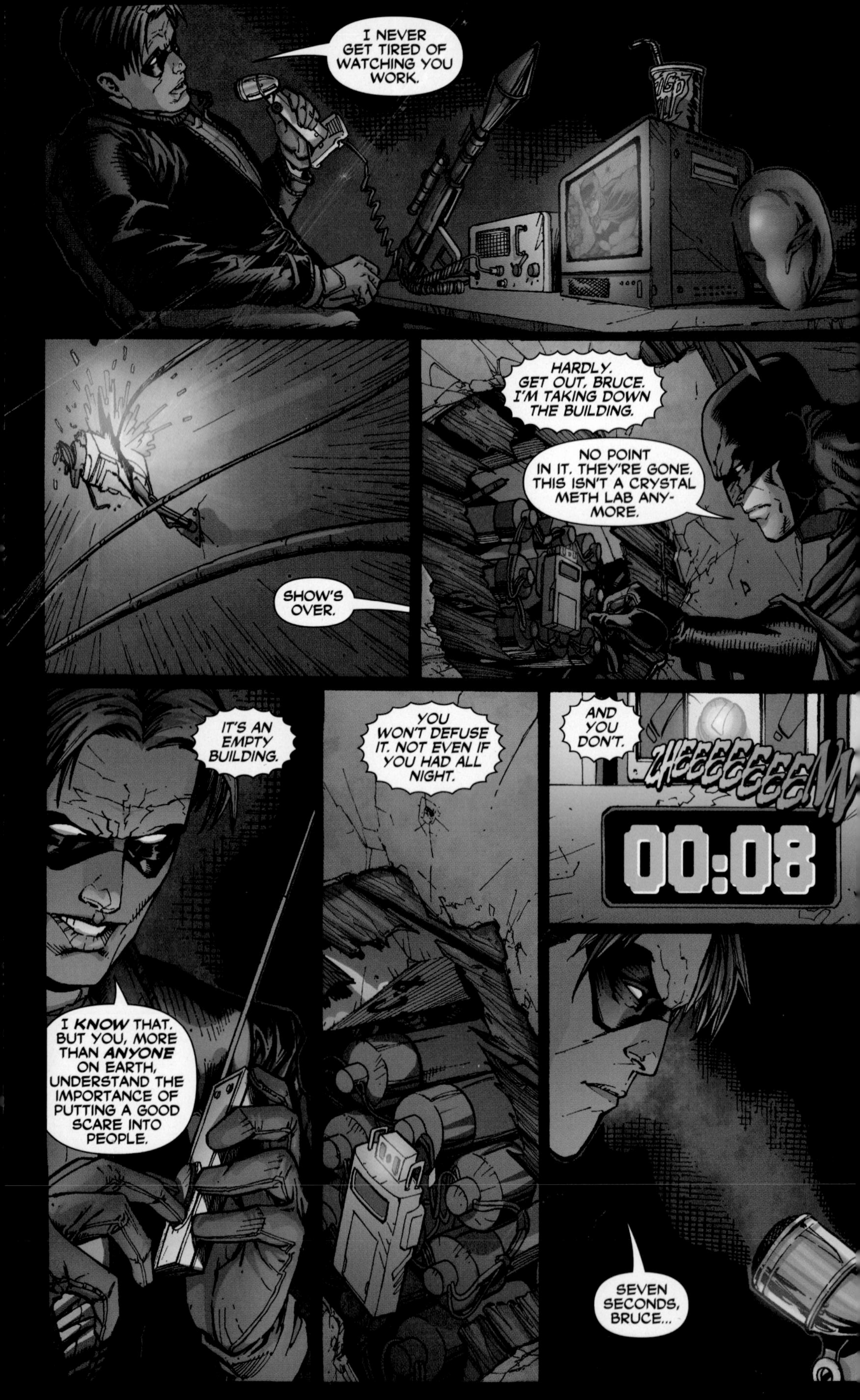

I NEVER GET TIRED OF WATCHING YOU WORK.
SHOW'S OVER.
HARDLY. GET OUT, BRUCE. I'M TAKING DOWN THE BUILDING.
NO POINT IN IT. THEY'RE GONE. THIS ISN'T A CRYSTAL METH LAB ANY-MORE.
IT'S AN EMPTY BUILDING.
I KNOW THAT. BUT YOU, MORE THAN ANYONE ON EARTH, UNDERSTAND THE IMPORTANCE OF PUTTING A GOOD SCARE INTO PEOPLE.
YOU WON'T DEFUSE IT. NOT EVEN IF YOU HAD ALL NIGHT.
AND YOU DON'T.
ZHEEEEEEEEM
00:08
SEVEN SECONDS, BRUCE...

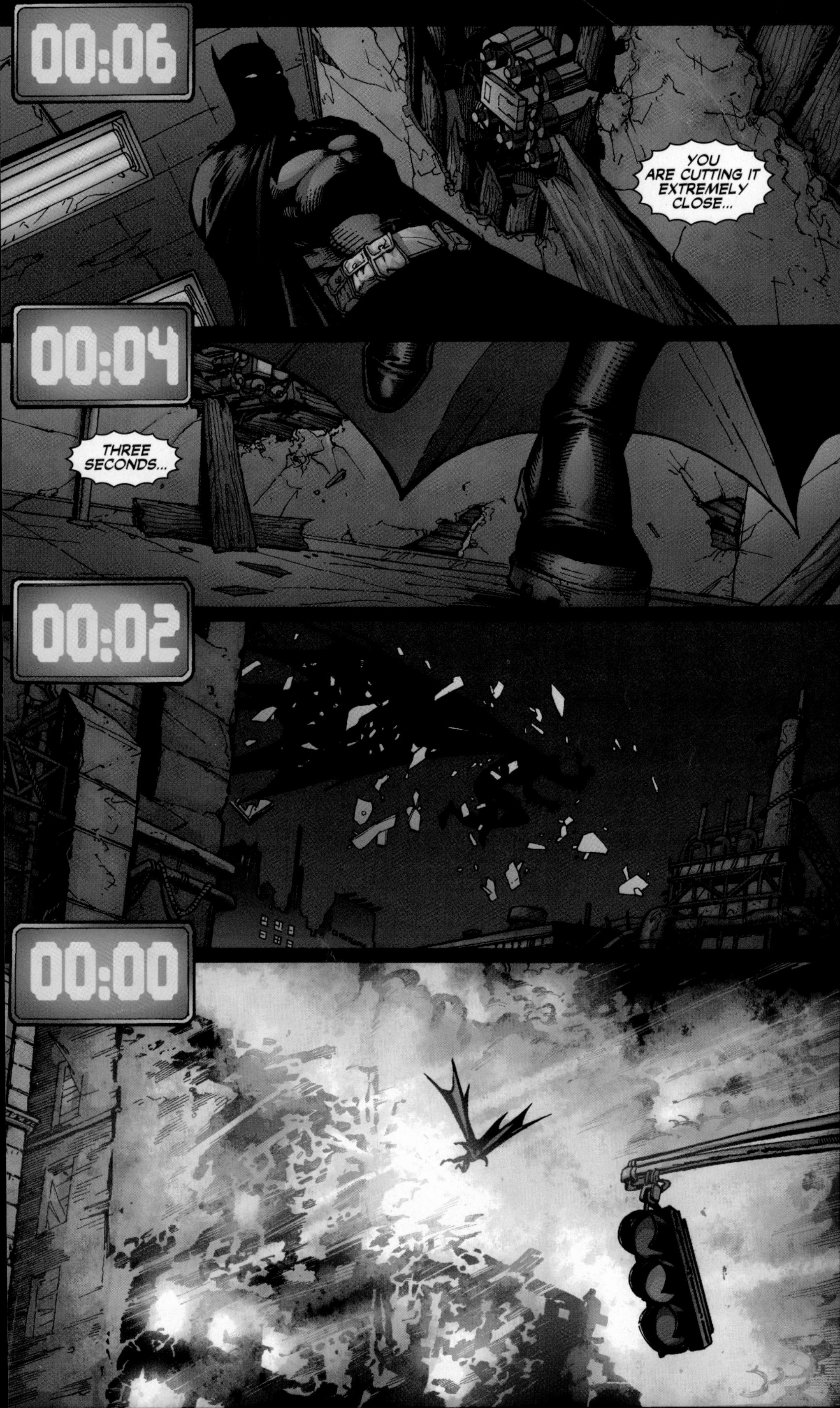
00:06
YOU ARE CUTTING IT EXTREMELY CLOSE...
00:04
THREE SECONDS...
00:02
00:00

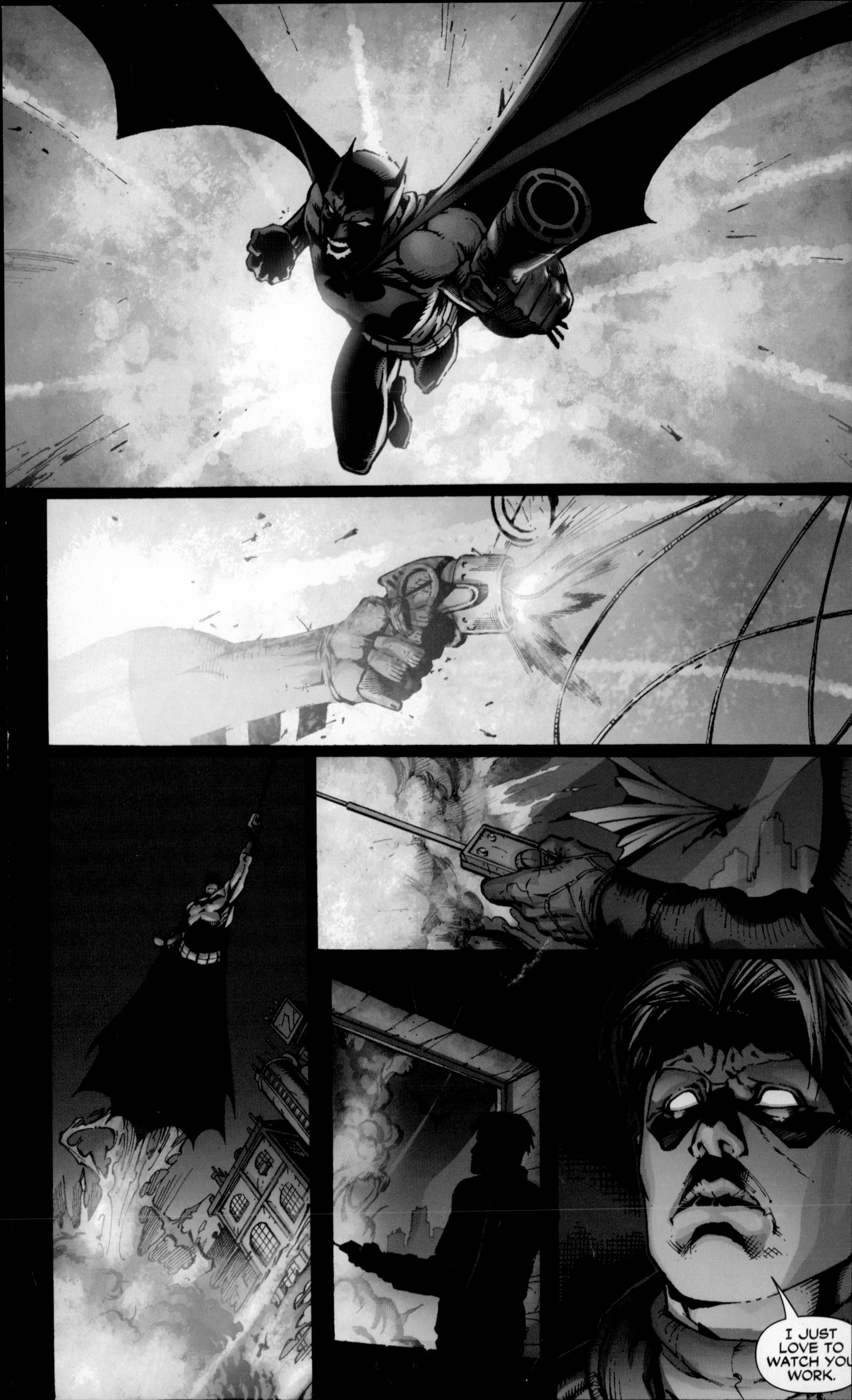
I JUST LOVE TO WATCH YOU WORK.

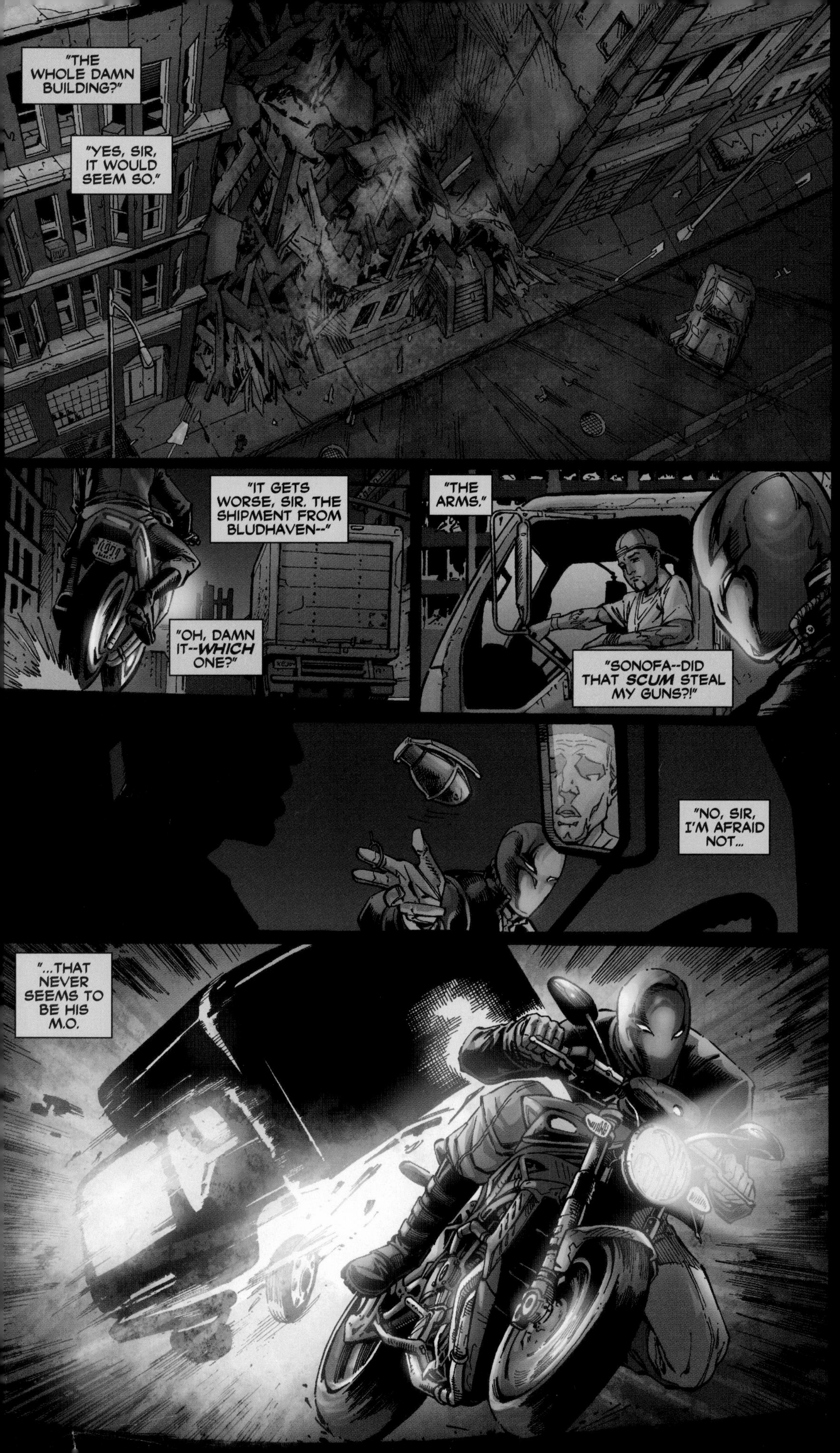
"THE WHOLE DAMN BUILDING?"
"YES, SIR, IT WOULD SEEM SO."
"IT GETS WORSE, SIR. THE SHIPMENT FROM BLUDHAVEN--"
"OH, DAMN IT--WHICH ONE?"
"THE ARMS."
"SONOFA--DID THAT SCUM STEAL MY GUNS?!"
"NO, SIR, I'M AFRAID NOT...
"...THAT NEVER SEEMS TO BE HIS M.O.

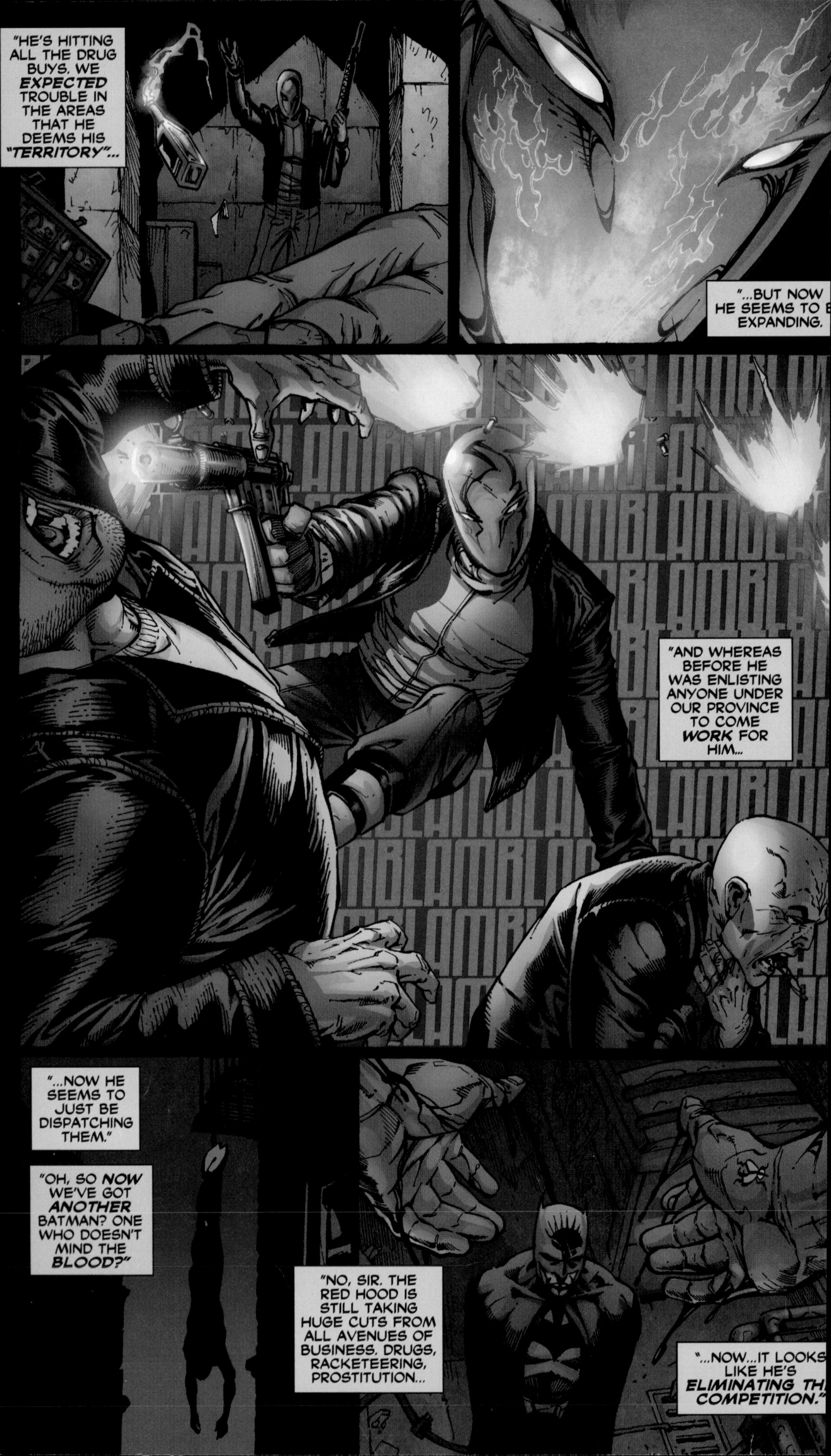
"HE'S HITTING ALL THE DRUG BUYS. WE **EXPECTED** TROUBLE IN THE AREAS THAT HE DEEMS HIS **"TERRITORY"**...
"...BUT NOW HE SEEMS TO B EXPANDING.
"AND WHEREAS BEFORE HE WAS ENLISTING ANYONE UNDER OUR PROVINCE TO COME **WORK** FOR HIM...
"...NOW HE SEEMS TO JUST BE DISPATCHING THEM."
"OH, SO **NOW** WE'VE GOT **ANOTHER** BATMAN? ONE WHO DOESN'T MIND THE **BLOOD?"**
"NO, SIR. THE RED HOOD IS STILL TAKING HUGE CUTS FROM ALL AVENUES OF BUSINESS. DRUGS, RACKETEERING, PROSTITUTION...
"...NOW...IT LOOKS LIKE HE'S **ELIMINATING TH COMPETITION."**

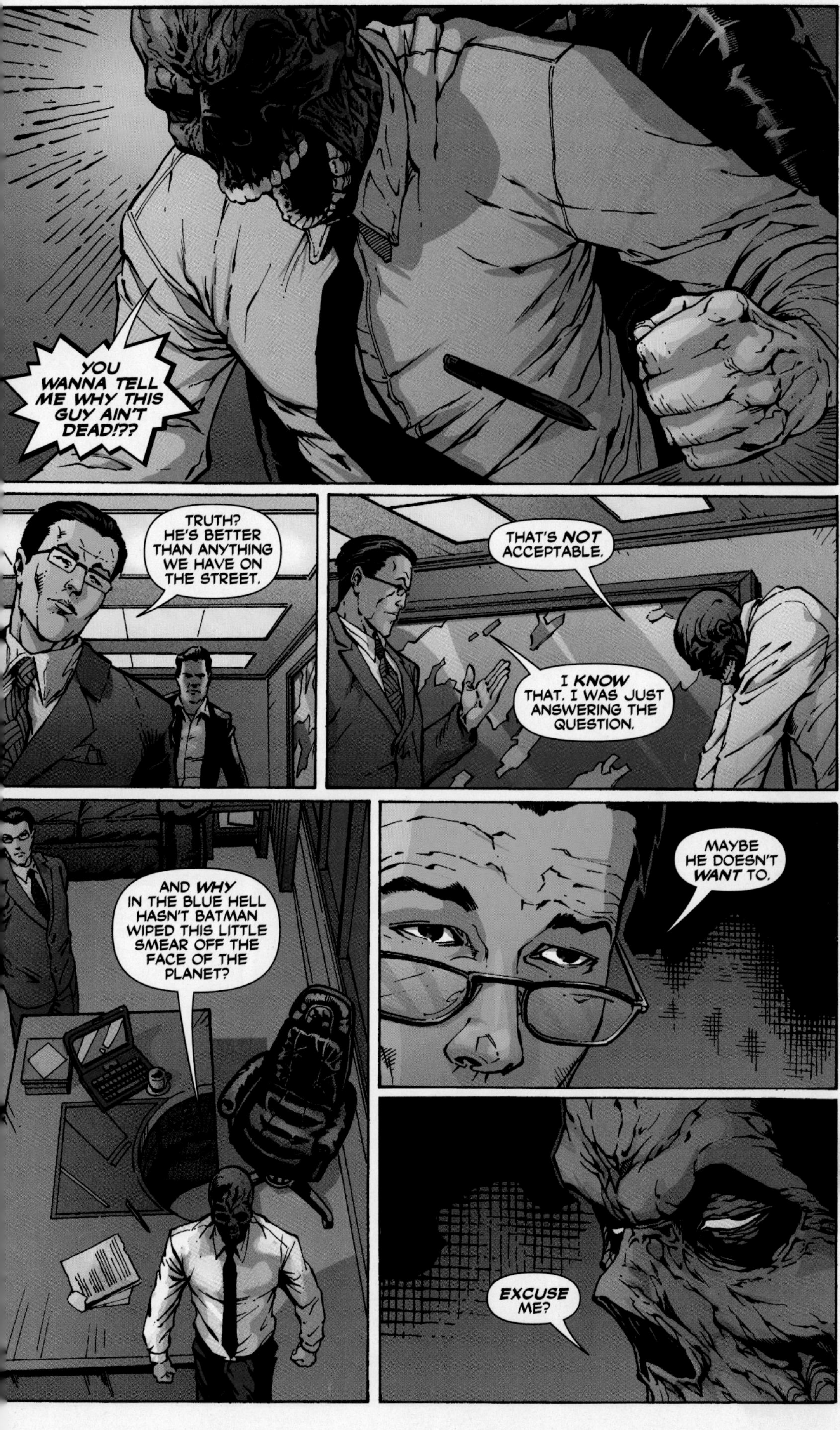
YOU WANNA TELL ME WHY THIS GUY AIN'T DEAD!??
TRUTH? HE'S BETTER THAN ANYTHING WE HAVE ON THE STREET.
THAT'S NOT ACCEPTABLE.
I KNOW THAT. I WAS JUST ANSWERING THE QUESTION.
AND WHY IN THE BLUE HELL HASN'T BATMAN WIPED THIS LITTLE SMEAR OFF THE FACE OF THE PLANET?
MAYBE HE DOESN'T WANT TO.
EXCUSE ME?

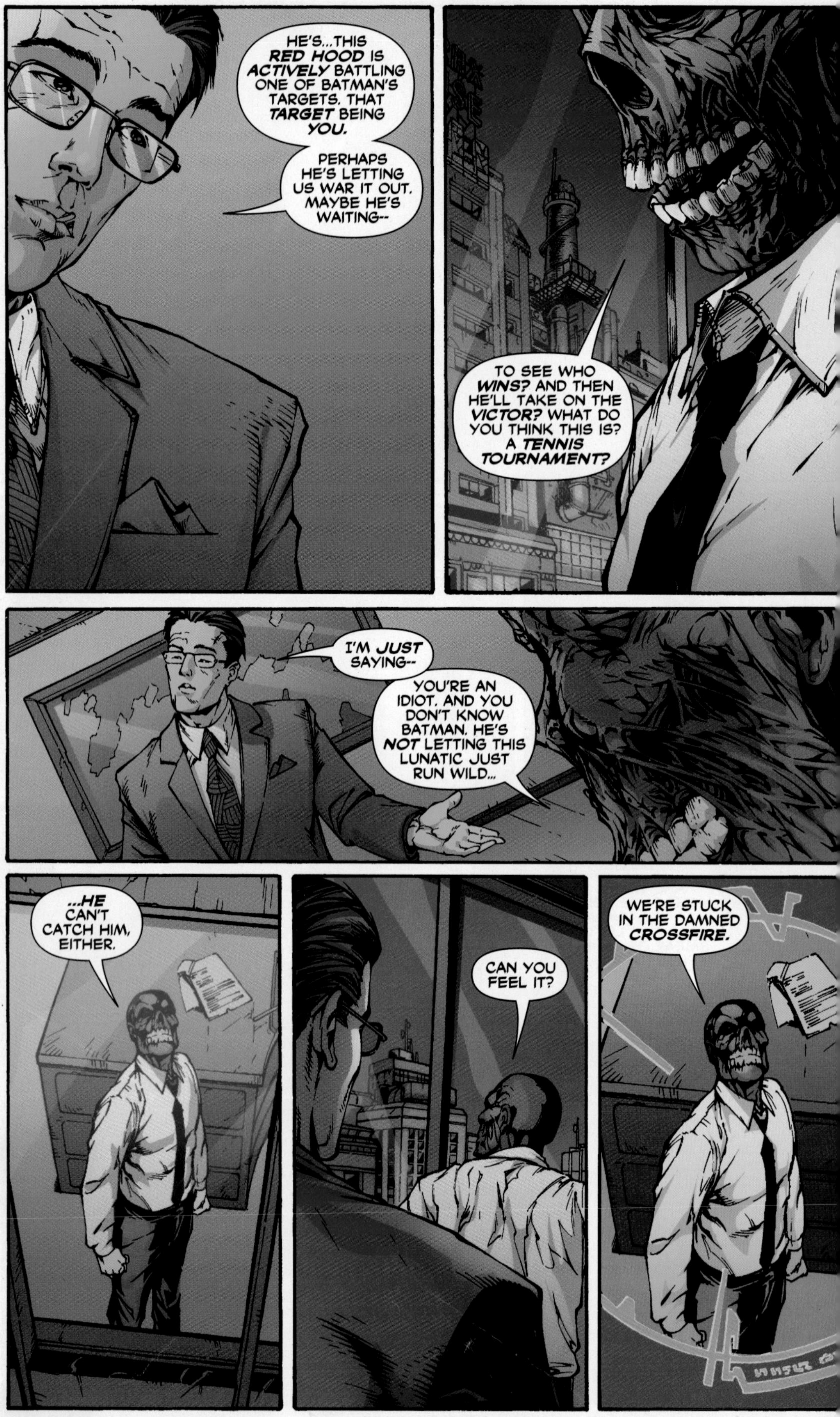
HE'S...THIS **RED HOOD** IS **ACTIVELY** BATTLING ONE OF BATMAN'S TARGETS. THAT **TARGET** BEING **YOU.**
PERHAPS HE'S LETTING US WAR IT OUT. MAYBE HE'S WAITING--
TO SEE WHO **WINS?** AND THEN HE'LL TAKE ON THE **VICTOR?** WHAT DO YOU THINK THIS IS? A **TENNIS TOURNAMENT?**
I'M **JUST** SAYING--
YOU'RE AN IDIOT. AND YOU DON'T KNOW BATMAN. HE'S **NOT** LETTING THIS LUNATIC JUST RUN WILD...
...HE CAN'T CATCH HIM, EITHER.
CAN YOU FEEL IT?
WE'RE STUCK IN THE DAMNED **CROSSFIRE.**

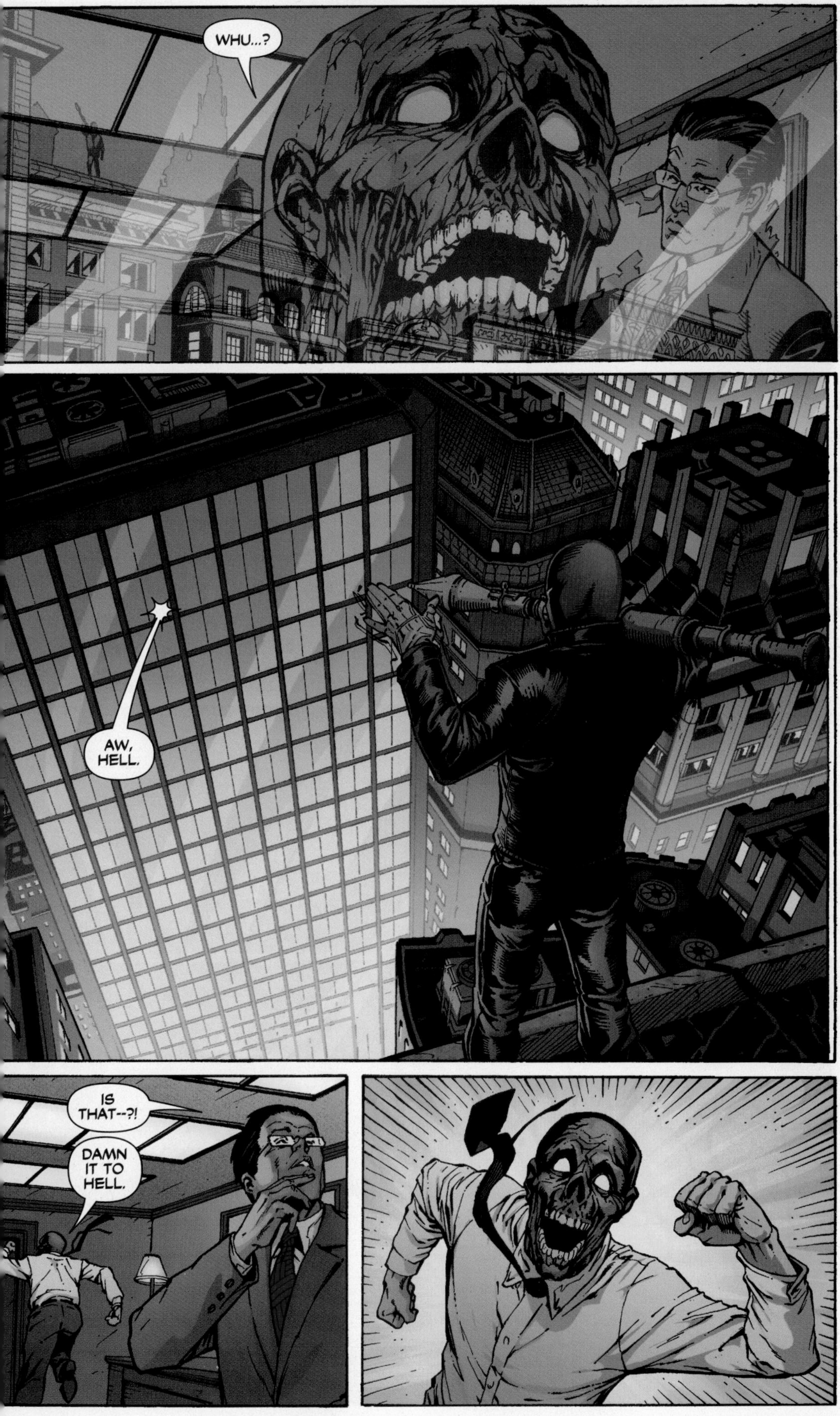
WHU...?
AW, HELL.
IS THAT--?!
DAMN IT TO HELL.

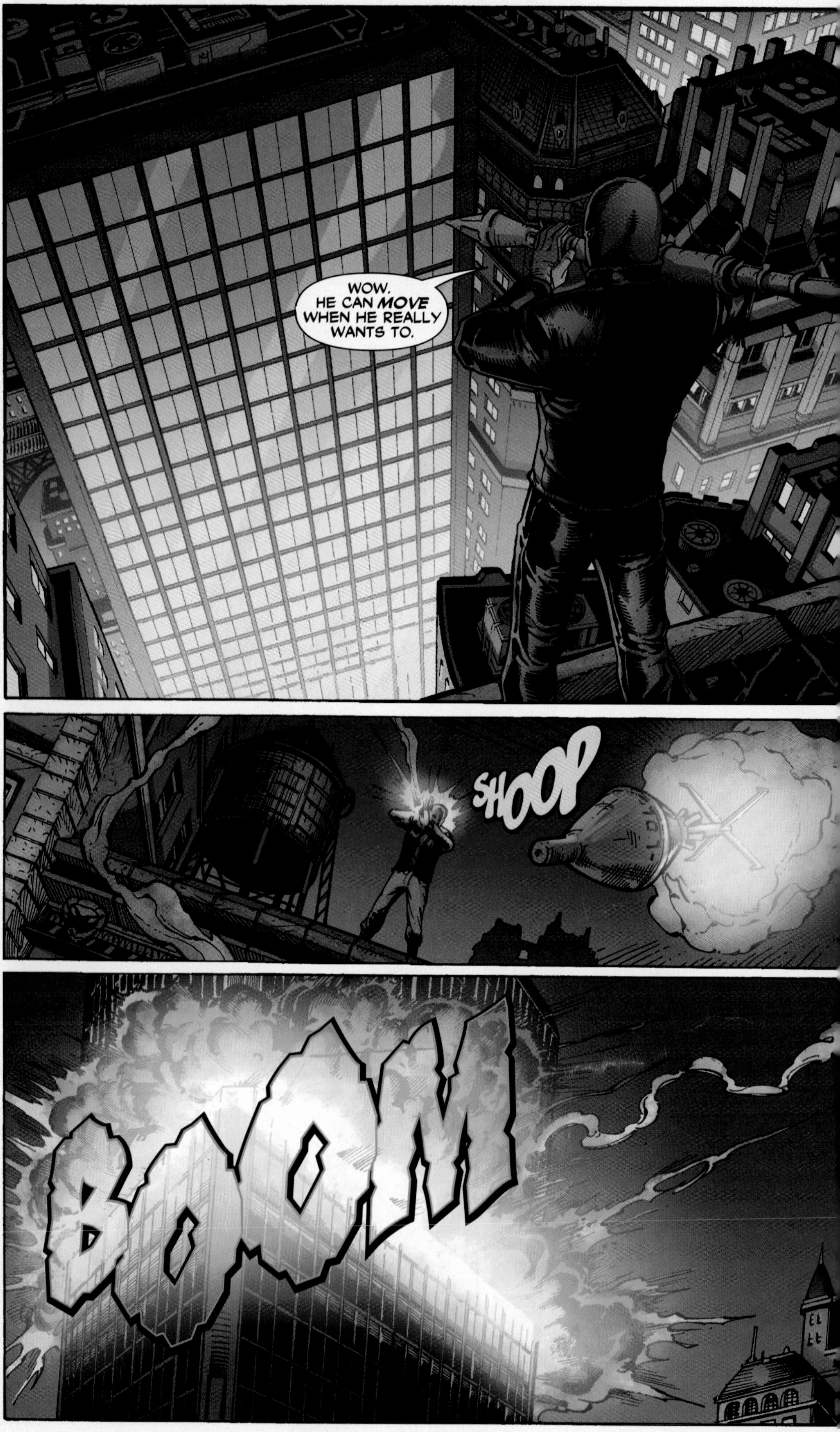
WOW, HE CAN MOVE WHEN HE REALLY WANTS TO.
SHOOP
BOOM

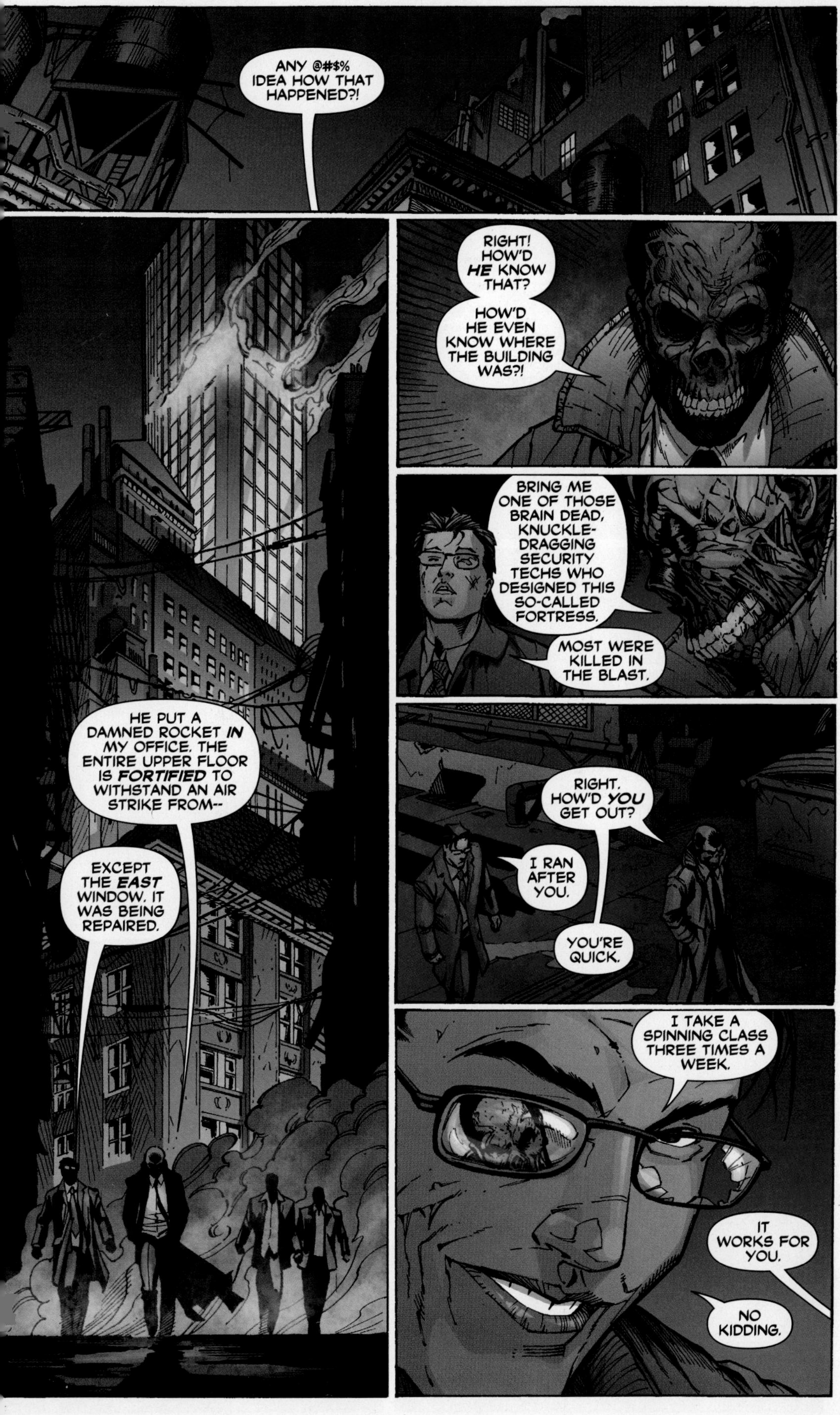
ANY @#$% IDEA HOW THAT HAPPENED?!
HE PUT A DAMNED ROCKET *IN* MY OFFICE. THE ENTIRE UPPER FLOOR IS *FORTIFIED* TO WITHSTAND AN AIR STRIKE FROM--
EXCEPT THE *EAST* WINDOW. IT WAS BEING REPAIRED.
RIGHT! HOW'D *HE* KNOW THAT?
HOW'D HE EVEN KNOW WHERE THE BUILDING WAS?!
BRING ME ONE OF THOSE BRAIN DEAD, KNUCKLE-DRAGGING SECURITY TECHS WHO DESIGNED THIS SO-CALLED FORTRESS.
MOST WERE KILLED IN THE BLAST.
RIGHT. HOW'D *YOU* GET OUT?
I RAN AFTER YOU.
YOU'RE QUICK.
I TAKE A SPINNING CLASS THREE TIMES A WEEK.
IT WORKS FOR YOU.
NO KIDDING.

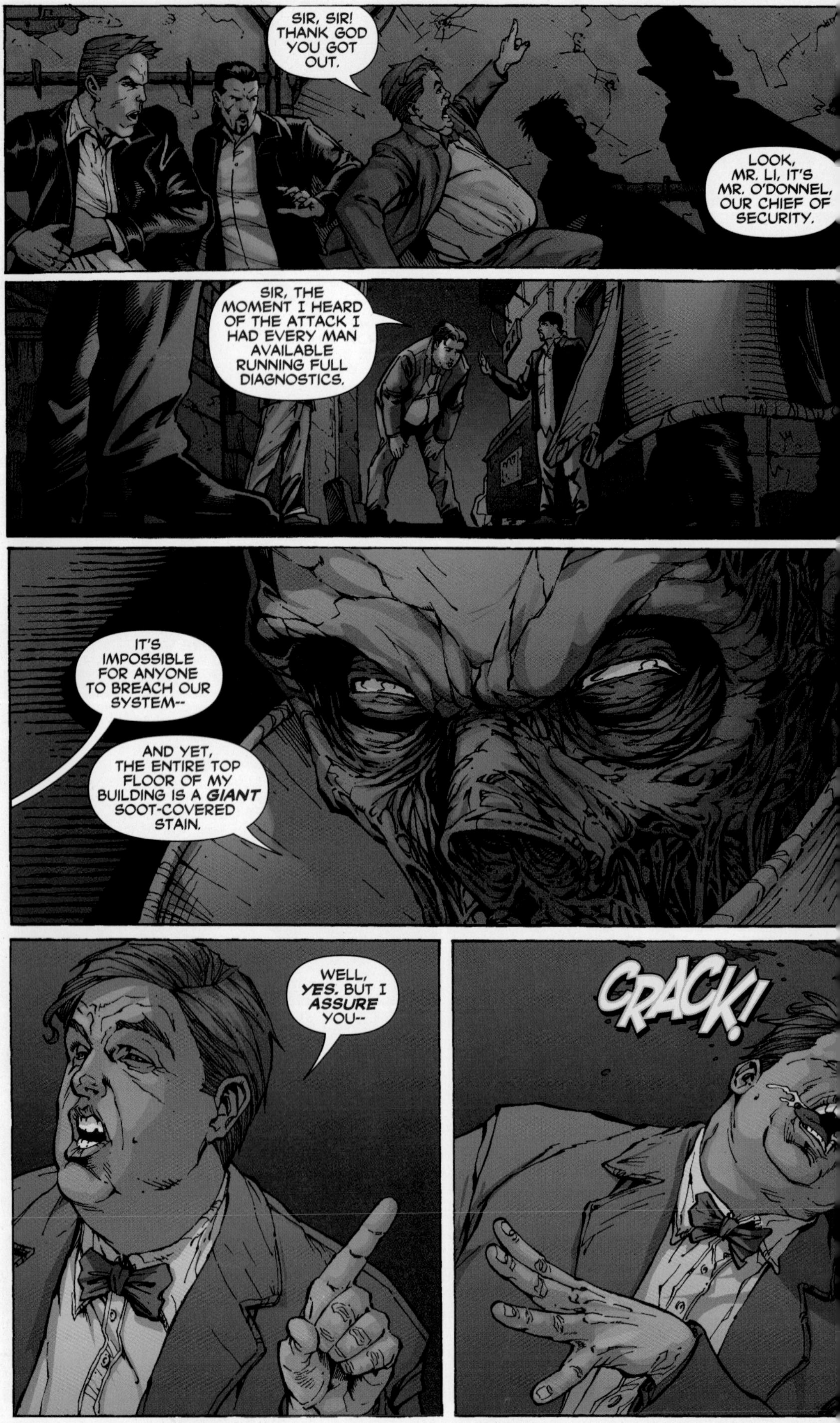
SIR, SIR! THANK GOD YOU GOT OUT.
LOOK, MR. LI, IT'S MR. O'DONNEL, OUR CHIEF OF SECURITY.
SIR, THE MOMENT I HEARD OF THE ATTACK I HAD EVERY MAN AVAILABLE RUNNING FULL DIAGNOSTICS.
IT'S IMPOSSIBLE FOR ANYONE TO BREACH OUR SYSTEM--
AND YET, THE ENTIRE TOP FLOOR OF MY BUILDING IS A GIANT SOOT-COVERED STAIN.
WELL, YES. BUT I ASSURE YOU--
CRACK!

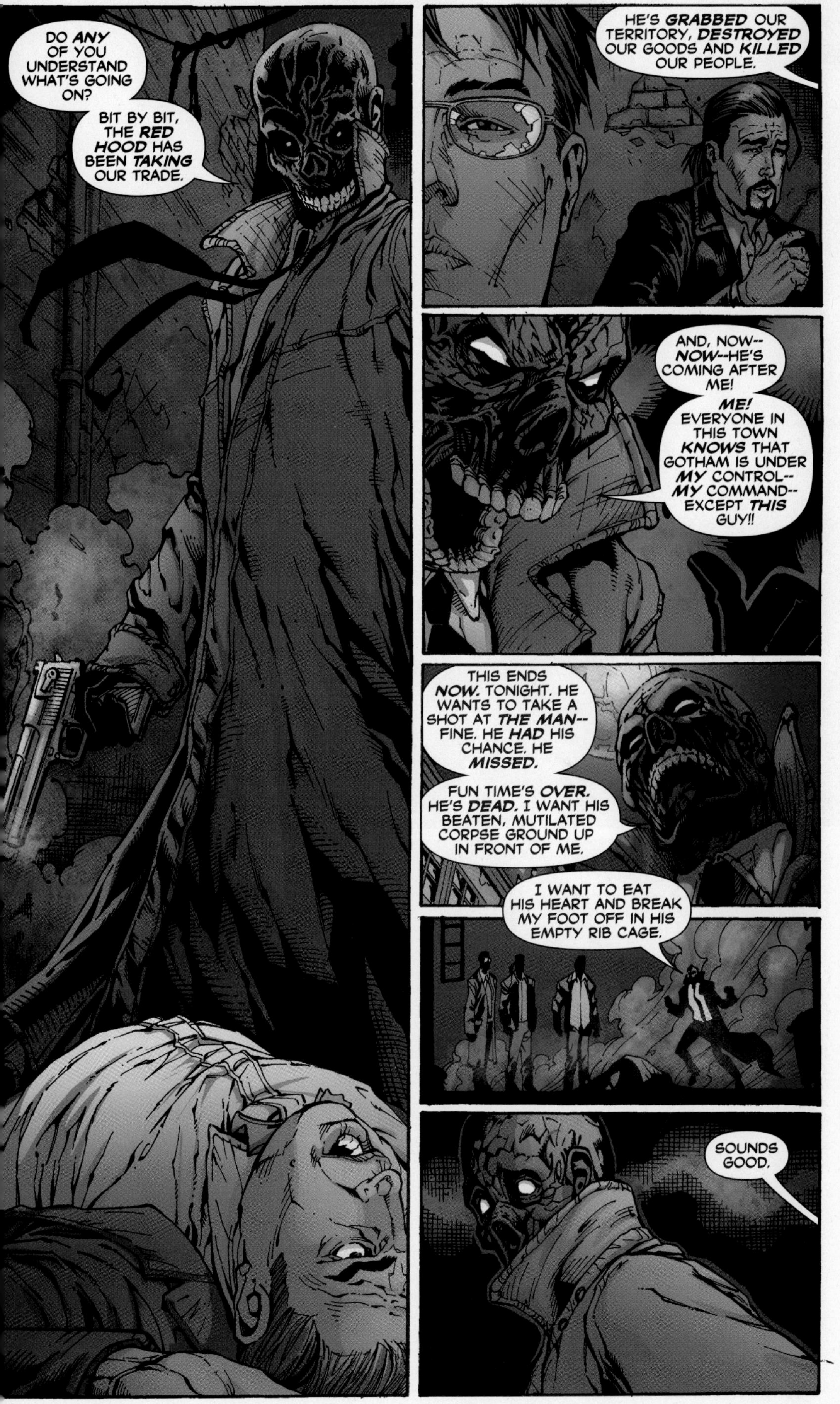
DO ANY OF YOU UNDERSTAND WHAT'S GOING ON?
BIT BY BIT, THE RED HOOD HAS BEEN TAKING OUR TRADE.
HE'S GRABBED OUR TERRITORY, DESTROYED OUR GOODS AND KILLED OUR PEOPLE.
AND, NOW-- NOW--HE'S COMING AFTER ME!
ME! EVERYONE IN THIS TOWN KNOWS THAT GOTHAM IS UNDER MY CONTROL-- MY COMMAND-- EXCEPT THIS GUY!!
THIS ENDS NOW. TONIGHT. HE WANTS TO TAKE A SHOT AT THE MAN-- FINE. HE HAD HIS CHANCE. HE MISSED.
FUN TIME'S OVER. HE'S DEAD. I WANT HIS BEATEN, MUTILATED CORPSE GROUND UP IN FRONT OF ME.
I WANT TO EAT HIS HEART AND BREAK MY FOOT OFF IN HIS EMPTY RIB CAGE.
SOUNDS GOOD.

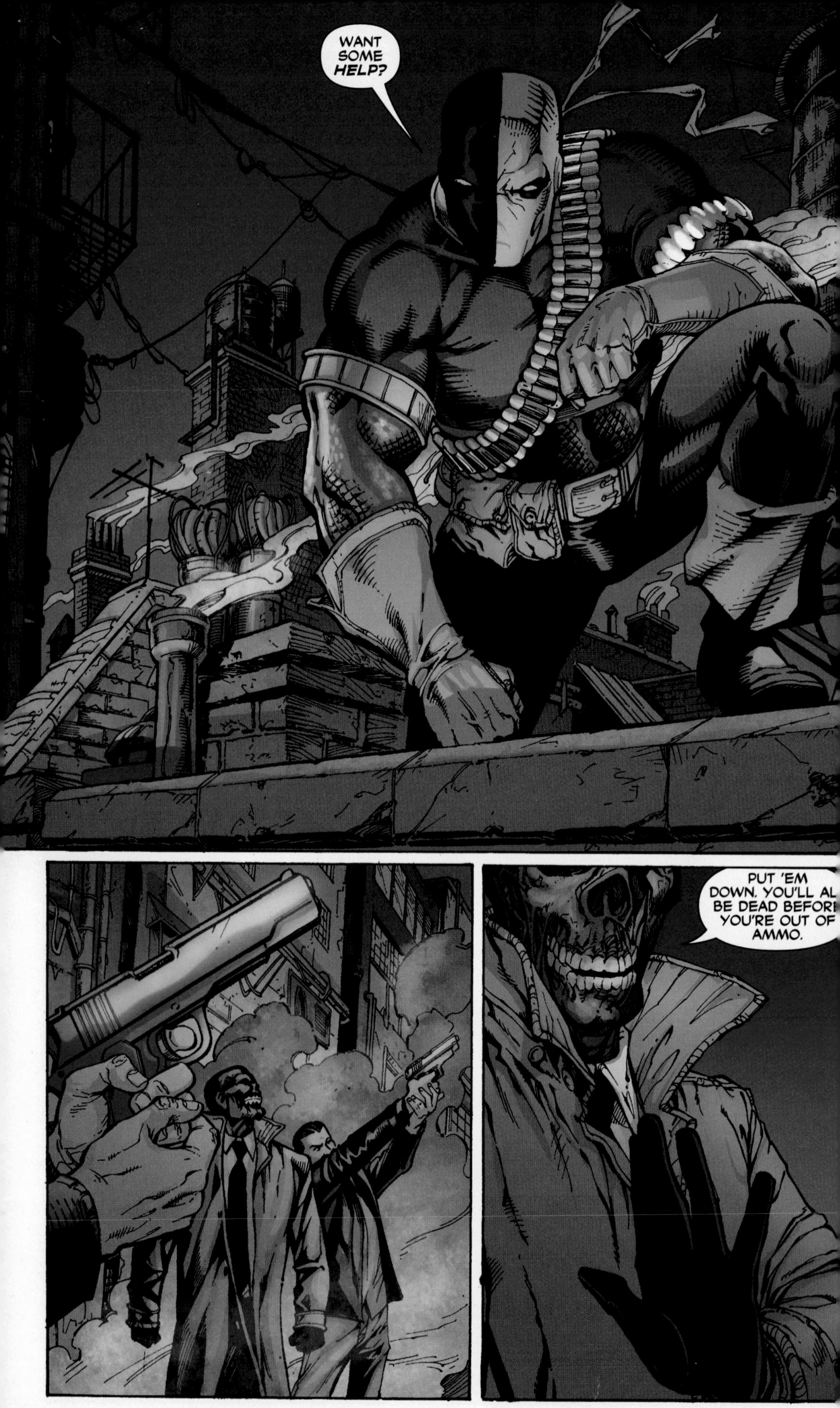
WANT SOME HELP?
PUT 'EM DOWN. YOU'LL AL BE DEAD BEFOR YOU'RE OUT OF AMMO.

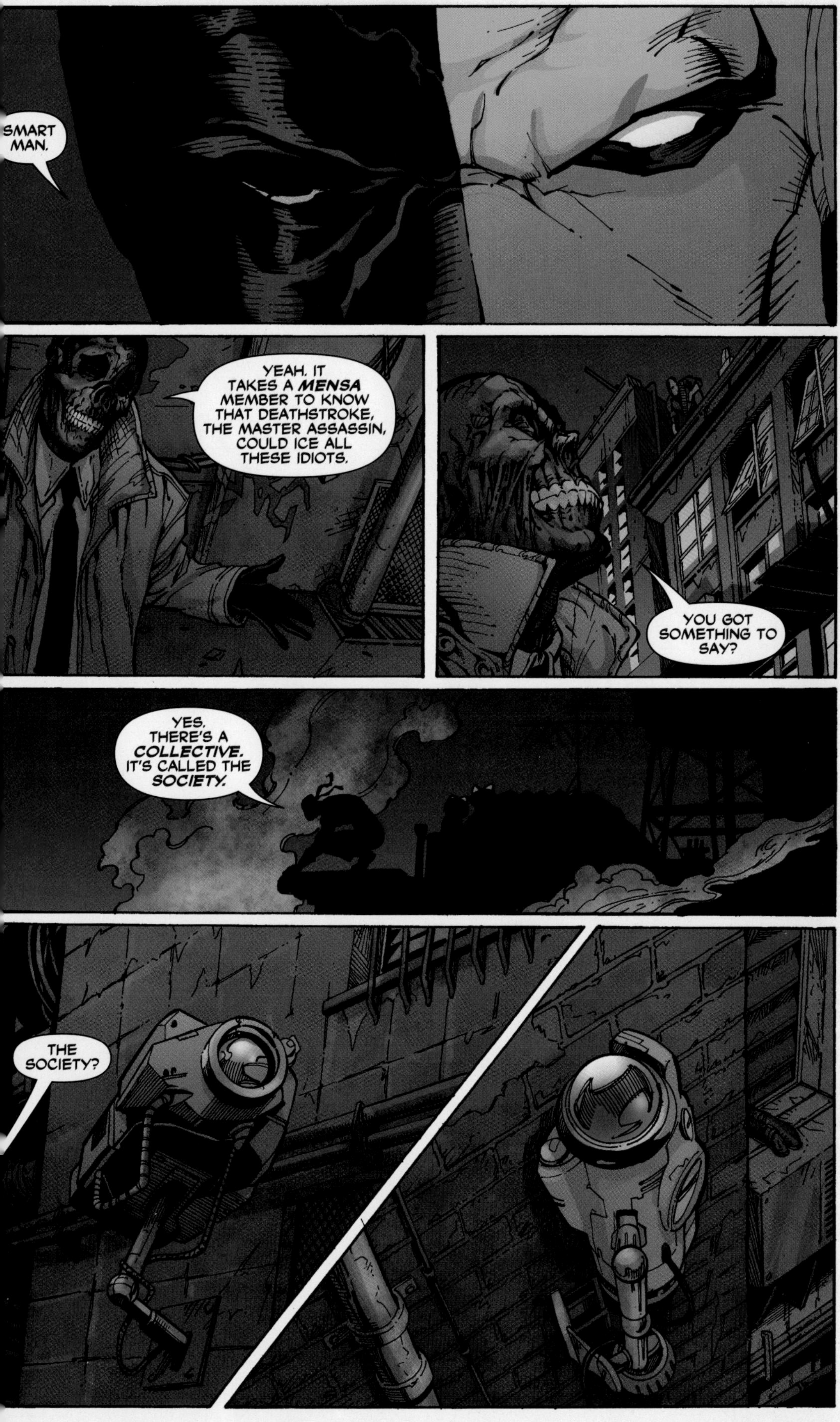
SMART MAN.
YEAH, IT TAKES A *MENSA* MEMBER TO KNOW THAT DEATHSTROKE, THE MASTER ASSASSIN, COULD ICE ALL THESE IDIOTS.
YOU GOT SOMETHING TO SAY?
YES, THERE'S A *COLLECTIVE*. IT'S CALLED THE *SOCIETY*.
THE SOCIETY?

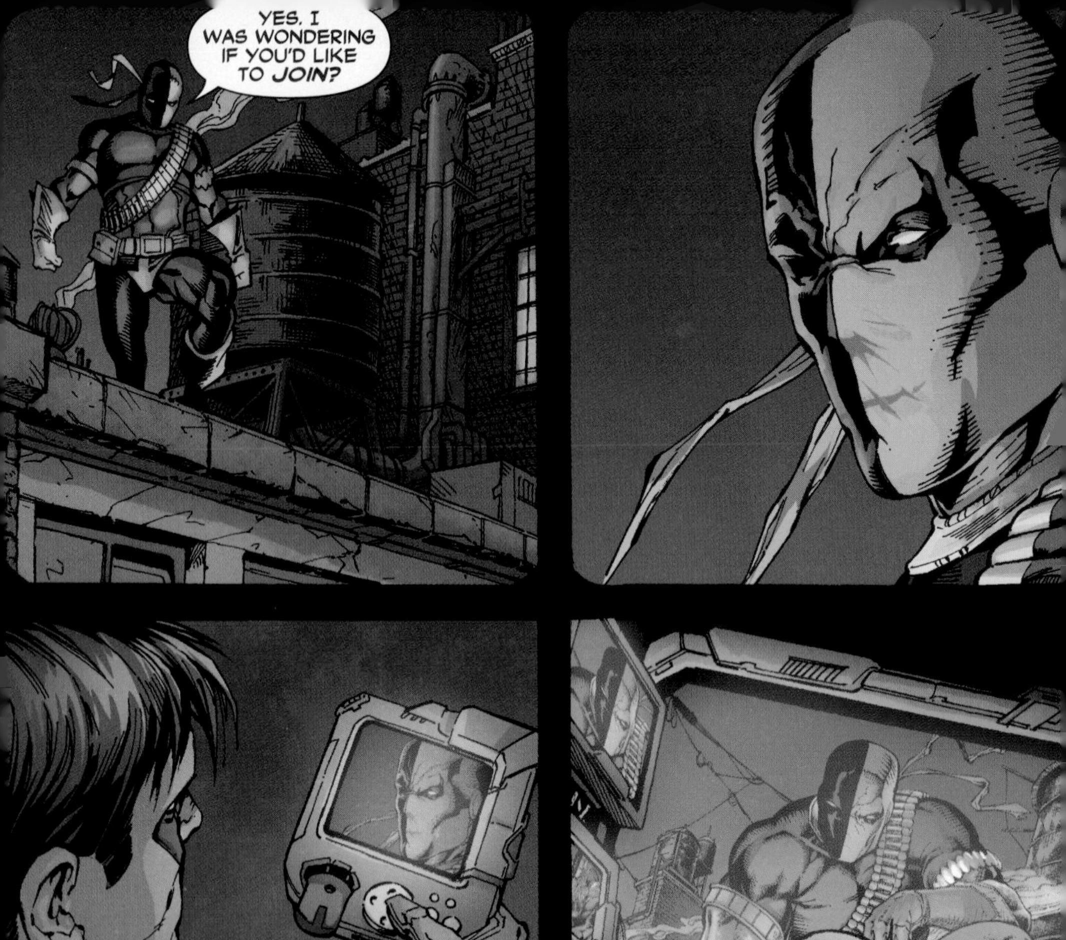
YES. I WAS WONDERING IF YOU'D LIKE TO *JOIN?*
DAMN IT.
DAMN IT.

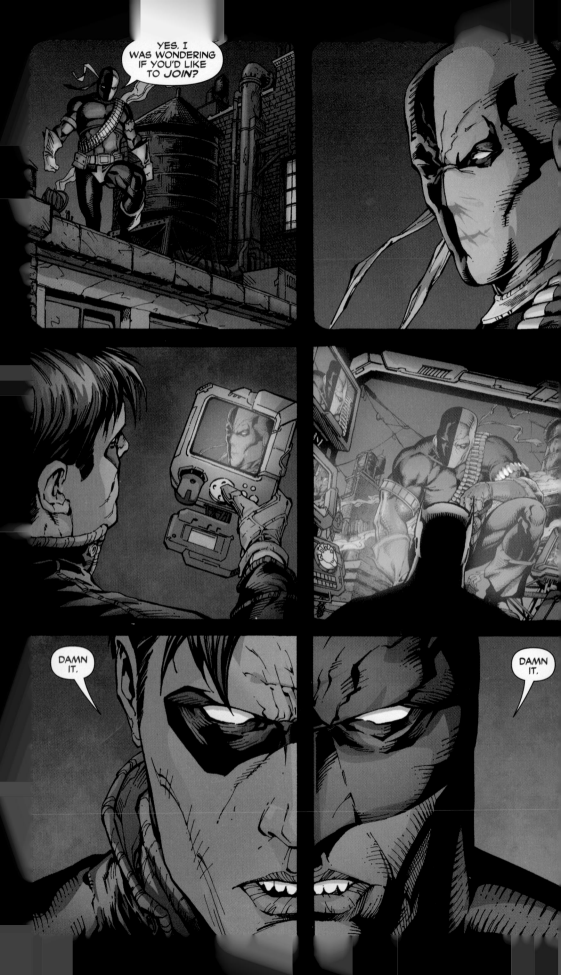

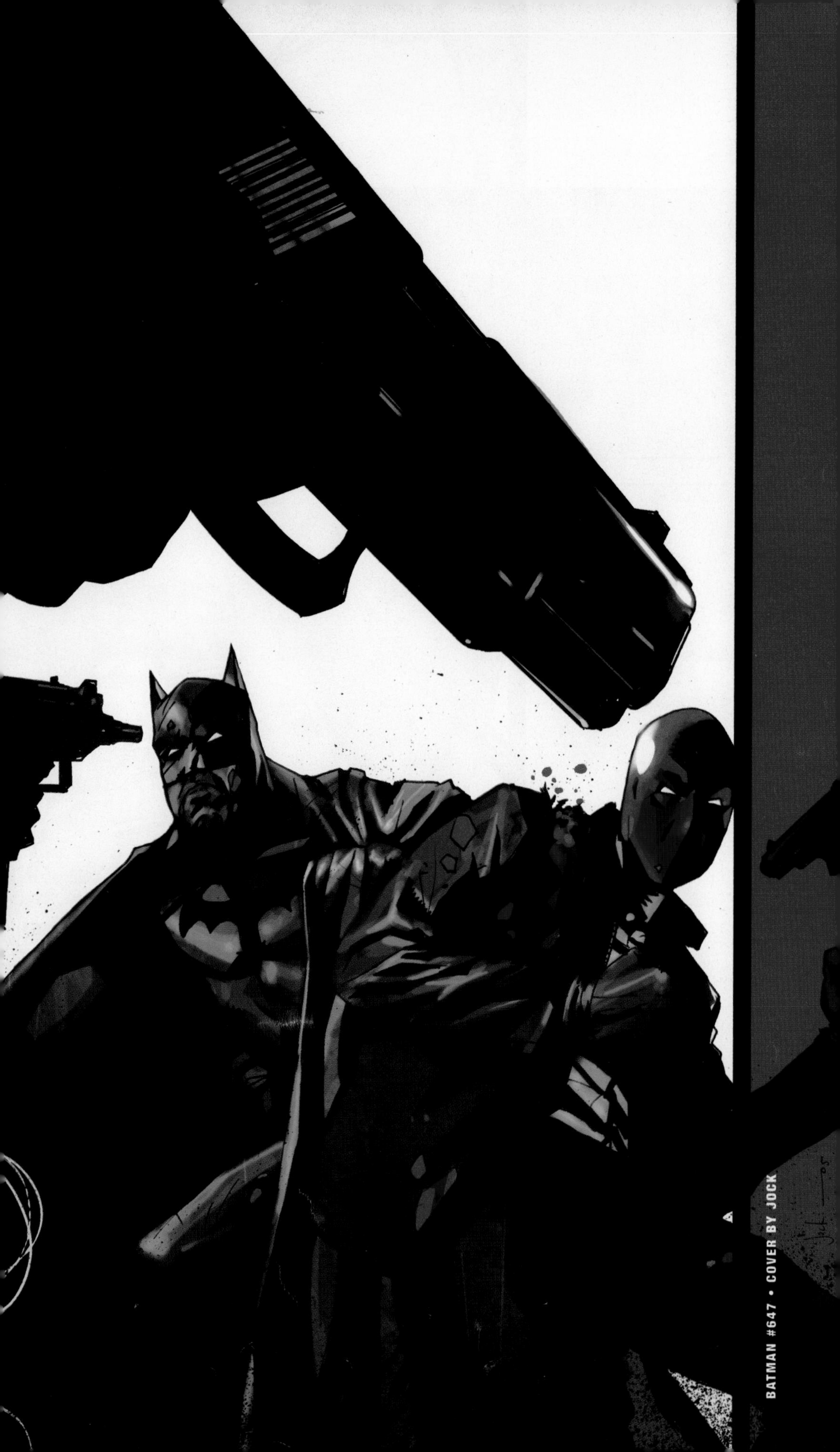

BATMAN #647 • COVER BY JOCK

CHAPTER 3

FRANCHISE PART 2: THE AWAY TEAM

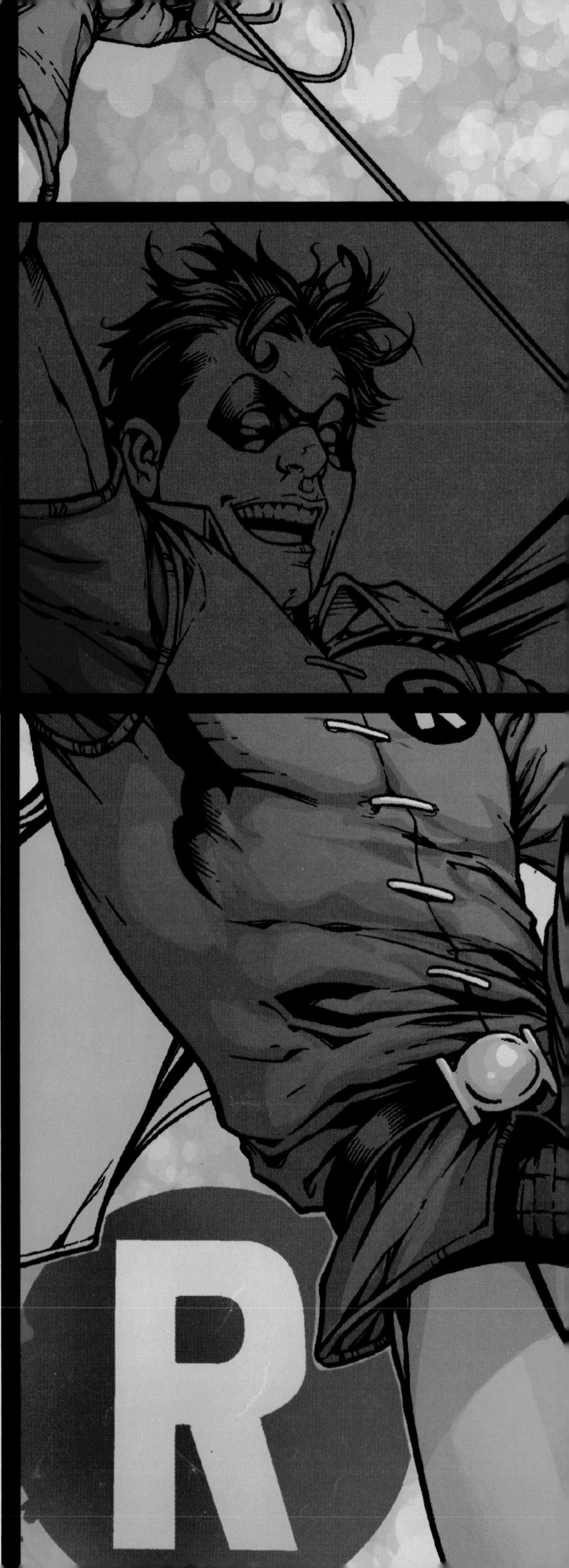

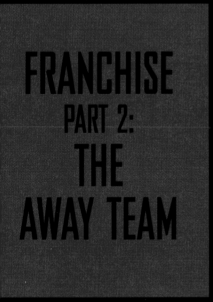

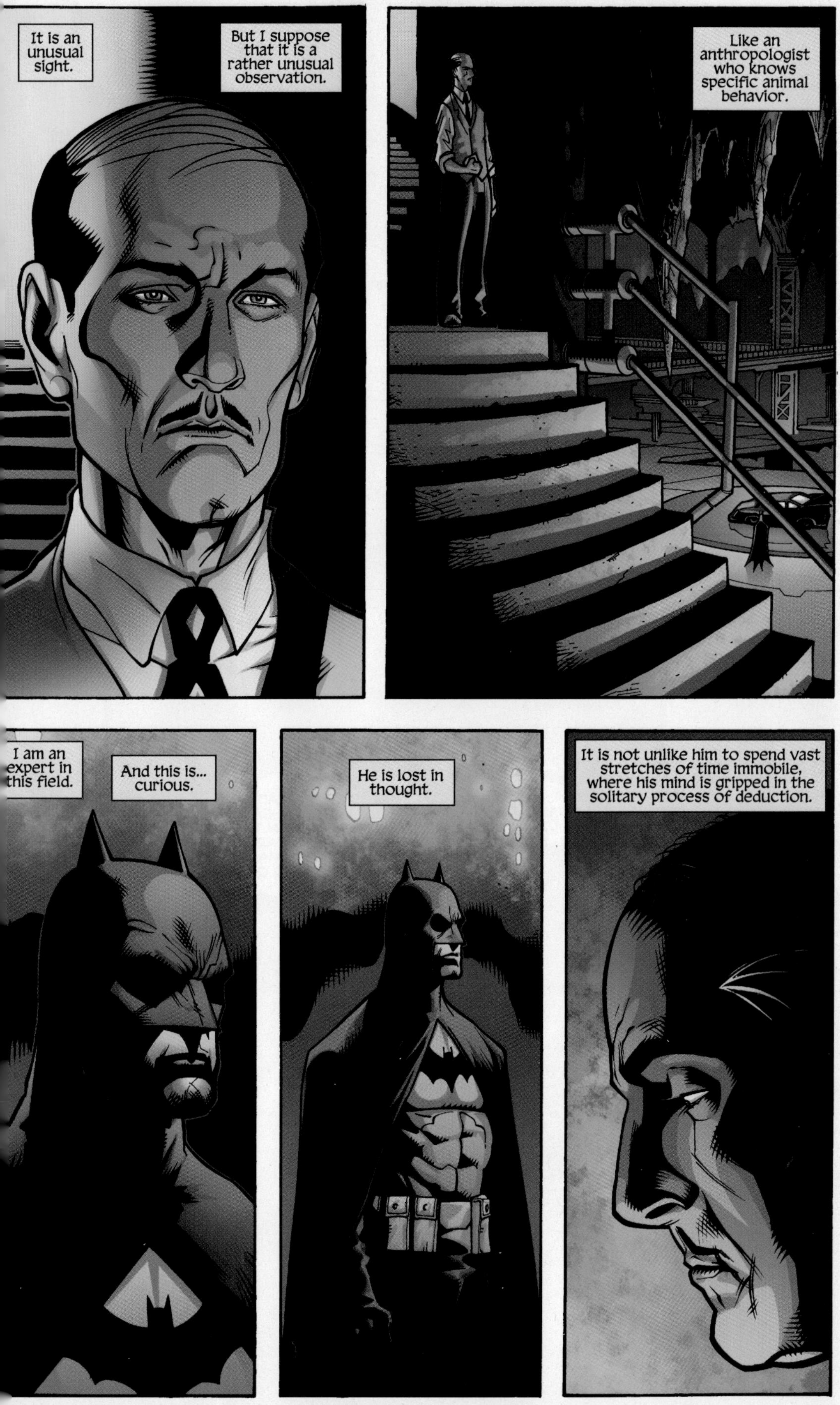
It is an unusual sight.
But I suppose that it is a rather unusual observation.
Like an anthropologist who knows specific animal behavior.
I am an expert in this field.
And this is... curious.
He is lost in thought.
It is not unlike him to spend vast stretches of time immobile, where his mind is gripped in the solitary process of deduction.

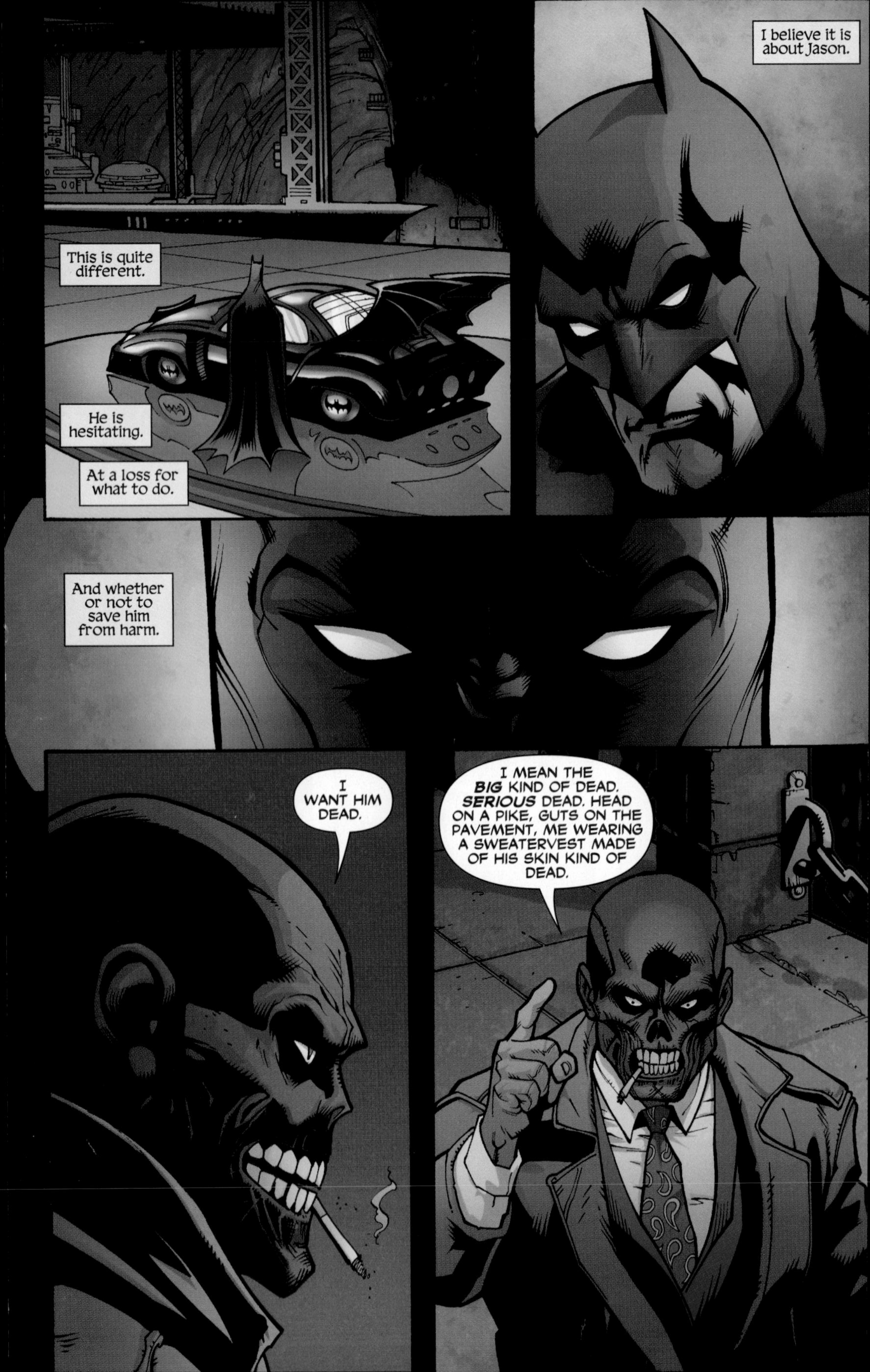

This is quite different.
He is hesitating.
At a loss for what to do.
I believe it is about Jason.
And whether or not to save him from harm.
I WANT HIM DEAD.
I MEAN THE BIG KIND OF DEAD. SERIOUS DEAD. HEAD ON A PIKE, GUTS ON THE PAVEMENT, ME WEARING A SWEATERVEST MADE OF HIS SKIN KIND OF DEAD.

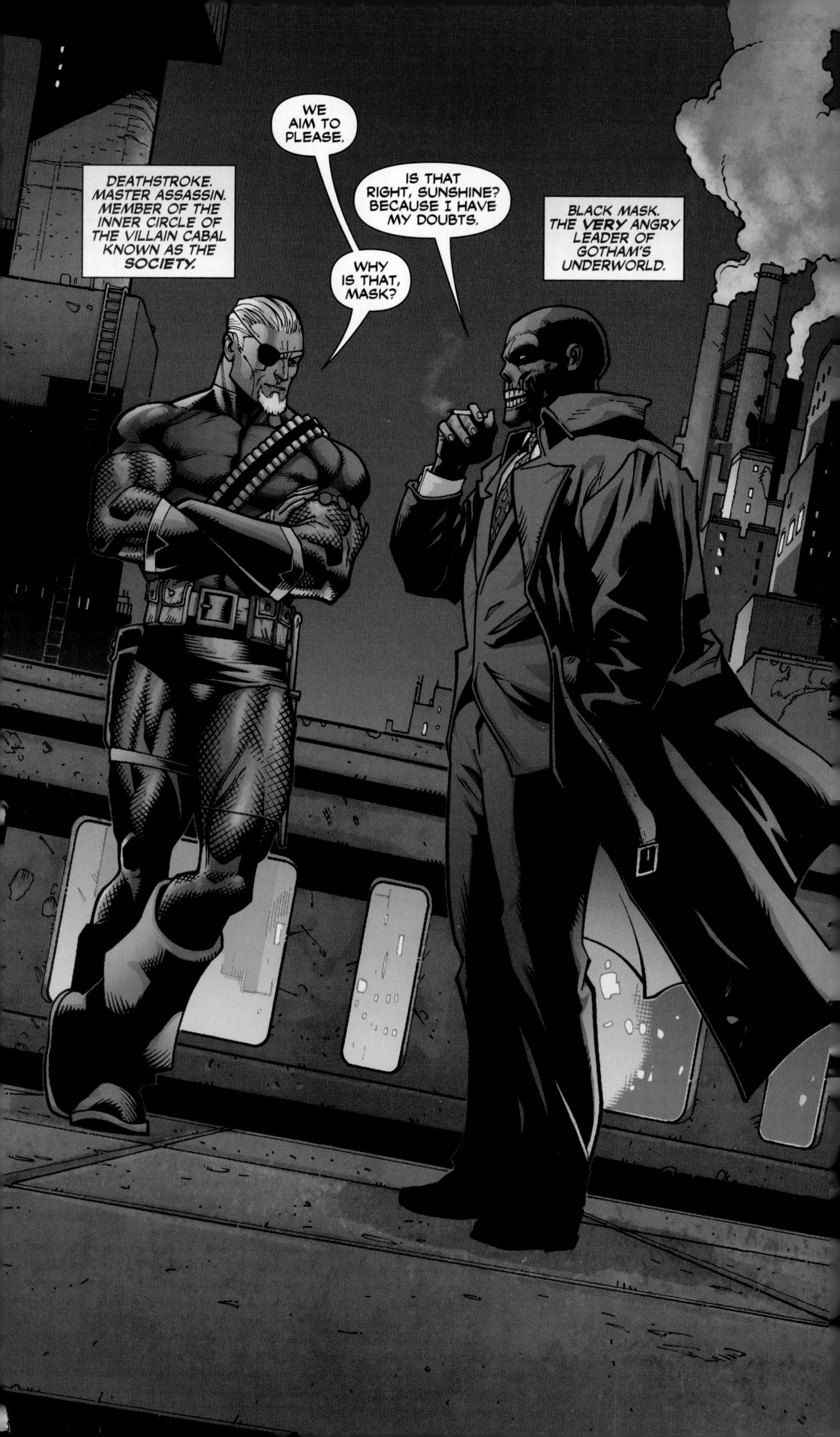
DEATHSTROKE. MASTER ASSASSIN. MEMBER OF THE INNER CIRCLE OF THE VILLAIN CABAL KNOWN AS THE SOCIETY.
WE AIM TO PLEASE.
IS THAT RIGHT, SUNSHINE? BECAUSE I HAVE MY DOUBTS.
BLACK MASK. THE VERY ANGRY LEADER OF GOTHAM'S UNDERWORLD.
WHY IS THAT, MASK?

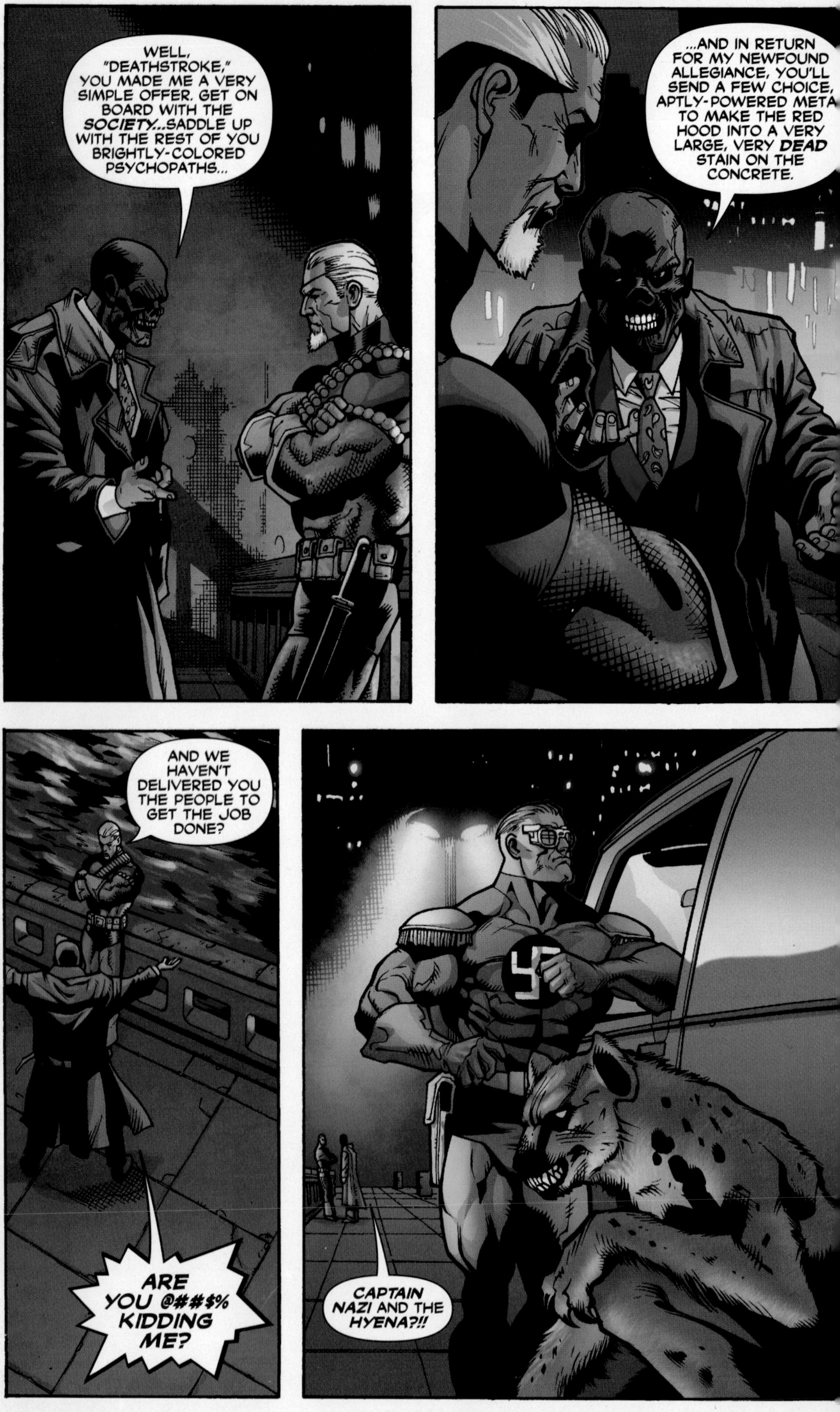
WELL, "DEATHSTROKE," YOU MADE ME A VERY SIMPLE OFFER. GET ON BOARD WITH THE *SOCIETY*...SADDLE UP WITH THE REST OF YOU BRIGHTLY-COLORED PSYCHOPATHS...
...AND IN RETURN FOR MY NEWFOUND ALLEGIANCE, YOU'LL SEND A FEW CHOICE, APTLY-POWERED META TO MAKE THE RED HOOD INTO A VERY LARGE, VERY *DEAD* STAIN ON THE CONCRETE.
AND WE HAVEN'T DELIVERED YOU THE PEOPLE TO GET THE JOB DONE?
ARE YOU @##$% KIDDING ME?
CAPTAIN NAZI AND THE *HYENA?!!*

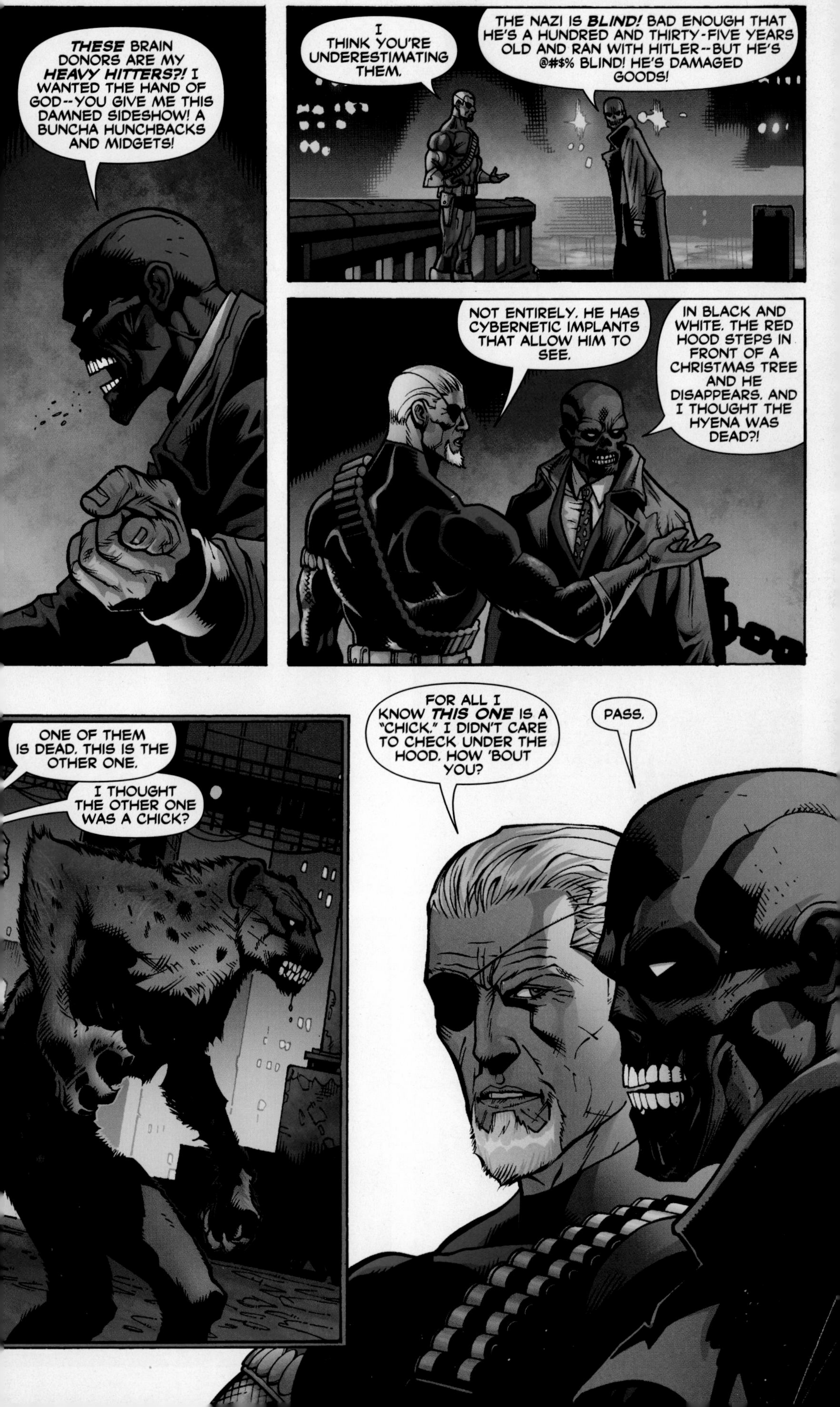
THESE BRAIN DONORS ARE MY HEAVY HITTERS?! I WANTED THE HAND OF GOD--YOU GIVE ME THIS DAMNED SIDESHOW! A BUNCHA HUNCHBACKS AND MIDGETS!
I THINK YOU'RE UNDERESTIMATING THEM.
THE NAZI IS BLIND! BAD ENOUGH THAT HE'S A HUNDRED AND THIRTY-FIVE YEARS OLD AND RAN WITH HITLER--BUT HE'S @#$% BLIND! HE'S DAMAGED GOODS!
NOT ENTIRELY. HE HAS CYBERNETIC IMPLANTS THAT ALLOW HIM TO SEE.
IN BLACK AND WHITE. THE RED HOOD STEPS IN FRONT OF A CHRISTMAS TREE AND HE DISAPPEARS. AND I THOUGHT THE HYENA WAS DEAD?!
ONE OF THEM IS DEAD. THIS IS THE OTHER ONE.
I THOUGHT THE OTHER ONE WAS A CHICK?
FOR ALL I KNOW THIS ONE IS A "CHICK." I DIDN'T CARE TO CHECK UNDER THE HOOD. HOW 'BOUT YOU?
PASS.

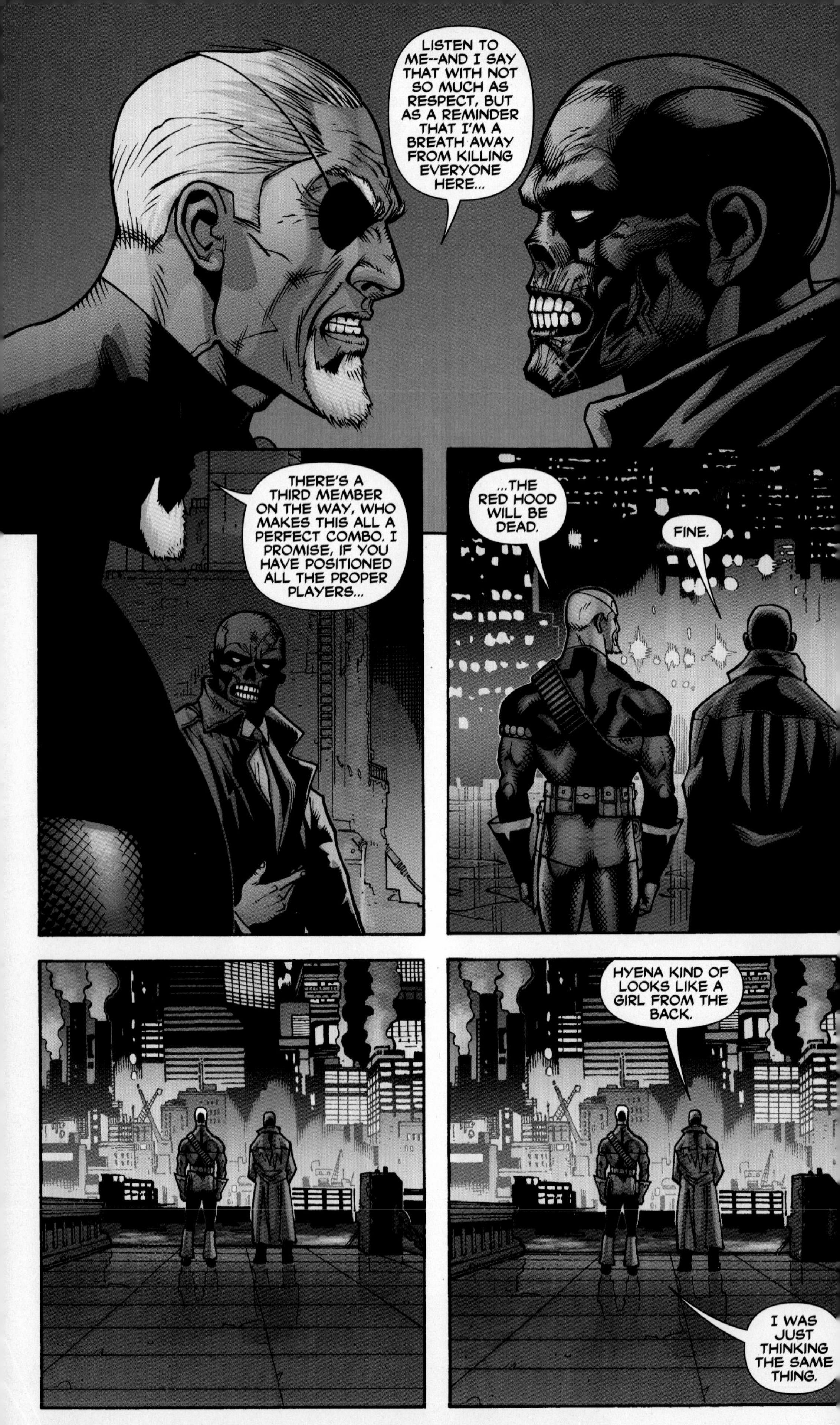
LISTEN TO ME--AND I SAY THAT WITH NOT SO MUCH AS RESPECT, BUT AS A REMINDER THAT I'M A BREATH AWAY FROM KILLING EVERYONE HERE...
THERE'S A THIRD MEMBER ON THE WAY, WHO MAKES THIS ALL A PERFECT COMBO. I PROMISE, IF YOU HAVE POSITIONED ALL THE PROPER PLAYERS...
...THE RED HOOD WILL BE DEAD.
FINE.
HYENA KIND OF LOOKS LIKE A GIRL FROM THE BACK.
I WAS JUST THINKING THE SAME THING.

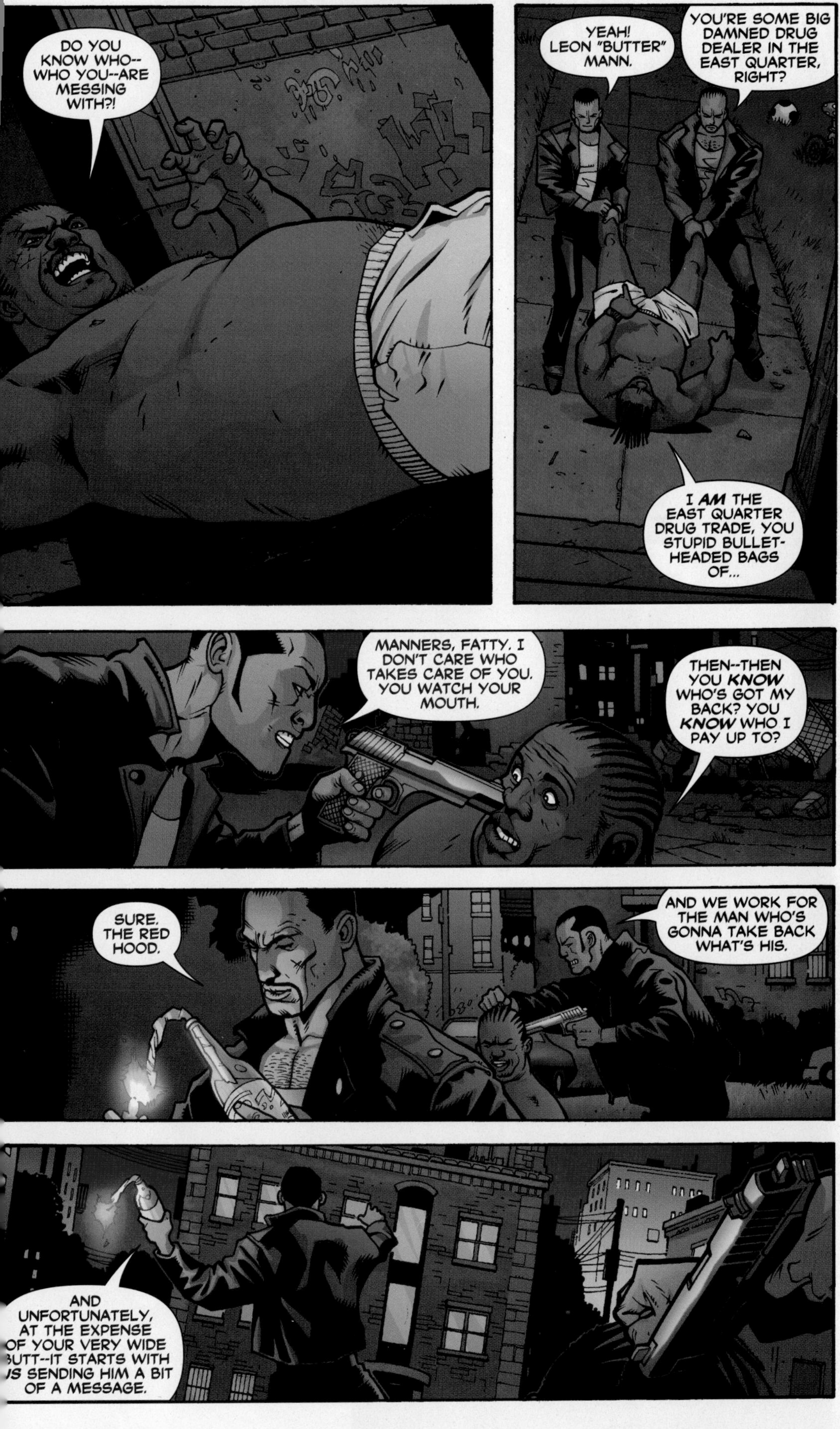
DO YOU KNOW WHO-- WHO YOU--ARE MESSING WITH?!
YEAH! LEON "BUTTER" MANN.
YOU'RE SOME BIG DAMNED DRUG DEALER IN THE EAST QUARTER, RIGHT?
I **AM** THE EAST QUARTER DRUG TRADE, YOU STUPID BULLET-HEADED BAGS OF...
MANNERS, FATTY. I DON'T CARE WHO TAKES CARE OF YOU. YOU WATCH YOUR MOUTH.
THEN--THEN YOU ***KNOW*** WHO'S GOT MY BACK? YOU ***KNOW*** WHO I PAY UP TO?
SURE. THE RED HOOD.
AND WE WORK FOR THE MAN WHO'S GONNA TAKE BACK WHAT'S HIS.
AND UNFORTUNATELY, AT THE EXPENSE OF YOUR VERY WIDE BUTT--IT STARTS WITH ***US*** SENDING HIM A BIT OF A MESSAGE.

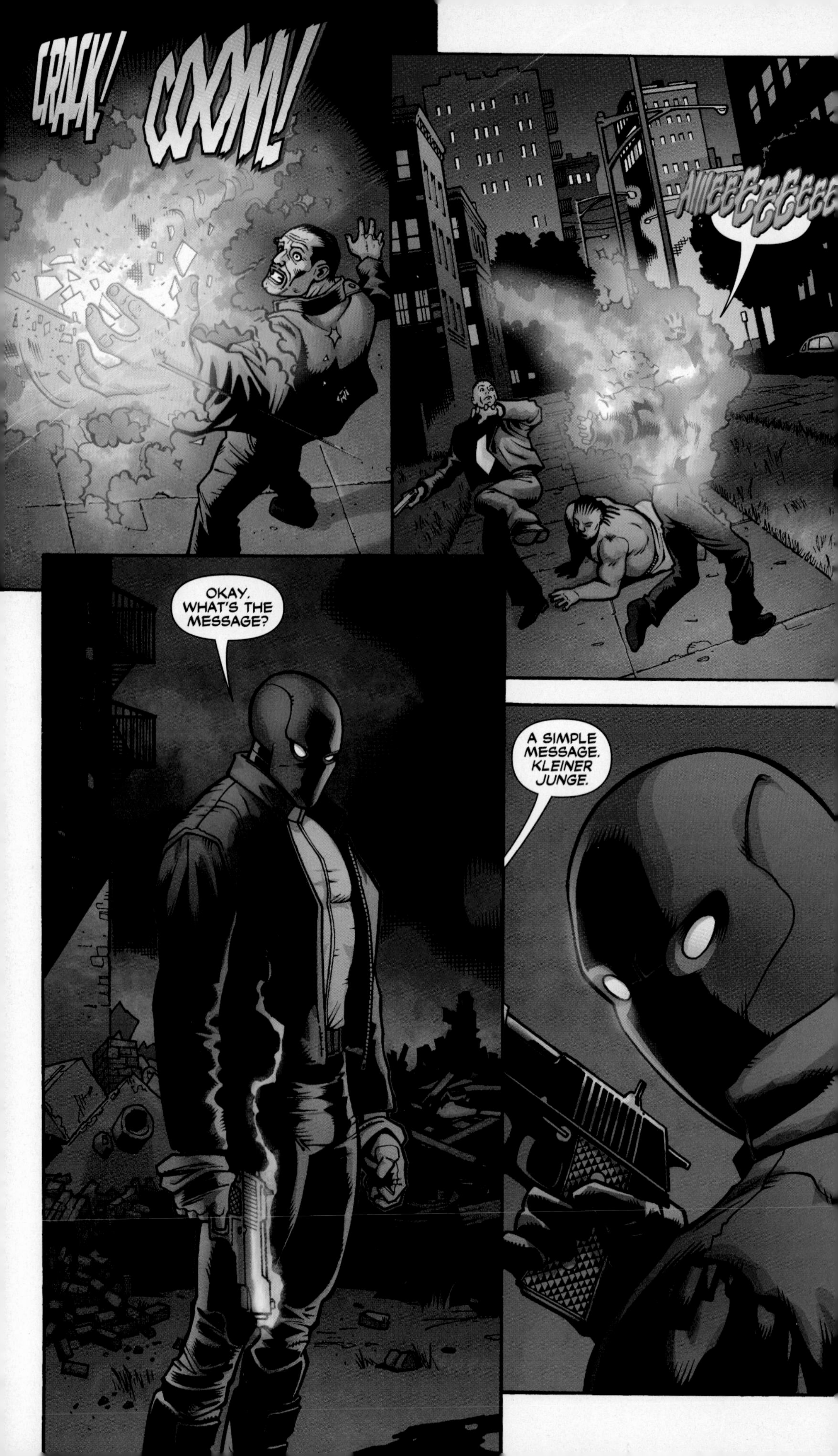
CRACK!
COOM!
AIIIEEEEEEEEE
OKAY. WHAT'S THE MESSAGE?
A SIMPLE MESSAGE. KLEINER JUNGE.

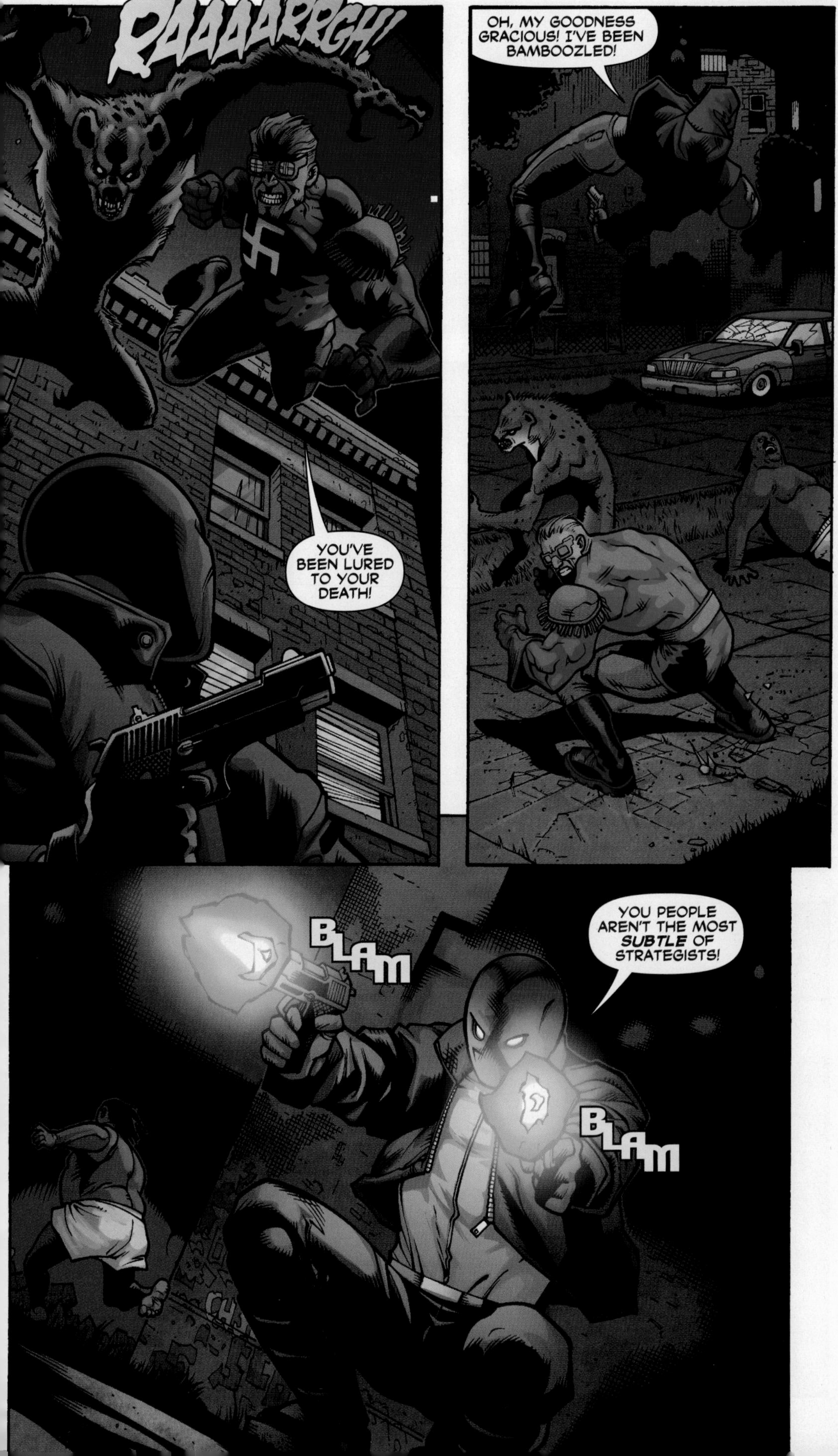
RAAAARRGH!
YOU'VE BEEN LURED TO YOUR DEATH!
OH, MY GOODNESS GRACIOUS! I'VE BEEN BAMBOOZLED!
BLAM
YOU PEOPLE AREN'T THE MOST *SUBTLE* OF STRATEGISTS!
BLAM

BUT I ASSUME SUBTLETY WASN'T PART OF THE PLAN.

Master Jason's had a condescending practice of referring to the costumed criminal elements as "dress ups."

NO, FEIGER HUND, YOUR DEATH IS OUR ONLY PLAN!

He also noted that such individuals did not fear the Batman the way the street toughs and mafioso did.

NO KIDDING? HERE I THOUGHT I WAS BEING GIVEN AN AUDITION.

BLAM

BLA

The "dress ups" did not believe that he was a monster.

PLING

PLING

PLING

I explained to Jason that he wa correct, but on to a certain degr

These individuals with their special abilities...these men who could do the unimaginable... these madmen...

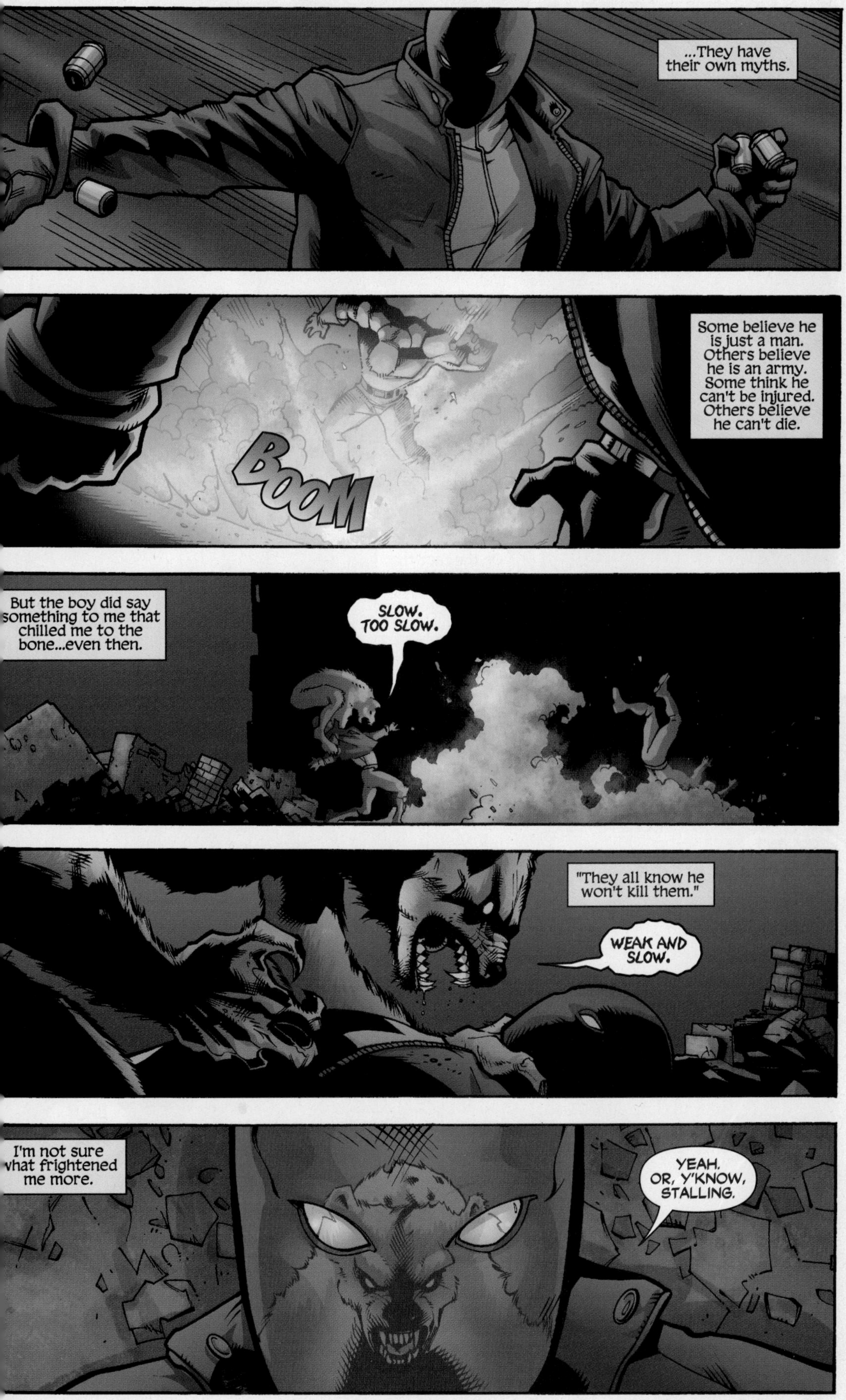

...They have their own myths.
Some believe he is just a man. Others believe he is an army. Some think he can't be injured. Others believe he can't die.
BOOM
But the boy did say something to me that chilled me to the bone...even then.
SLOW. TOO SLOW.
"They all know he won't kill them."
WEAK AND SLOW.
I'm not sure what frightened me more.
YEAH. OR, Y'KNOW, STALLING.

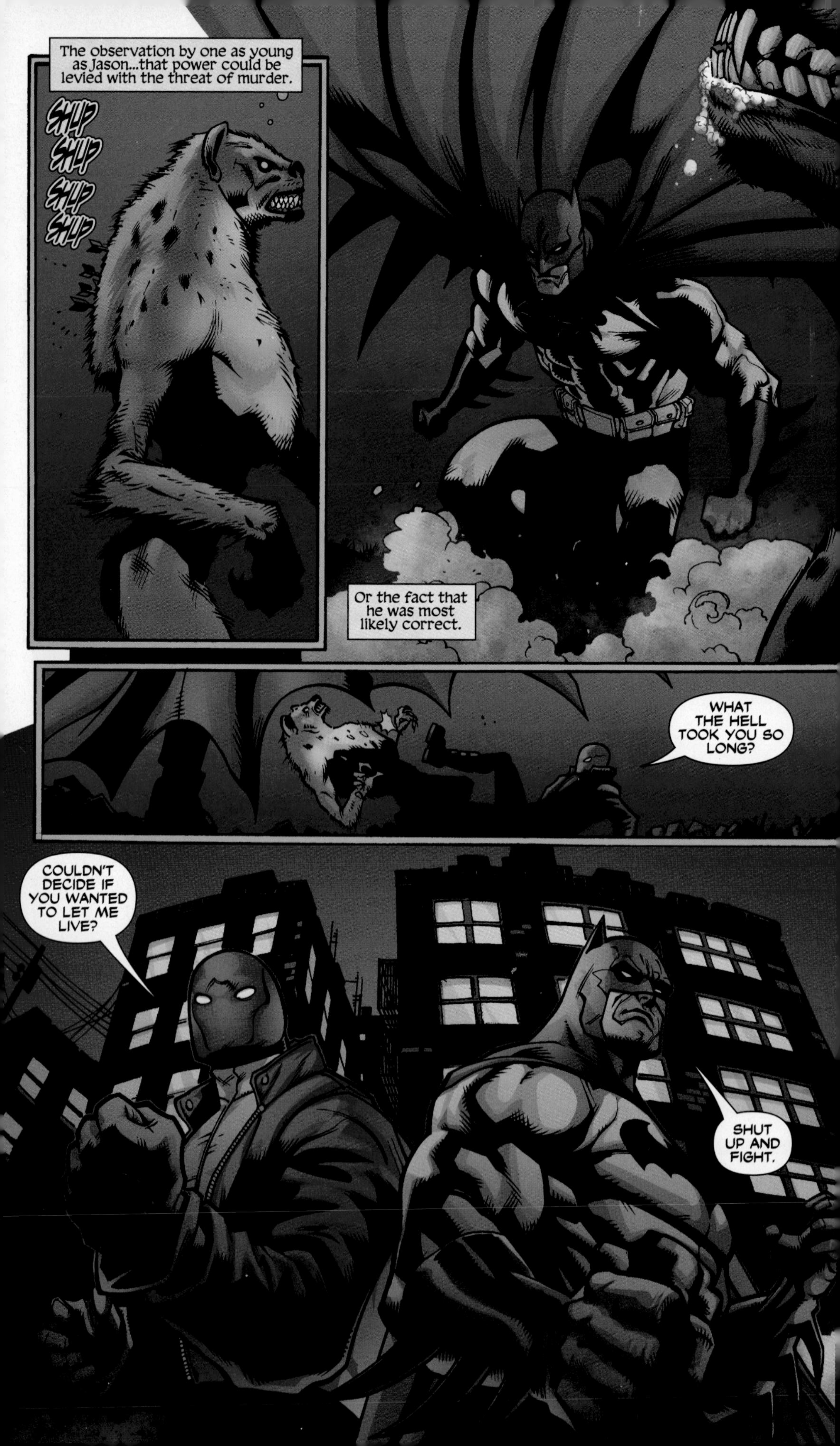
The observation by one as young as Jason...that power could be levied with the threat of murder.
SHUP SHUP SHUP SHUP
Or the fact that he was most likely correct.
WHAT THE HELL TOOK YOU SO LONG?
COULDN'T DECIDE IF YOU WANTED TO LET ME LIVE?
SHUT UP AND FIGHT.

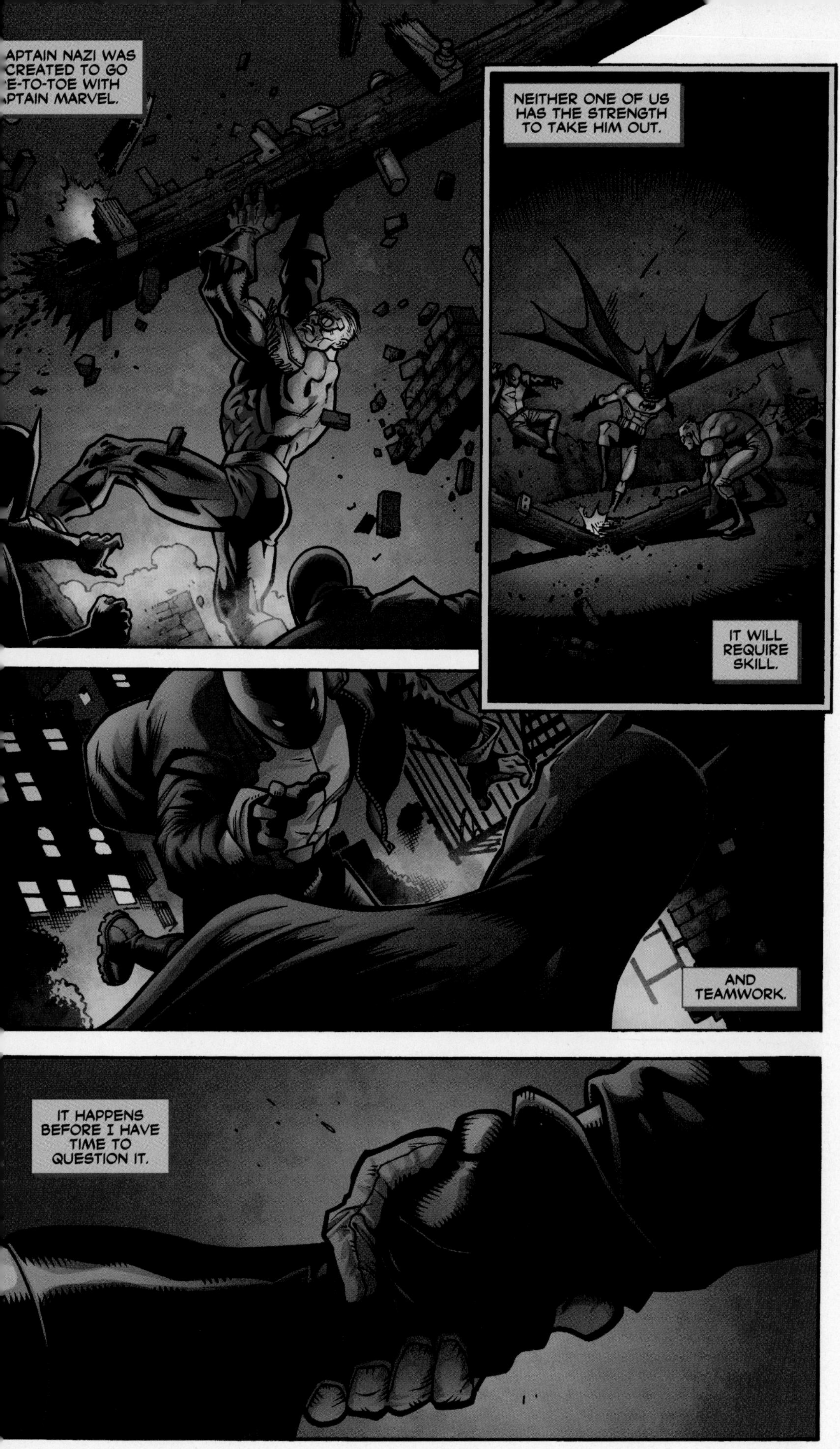
APTAIN NAZI WAS CREATED TO GO E-TO-TOE WITH PTAIN MARVEL.
NEITHER ONE OF US HAS THE STRENGTH TO TAKE HIM OUT.
IT WILL REQUIRE SKILL.
AND TEAMWORK.
IT HAPPENS BEFORE I HAVE TIME TO QUESTION IT.

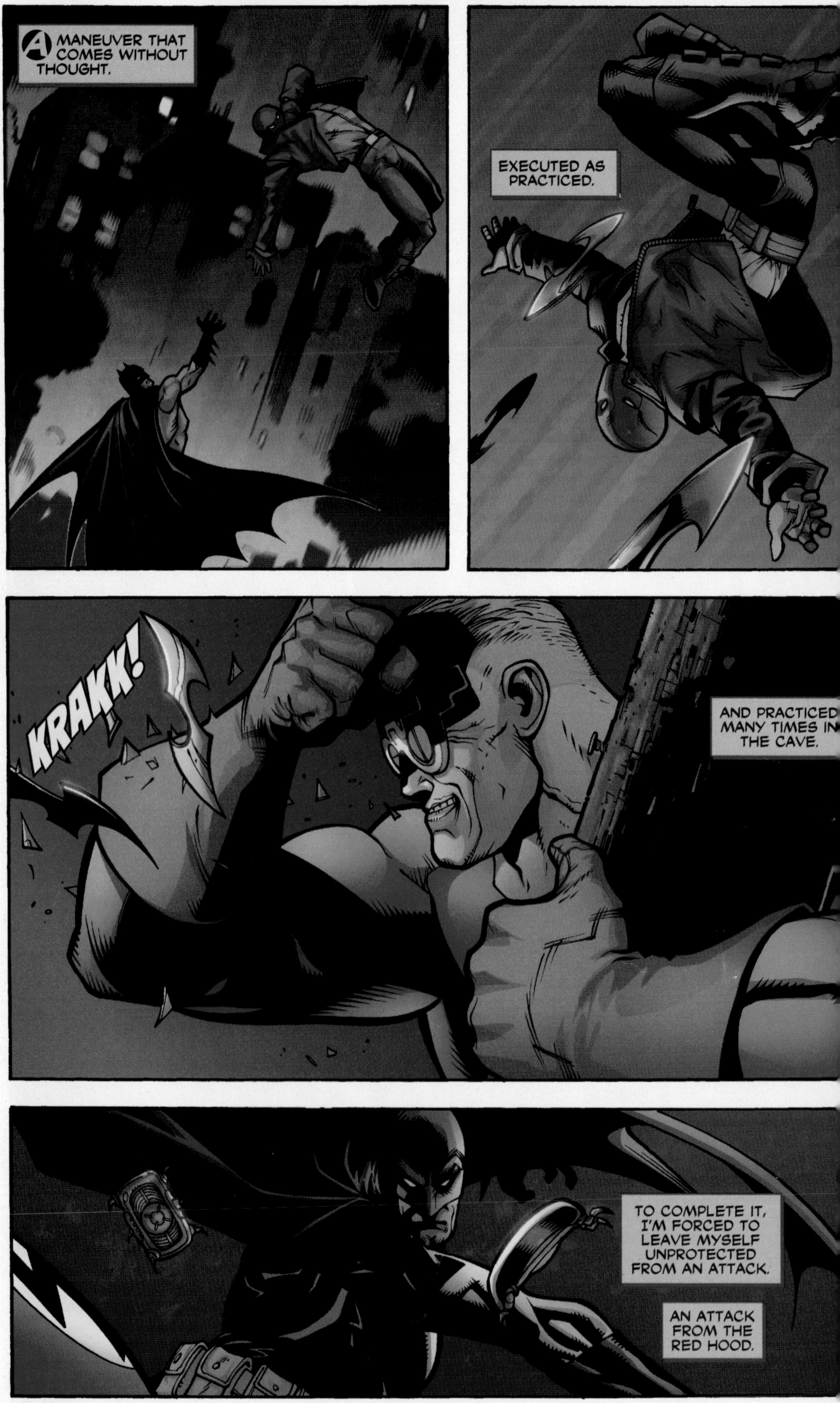
A MANEUVER THAT COMES WITHOUT THOUGHT.
EXECUTED AS PRACTICED.
KRAKK!
AND PRACTICED MANY TIMES IN THE CAVE.
TO COMPLETE IT, I'M FORCED TO LEAVE MYSELF UNPROTECTED FROM AN ATTACK.
AN ATTACK FROM THE RED HOOD.

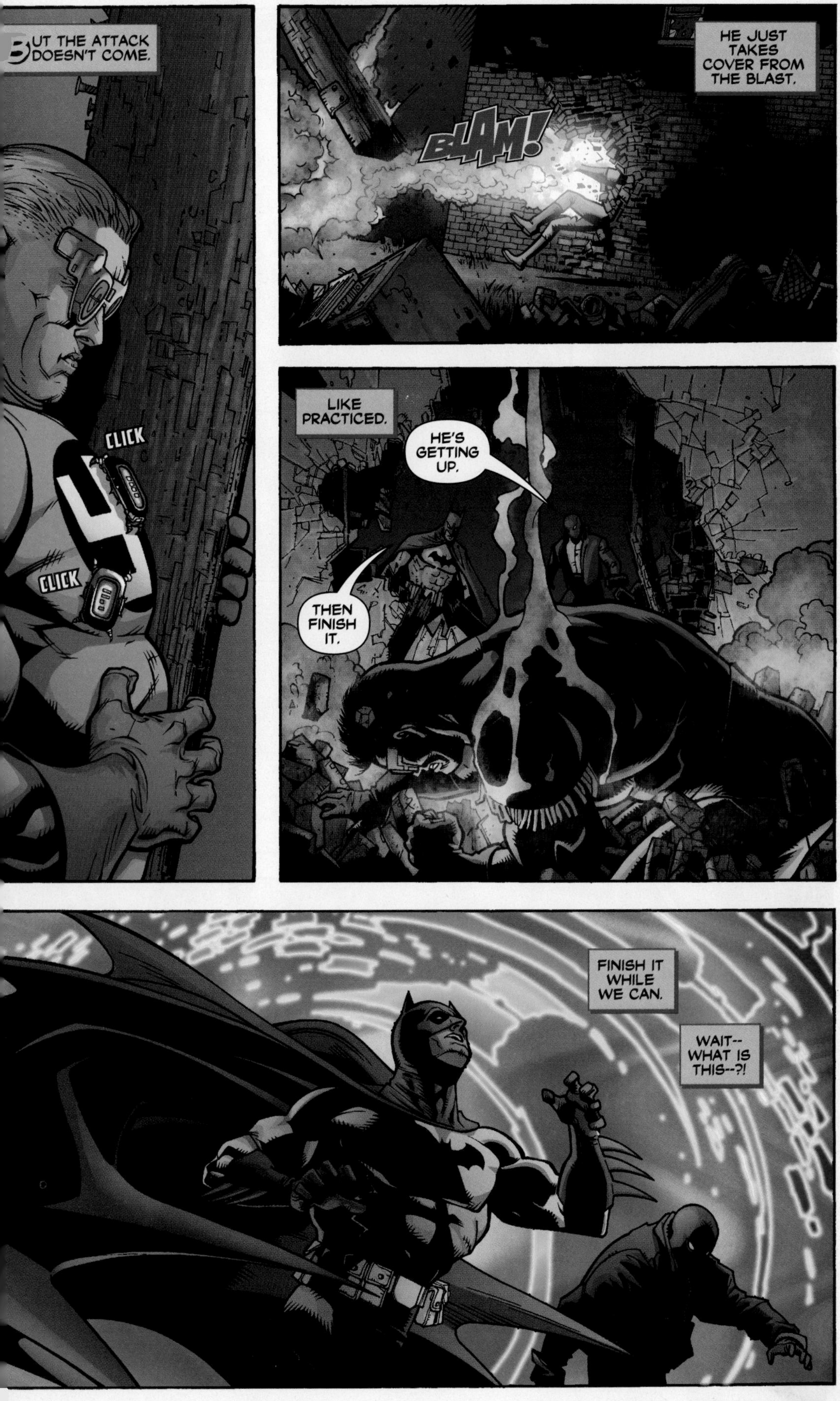
BUT THE ATTACK DOESN'T COME.
CLICK
CLICK
HE JUST TAKES COVER FROM THE BLAST.
BLAM!
LIKE PRACTICED.
HE'S GETTING UP.
THEN FINISH IT.
FINISH IT WHILE WE CAN.
WAIT-- WHAT IS THIS--?!

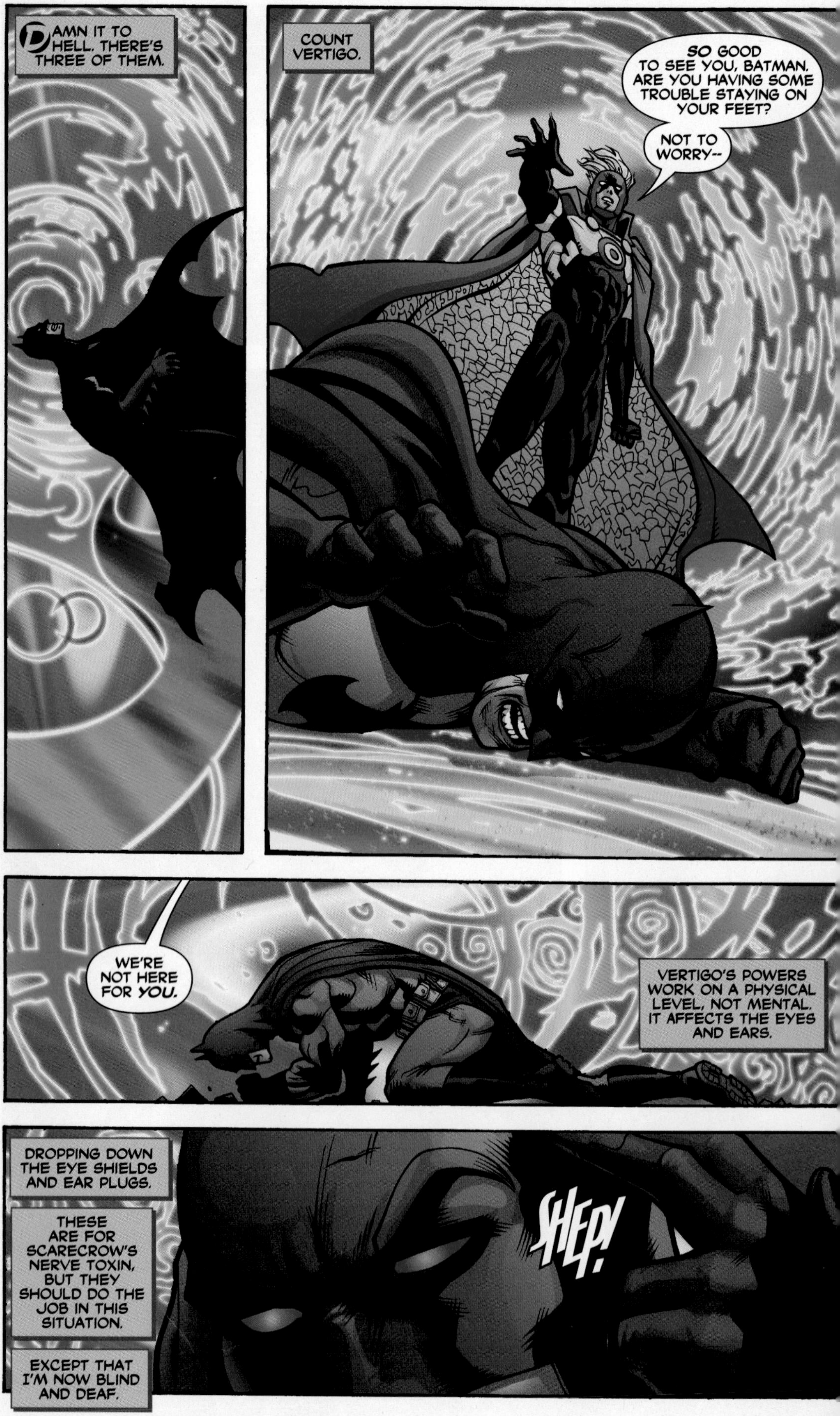
DAMN IT TO HELL. THERE'S THREE OF THEM.
COUNT VERTIGO.
SO GOOD TO SEE YOU, BATMAN. ARE YOU HAVING SOME TROUBLE STAYING ON YOUR FEET?
NOT TO WORRY--
WE'RE NOT HERE FOR YOU.
VERTIGO'S POWERS WORK ON A PHYSICAL LEVEL, NOT MENTAL. IT AFFECTS THE EYES AND EARS.
DROPPING DOWN THE EYE SHIELDS AND EAR PLUGS.
THESE ARE FOR SCARECROW'S NERVE TOXIN, BUT THEY SHOULD DO THE JOB IN THIS SITUATION.
SHEP!
EXCEPT THAT I'M NOW BLIND AND DEAF.

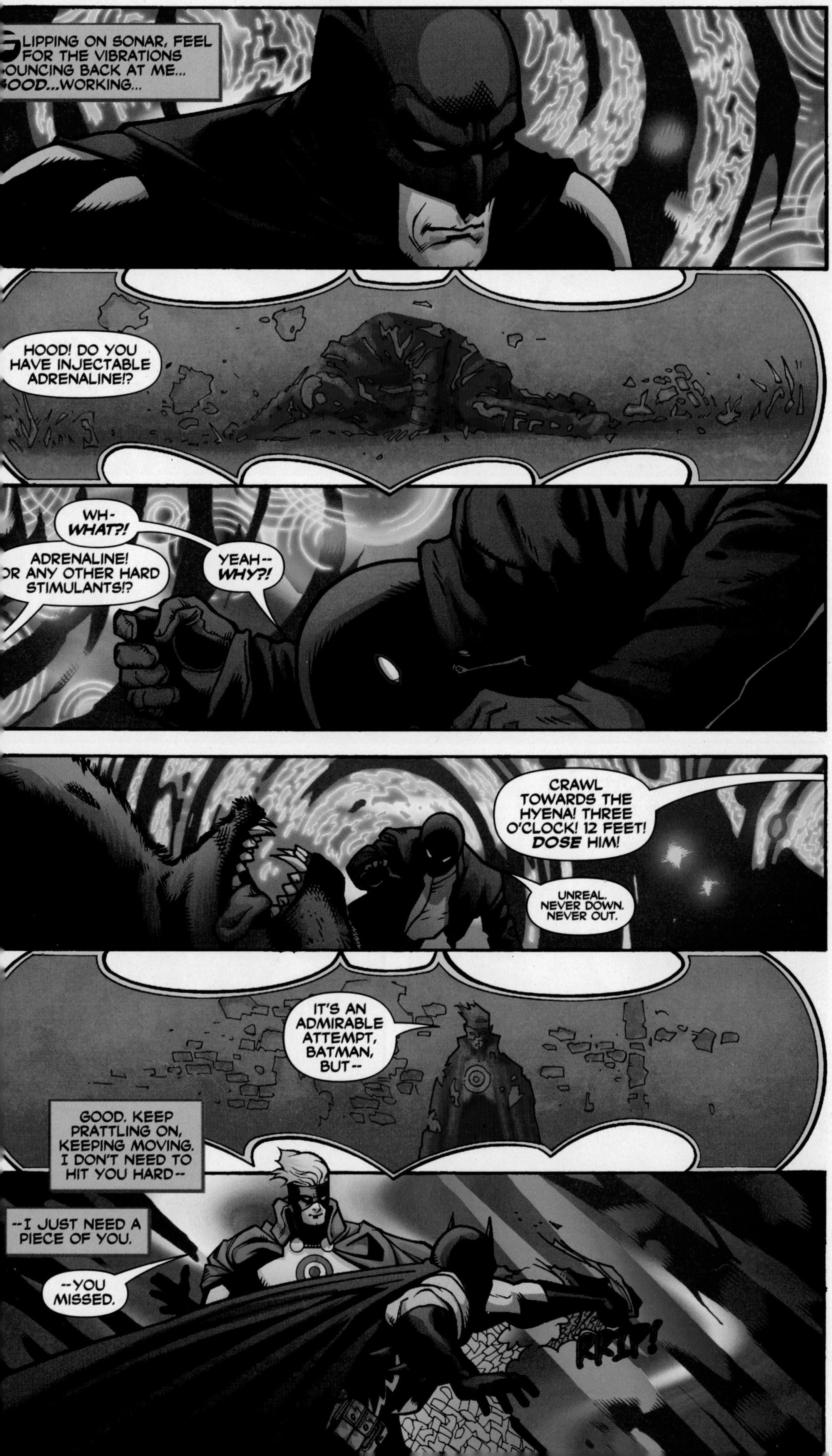
SLIPPING ON SONAR, FEEL FOR THE VIBRATIONS BOUNCING BACK AT ME... GOOD...WORKING...
HOOD! DO YOU HAVE INJECTABLE ADRENALINE!?
WH- WHAT?!
ADRENALINE! OR ANY OTHER HARD STIMULANTS!?
YEAH-- WHY?!
CRAWL TOWARDS THE HYENA! THREE O'CLOCK! 12 FEET! DOSE HIM!
UNREAL. NEVER DOWN. NEVER OUT.
IT'S AN ADMIRABLE ATTEMPT, BATMAN, BUT--
GOOD. KEEP PRATTLING ON, KEEPING MOVING. I DON'T NEED TO HIT YOU HARD--
--I JUST NEED A PIECE OF YOU.
--YOU MISSED.
RRIP!

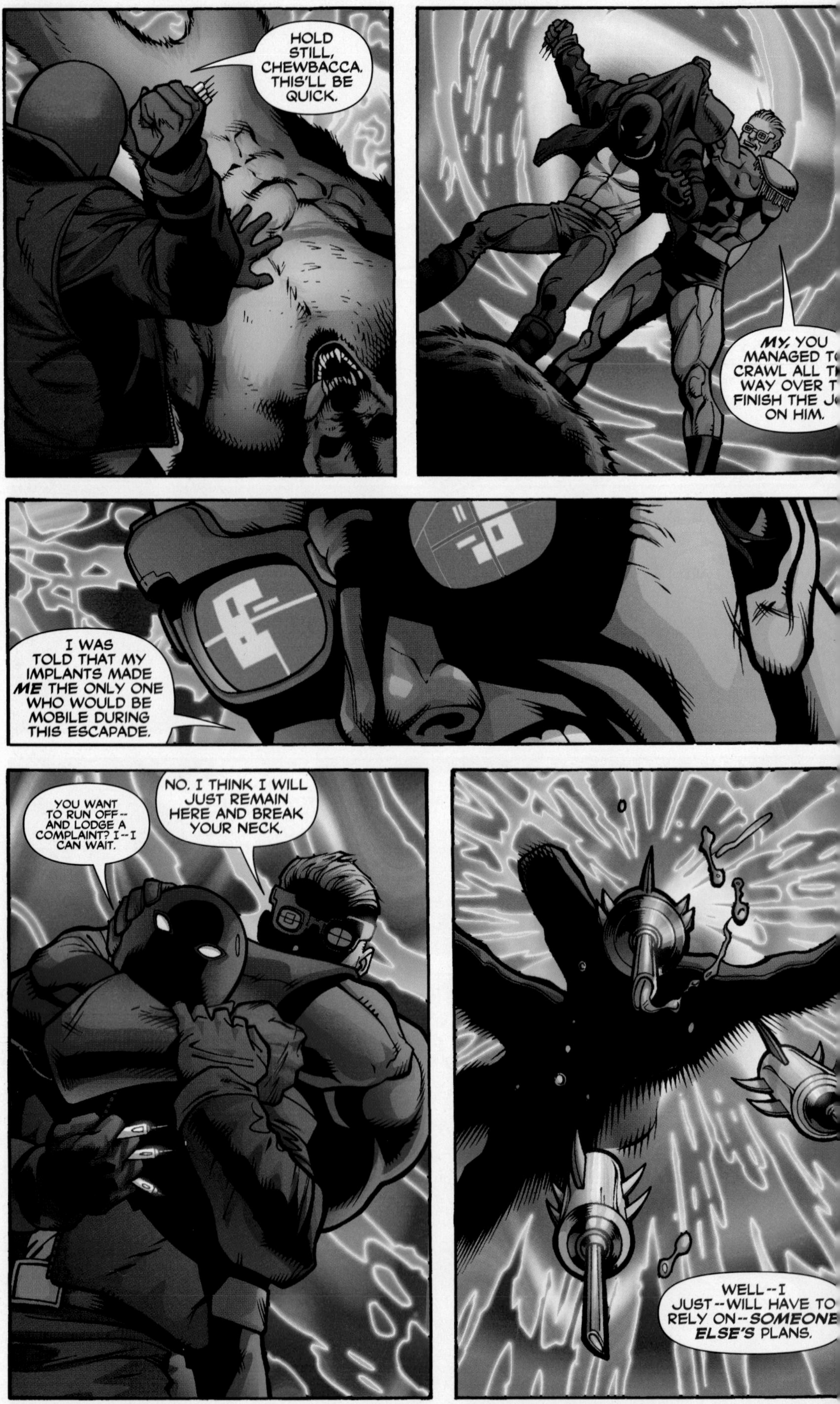
HOLD STILL, CHEWBACCA. THIS'LL BE QUICK.
MY, YOU MANAGED T
CRAWL ALL T
WAY OVER T
FINISH THE J
ON HIM.
I WAS TOLD THAT MY IMPLANTS MADE ME THE ONLY ONE WHO WOULD BE MOBILE DURING THIS ESCAPADE.
YOU WANT TO RUN OFF-- AND LODGE A COMPLAINT? I--I CAN WAIT.
NO. I THINK I WILL JUST REMAIN HERE AND BREAK YOUR NECK.
WELL--I JUST--WILL HAVE TO RELY ON--SOMEONE ELSE'S PLANS.

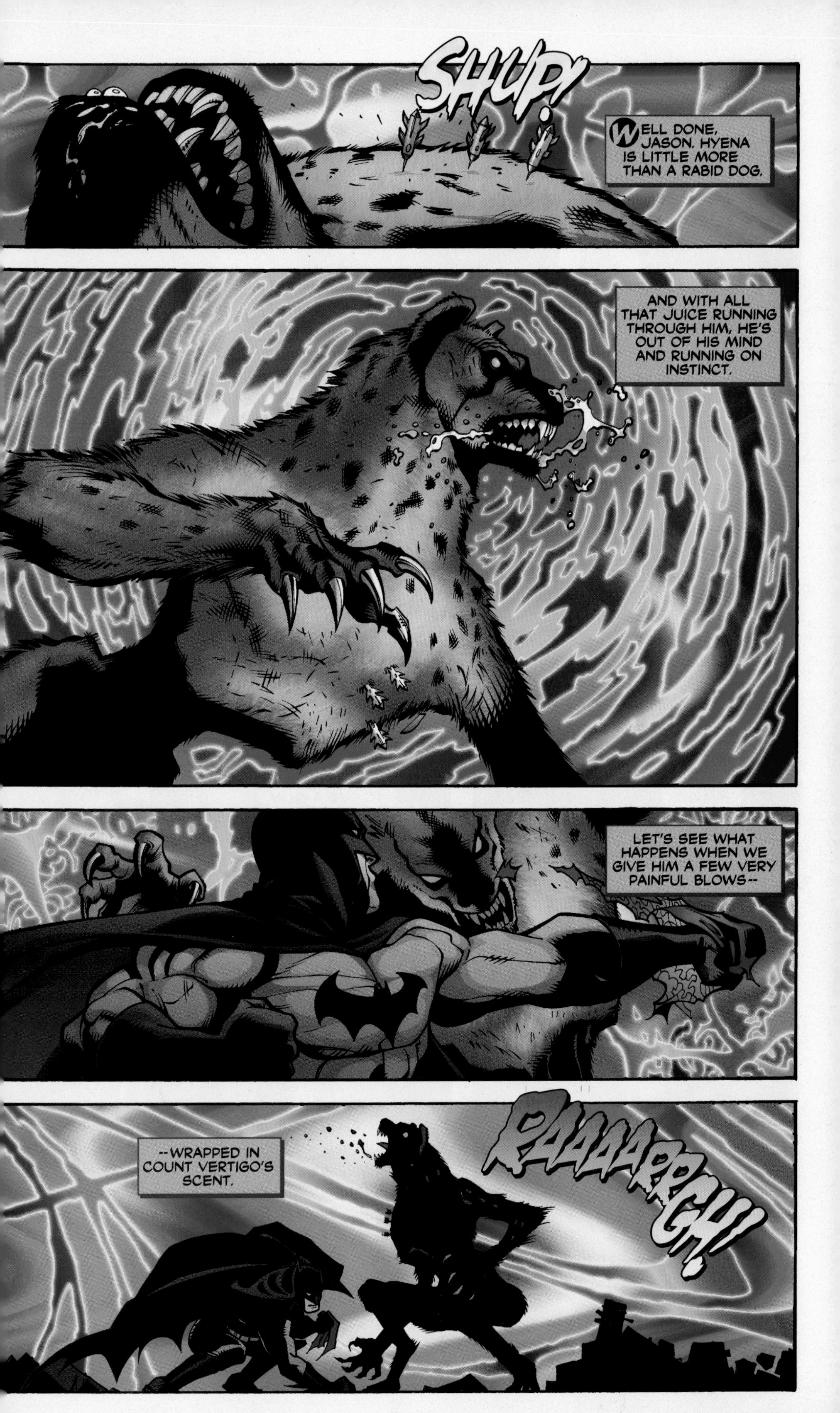
SHUP!
WELL DONE, JASON. HYENA IS LITTLE MORE THAN A RABID DOG.
AND WITH ALL THAT JUICE RUNNING THROUGH HIM, HE'S OUT OF HIS MIND AND RUNNING ON INSTINCT.
LET'S SEE WHAT HAPPENS WHEN WE GIVE HIM A FEW VERY PAINFUL BLOWS--
--WRAPPED IN COUNT VERTIGO'S SCENT.
RAAAARRGH!!

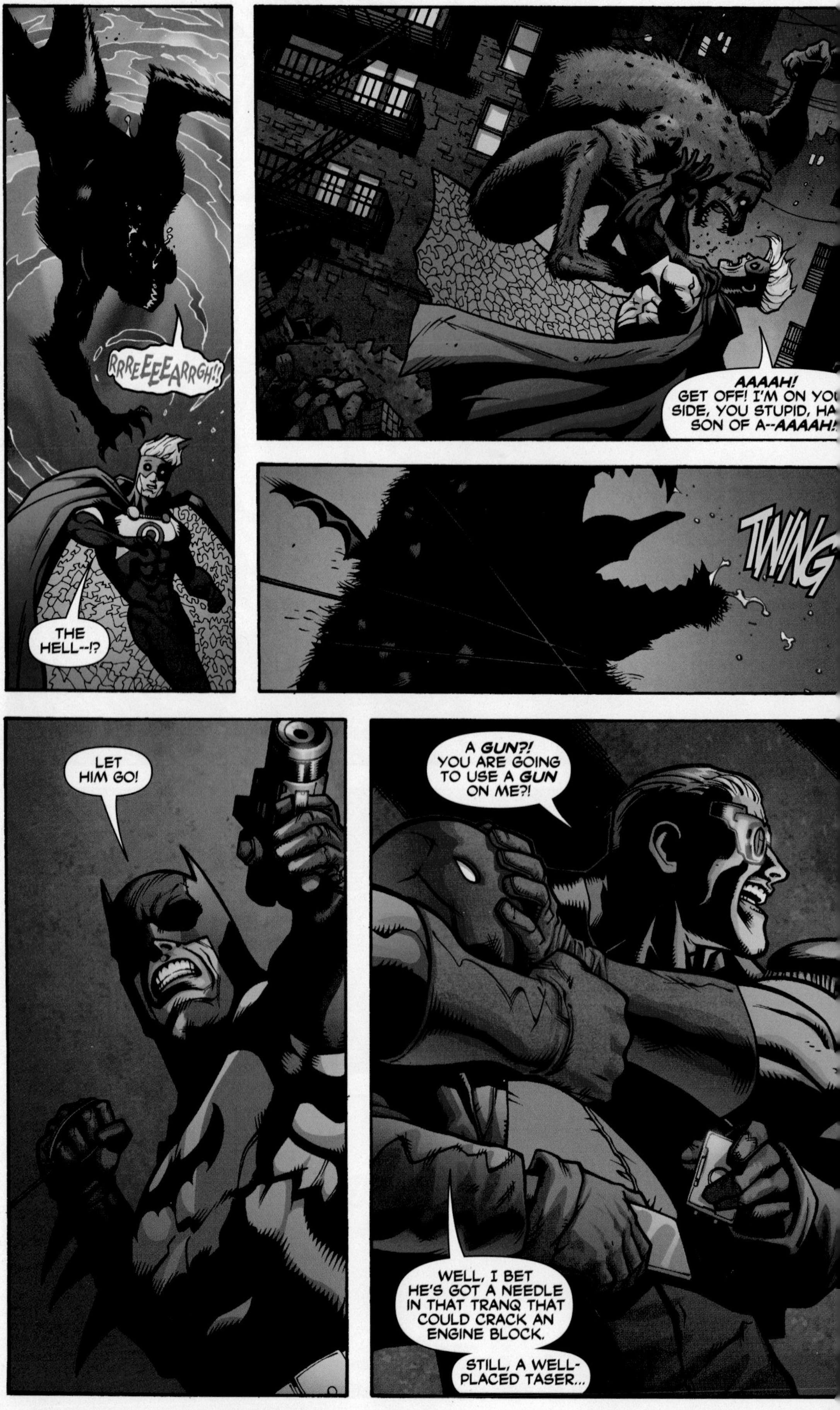
RRREEEEARRGH!!
THE HELL--!?
AAAAH! GET OFF! I'M ON YOU SIDE, YOU STUPID, HA SON OF A--AAAAH!
TWING
LET HIM GO!
A GUN?! YOU ARE GOING TO USE A GUN ON ME?!
WELL, I BET HE'S GOT A NEEDLE IN THAT TRANQ THAT COULD CRACK AN ENGINE BLOCK.
STILL, A WELL-PLACED TASER...

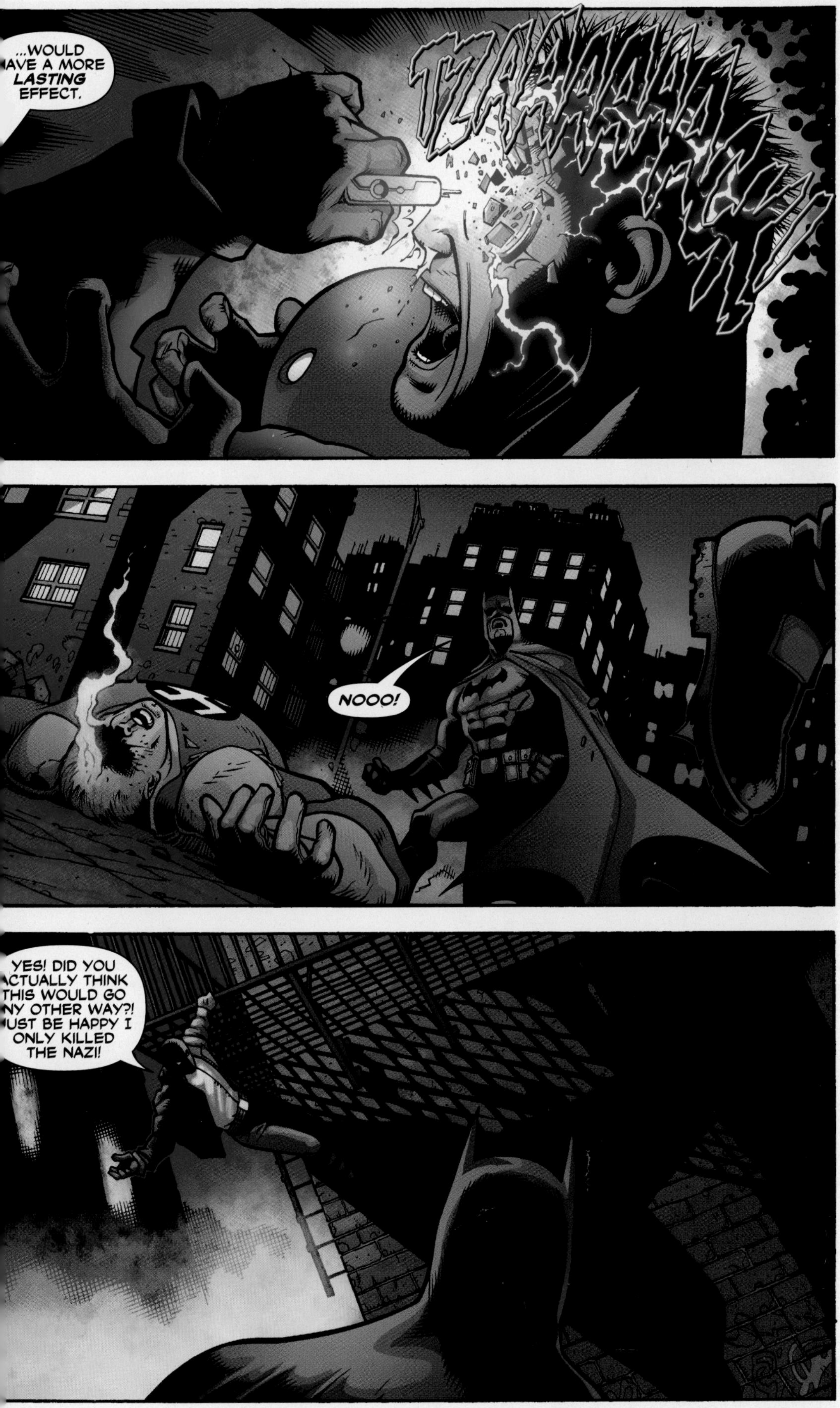
...WOULD AVE A MORE *LASTING* EFFECT.
NOOO!
YES! DID YOU CTUALLY THINK THIS WOULD GO NY OTHER WAY?! UST BE HAPPY I ONLY KILLED THE NAZI!

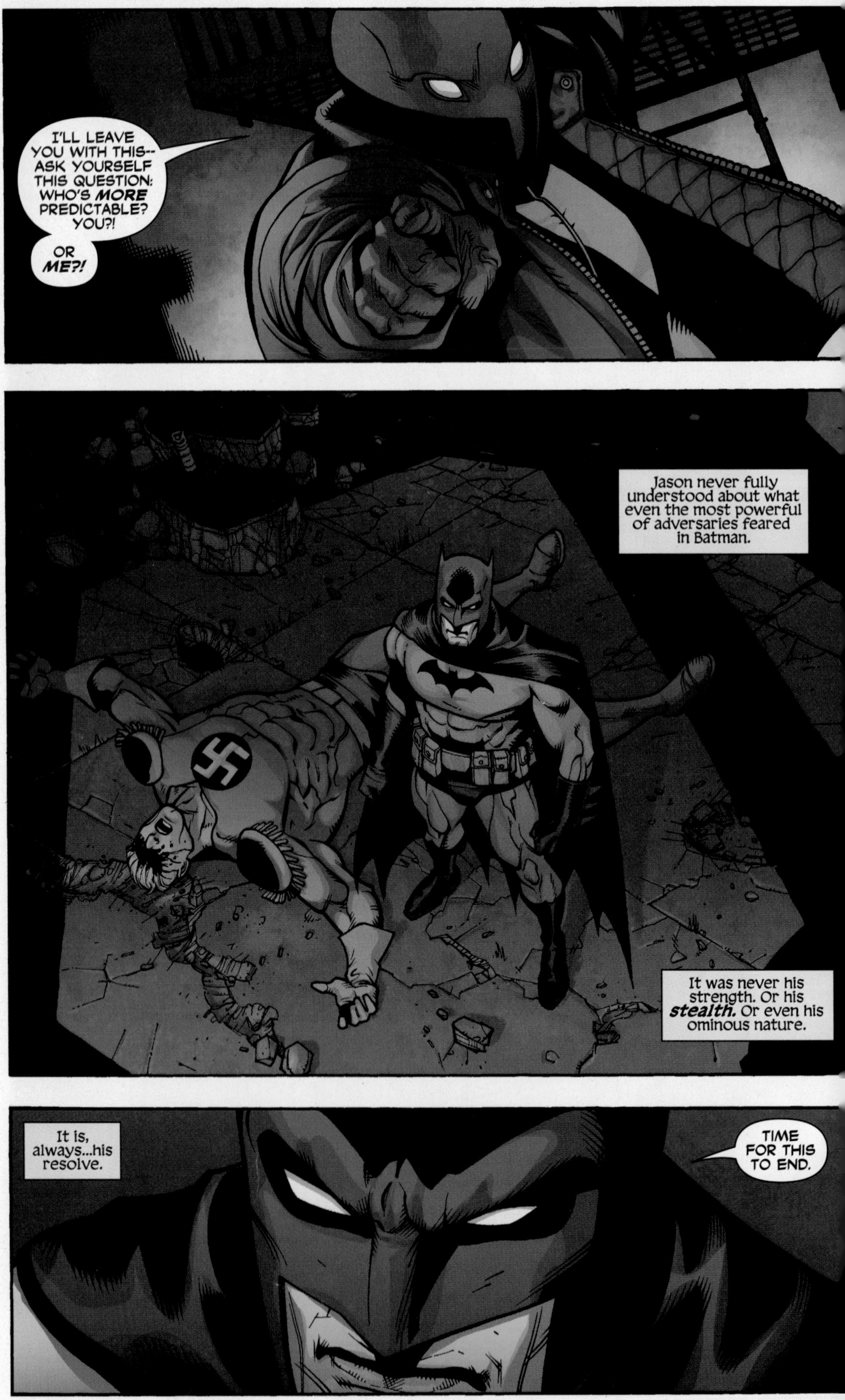
I'LL LEAVE YOU WITH THIS-- ASK YOURSELF THIS QUESTION: WHO'S MORE PREDICTABLE? YOU?!
OR ME?!
Jason never fully understood about what even the most powerful of adversaries feared in Batman.
It was never his strength. Or his stealth. Or even his ominous nature.
It is, always...his resolve.
TIME FOR THIS TO END.

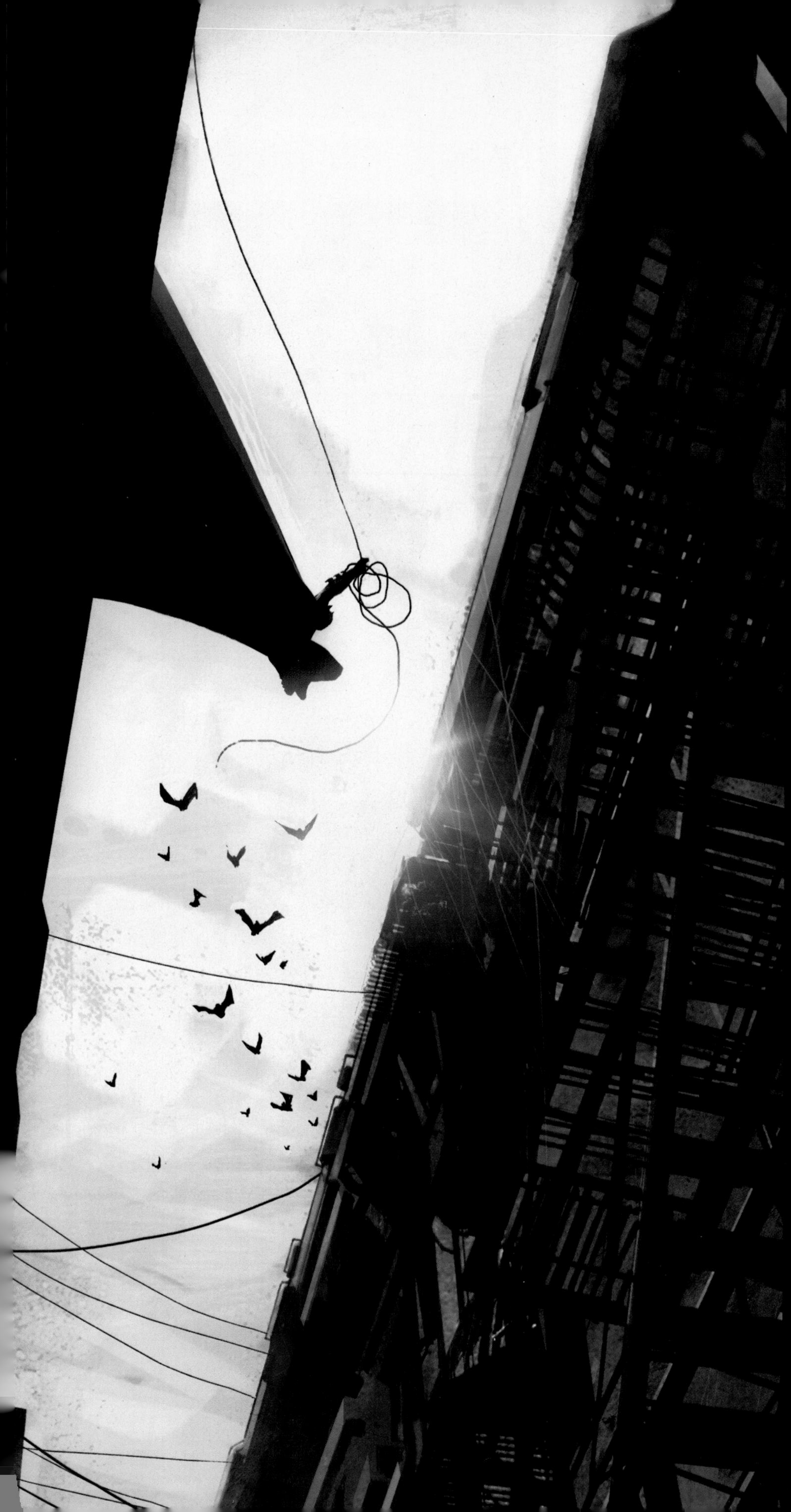

BATMAN #648 • COVER BY JOCK

CHAPTER 4

ALL THEY DO IS WATCH US KILL

PART 1

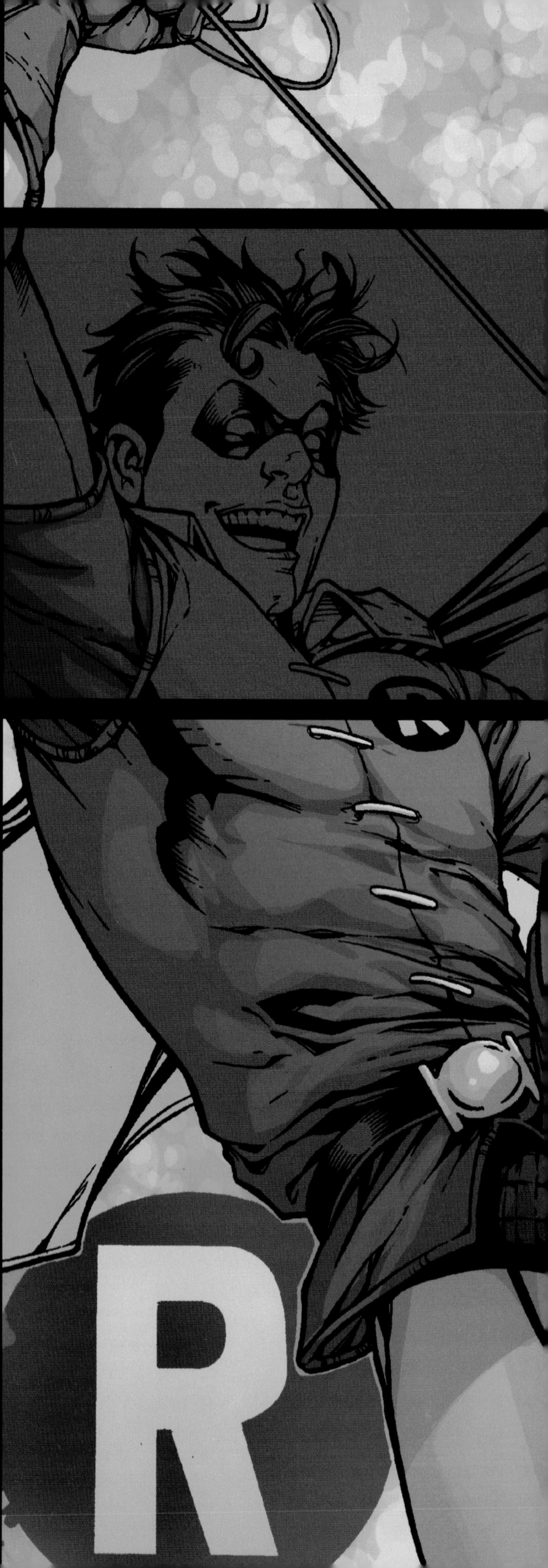

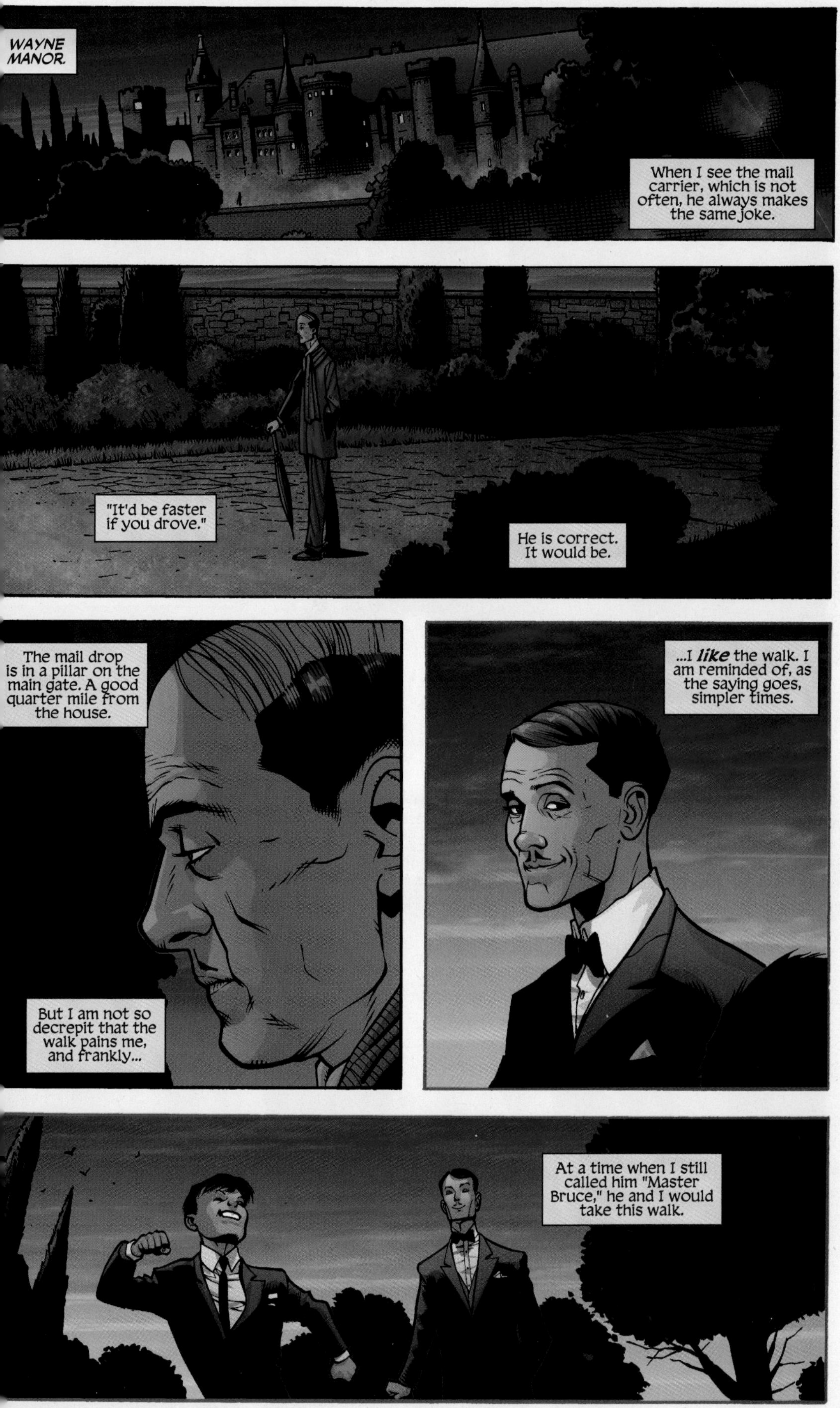
WAYNE MANOR.
When I see the mail carrier, which is not often, he always makes the same joke.
"It'd be faster if you drove."
He is correct. It would be.
The mail drop is in a pillar on the main gate. A good quarter mile from the house.
But I am not so decrepit that the walk pains me, and frankly...
...I *like* the walk. I am reminded of, as the saying goes, simpler times.
At a time when I still called him "Master Bruce," he and I would take this walk.

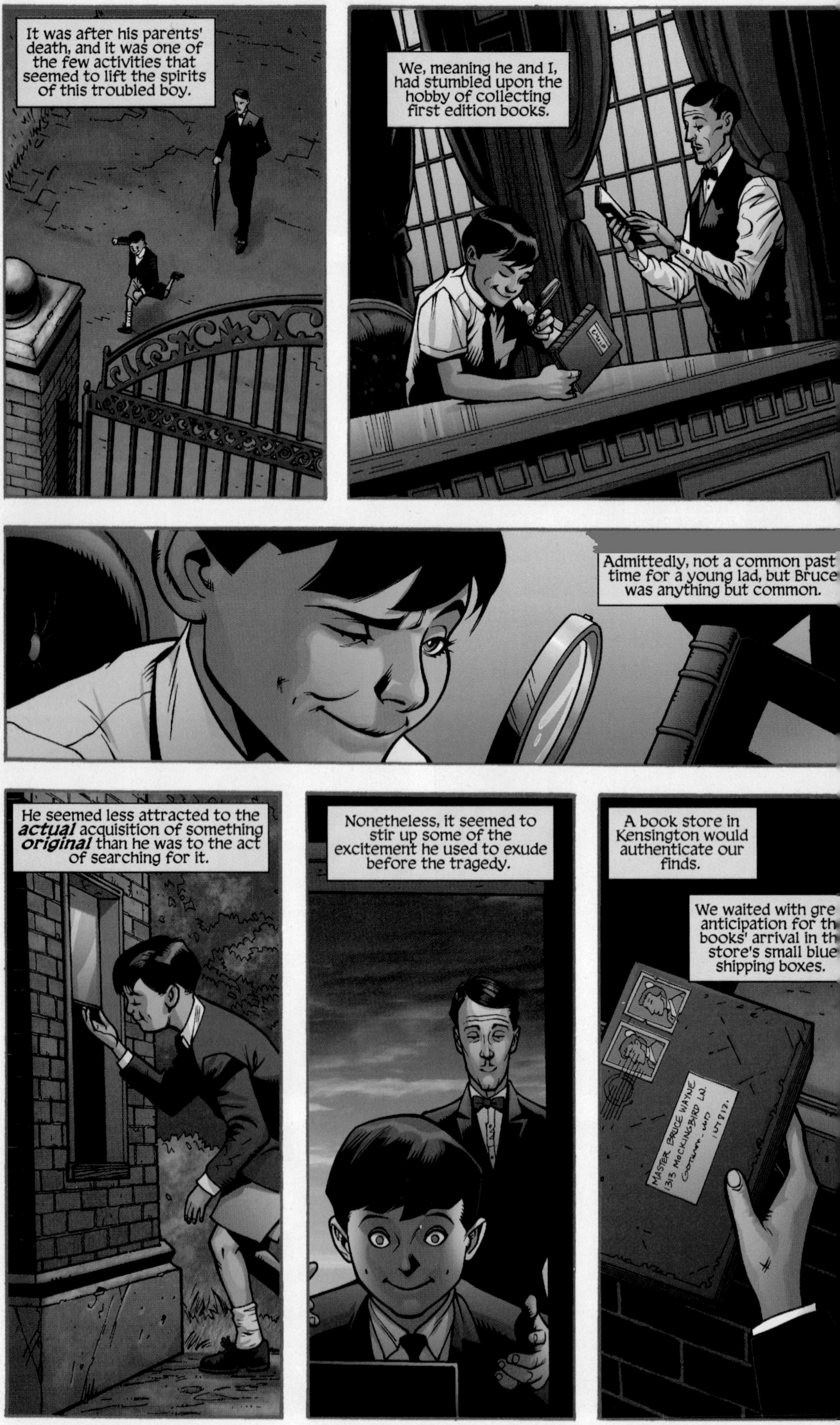
It was after his parents' death, and it was one of the few activities that seemed to lift the spirits of this troubled boy.
We, meaning he and I, had stumbled upon the hobby of collecting first edition books.
Admittedly, not a common past time for a young lad, but Bruce was anything but common.
He seemed less attracted to the ***actual*** acquisition of something ***original*** than he was to the act of searching for it.
Nonetheless, it seemed to stir up some of the excitement he used to exude before the tragedy.
A book store in Kensington would authenticate our finds.
We waited with gre anticipation for th books' arrival in th store's small blue shipping boxes.
MASTER BRUCE WAYNE
1313 MOCKINGBIRD LN.

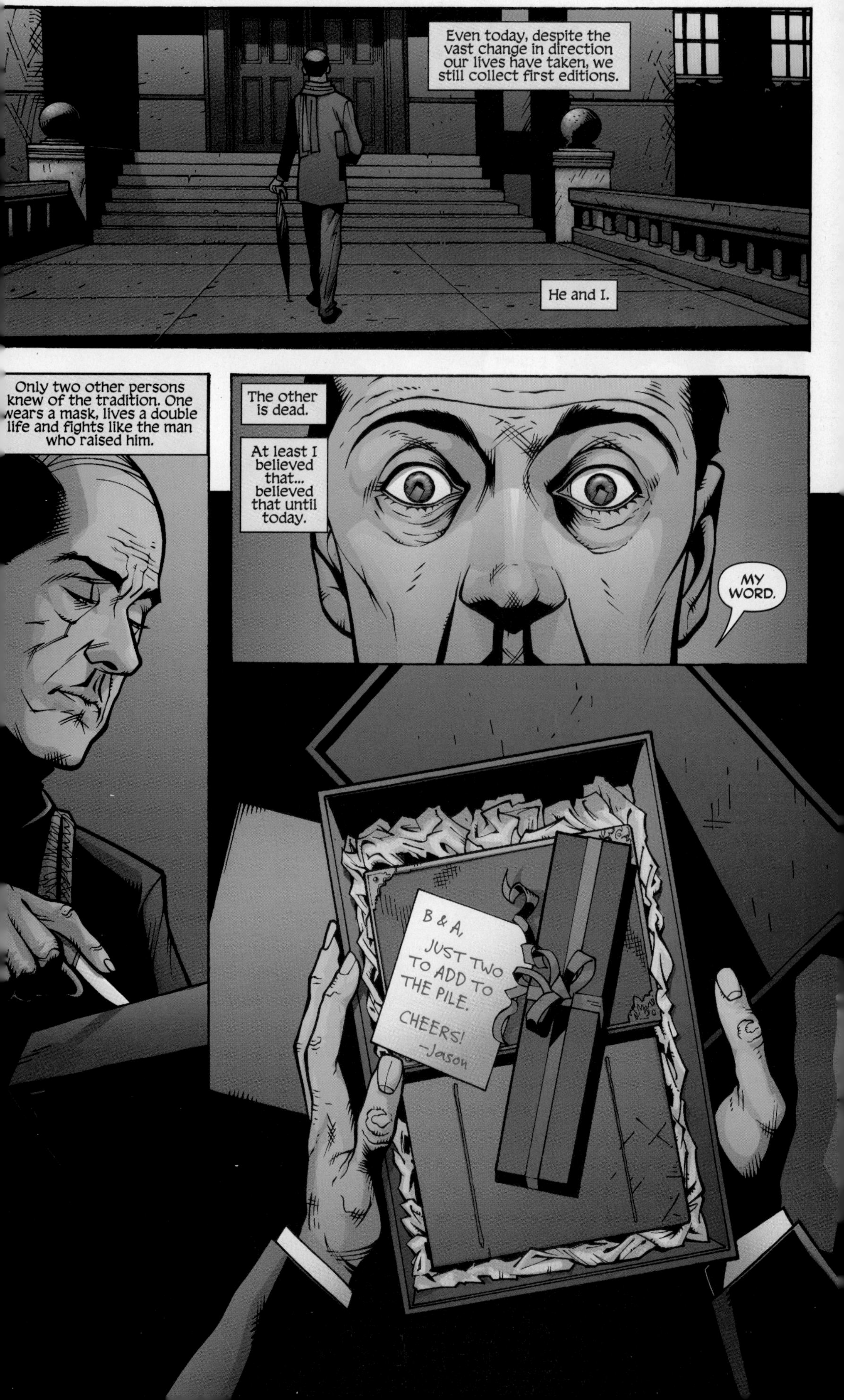
Even today, despite the vast change in direction our lives have taken, we still collect first editions.
He and I.
Only two other persons knew of the tradition. One wears a mask, lives a double life and fights like the man who raised him.
The other is dead.
At least I believed that... believed that until today.
MY WORD.
B & A,
JUST TWO TO ADD TO THE PILE.
CHEERS!
-Jason

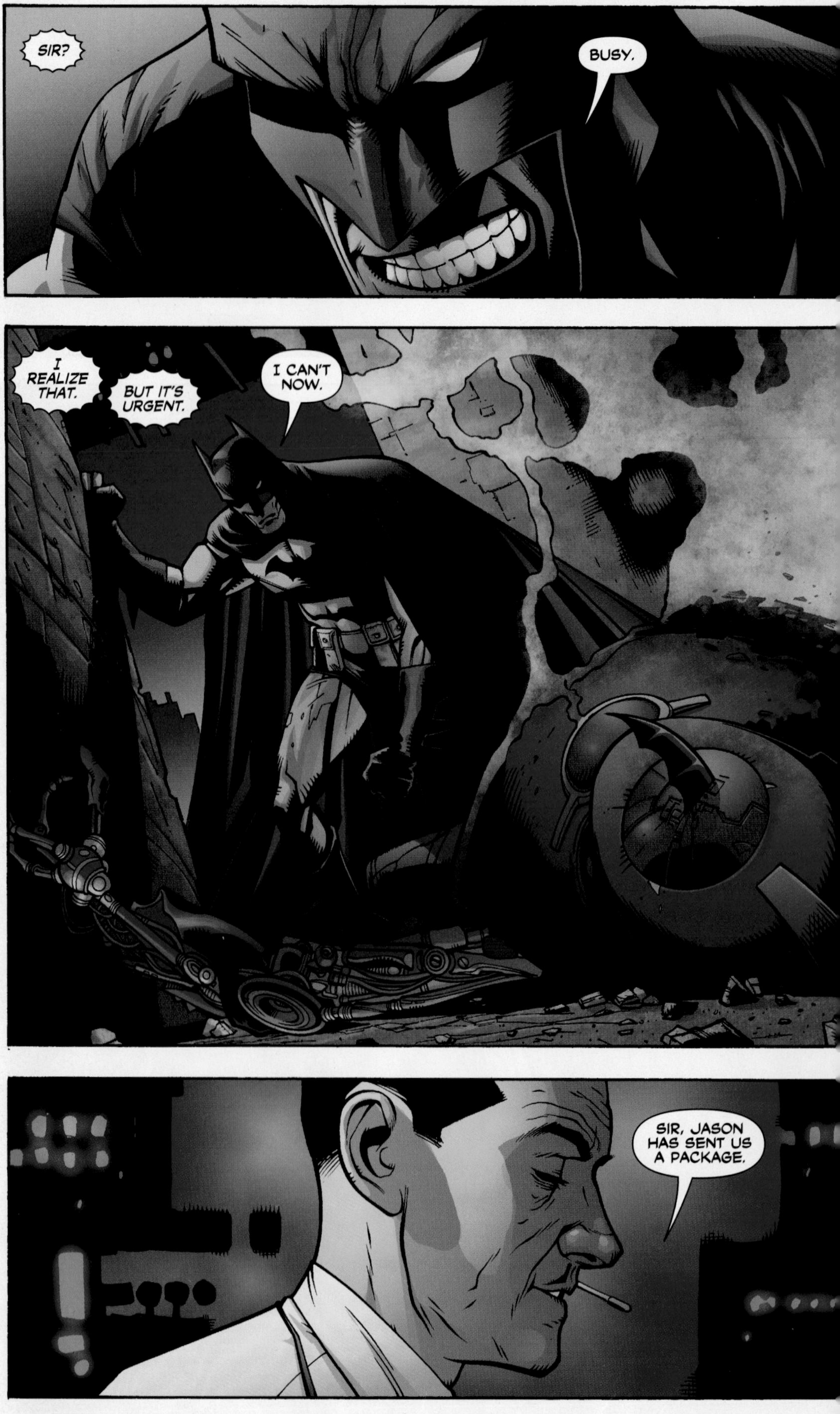
SIR?
BUSY.
I REALIZE THAT.
BUT IT'S URGENT.
I CAN'T NOW.
SIR, JASON HAS SENT US A PACKAGE.

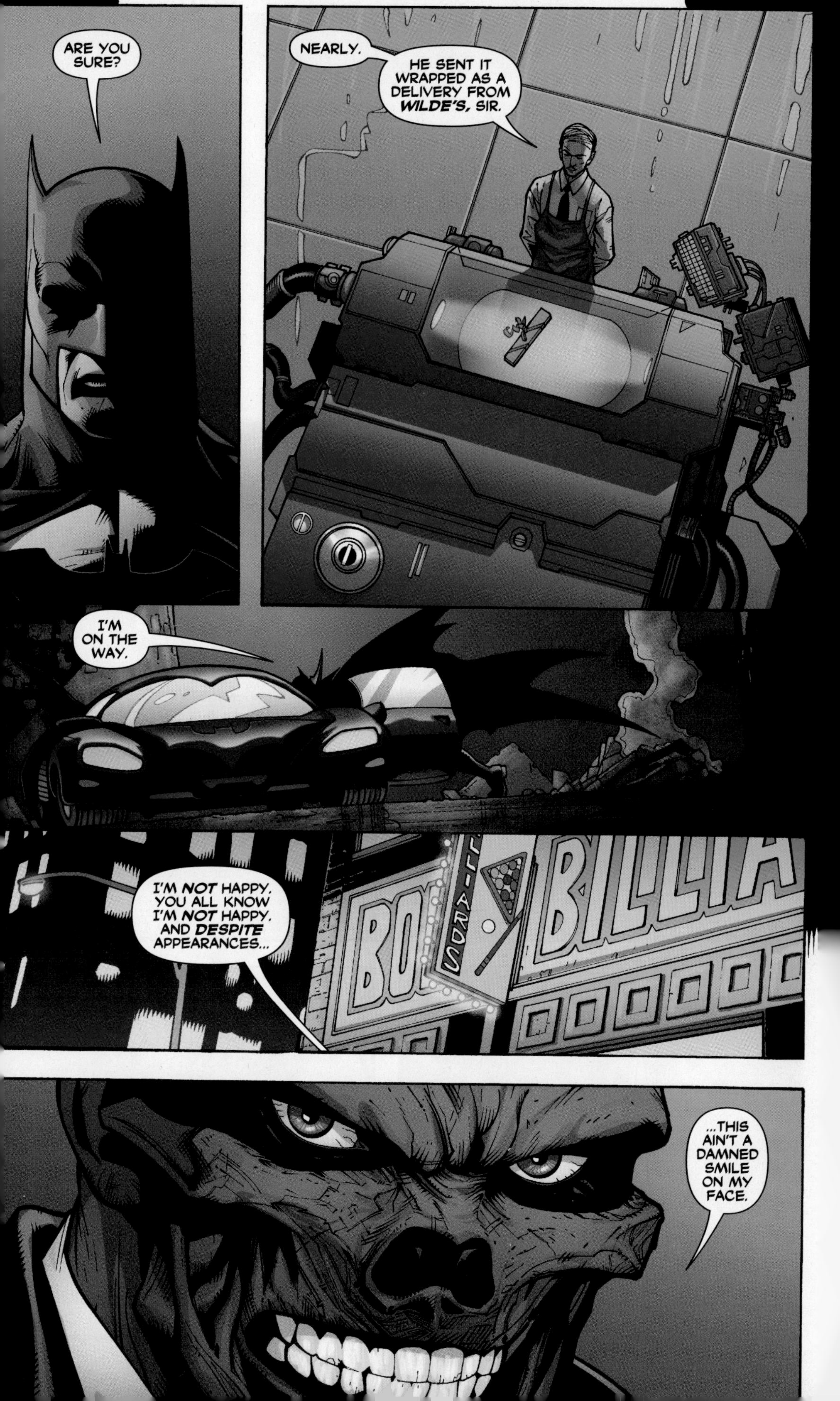
ARE YOU SURE?
NEARLY.
HE SENT IT WRAPPED AS A DELIVERY FROM *WILDE'S,* SIR.
I'M ON THE WAY.
I'M *NOT* HAPPY. YOU ALL KNOW I'M *NOT* HAPPY. AND *DESPITE* APPEARANCES...
BILLIARDS
...THIS AIN'T A DAMNED SMILE ON MY FACE.

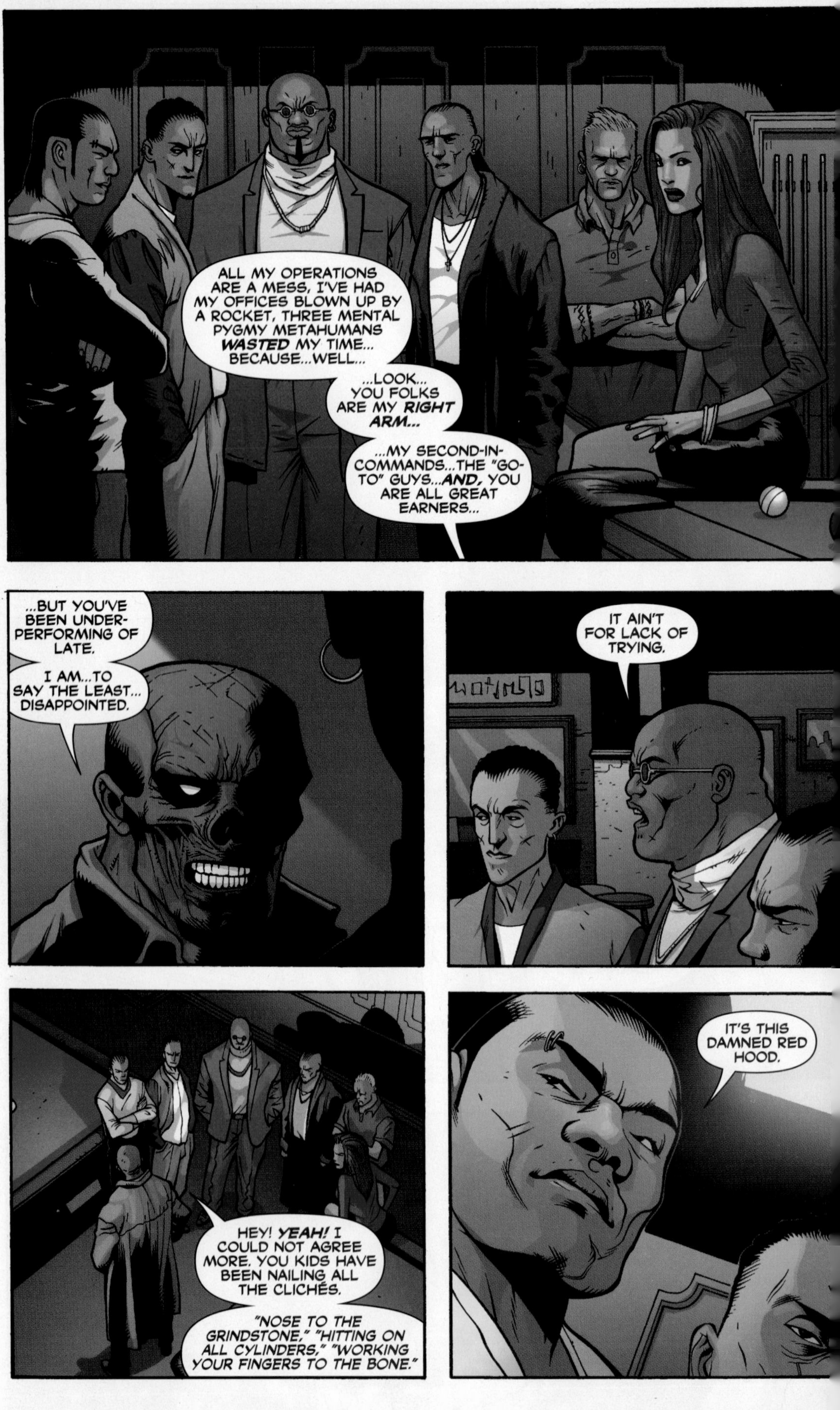
ALL MY OPERATIONS ARE A MESS, I'VE HAD MY OFFICES BLOWN UP BY A ROCKET, THREE MENTAL PYGMY METAHUMANS WASTED MY TIME... BECAUSE...WELL...
...LOOK... YOU FOLKS ARE MY RIGHT ARM...
...MY SECOND-IN-COMMANDS...THE "GO-TO" GUYS...AND, YOU ARE ALL GREAT EARNERS...
...BUT YOU'VE BEEN UNDER-PERFORMING OF LATE.
I AM...TO SAY THE LEAST... DISAPPOINTED.
IT AIN'T FOR LACK OF TRYING.
HEY! YEAH! I COULD NOT AGREE MORE. YOU KIDS HAVE BEEN NAILING ALL THE CLICHÉS.
"NOSE TO THE GRINDSTONE," "HITTING ON ALL CYLINDERS," "WORKING YOUR FINGERS TO THE BONE."
IT'S THIS DAMNED RED HOOD.

HE HITS US *HARD*, HE HITS US *DIRTY*. HOW ARE WE SUPPOSED TO *DEAL* WITH A GUY WHO *WON'T* DEAL?

HE'S GOTTA DIE.

YEAH. BUT THAT'S THE THING, HE'S A DAMN COCKROACH, MAN. HE JUST *WON'T* DIE.

RIGHT. I THINK WE GOTTA FIND A WAY TO...TO REACH SOME KIND OF MIDDLE GROUND. SOME WAY THAT HE WILL TAKE A DEAL WITH US.

I HAVE.

YEAH?! WHAT IS IT?

MONEY OR TERRITORY?

IT BETTER BE MONEY BECAUSE IT AIN'T GONNA BE TERRITORY...

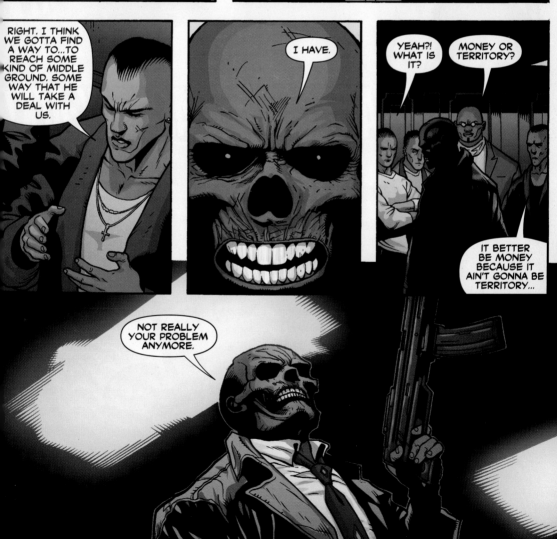

NOT REALLY YOUR PROBLEM ANYMORE.

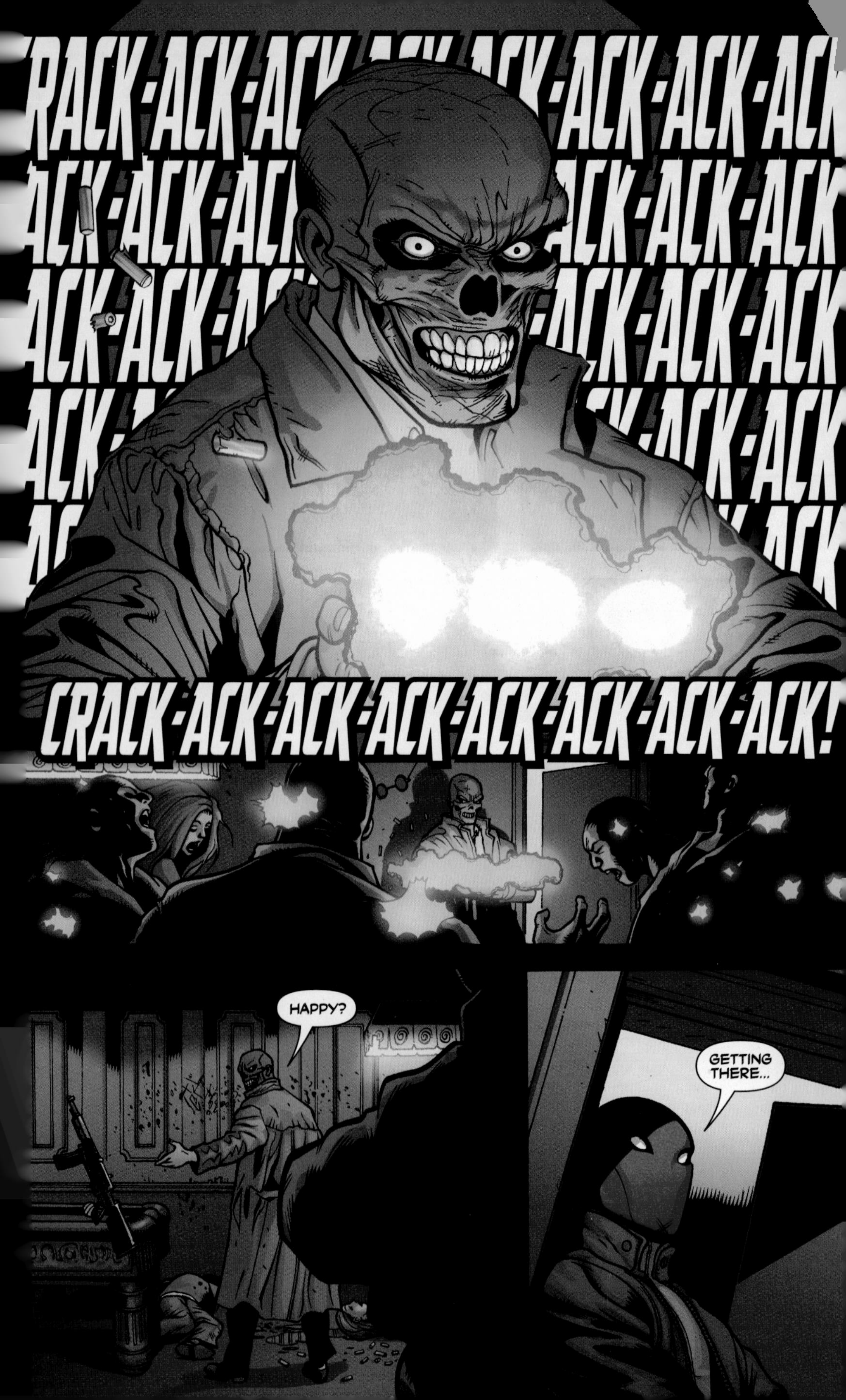
CRACK-ACK-ACK-ACK-ACK-ACK-ACK-ACK!
HAPPY?
GETTING THERE...

ALFRED, WE SHOULDN'T WASTE TIME.

I'M GOING TO NEED YOU TO--

YES, SIR, OPEN THE REMAINING BOX.

BE SURE TO--

AND AS YOU KNOW, SIR, I AM QUITE ADEPT WITH INCENDIARIES.

I KNOW.

I'VE DONE AT LEAST SIX SCANS SINCE IT ARRIVED, SIR. IT APPEARS TO BE COMPLETELY FREE OF EXPLOSIVES OR CHEMICAL AGENTS OF ANY KIND.

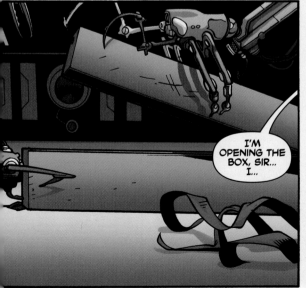

I'M OPENING THE BOX, SIR... I...

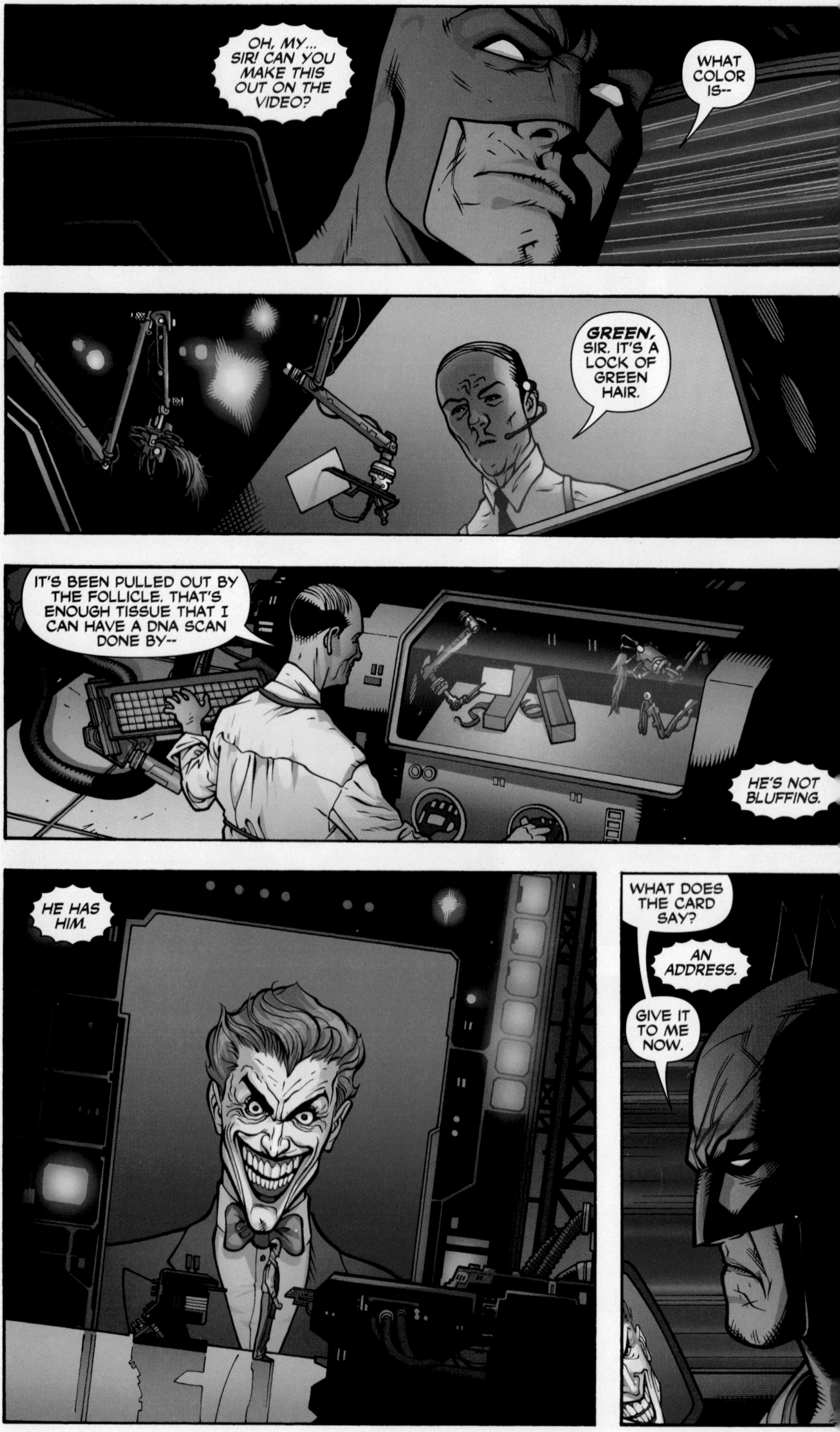
OH, MY... SIR! CAN YOU MAKE THIS OUT ON THE VIDEO?
WHAT COLOR IS--
GREEN, SIR. IT'S A LOCK OF GREEN HAIR.
IT'S BEEN PULLED OUT BY THE FOLLICLE. THAT'S ENOUGH TISSUE THAT I CAN HAVE A DNA SCAN DONE BY--
HE'S NOT BLUFFING.
HE HAS HIM.
WHAT DOES THE CARD SAY?
AN ADDRESS.
GIVE IT TO ME NOW.

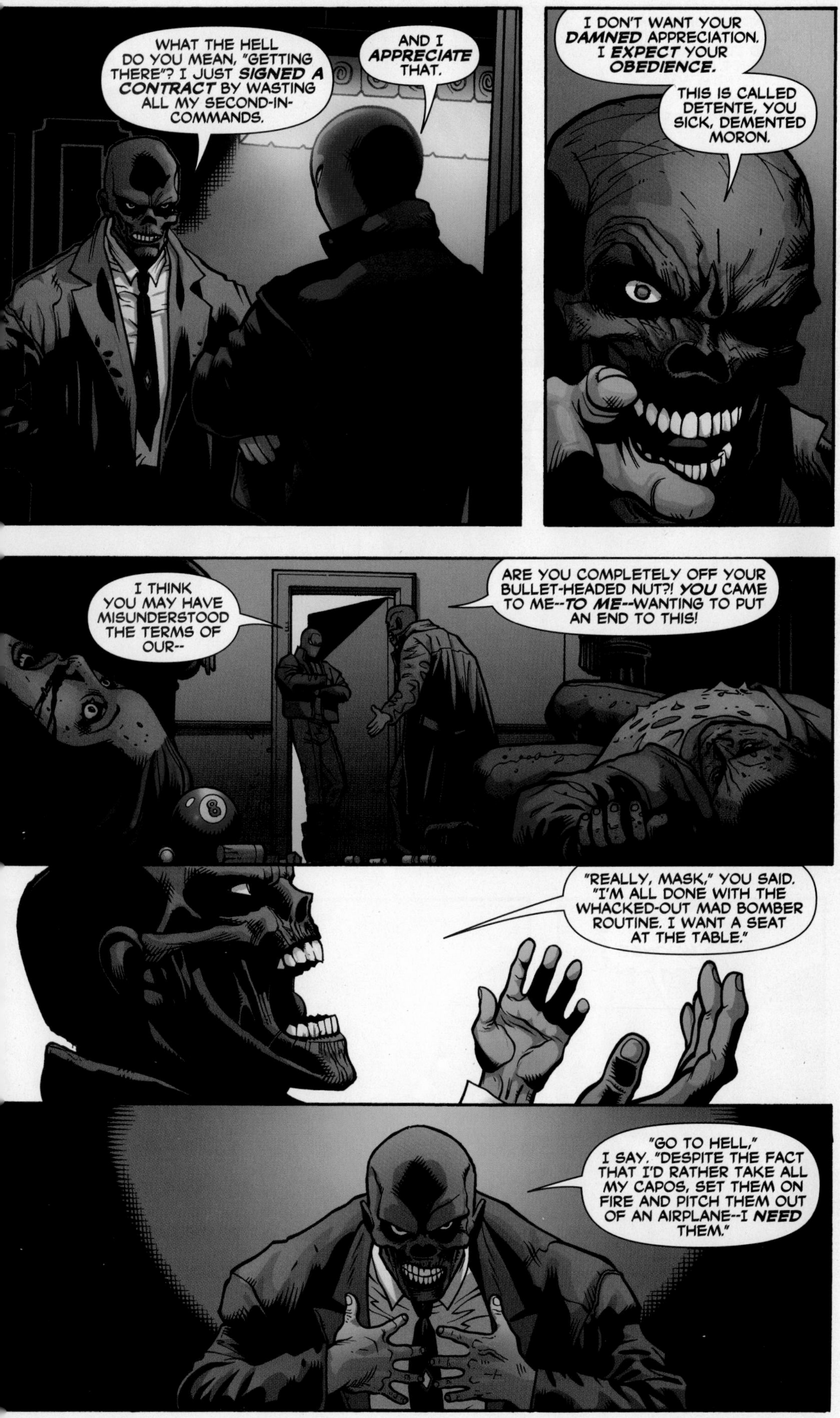
WHAT THE HELL DO YOU MEAN, "GETTING THERE"? I JUST SIGNED A CONTRACT BY WASTING ALL MY SECOND-IN-COMMANDS.
AND I APPRECIATE THAT.
I DON'T WANT YOUR DAMNED APPRECIATION. I EXPECT YOUR OBEDIENCE.
THIS IS CALLED DETENTE, YOU SICK, DEMENTED MORON.
I THINK YOU MAY HAVE MISUNDERSTOOD THE TERMS OF OUR--
ARE YOU COMPLETELY OFF YOUR BULLET-HEADED NUT?! YOU CAME TO ME--TO ME--WANTING TO PUT AN END TO THIS!
"REALLY, MASK," YOU SAID. "I'M ALL DONE WITH THE WHACKED-OUT MAD BOMBER ROUTINE. I WANT A SEAT AT THE TABLE."
"GO TO HELL," I SAY. "DESPITE THE FACT THAT I'D RATHER TAKE ALL MY CAPOS, SET THEM ON FIRE AND PITCH THEM OUT OF AN AIRPLANE--I NEED THEM."

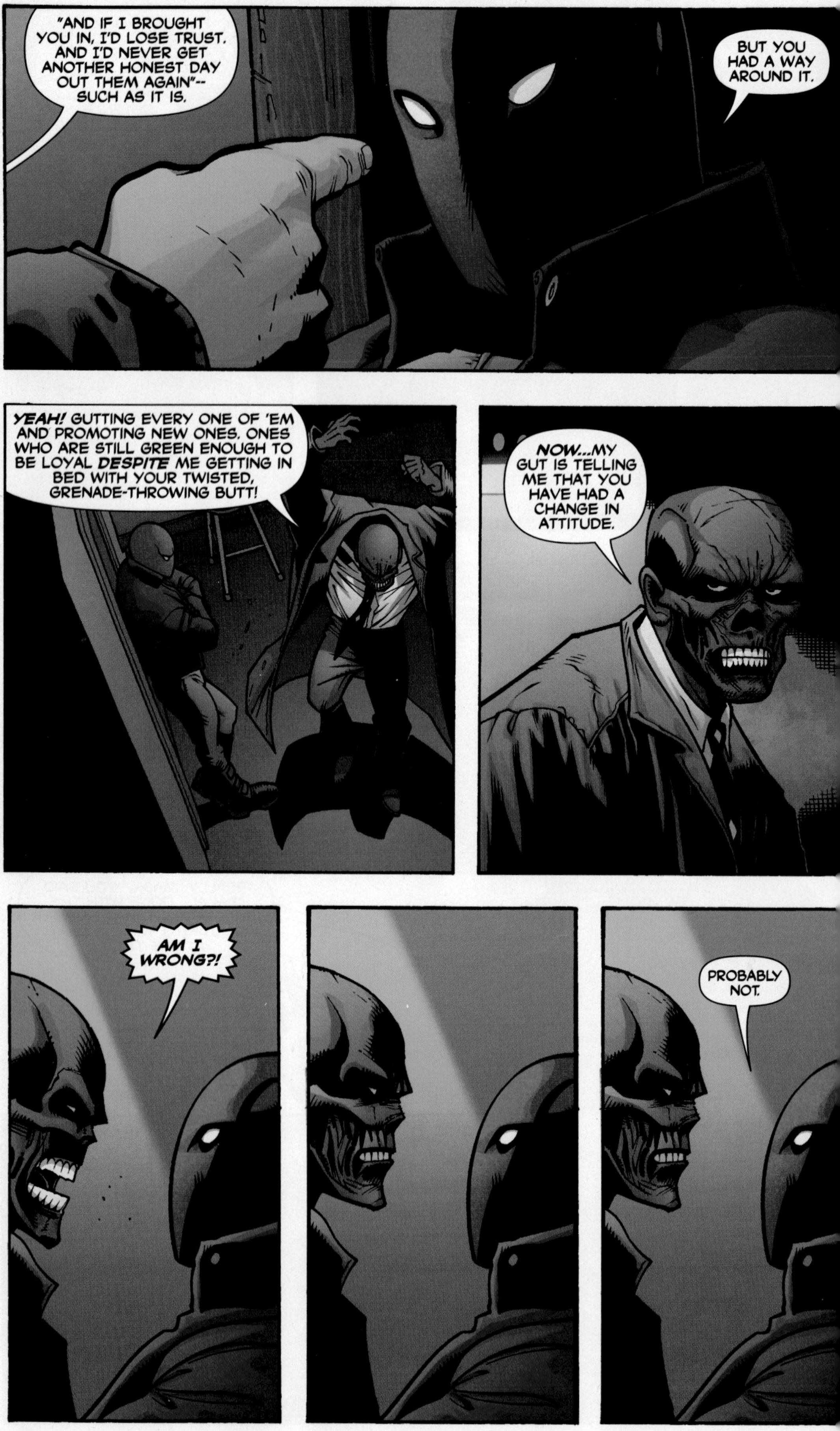
"AND IF I BROUGHT YOU IN, I'D LOSE TRUST. AND I'D NEVER GET ANOTHER HONEST DAY OUT THEM AGAIN"-- SUCH AS IT IS.
BUT YOU HAD A WAY AROUND IT.
YEAH! GUTTING EVERY ONE OF 'EM AND PROMOTING NEW ONES. ONES WHO ARE STILL GREEN ENOUGH TO BE LOYAL DESPITE ME GETTING IN BED WITH YOUR TWISTED, GRENADE-THROWING BUTT!
NOW...MY GUT IS TELLING ME THAT YOU HAVE HAD A CHANGE IN ATTITUDE.
AM I WRONG?!
PROBABLY NOT.

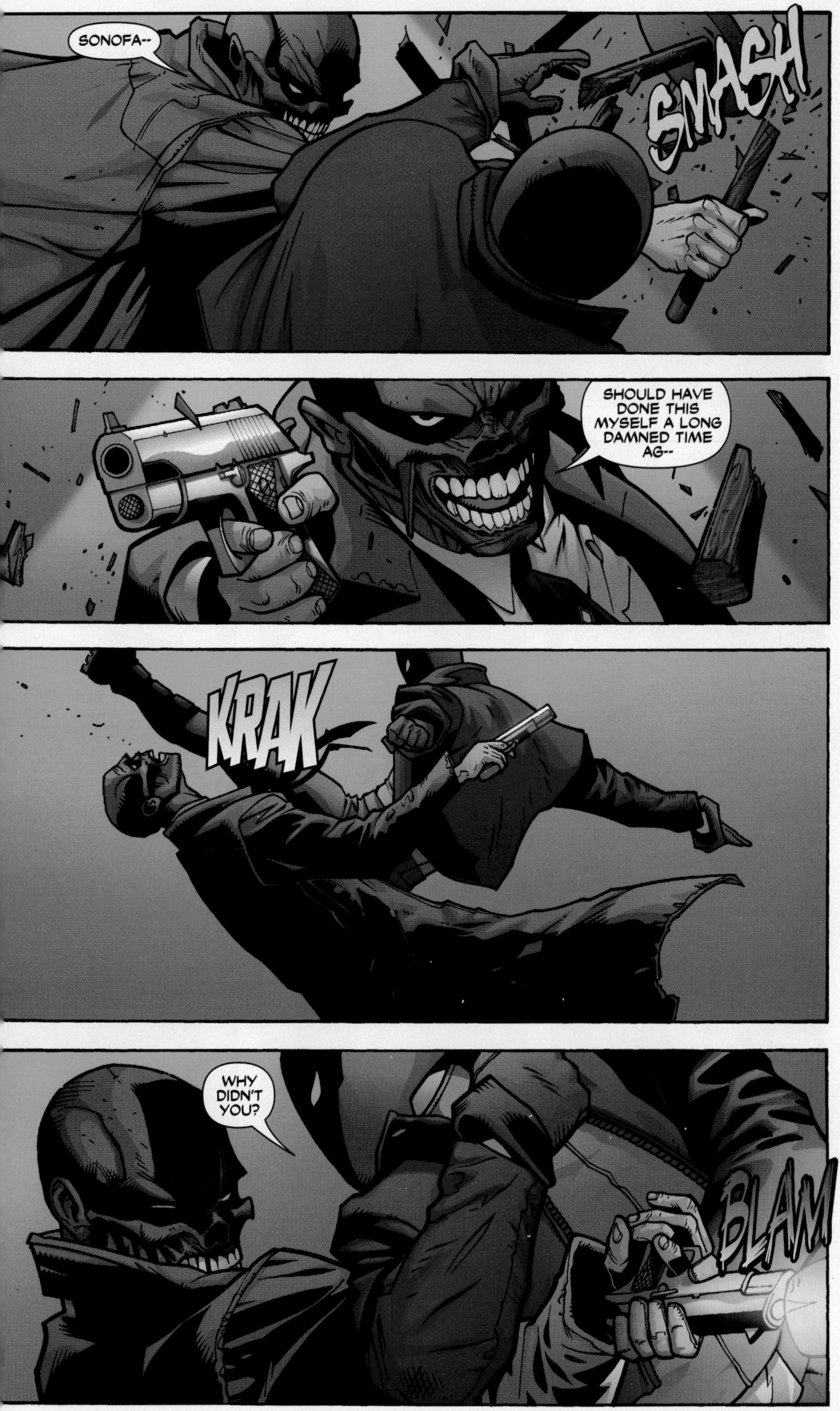
SONOFA--
SMASH
SHOULD HAVE DONE THIS MYSELF A LONG DAMNED TIME AG--
KRAK
WHY DIDN'T YOU?
BLAM

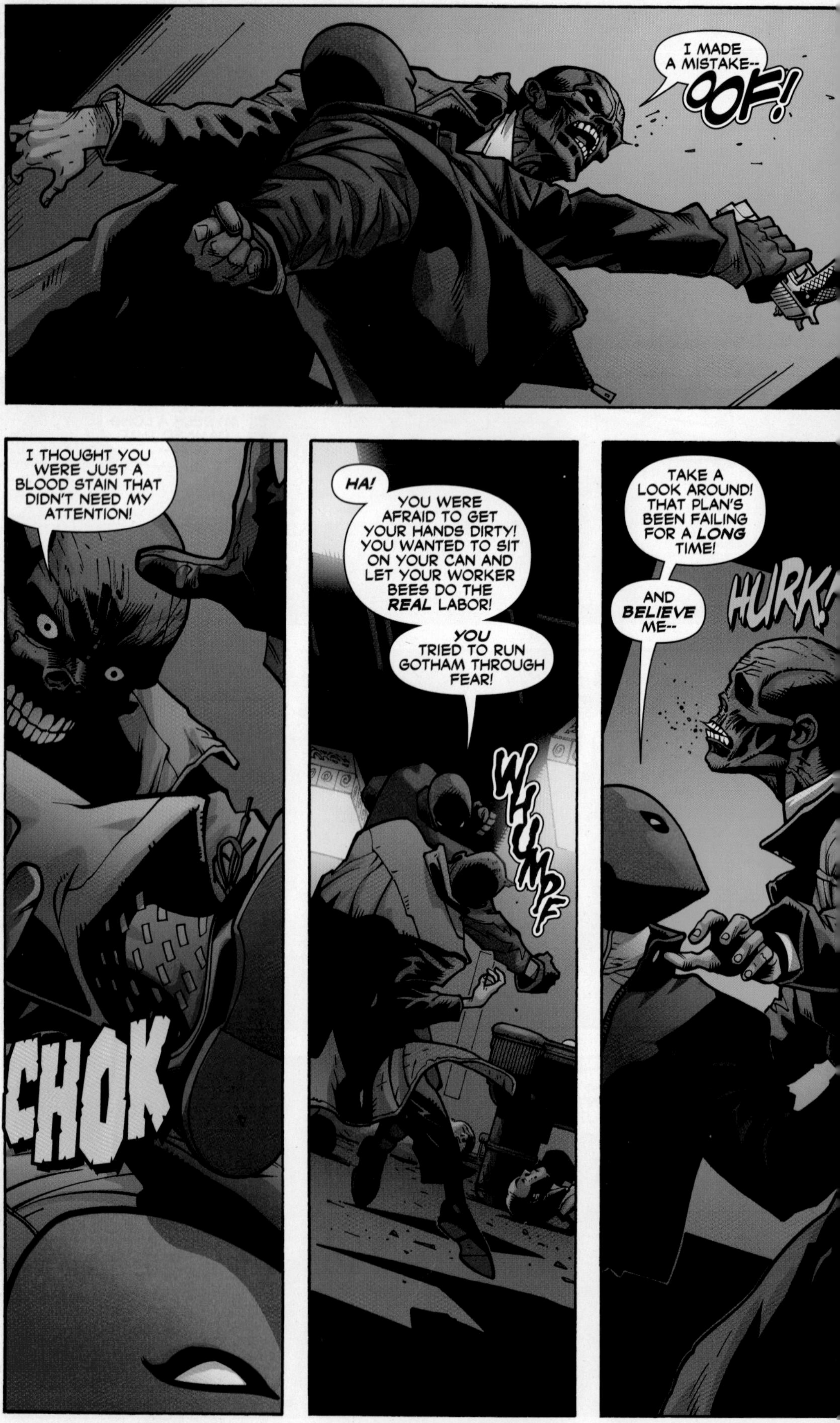

I MADE A MISTAKE--
OOF!
I THOUGHT YOU WERE JUST A BLOOD STAIN THAT DIDN'T NEED MY ATTENTION!
CHOK
HA!
YOU WERE AFRAID TO GET YOUR HANDS DIRTY! YOU WANTED TO SIT ON YOUR CAN AND LET YOUR WORKER BEES DO THE REAL LABOR!
YOU TRIED TO RUN GOTHAM THROUGH FEAR!
WHUMPF
TAKE A LOOK AROUND! THAT PLAN'S BEEN FAILING FOR A LONG TIME!
AND BELIEVE ME--
HURK!

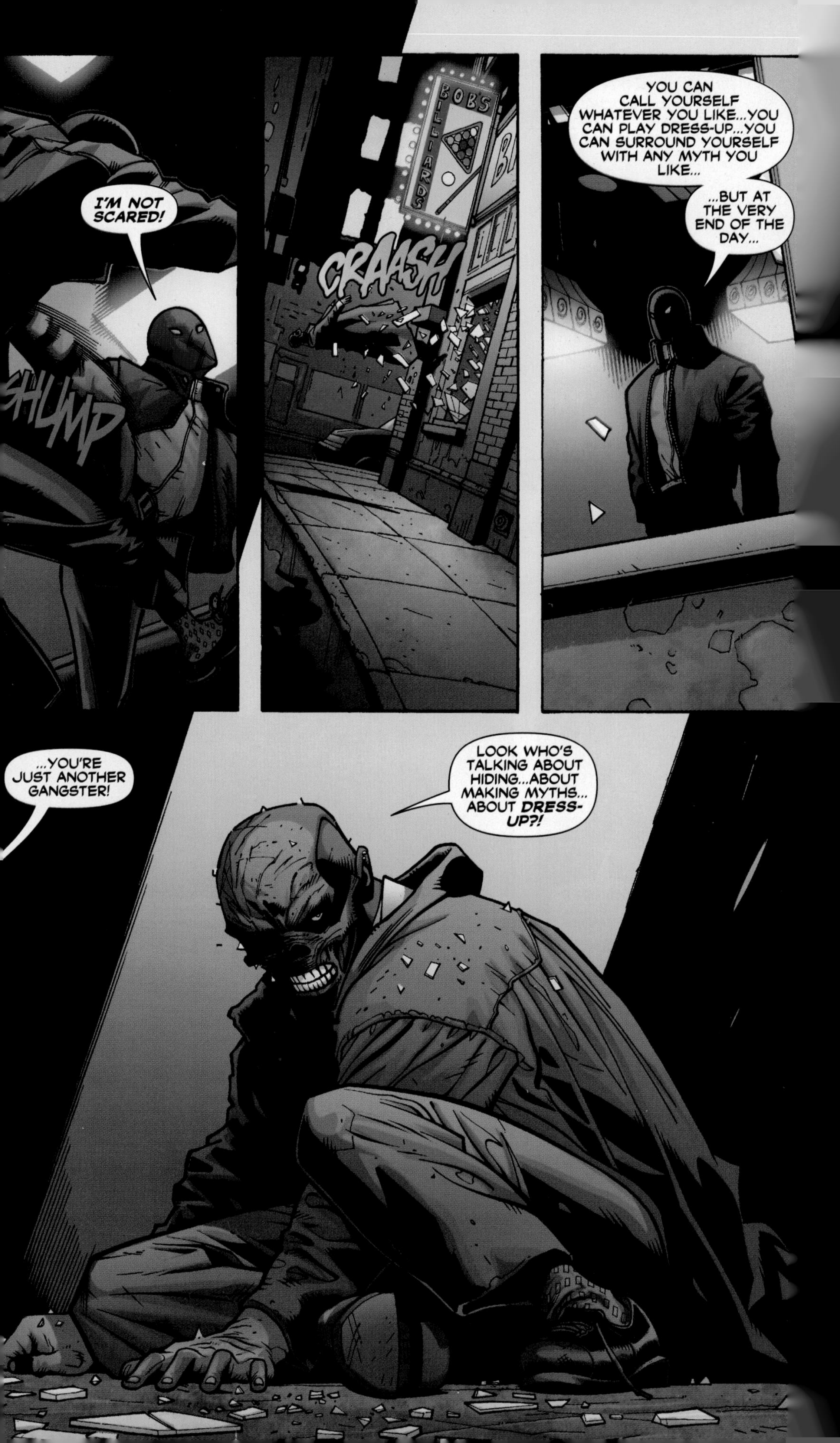
I'M NOT SCARED!
SHUMP
BOB'S BILLIARDS
CRAASH
YOU CAN CALL YOURSELF WHATEVER YOU LIKE...YOU CAN PLAY DRESS-UP...YOU CAN SURROUND YOURSELF WITH ANY MYTH YOU LIKE...
...BUT AT THE VERY END OF THE DAY...
...YOU'RE JUST ANOTHER GANGSTER!
LOOK WHO'S TALKING ABOUT HIDING...ABOUT MAKING MYTHS... ABOUT DRESS-UP?!

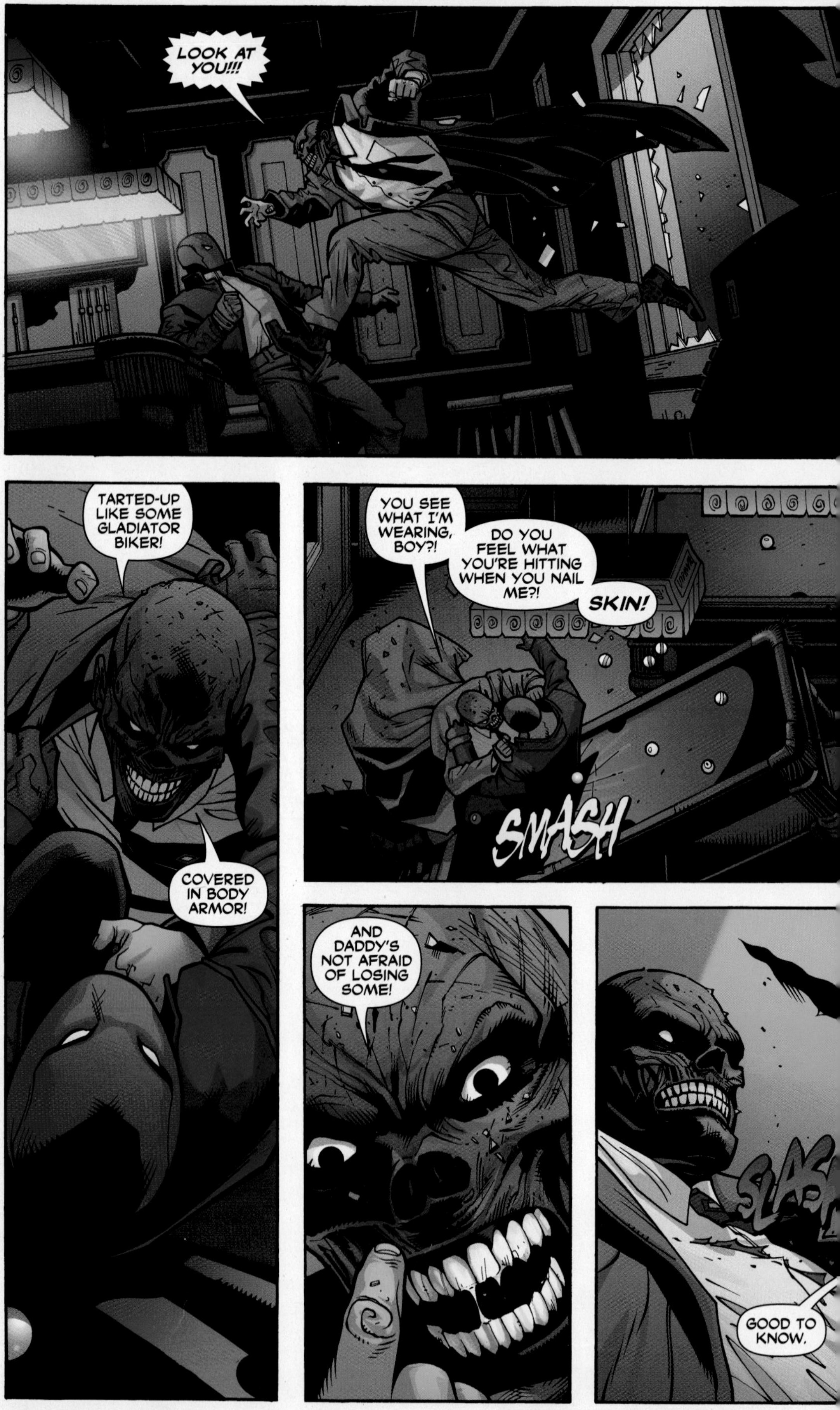
LOOK AT YOU!!!
TARTED-UP LIKE SOME GLADIATOR BIKER!
COVERED IN BODY ARMOR!
YOU SEE WHAT I'M WEARING, BOY?!
DO YOU FEEL WHAT YOU'RE HITTING WHEN YOU NAIL ME?!
SKIN!
SMASH
AND DADDY'S NOT AFRAID OF LOSING SOME!
GOOD TO KNOW.

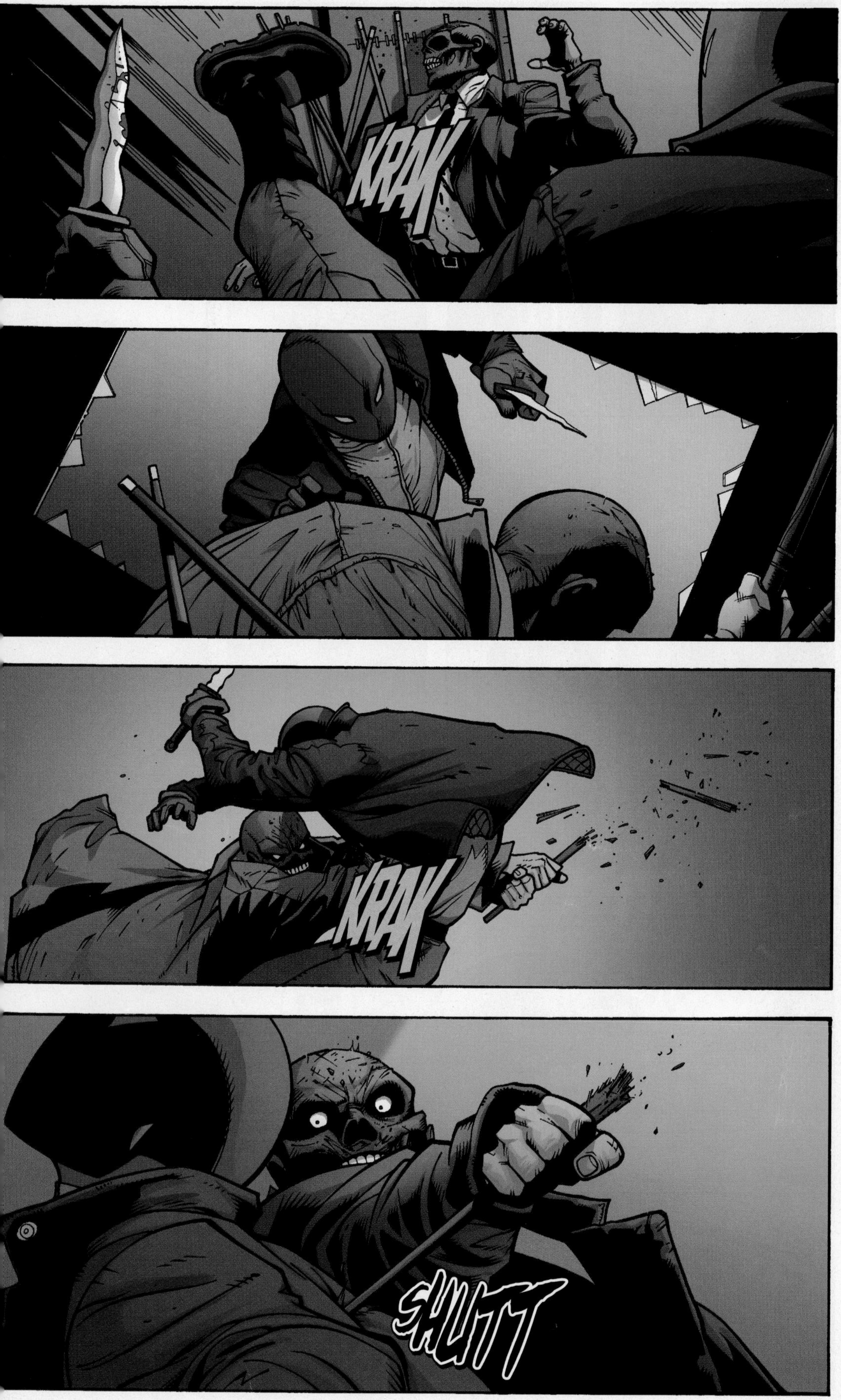
KRAK
KRAK
SHUTT

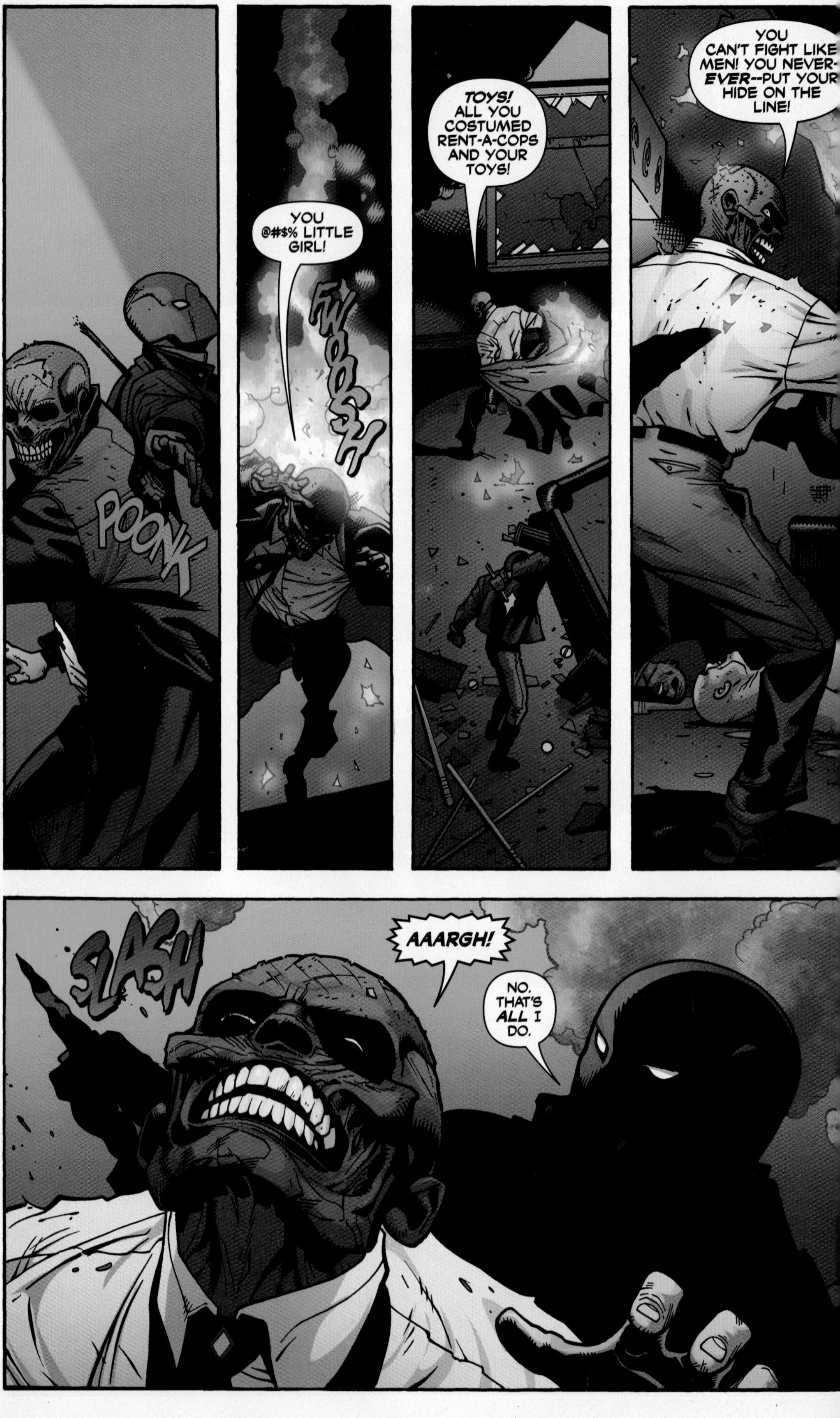
POONK
YOU @#$% LITTLE GIRL!
FWOOSH
TOYS! ALL YOU COSTUMED RENT-A-COPS AND YOUR TOYS!
YOU CAN'T FIGHT LIKE MEN! YOU NEVER-EVER--PUT YOUR HIDE ON THE LINE!
SLASH
AAARGH!
NO. THAT'S ALL I DO.

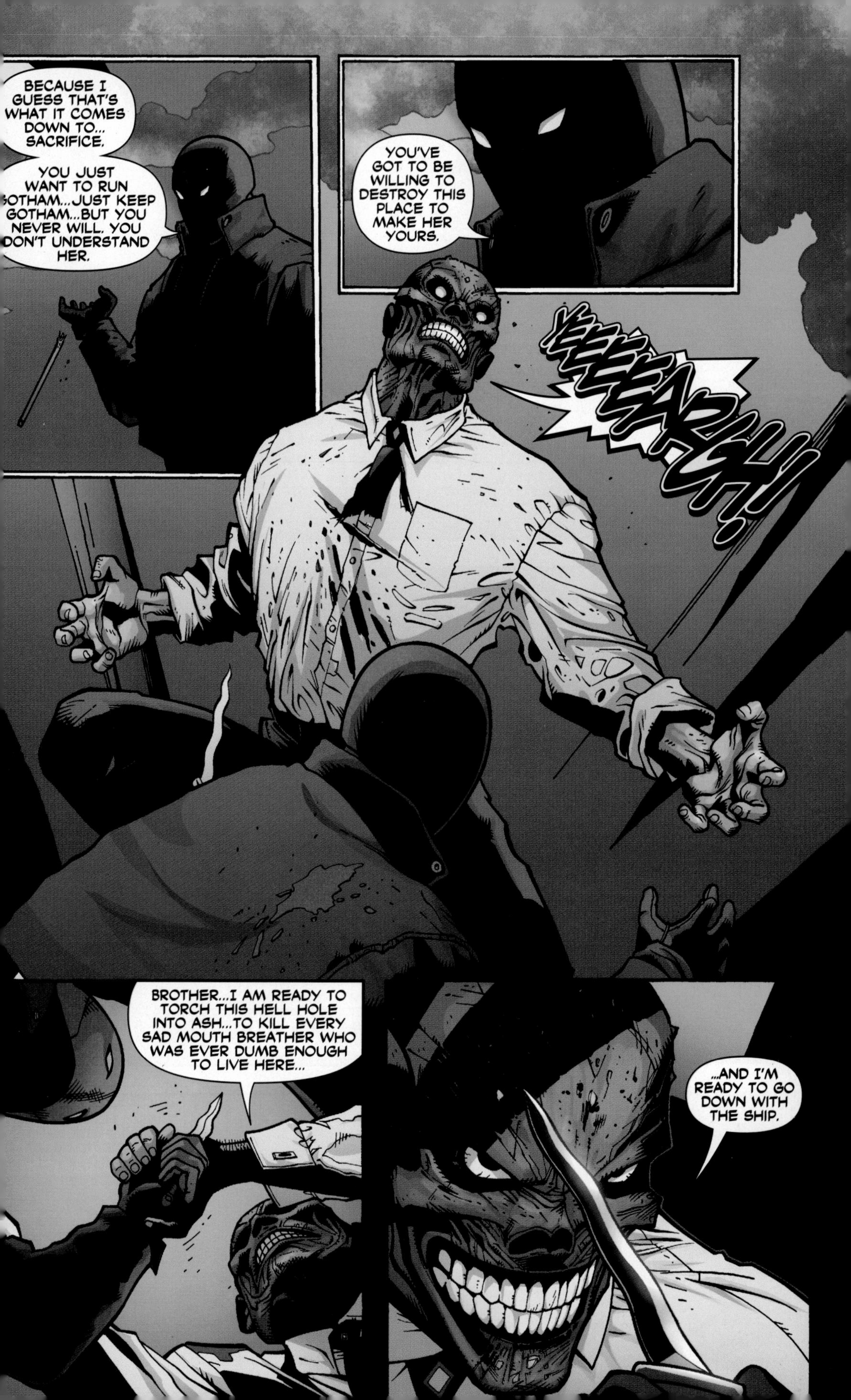
BECAUSE I GUESS THAT'S WHAT IT COMES DOWN TO... SACRIFICE.
YOU JUST WANT TO RUN GOTHAM...JUST KEEP GOTHAM...BUT YOU NEVER WILL. YOU DON'T UNDERSTAND HER.
YOU'VE GOT TO BE WILLING TO DESTROY THIS PLACE TO MAKE HER YOURS.
YEEEAARGH!!
BROTHER...I AM READY TO TORCH THIS HELL HOLE INTO ASH...TO KILL EVERY SAD MOUTH BREATHER WHO WAS EVER DUMB ENOUGH TO LIVE HERE...
...AND I'M READY TO GO DOWN WITH THE SHIP.

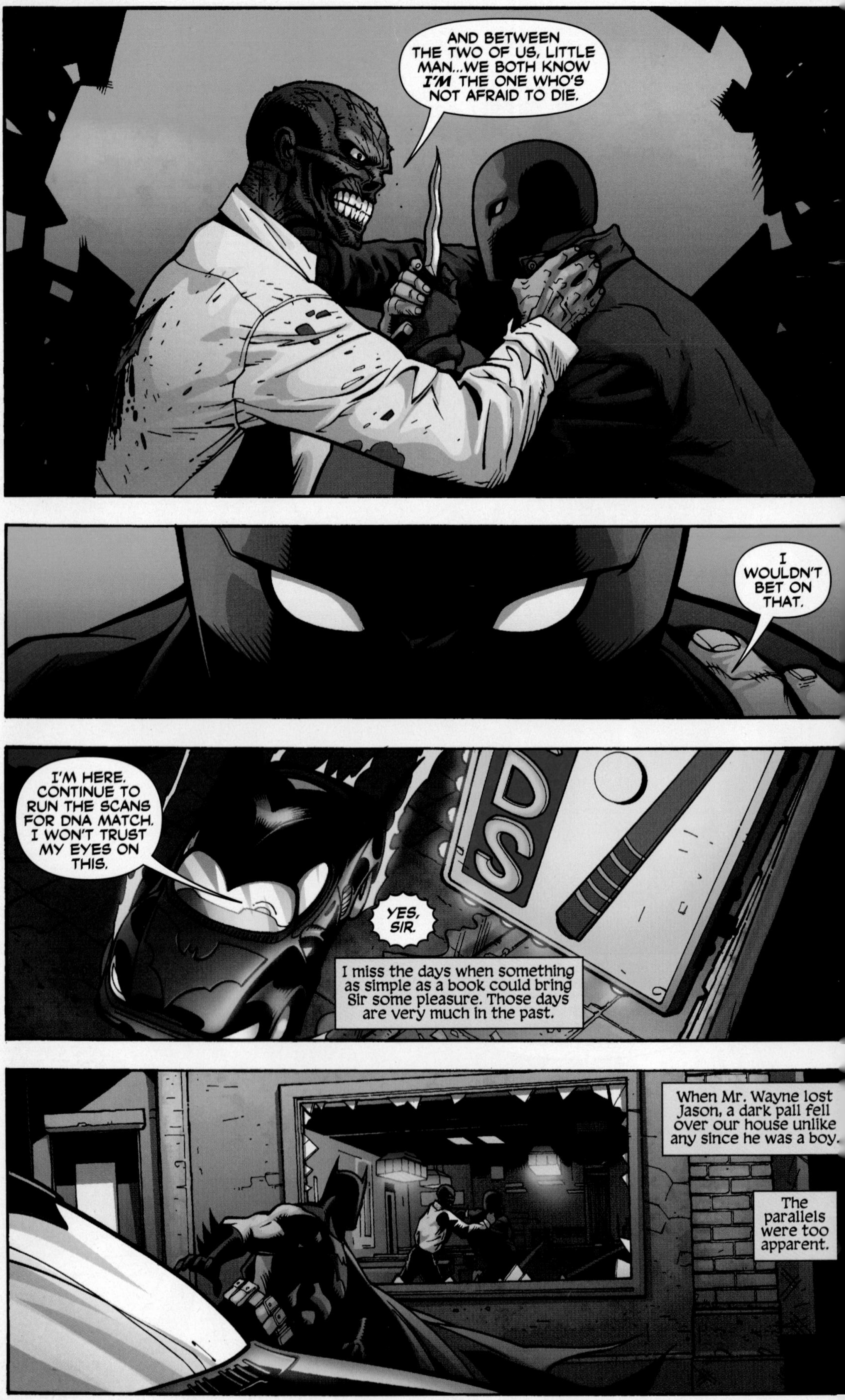
AND BETWEEN THE TWO OF US, LITTLE MAN...WE BOTH KNOW I'M THE ONE WHO'S NOT AFRAID TO DIE.
I WOULDN'T BET ON THAT.
I'M HERE. CONTINUE TO RUN THE SCANS FOR DNA MATCH. I WON'T TRUST MY EYES ON THIS.
YES, SIR.
I miss the days when something as simple as a book could bring Sir some pleasure. Those days are very much in the past.
When Mr. Wayne lost Jason, a dark pall fell over our house unlike any since he was a boy.
The parallels were too apparent.

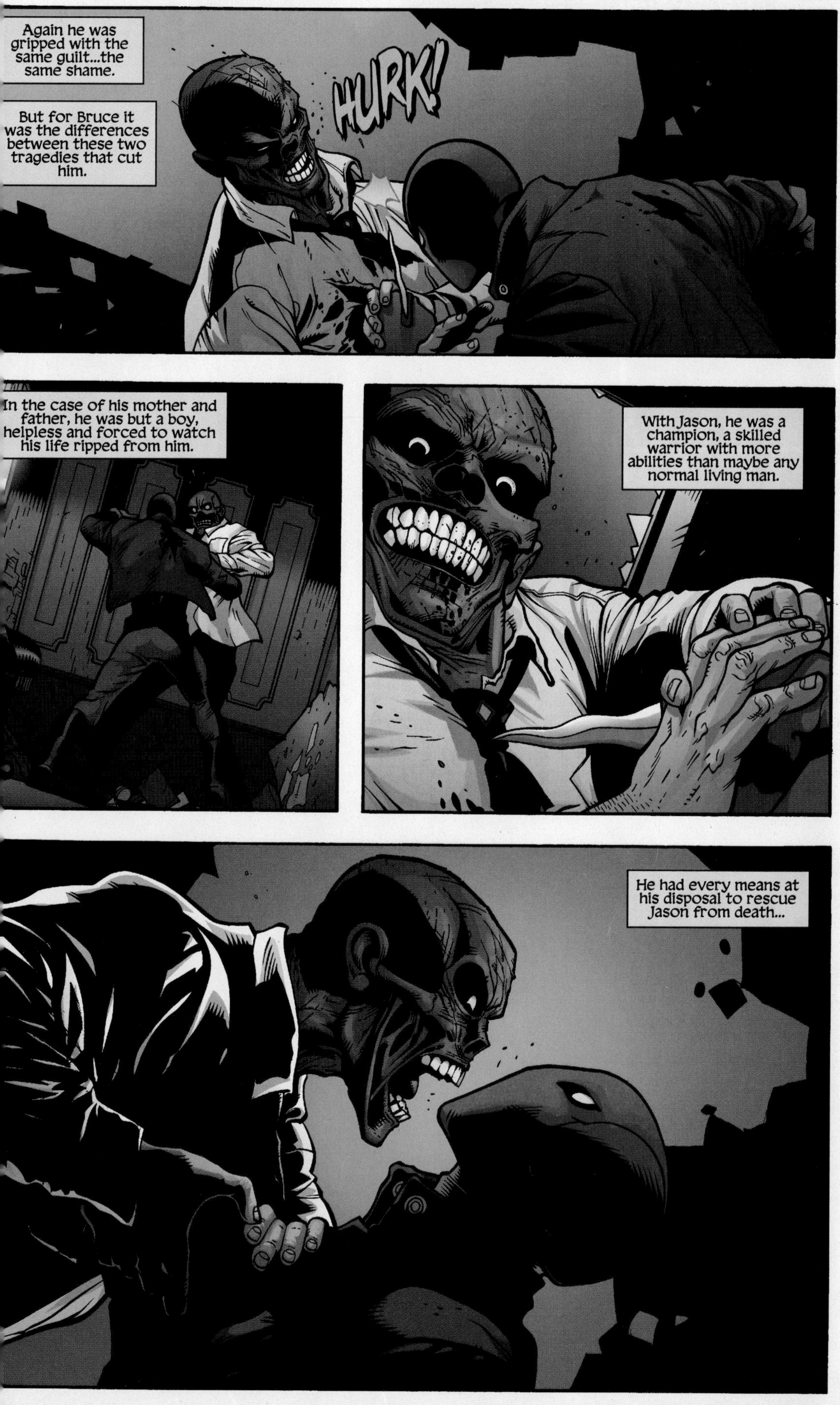

Again he was gripped with the same guilt...the same shame.
HURK!
But for Bruce it was the differences between these two tragedies that cut him.
In the case of his mother and father, he was but a boy, helpless and forced to watch his life ripped from him.
With Jason, he was a champion, a skilled warrior with more abilities than maybe any normal living man.
He had every means at his disposal to rescue Jason from death...

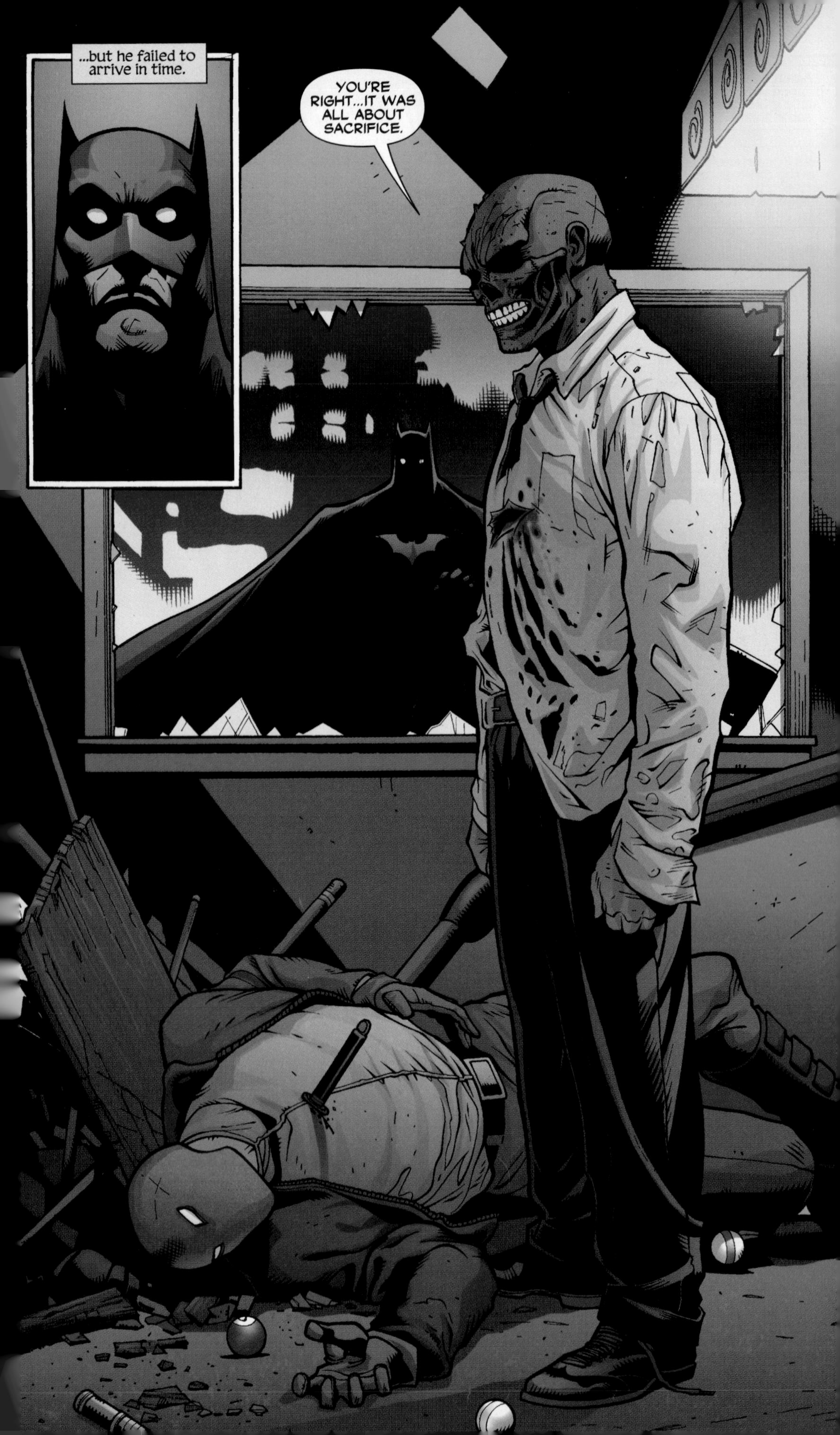
...but he failed to arrive in time.
YOU'RE RIGHT...IT WAS ALL ABOUT SACRIFICE.

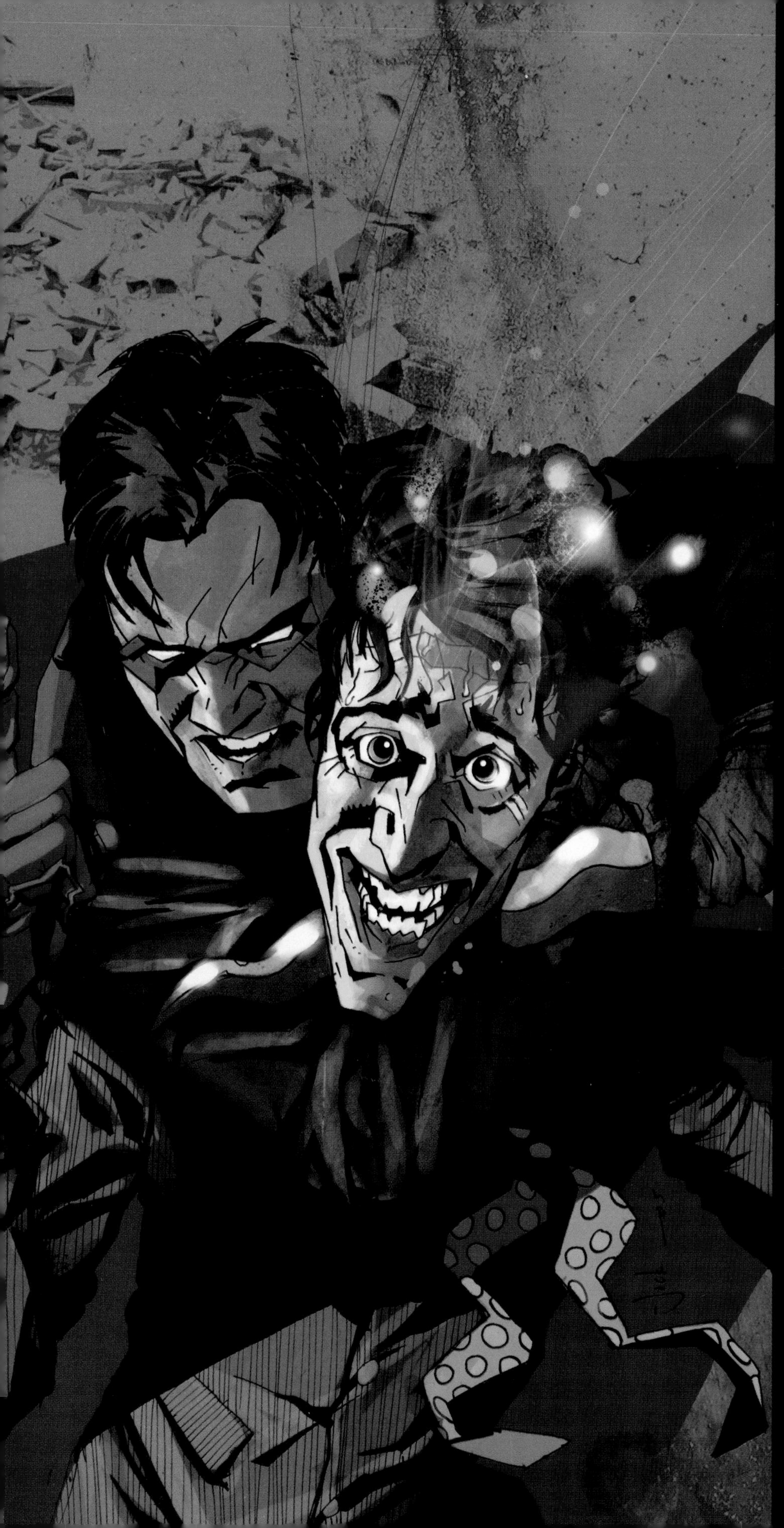

BATMAN #649 • COVER BY JOCK

CHAPTER 5

ALL THEY DO IS WATCH US KILL
PART 2

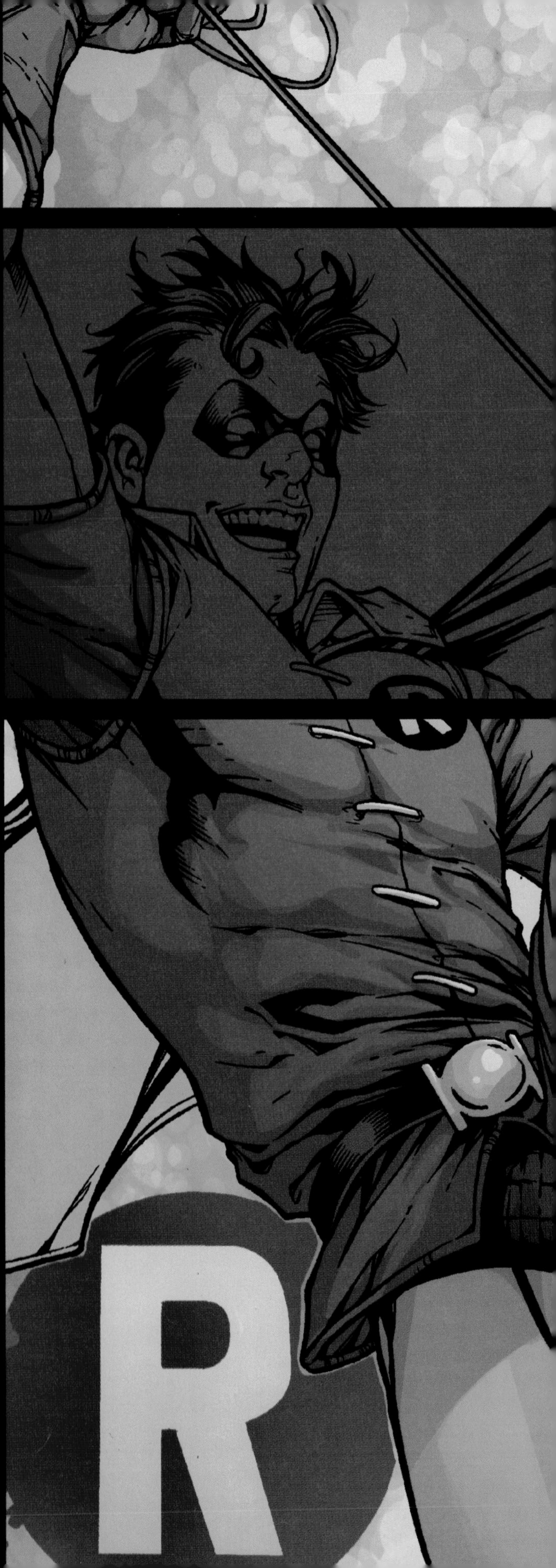

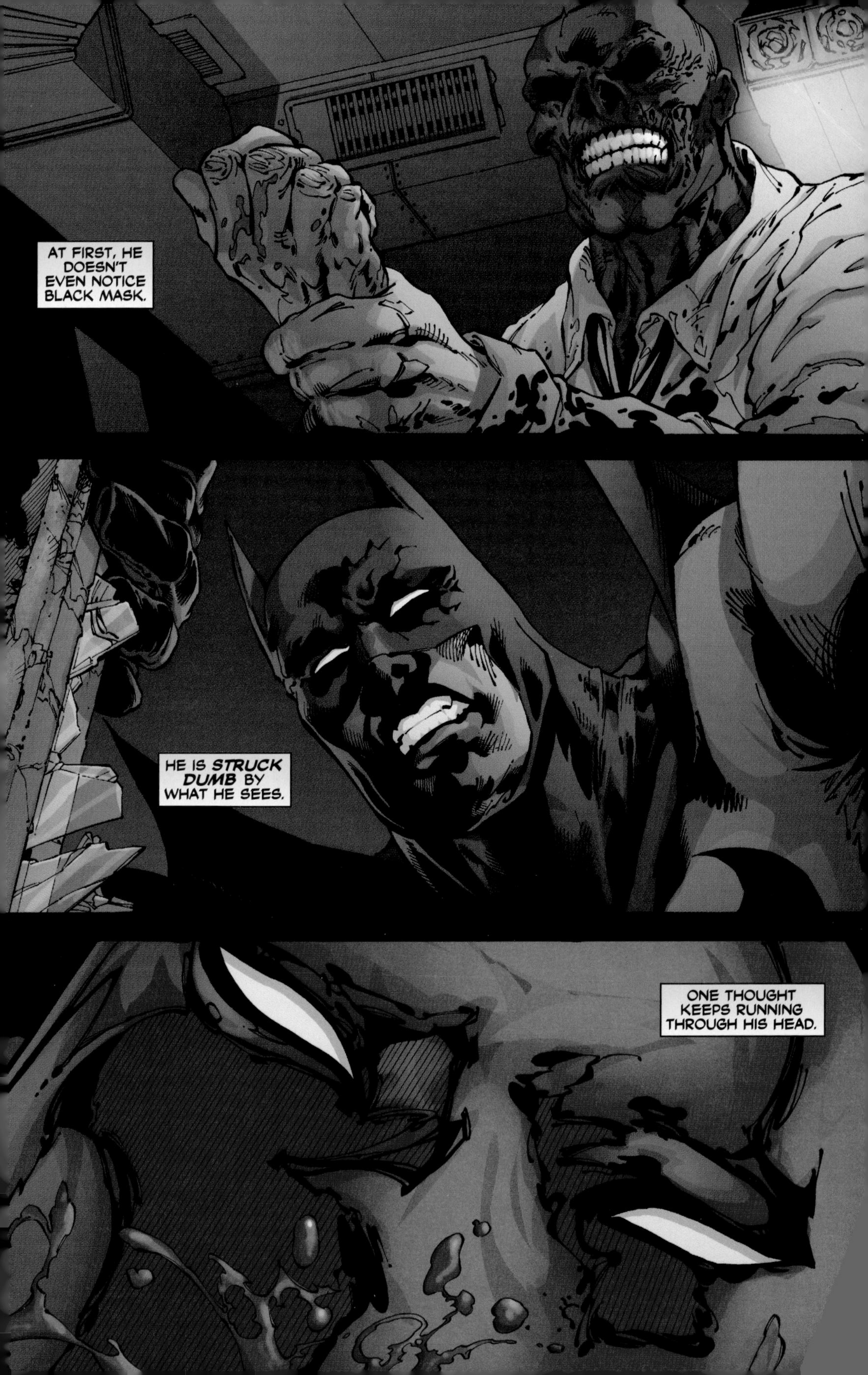
AT FIRST, HE DOESN'T EVEN NOTICE BLACK MASK.
HE IS STRUCK DUMB BY WHAT HE SEES.
ONE THOUGHT KEEPS RUNNING THROUGH HIS HEAD.

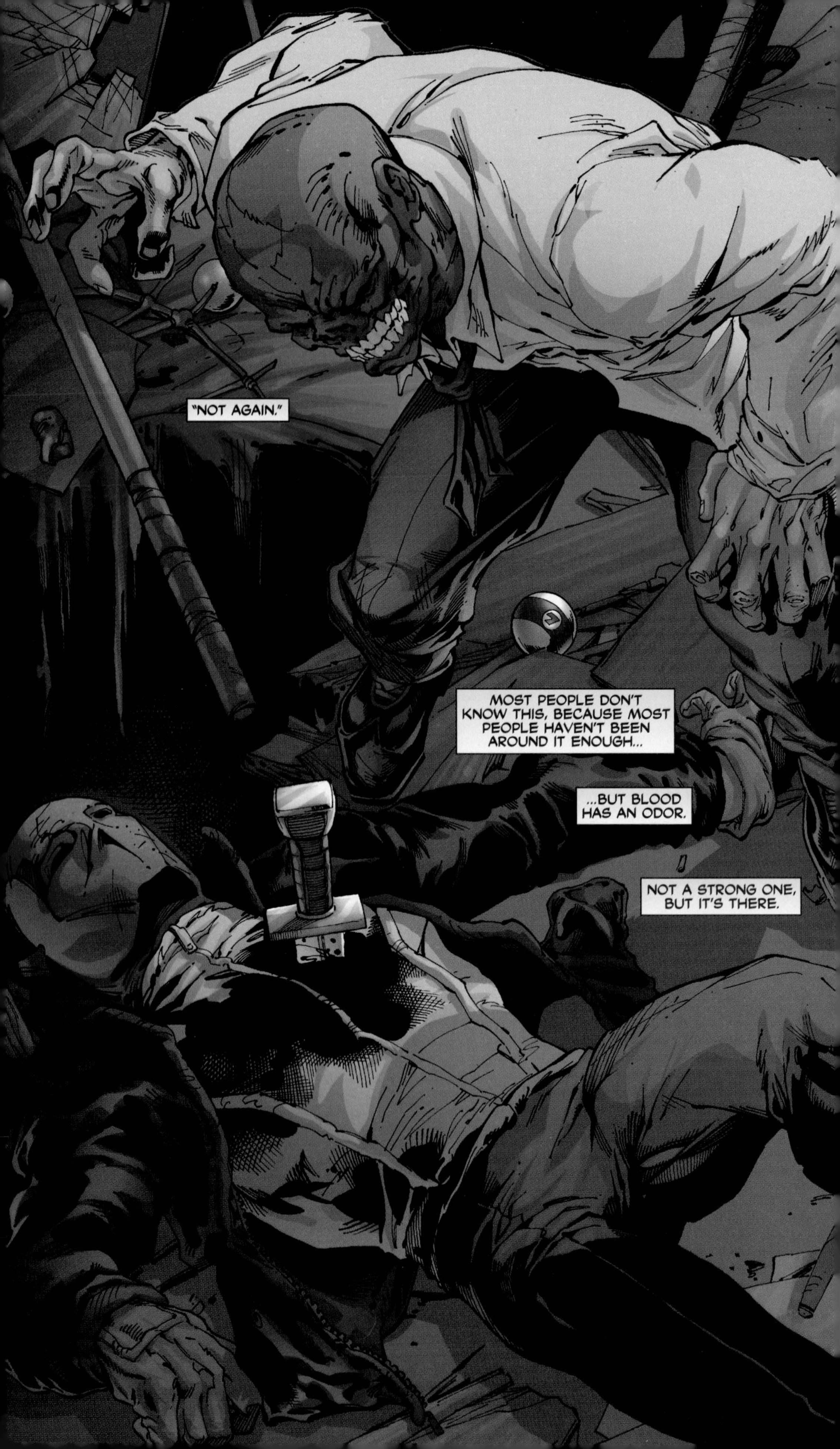
"NOT AGAIN."
MOST PEOPLE DON'T KNOW THIS, BECAUSE MOST PEOPLE HAVEN'T BEEN AROUND IT ENOUGH...
...BUT BLOOD HAS AN ODOR.
NOT A STRONG ONE, BUT IT'S THERE.

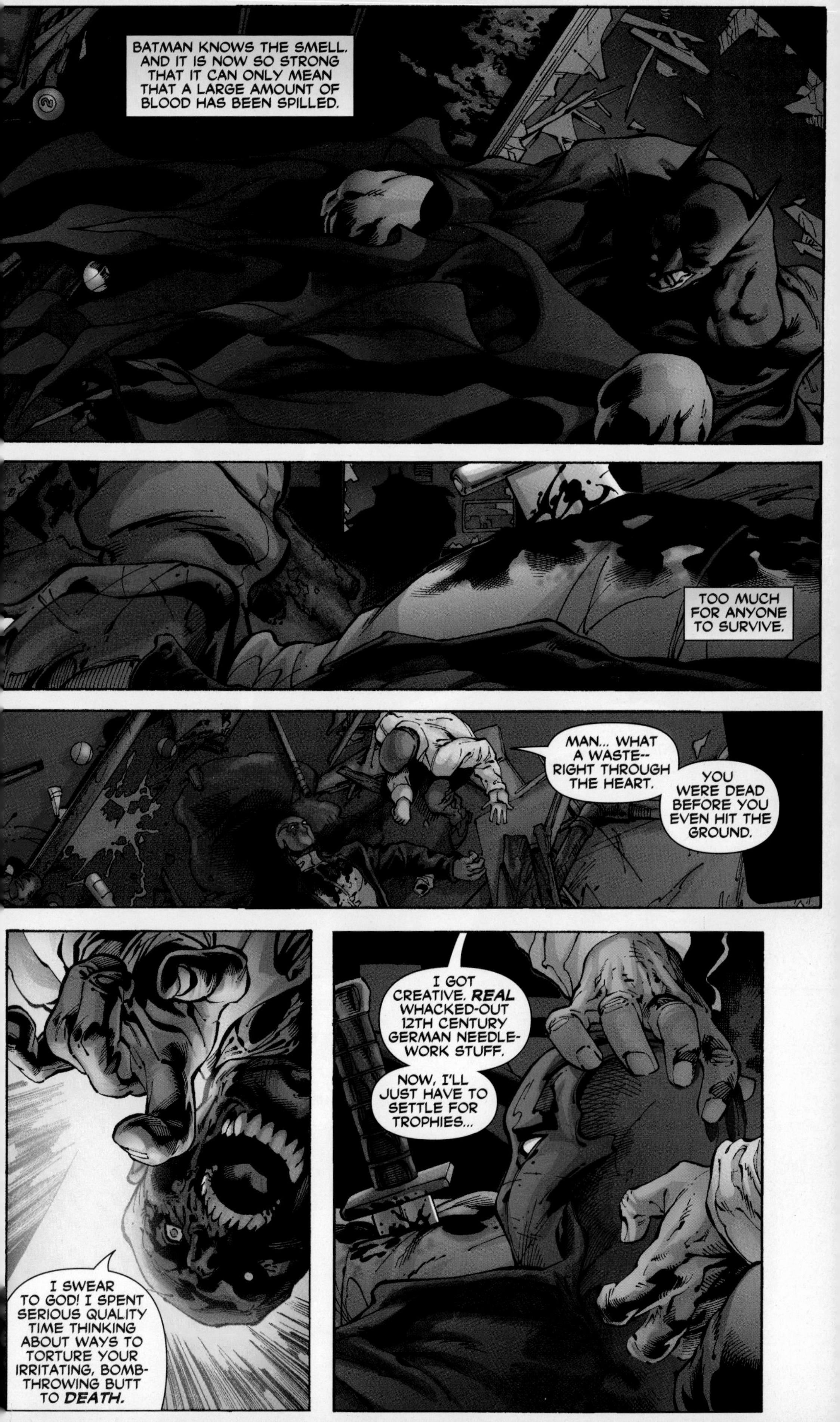
BATMAN KNOWS THE SMELL. AND IT IS NOW SO STRONG THAT IT CAN ONLY MEAN THAT A LARGE AMOUNT OF BLOOD HAS BEEN SPILLED.
TOO MUCH FOR ANYONE TO SURVIVE.
MAN... WHAT A WASTE-- RIGHT THROUGH THE HEART.
YOU WERE DEAD BEFORE YOU EVEN HIT THE GROUND.
I SWEAR TO GOD! I SPENT SERIOUS QUALITY TIME THINKING ABOUT WAYS TO TORTURE YOUR IRRITATING, BOMB-THROWING BUTT TO *DEATH.*
I GOT CREATIVE. *REAL* WHACKED-OUT 12TH CENTURY GERMAN NEEDLE-WORK STUFF.
NOW, I'LL JUST HAVE TO SETTLE FOR TROPHIES...

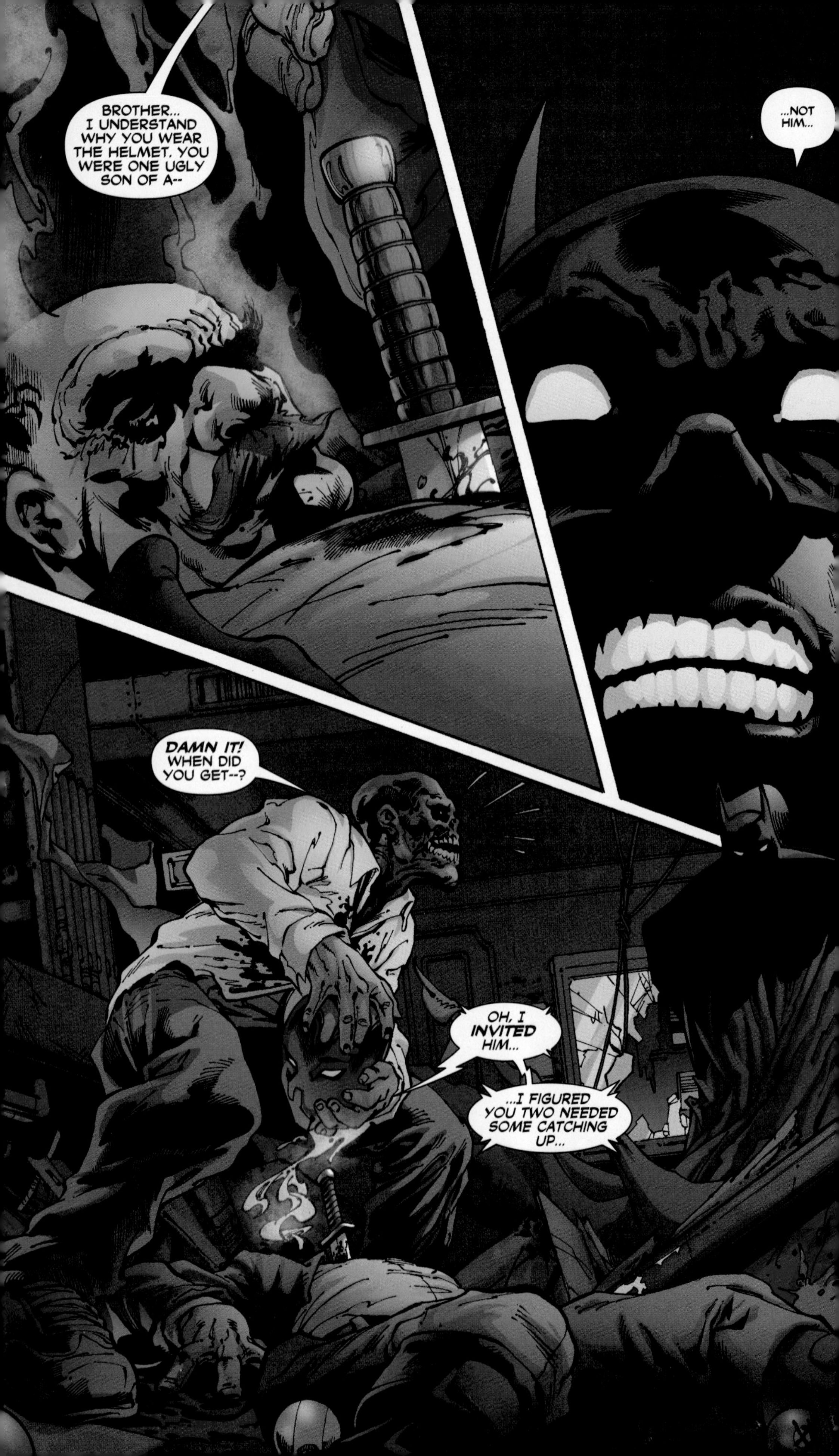

BROTHER... I UNDERSTAND WHY YOU WEAR THE HELMET. YOU WERE ONE UGLY SON OF A--
...NOT HIM...
DAMN IT! WHEN DID YOU GET--?
OH, I INVITED HIM...
...I FIGURED YOU TWO NEEDED SOME CATCHING UP...

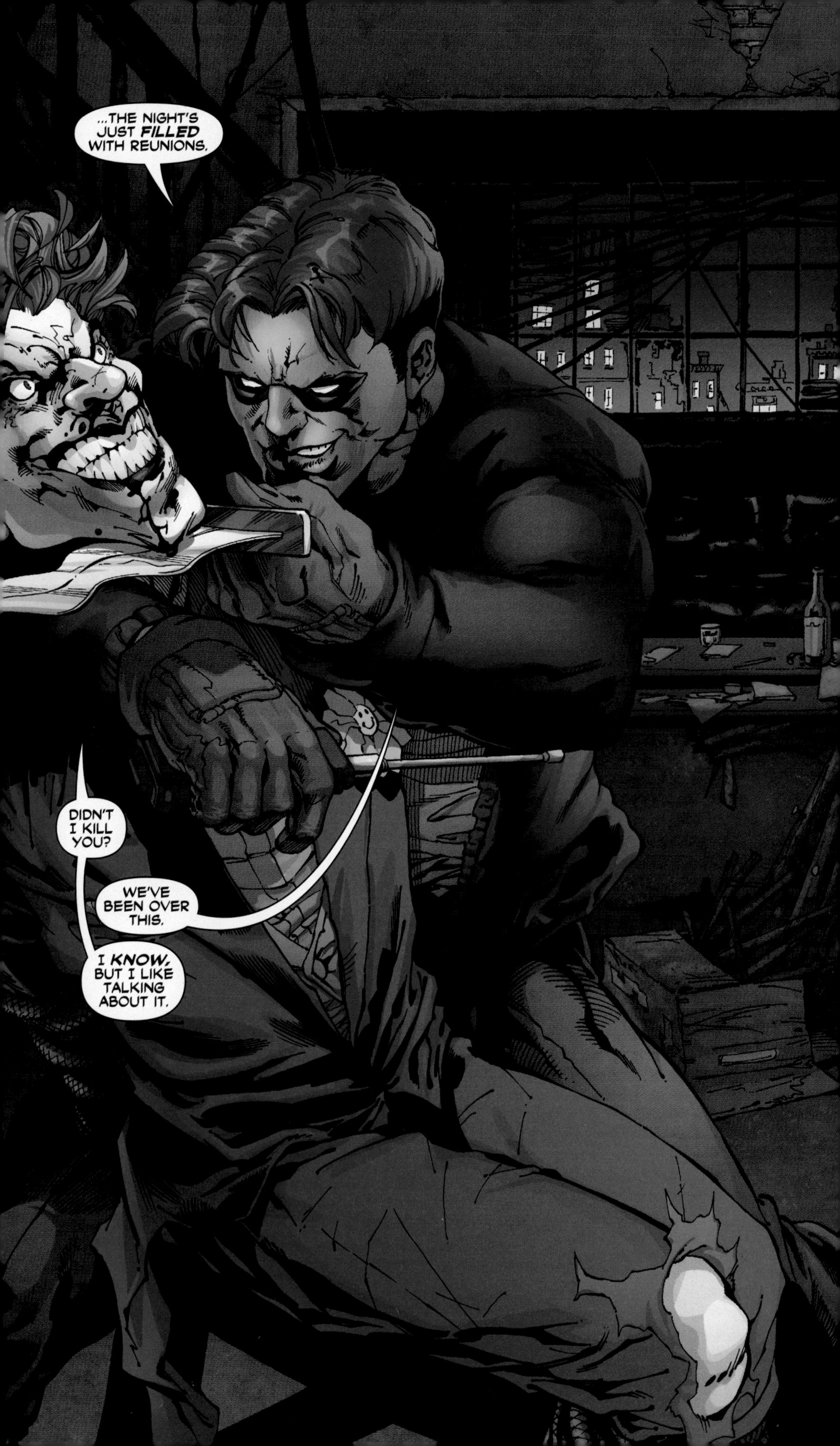
...THE NIGHT'S JUST *FILLED* WITH REUNIONS.
DIDN'T I KILL YOU?
WE'VE BEEN OVER THIS.
I *KNOW*, BUT I LIKE TALKING ABOUT IT.

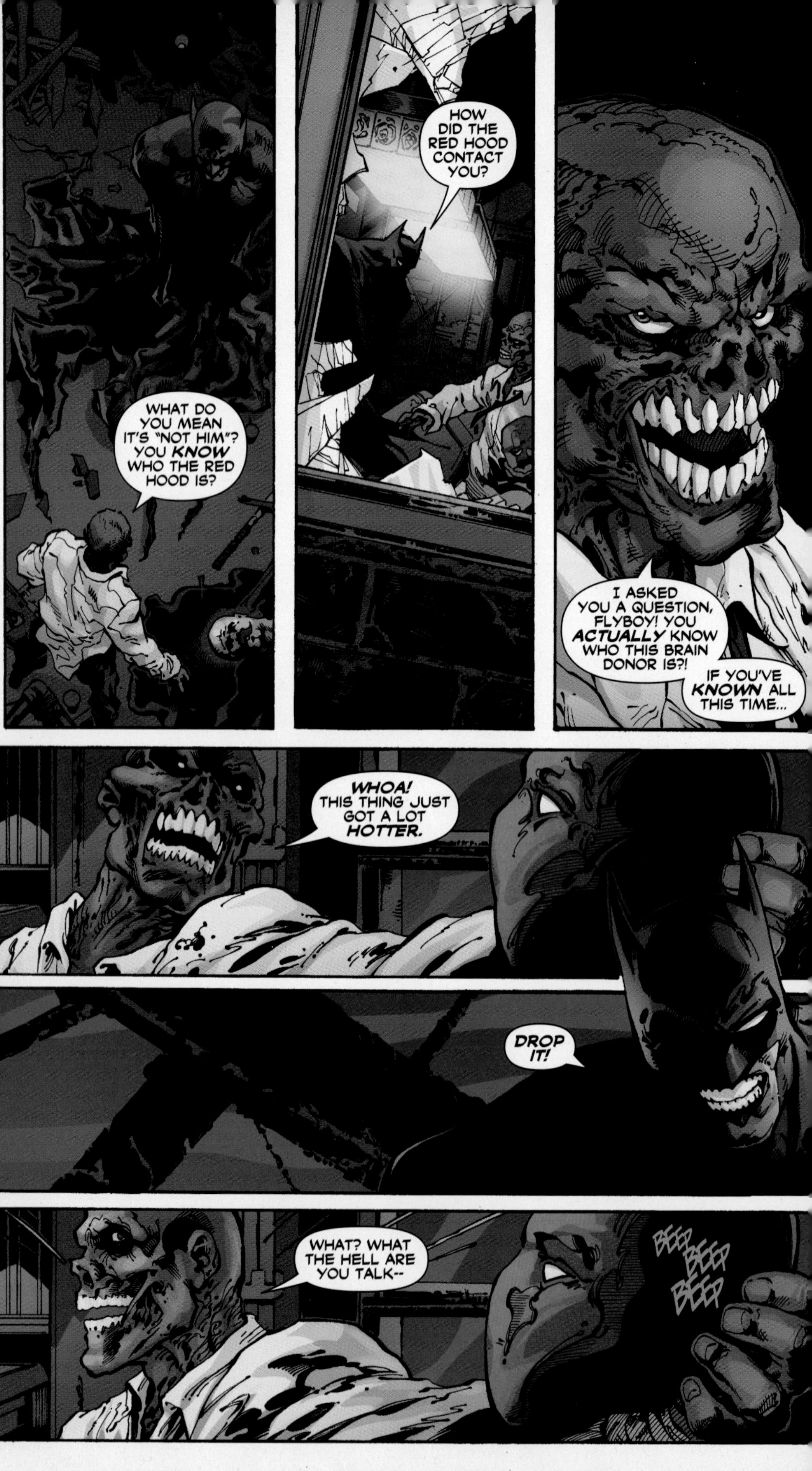
WHAT DO YOU MEAN IT'S "NOT HIM"? YOU KNOW WHO THE RED HOOD IS?
HOW DID THE RED HOOD CONTACT YOU?
I ASKED YOU A QUESTION, FLYBOY! YOU ACTUALLY KNOW WHO THIS BRAIN DONOR IS?!
IF YOU'VE KNOWN ALL THIS TIME...
WHOA! THIS THING JUST GOT A LOT HOTTER.
DROP IT!
WHAT? WHAT THE HELL ARE YOU TALK--
BEEP BEEP BEEP

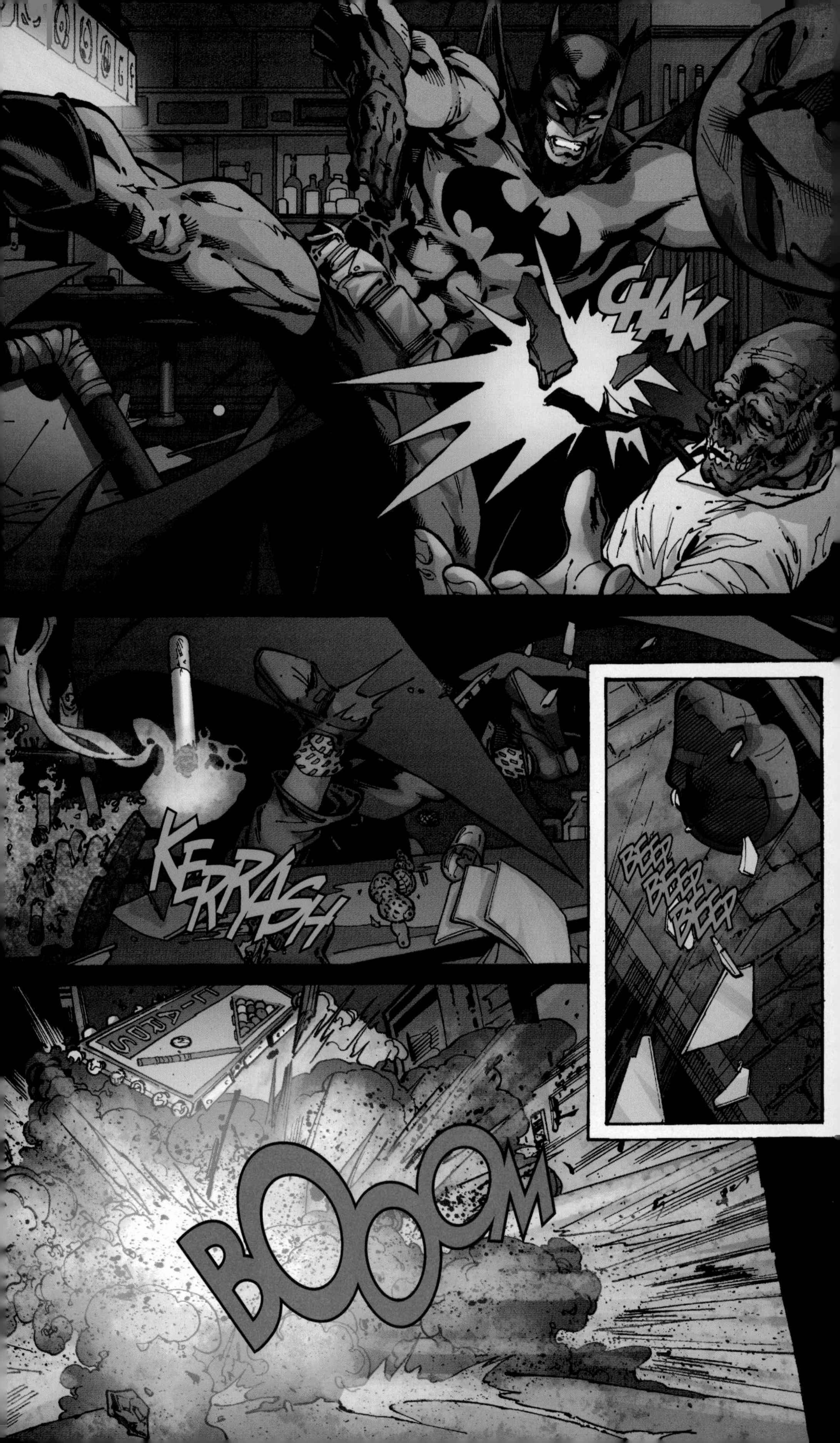
CHAK
KERRASH
BEEP
BEEP
BEEP
BOOOM

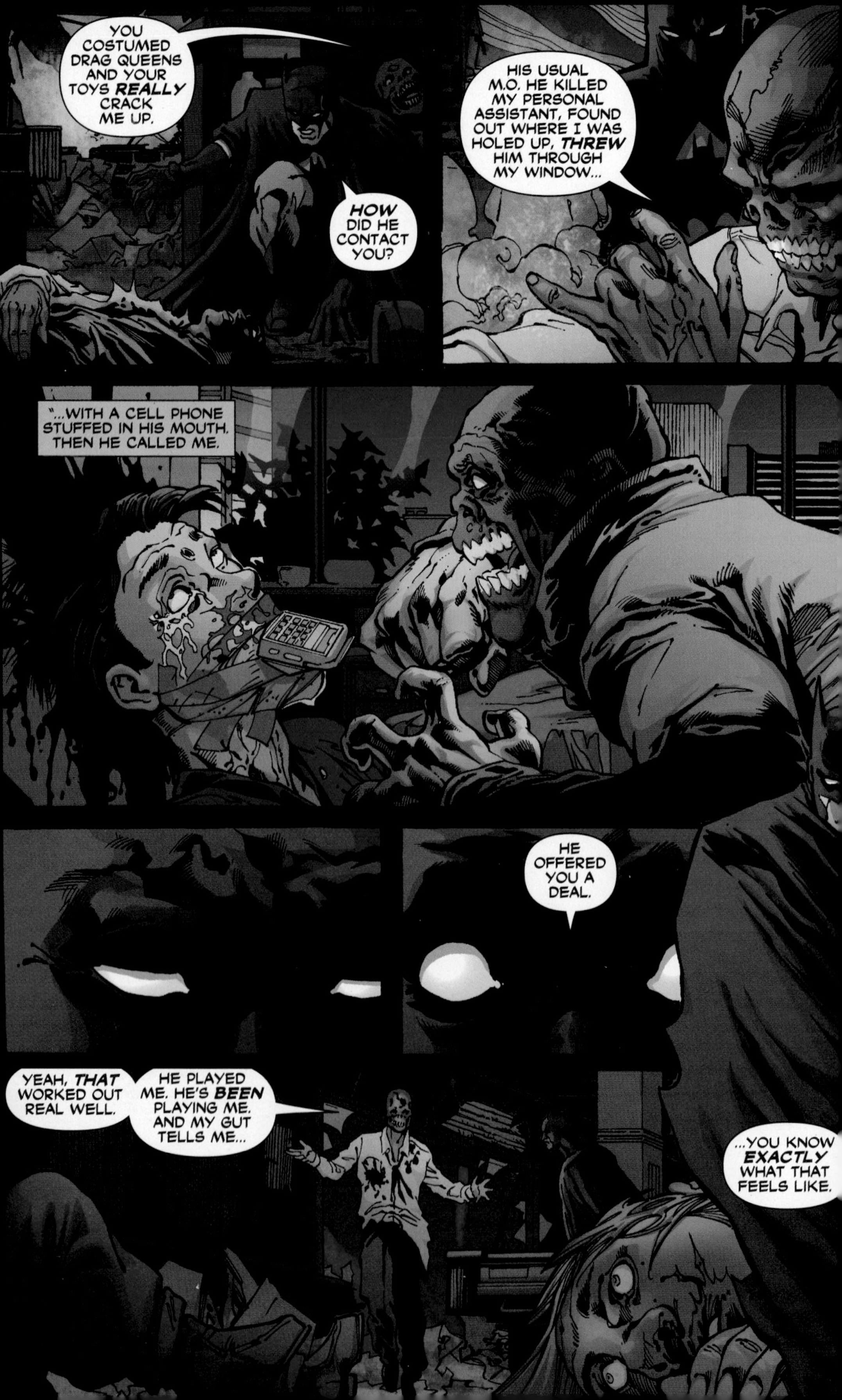
YOU COSTUMED DRAG QUEENS AND YOUR TOYS REALLY CRACK ME UP.
HOW DID HE CONTACT YOU?
HIS USUAL M.O. HE KILLED MY PERSONAL ASSISTANT, FOUND OUT WHERE I WAS HOLED UP, THREW HIM THROUGH MY WINDOW...
"...WITH A CELL PHONE STUFFED IN HIS MOUTH. THEN HE CALLED ME.
HE OFFERED YOU A DEAL.
YEAH, THAT WORKED OUT REAL WELL.
HE PLAYED ME. HE'S BEEN PLAYING ME. AND MY GUT TELLS ME...
...YOU KNOW EXACTLY WHAT THAT FEELS LIKE.

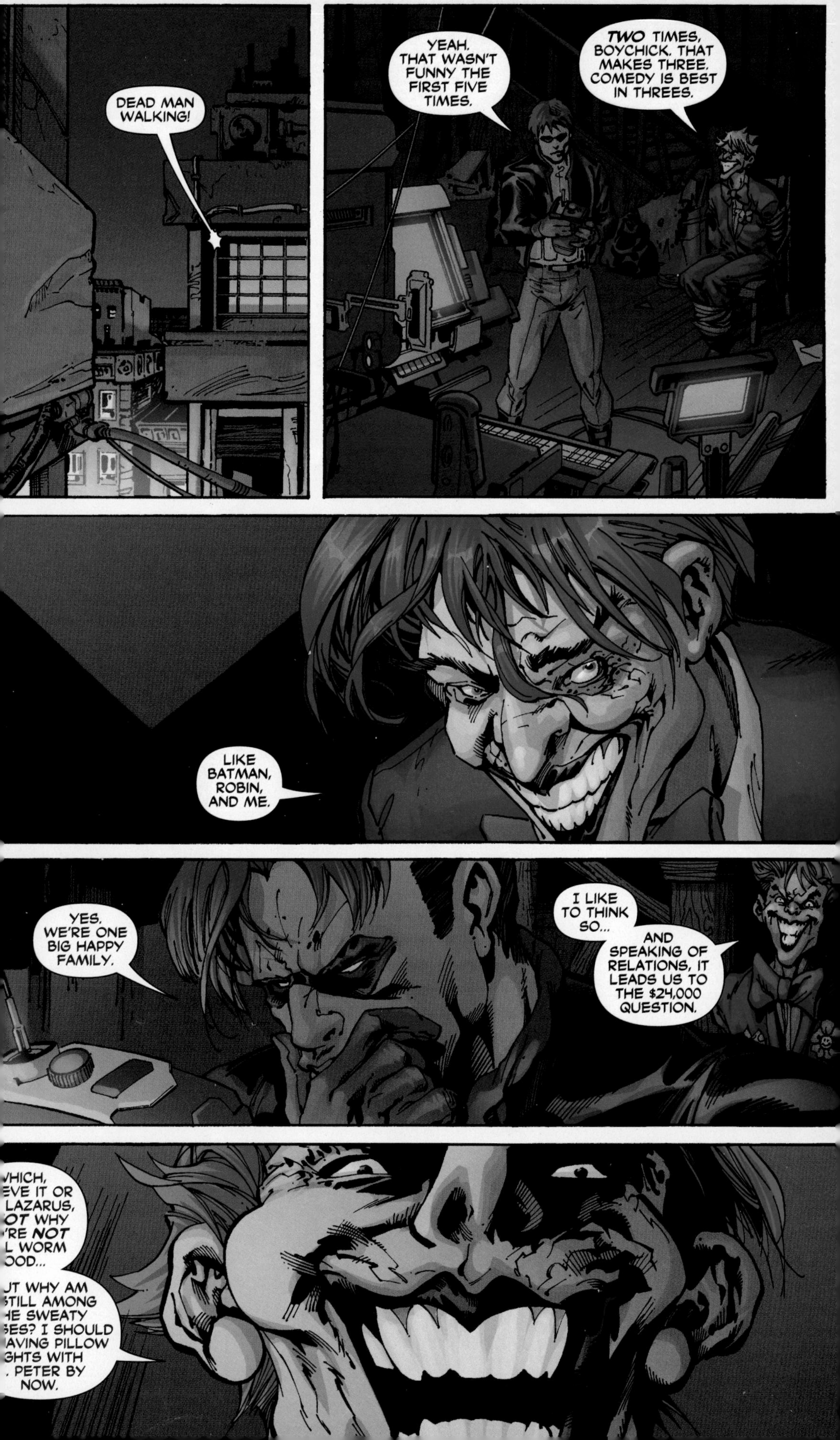
DEAD MAN WALKING!
YEAH. THAT WASN'T FUNNY THE FIRST FIVE TIMES.
TWO TIMES, BOYCHICK. THAT MAKES THREE. COMEDY IS BEST IN THREES.
LIKE BATMAN, ROBIN, AND ME.
YES. WE'RE ONE BIG HAPPY FAMILY.
I LIKE TO THINK SO...
AND SPEAKING OF RELATIONS, IT LEADS US TO THE $24,000 QUESTION.
VHICH, EVE IT OR LAZARUS, OT WHY 'RE NOT L WORM OOD...
UT WHY AM STILL AMONG HE SWEATY SES? I SHOULD AVING PILLOW GHTS WITH . PETER BY NOW.

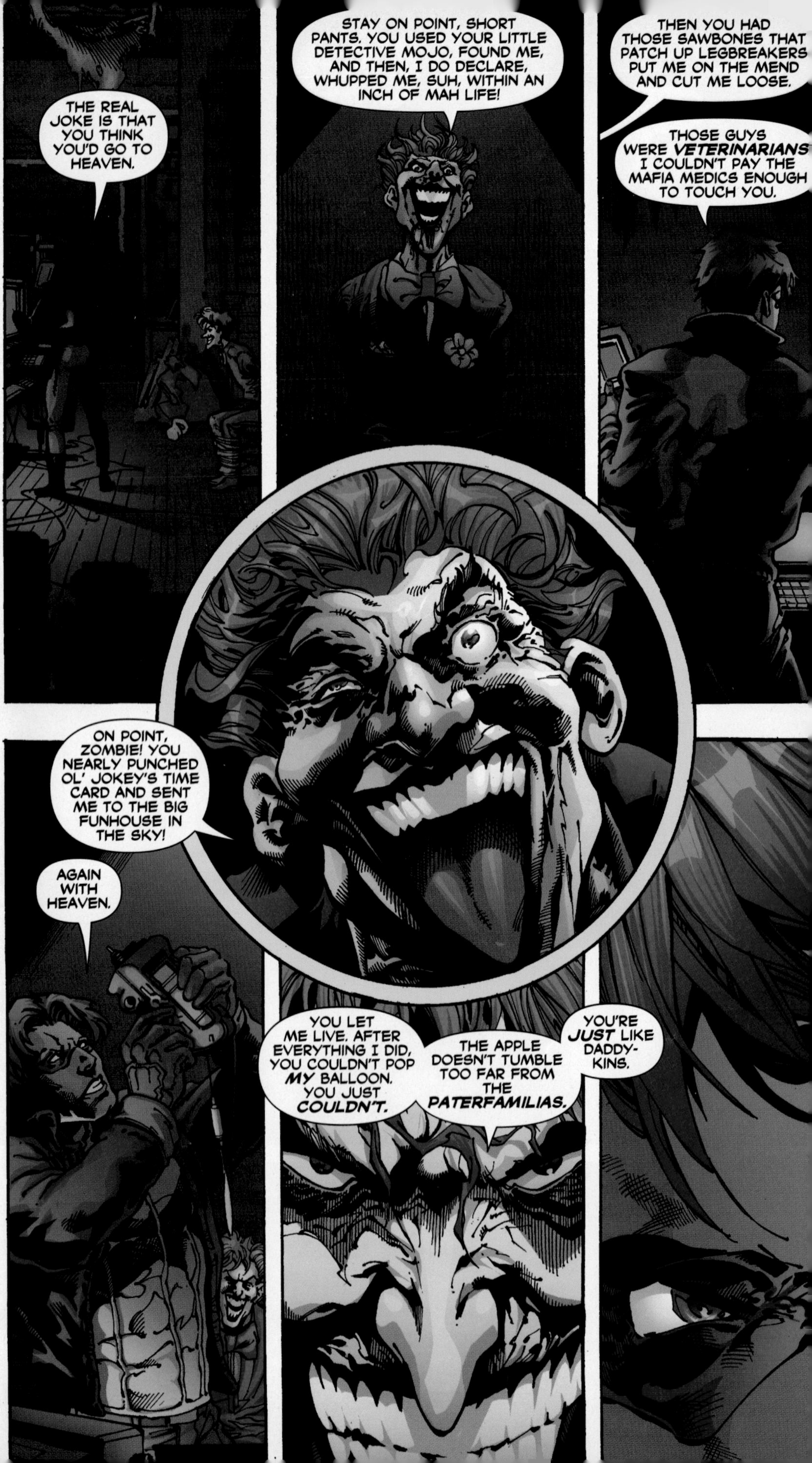
THE REAL JOKE IS THAT YOU THINK YOU'D GO TO HEAVEN.
STAY ON POINT, SHORT PANTS. YOU USED YOUR LITTLE DETECTIVE MOJO, FOUND ME, AND THEN, I DO DECLARE, WHUPPED ME, SUH, WITHIN AN INCH OF MAH LIFE!
THEN YOU HAD THOSE SAWBONES THAT PATCH UP LEGBREAKERS PUT ME ON THE MEND AND CUT ME LOOSE.
THOSE GUYS WERE *VETERINARIANS.* I COULDN'T PAY THE MAFIA MEDICS ENOUGH TO TOUCH YOU.
ON POINT, ZOMBIE! YOU NEARLY PUNCHED OL' JOKEY'S TIME CARD AND SENT ME TO THE BIG FUNHOUSE IN THE SKY!
AGAIN WITH HEAVEN.
YOU LET ME LIVE. AFTER EVERYTHING I DID, YOU COULDN'T POP *MY* BALLOON. YOU JUST *COULDN'T.*
THE APPLE DOESN'T TUMBLE TOO FAR FROM THE *PATERFAMILIAS.*
YOU'RE *JUST* LIKE DADDY-KINS.

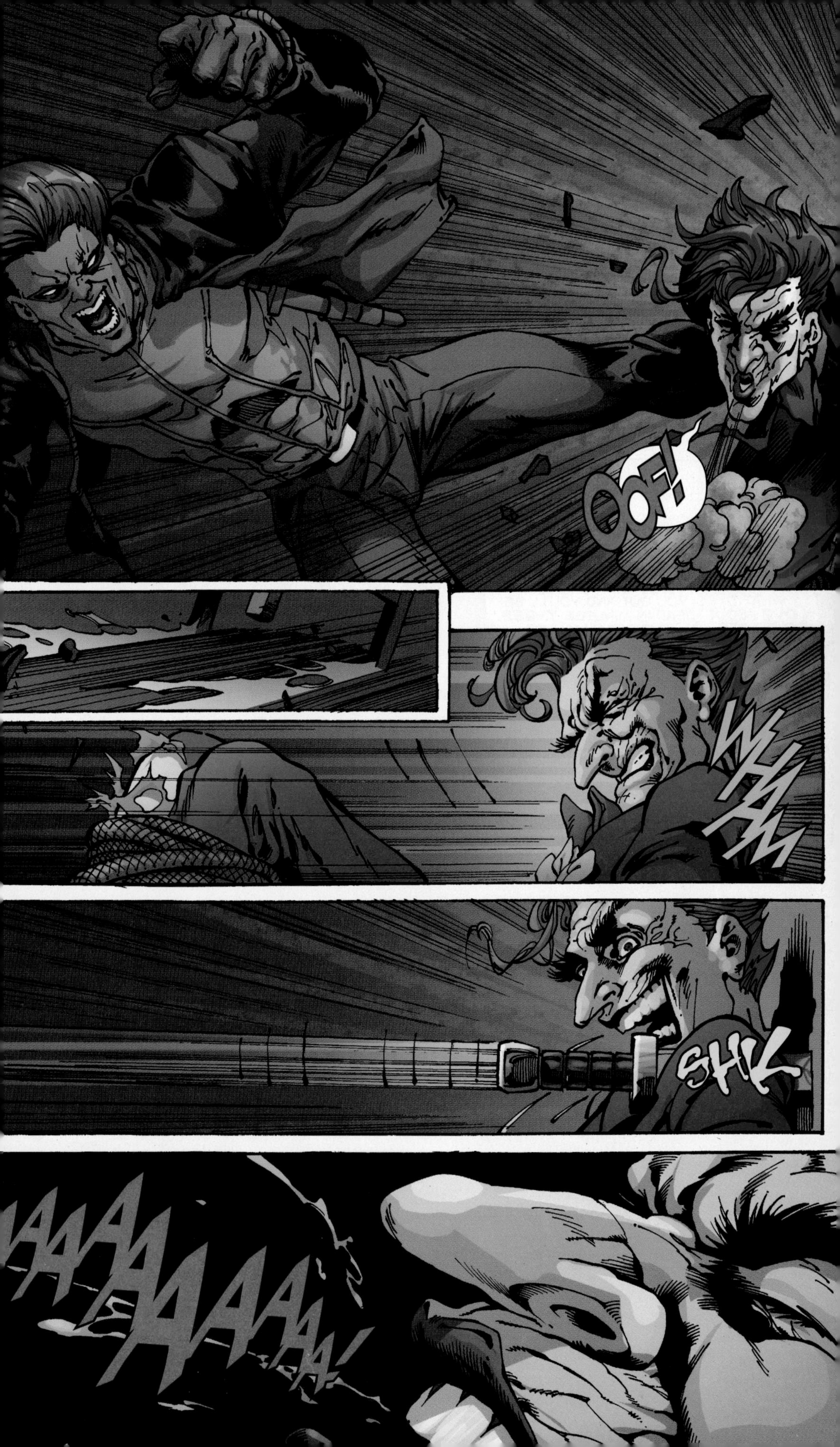
OOF!
WHAM
SHK
AAAAAAAAAAAAAAAAAAAA!

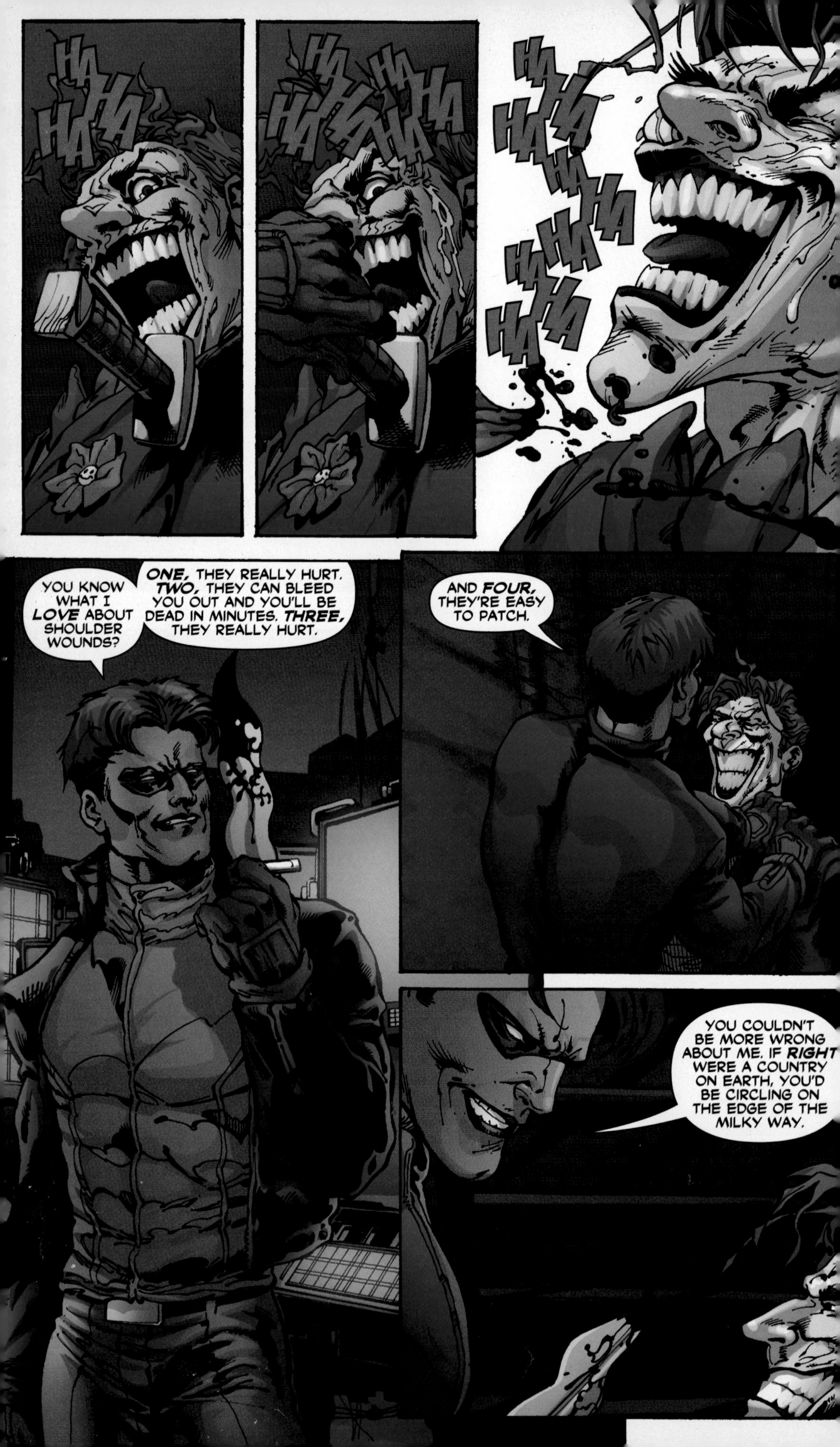
HA HA HA HA
HA HA HA HA HA HA HA
HA HA HA HA HA HA HA HA HA HA HA
YOU KNOW WHAT I LOVE ABOUT SHOULDER WOUNDS?
ONE, THEY REALLY HURT. TWO, THEY CAN BLEED YOU OUT AND YOU'LL BE DEAD IN MINUTES. THREE, THEY REALLY HURT.
AND FOUR, THEY'RE EASY TO PATCH.
YOU COULDN'T BE MORE WRONG ABOUT ME. IF RIGHT WERE A COUNTRY ON EARTH, YOU'D BE CIRCLING ON THE EDGE OF THE MILKY WAY.

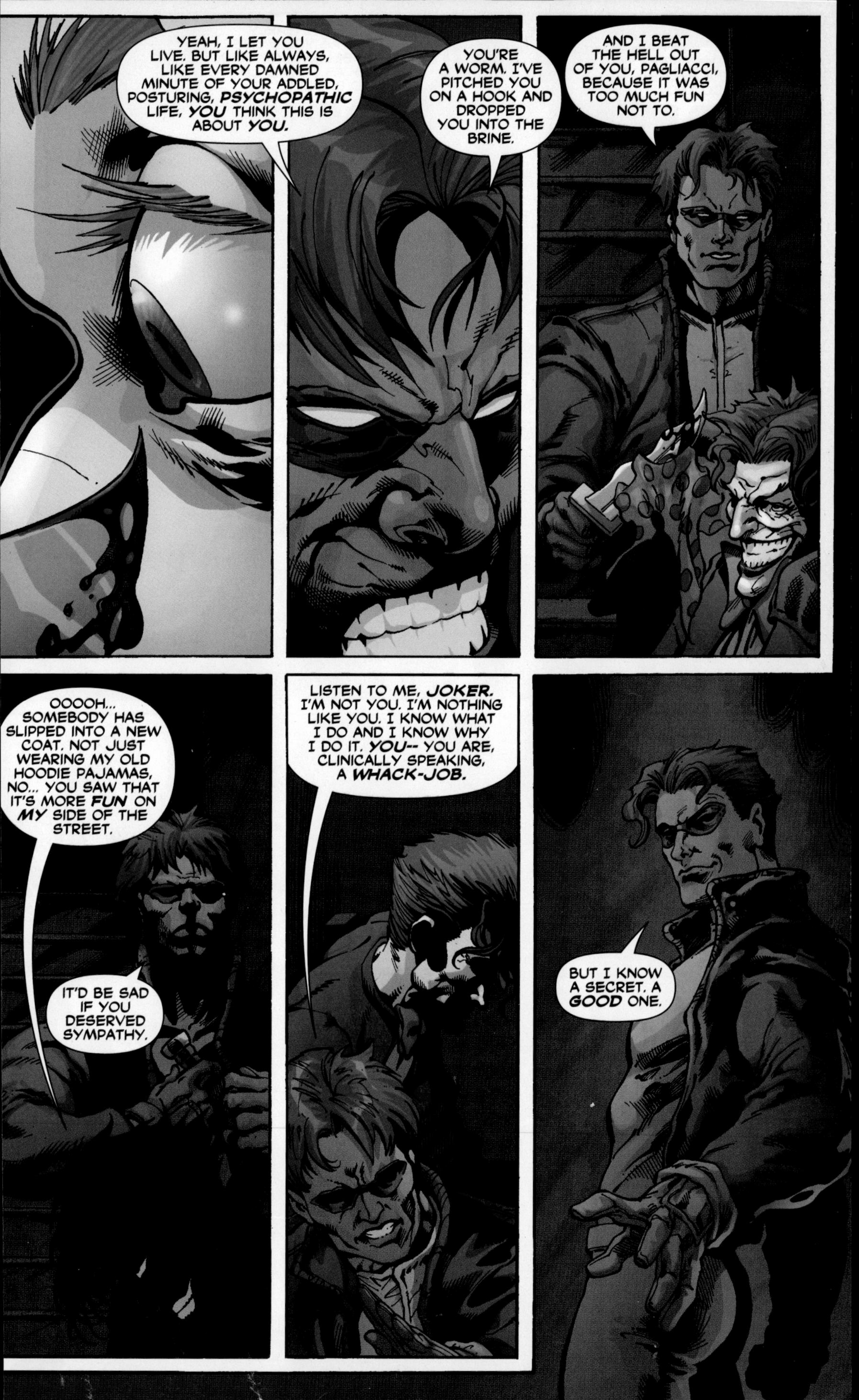
YEAH, I LET YOU LIVE. BUT LIKE ALWAYS, LIKE EVERY DAMNED MINUTE OF YOUR ADDLED, POSTURING, PSYCHOPATHIC LIFE, YOU THINK THIS IS ABOUT YOU.
YOU'RE A WORM. I'VE PITCHED YOU ON A HOOK AND DROPPED YOU INTO THE BRINE.
AND I BEAT THE HELL OUT OF YOU, PAGLIACCI, BECAUSE IT WAS TOO MUCH FUN NOT TO.
OOOOH... SOMEBODY HAS SLIPPED INTO A NEW COAT. NOT JUST WEARING MY OLD HOODIE PAJAMAS, NO... YOU SAW THAT IT'S MORE FUN ON MY SIDE OF THE STREET.
IT'D BE SAD IF YOU DESERVED SYMPATHY.
LISTEN TO ME, JOKER. I'M NOT YOU. I'M NOTHING LIKE YOU. I KNOW WHAT I DO AND I KNOW WHY I DO IT. YOU-- YOU ARE, CLINICALLY SPEAKING, A WHACK-JOB.
BUT I KNOW A SECRET. A GOOD ONE.

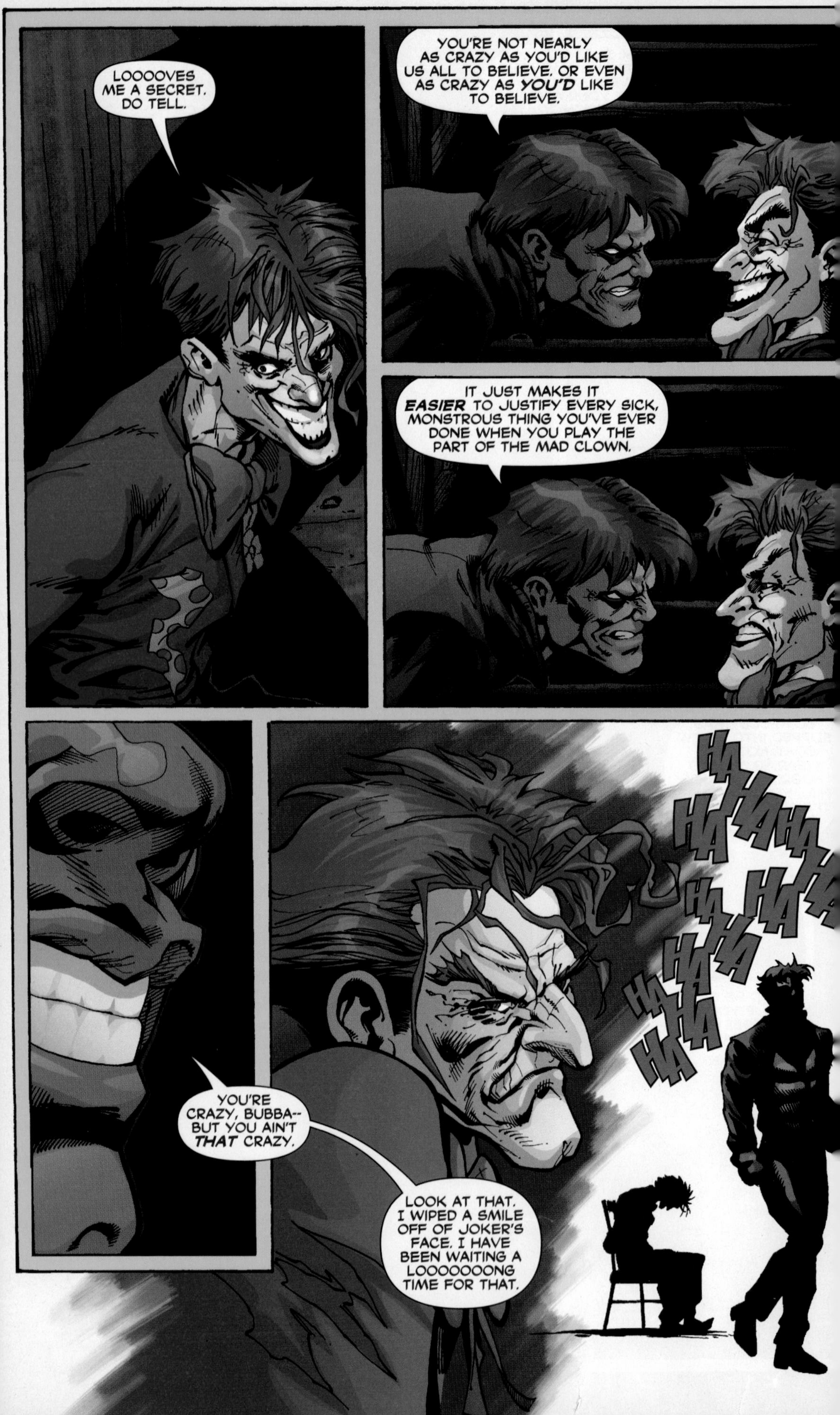
LOOOOVES ME A SECRET. DO TELL.
YOU'RE NOT NEARLY AS CRAZY AS YOU'D LIKE US ALL TO BELIEVE. OR EVEN AS CRAZY AS *YOU'D* LIKE TO BELIEVE.
IT JUST MAKES IT ***EASIER*** TO JUSTIFY EVERY SICK, MONSTROUS THING YOU'VE EVER DONE WHEN YOU PLAY THE PART OF THE MAD CLOWN.
YOU'RE CRAZY, BUBBA-- BUT YOU AIN'T *THAT* CRAZY.
HA HA HA HA HA HA HA HA HA HA HA HA HA
LOOK AT THAT. I WIPED A SMILE OFF OF JOKER'S FACE. I HAVE BEEN WAITING A LOOOOOOONG TIME FOR THAT.

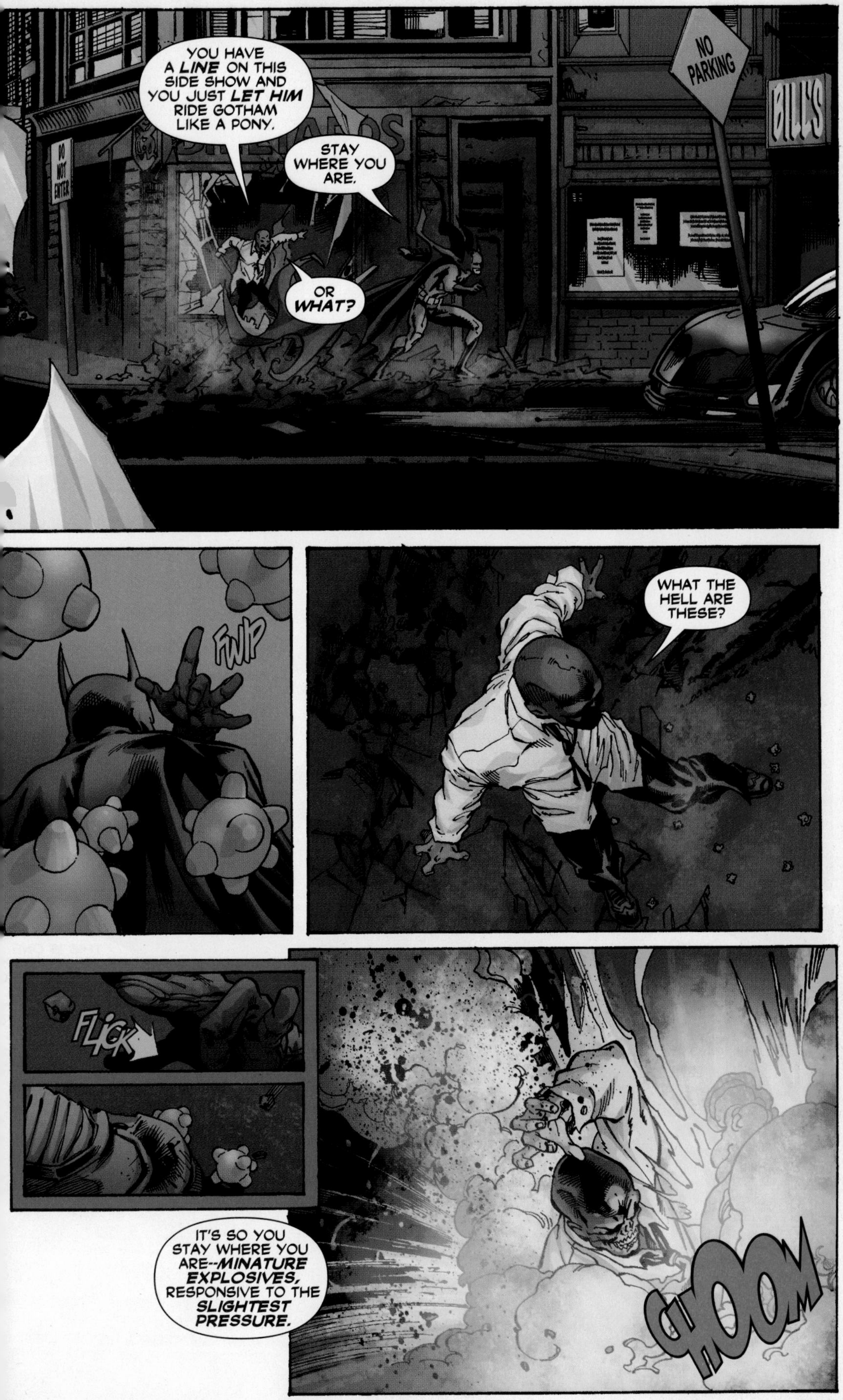

NO PARKING
BILL'S
DO NOT ENTER
YOU HAVE A LINE ON THIS SIDE SHOW AND YOU JUST LET HIM RIDE GOTHAM LIKE A PONY.
STAY WHERE YOU ARE.
OR WHAT?
FWIP
WHAT THE HELL ARE THESE?
FLICK
IT'S SO YOU STAY WHERE YOU ARE--MINATURE EXPLOSIVES, RESPONSIVE TO THE SLIGHTEST PRESSURE.
CHOOOM

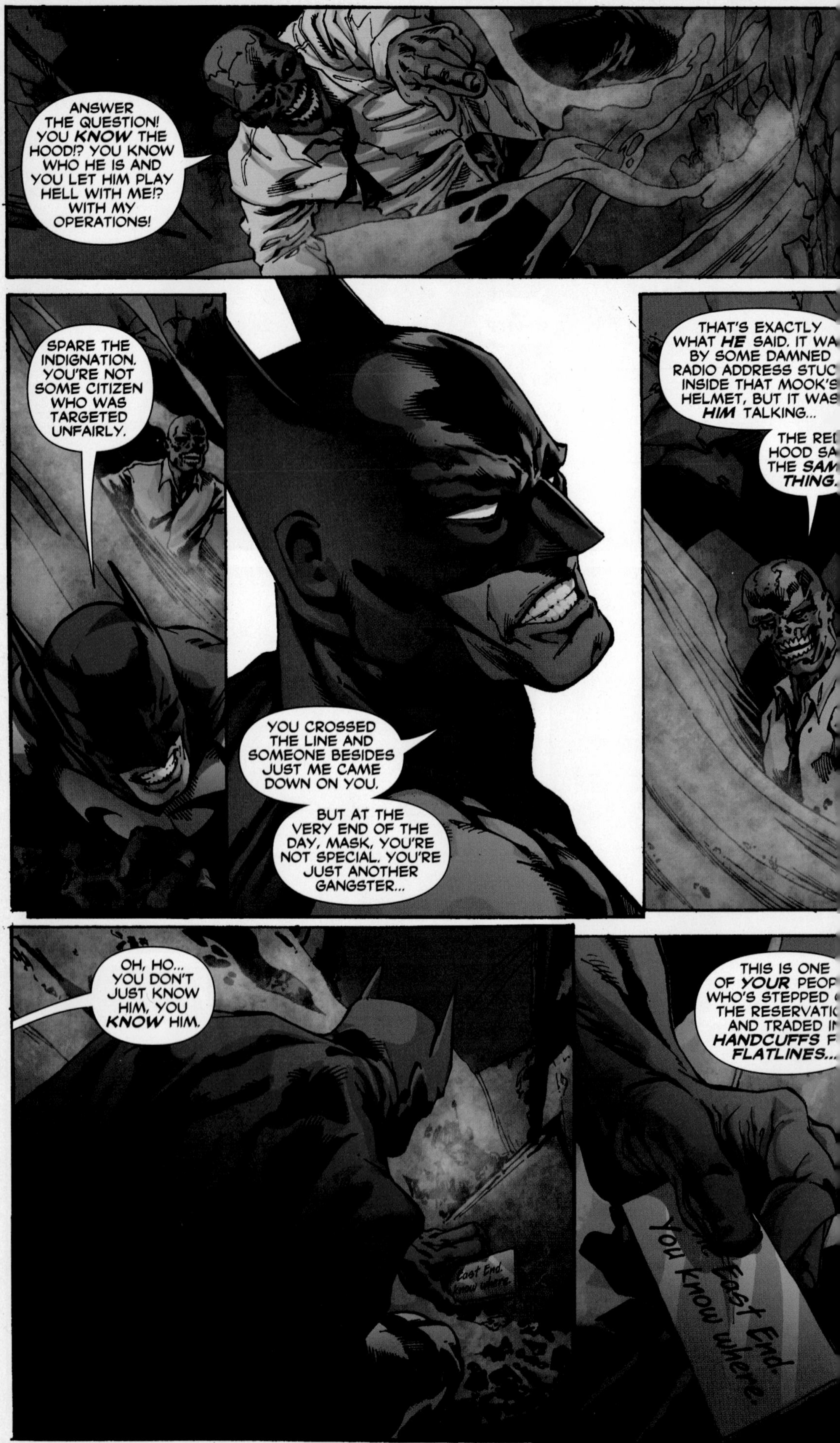

ANSWER THE QUESTION! YOU KNOW THE HOOD!? YOU KNOW WHO HE IS AND YOU LET HIM PLAY HELL WITH ME!? WITH MY OPERATIONS!
SPARE THE INDIGNATION. YOU'RE NOT SOME CITIZEN WHO WAS TARGETED UNFAIRLY.
YOU CROSSED THE LINE AND SOMEONE BESIDES JUST ME CAME DOWN ON YOU.
BUT AT THE VERY END OF THE DAY, MASK, YOU'RE NOT SPECIAL. YOU'RE JUST ANOTHER GANGSTER...
THAT'S EXACTLY WHAT HE SAID. IT WA BY SOME DAMNED RADIO ADDRESS STUC INSIDE THAT MOOK'S HELMET, BUT IT WAS HIM TALKING...
THE RE HOOD SA THE SAM THING.
OH, HO... YOU DON'T JUST KNOW HIM, YOU KNOW HIM.
THIS IS ONE OF YOUR PEOP WHO'S STEPPED THE RESERVATI AND TRADED I HANDCUFFS F FLATLINES...
East End. You know where

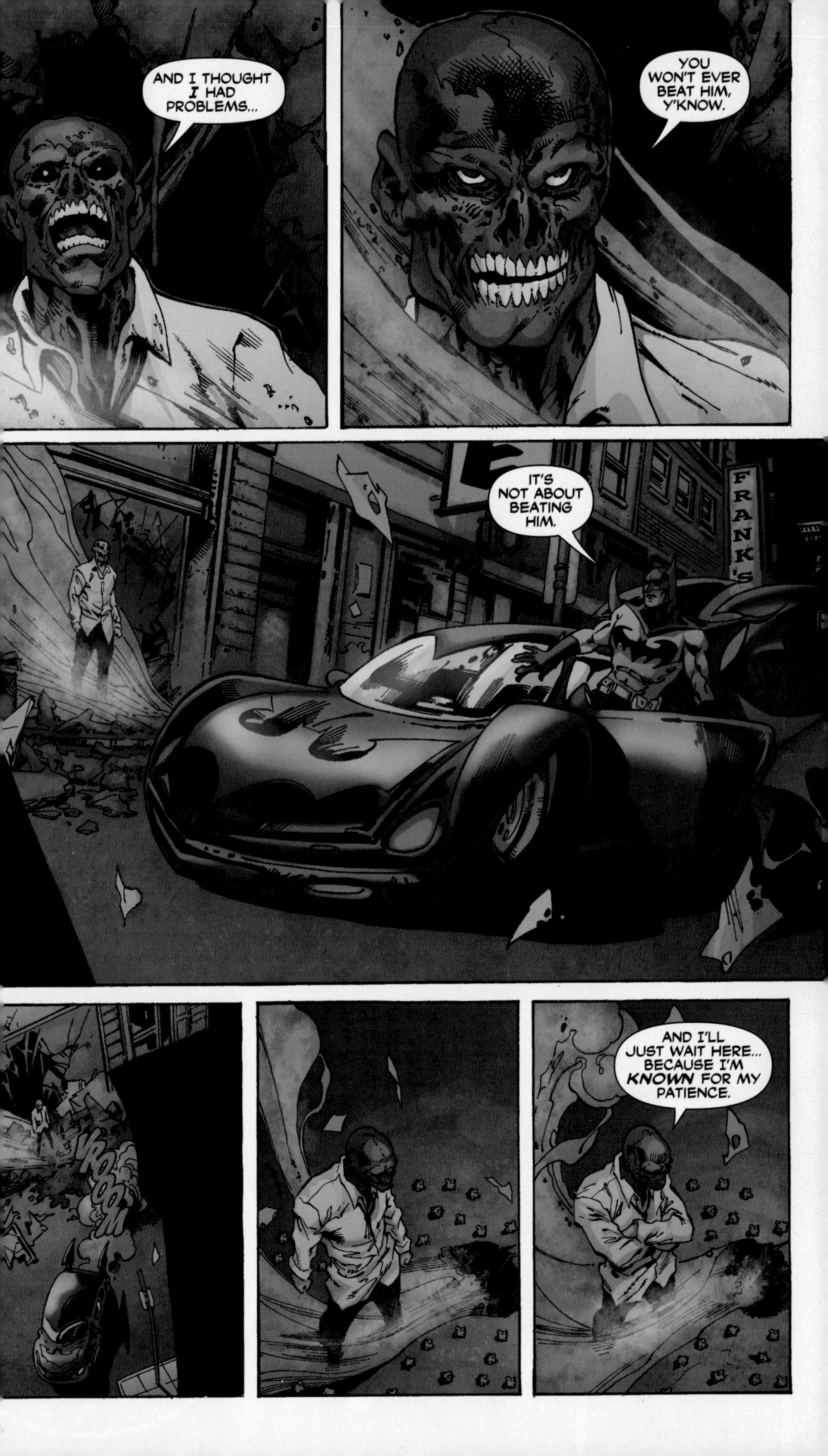
AND I THOUGHT *I* HAD PROBLEMS...
YOU WON'T EVER BEAT HIM, Y'KNOW.
IT'S NOT ABOUT BEATING HIM.
FRANK'S
VROOOM
AND I'LL JUST WAIT HERE... BECAUSE I'M ***KNOWN*** FOR MY PATIENCE.

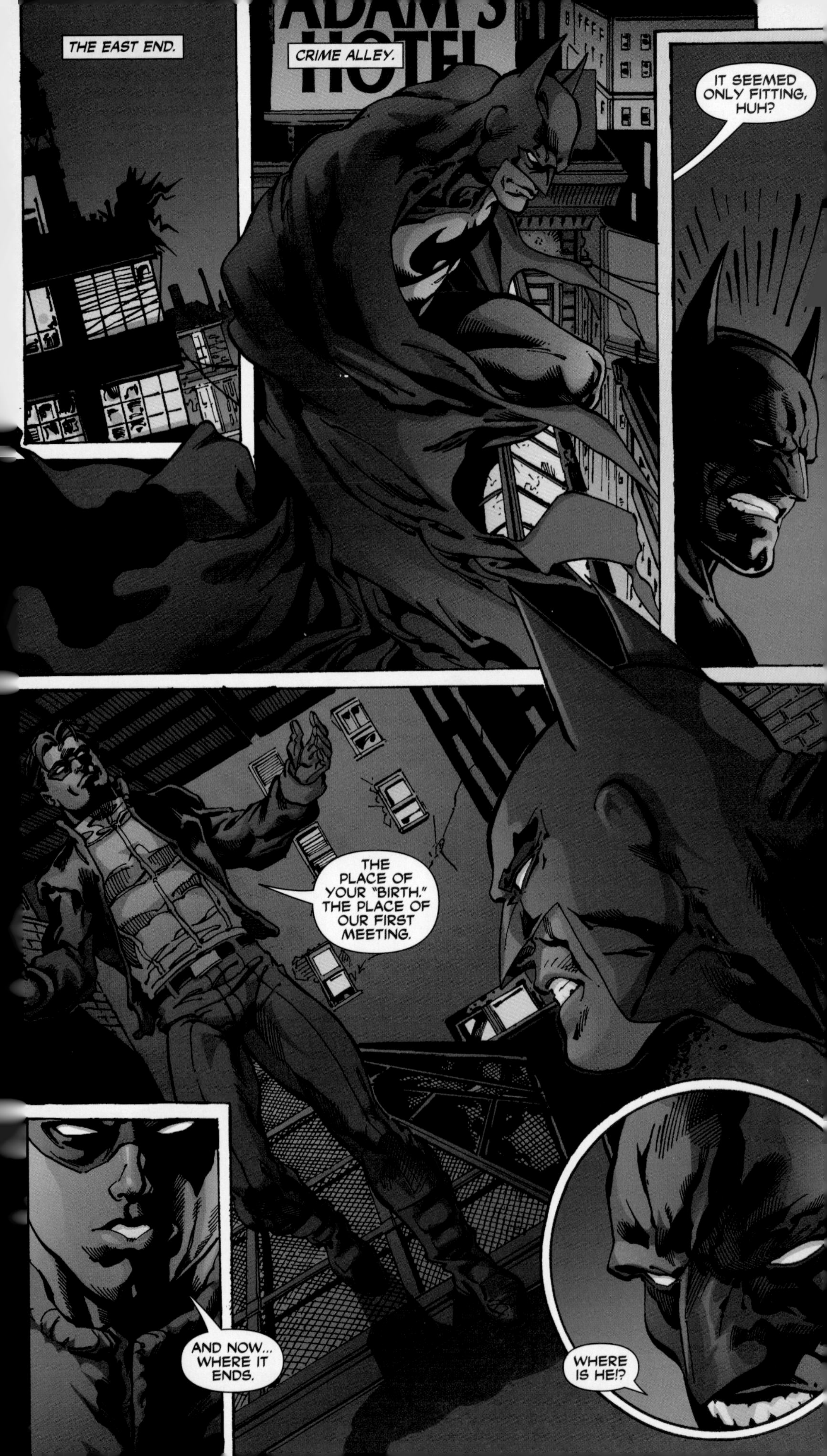

THE EAST END.
CRIME ALLEY.
ADAM'S HOTEL
IT SEEMED ONLY FITTING, HUH?
THE PLACE OF YOUR "BIRTH." THE PLACE OF OUR FIRST MEETING.
AND NOW... WHERE IT ENDS.
WHERE IS HE!?

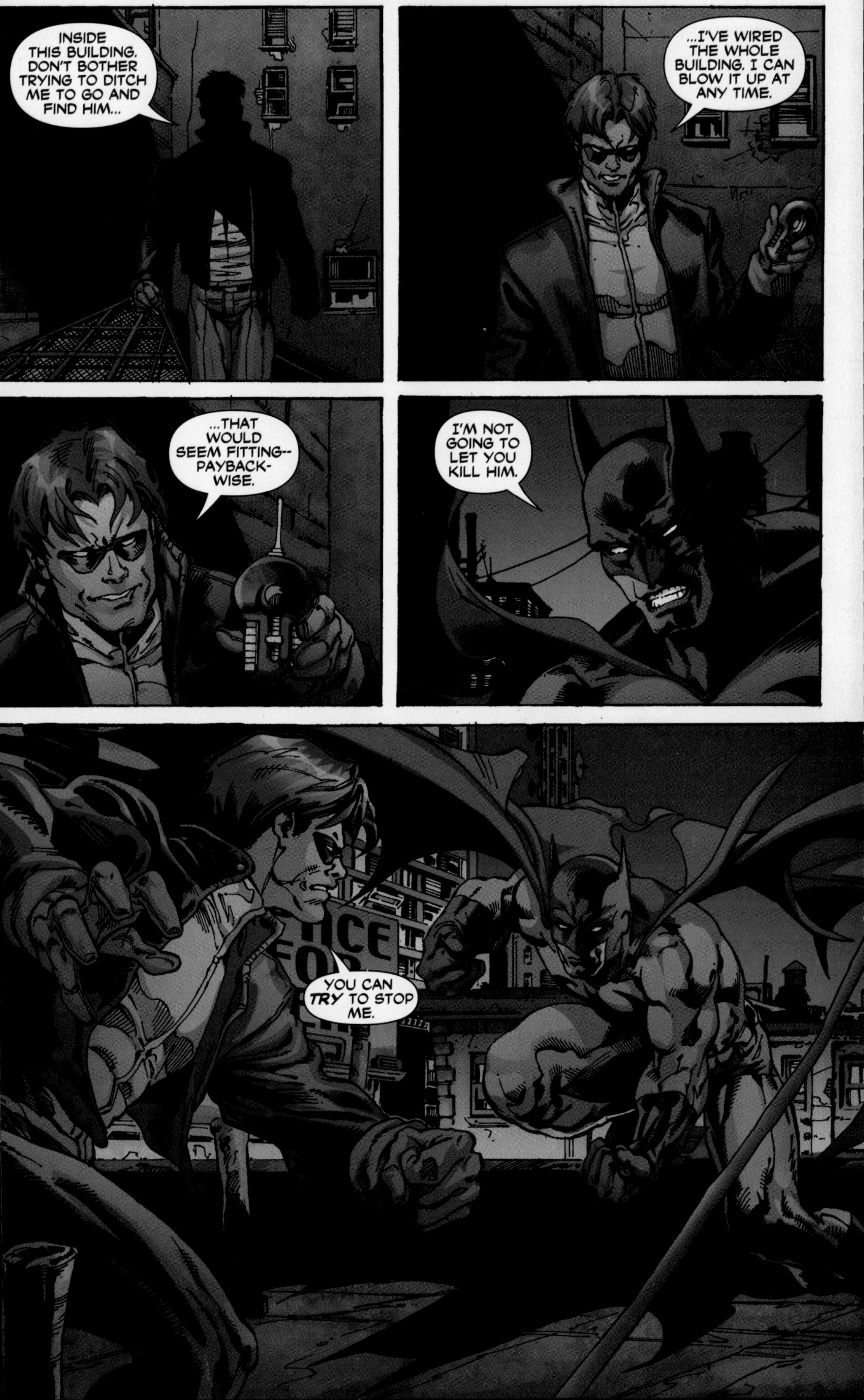
INSIDE THIS BUILDING. DON'T BOTHER TRYING TO DITCH ME TO GO AND FIND HIM...
...I'VE WIRED THE WHOLE BUILDING. I CAN BLOW IT UP AT ANY TIME.
...THAT WOULD SEEM FITTING-- PAYBACK-WISE.
I'M NOT GOING TO LET YOU KILL HIM.
YOU CAN *TRY* TO STOP ME.

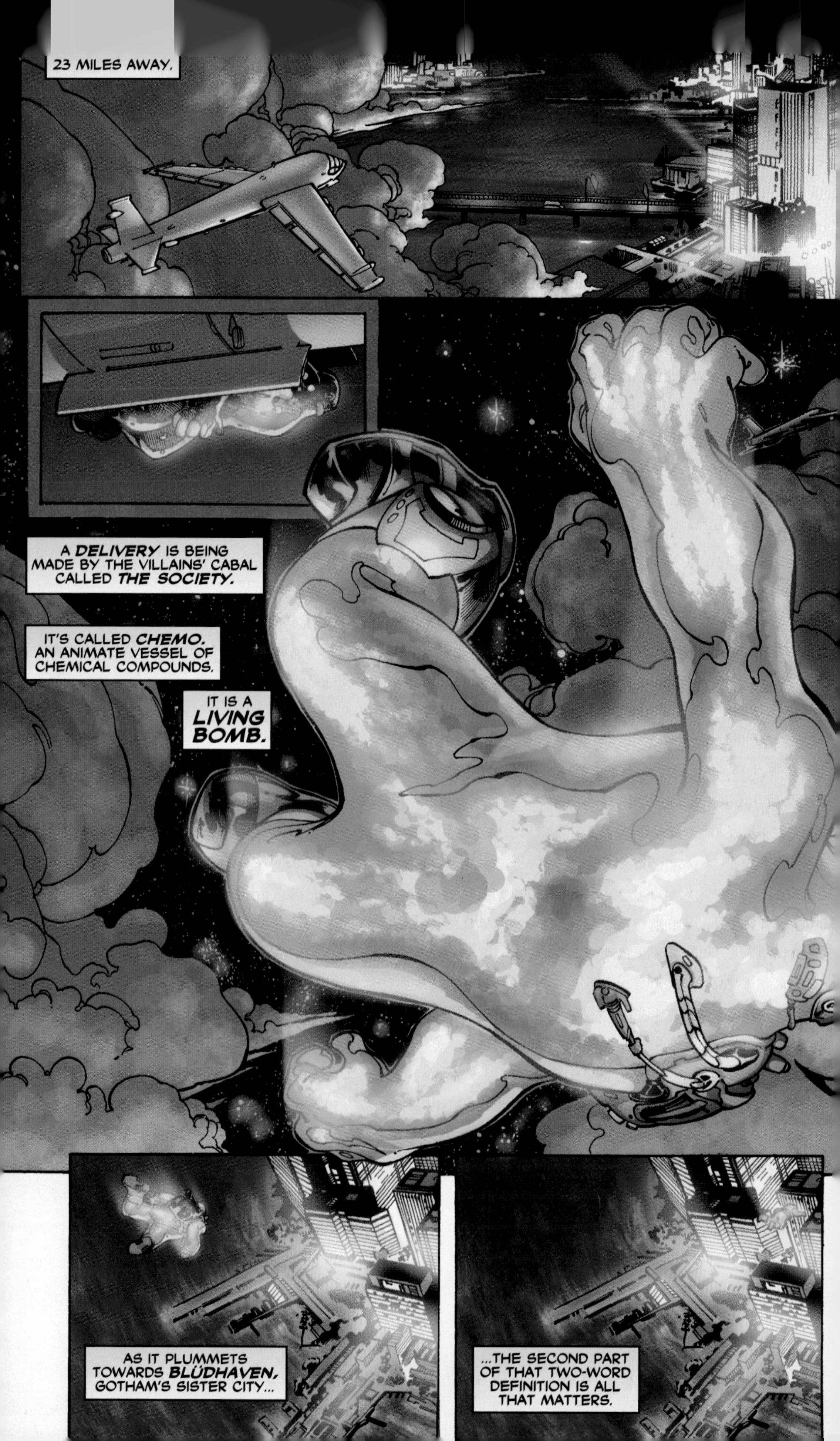
23 MILES AWAY.
A DELIVERY IS BEING MADE BY THE VILLAINS' CABAL CALLED THE SOCIETY.
IT'S CALLED CHEMO. AN ANIMATE VESSEL OF CHEMICAL COMPOUNDS.
IT IS A LIVING BOMB.
AS IT PLUMMETS TOWARDS BLÜDHAVEN, GOTHAM'S SISTER CITY...
...THE SECOND PART OF THAT TWO-WORD DEFINITION IS ALL THAT MATTERS.

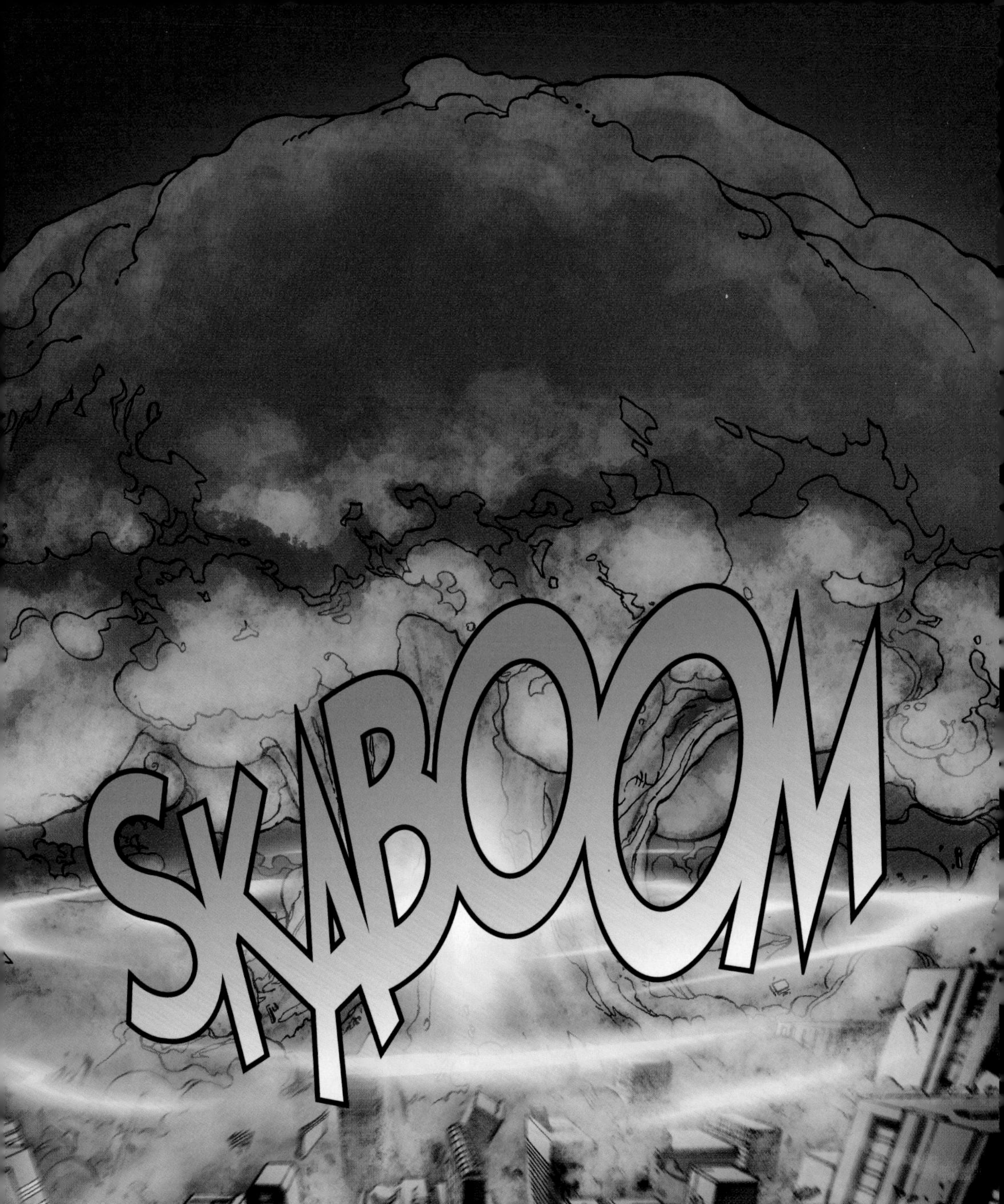
SKABOOM
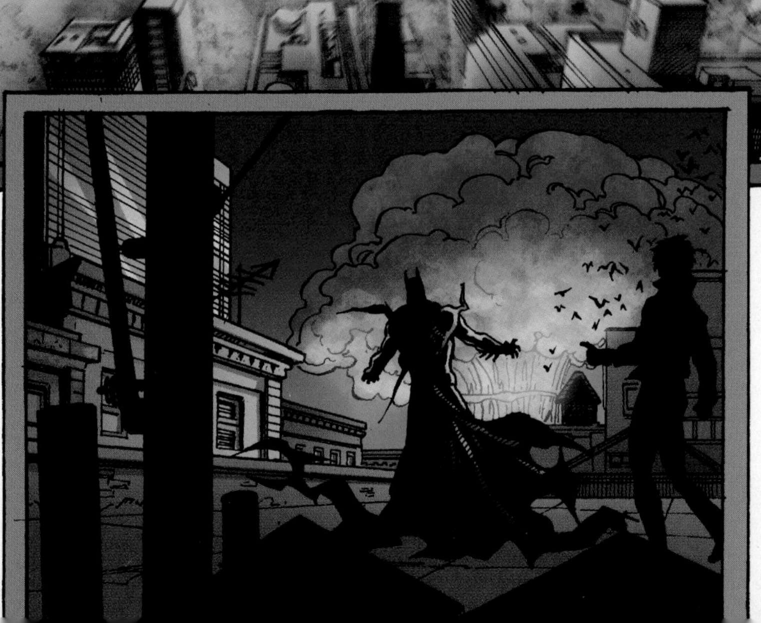

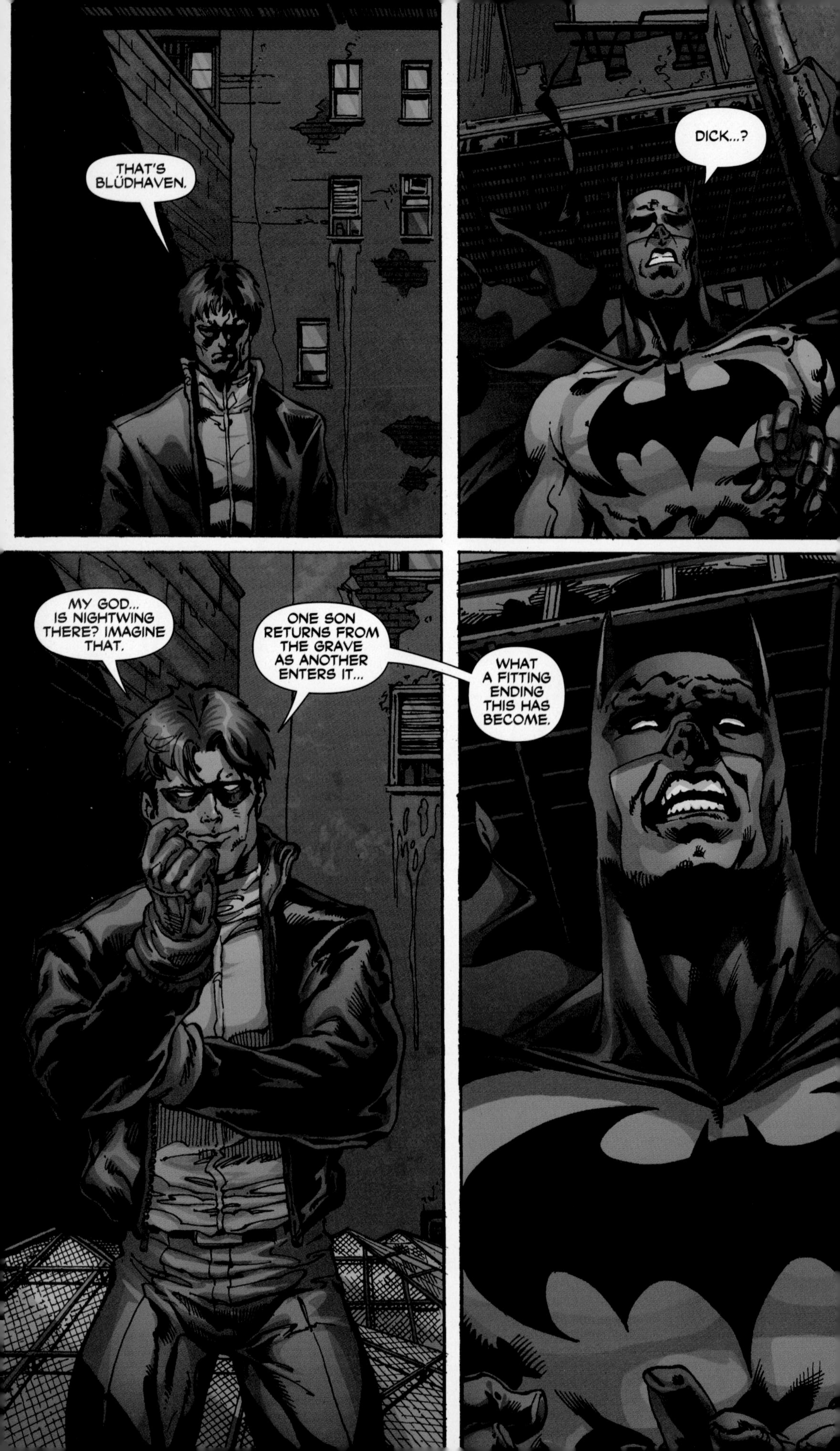
THAT'S BLÜDHAVEN.
DICK...?
MY GOD... IS NIGHTWING THERE? IMAGINE THAT.
ONE SON RETURNS FROM THE GRAVE AS ANOTHER ENTERS IT...
WHAT A FITTING ENDING THIS HAS BECOME.

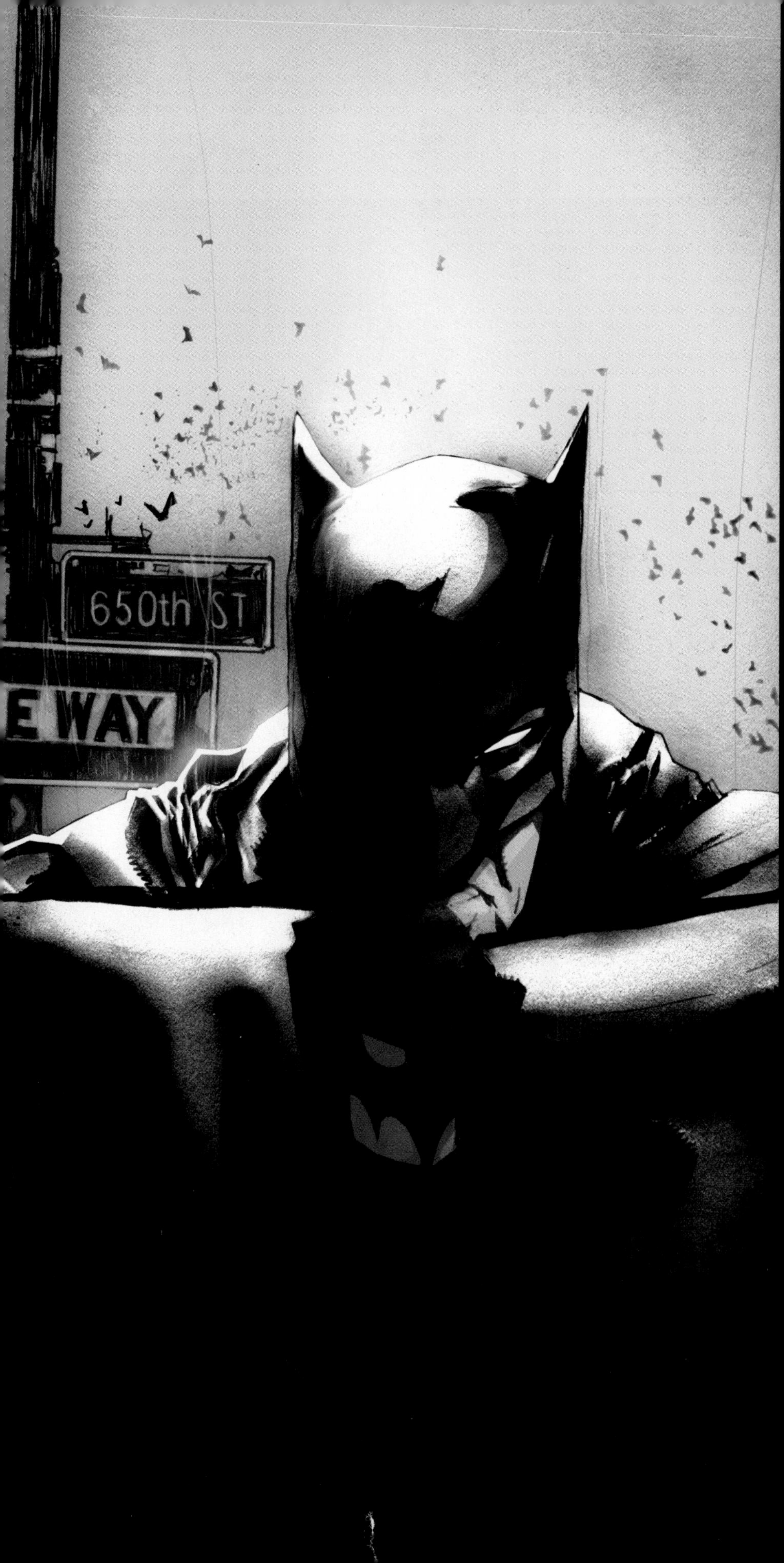
650th ST
E WAY

BATMAN #650 • COVER BY JOCK

CHAPTER 6

ALL THEY DO IS WATCH US KILL
PART 3

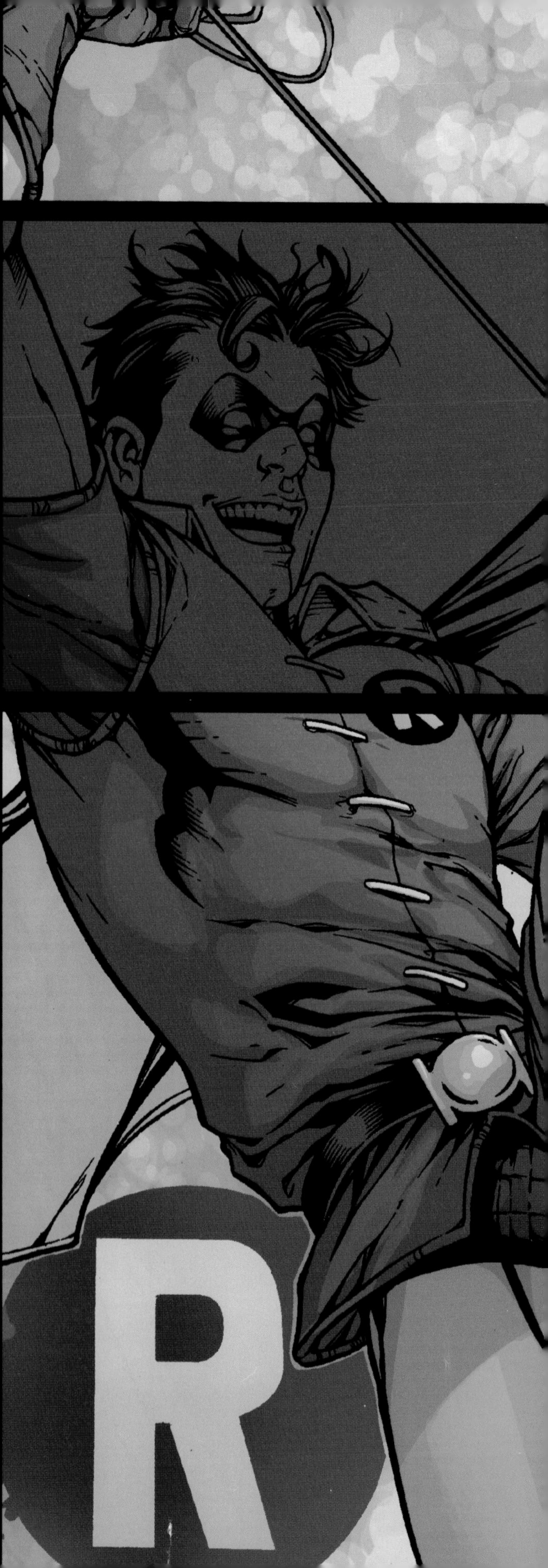

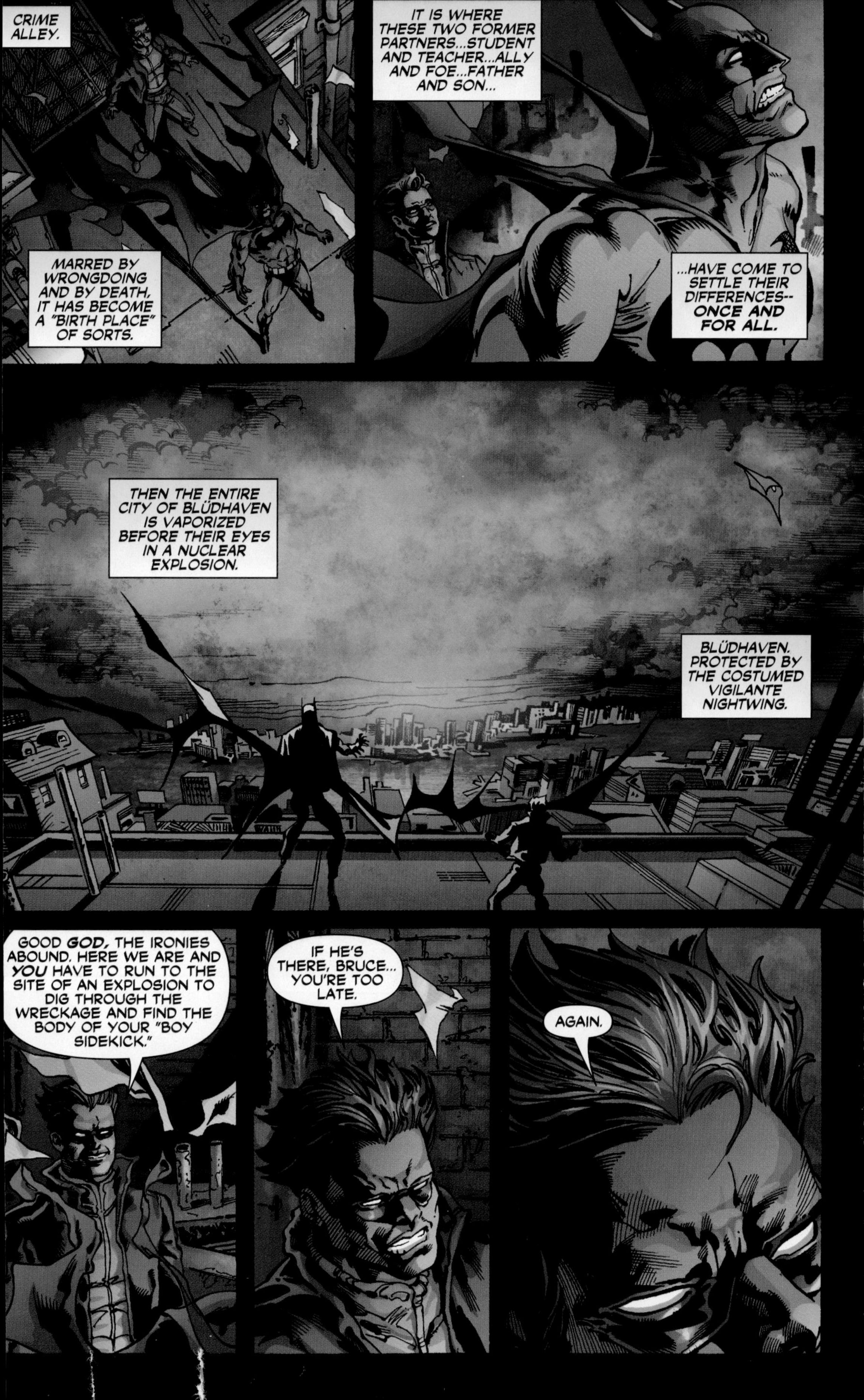

CRIME ALLEY.
MARRED BY WRONGDOING AND BY DEATH, IT HAS BECOME A "BIRTH PLACE" OF SORTS.
IT IS WHERE THESE TWO FORMER PARTNERS...STUDENT AND TEACHER...ALLY AND FOE...FATHER AND SON...
...HAVE COME TO SETTLE THEIR DIFFERENCES-- ONCE AND FOR ALL.
THEN THE ENTIRE CITY OF BLÜDHAVEN IS VAPORIZED BEFORE THEIR EYES IN A NUCLEAR EXPLOSION.
BLÜDHAVEN. PROTECTED BY THE COSTUMED VIGILANTE NIGHTWING.
GOOD GOD, THE IRONIES ABOUND. HERE WE ARE AND YOU HAVE TO RUN TO THE SITE OF AN EXPLOSION TO DIG THROUGH THE WRECKAGE AND FIND THE BODY OF YOUR "BOY SIDEKICK."
IF HE'S THERE, BRUCE... YOU'RE TOO LATE.
AGAIN.

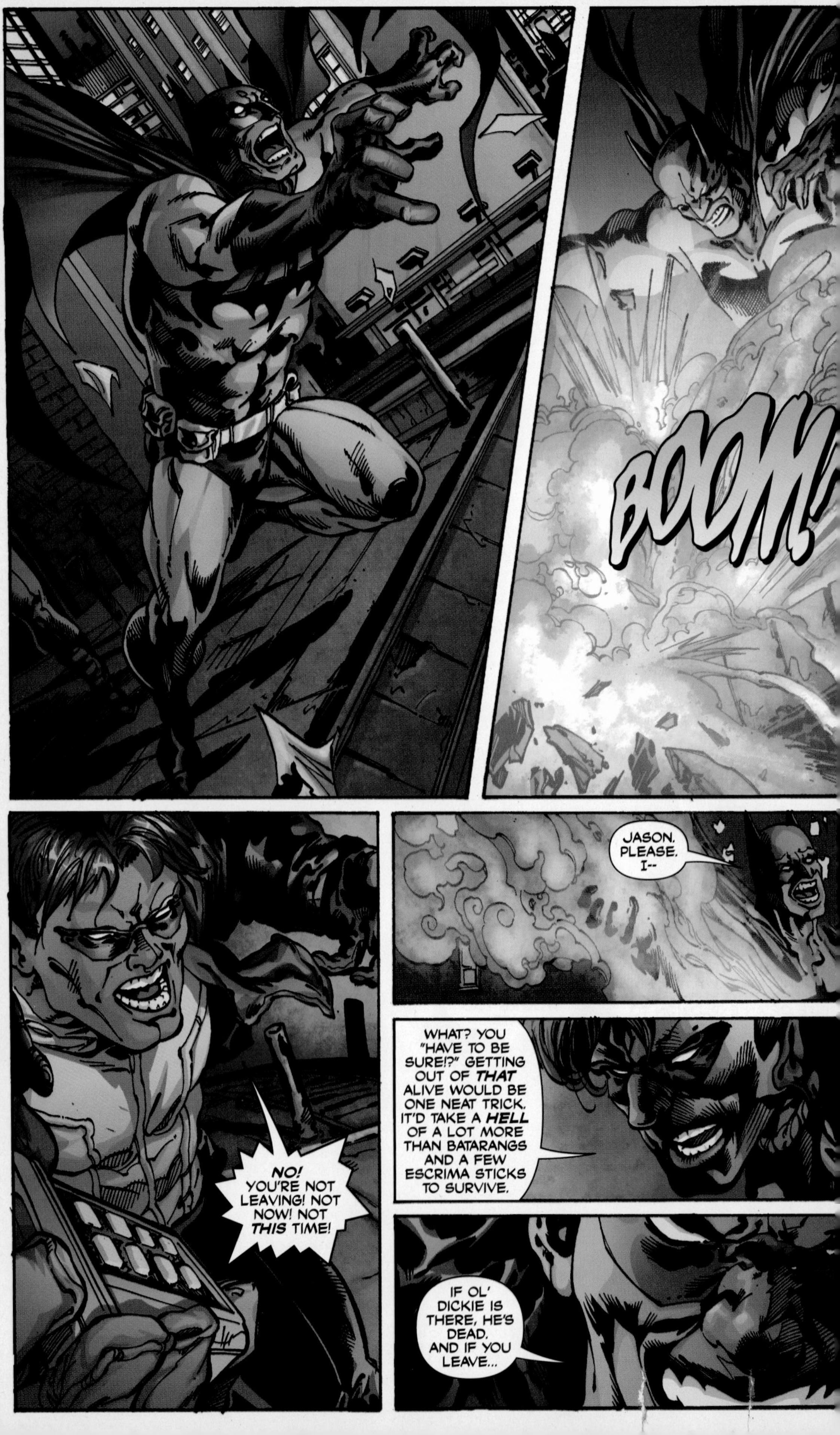
BOOM!
JASON. PLEASE. I--
NO! YOU'RE NOT LEAVING! NOT NOW! NOT THIS TIME!
WHAT? YOU "HAVE TO BE SURE!?" GETTING OUT OF THAT ALIVE WOULD BE ONE NEAT TRICK. IT'D TAKE A HELL OF A LOT MORE THAN BATARANGS AND A FEW ESCRIMA STICKS TO SURVIVE.
IF OL' DICKIE IS THERE, HE'S DEAD. AND IF YOU LEAVE...

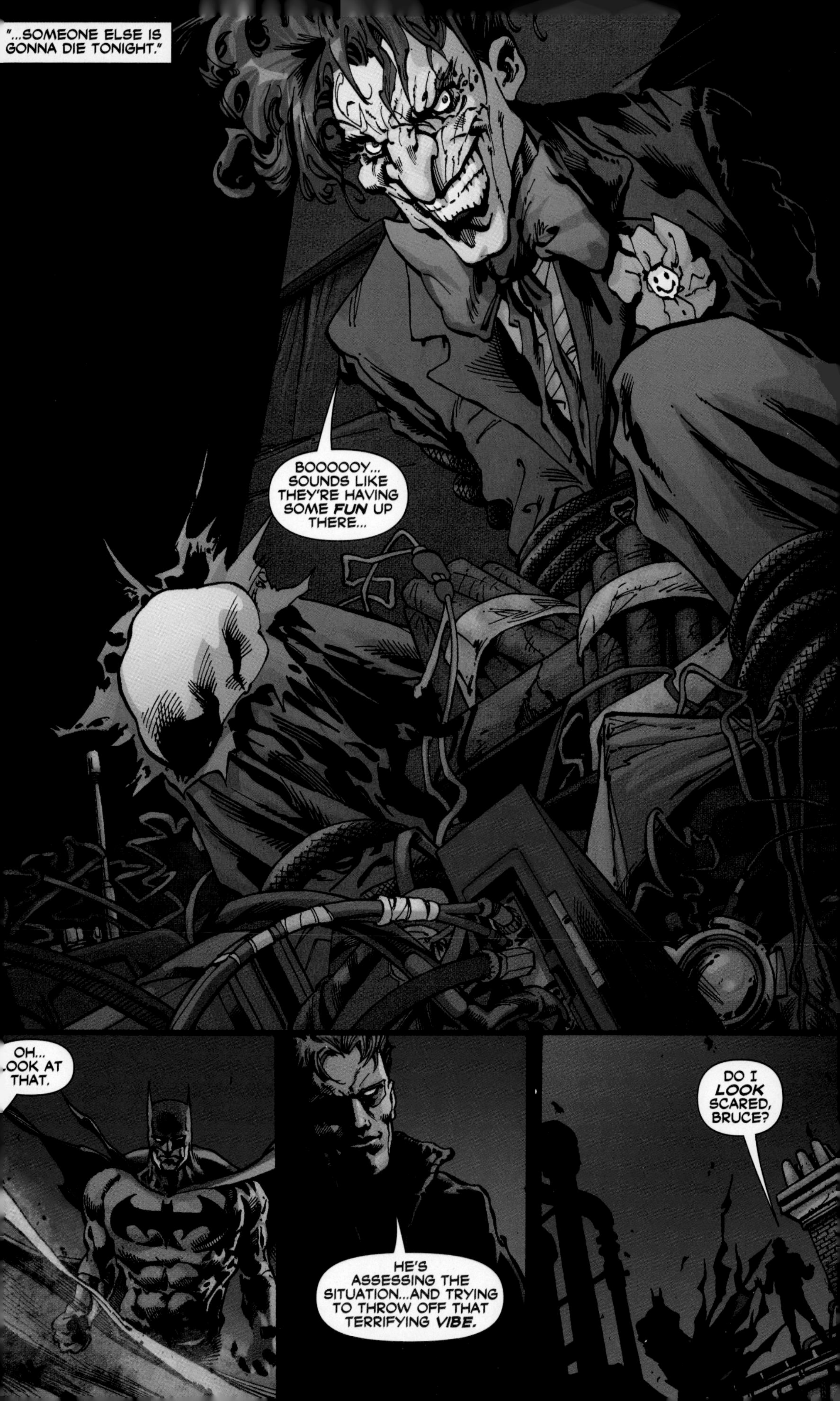
"...SOMEONE ELSE IS GONNA DIE TONIGHT."
BOOOOOY... SOUNDS LIKE THEY'RE HAVING SOME FUN UP THERE...
OH... LOOK AT THAT.
HE'S ASSESSING THE SITUATION...AND TRYING TO THROW OFF THAT TERRIFYING VIBE.
DO I LOOK SCARED, BRUCE?

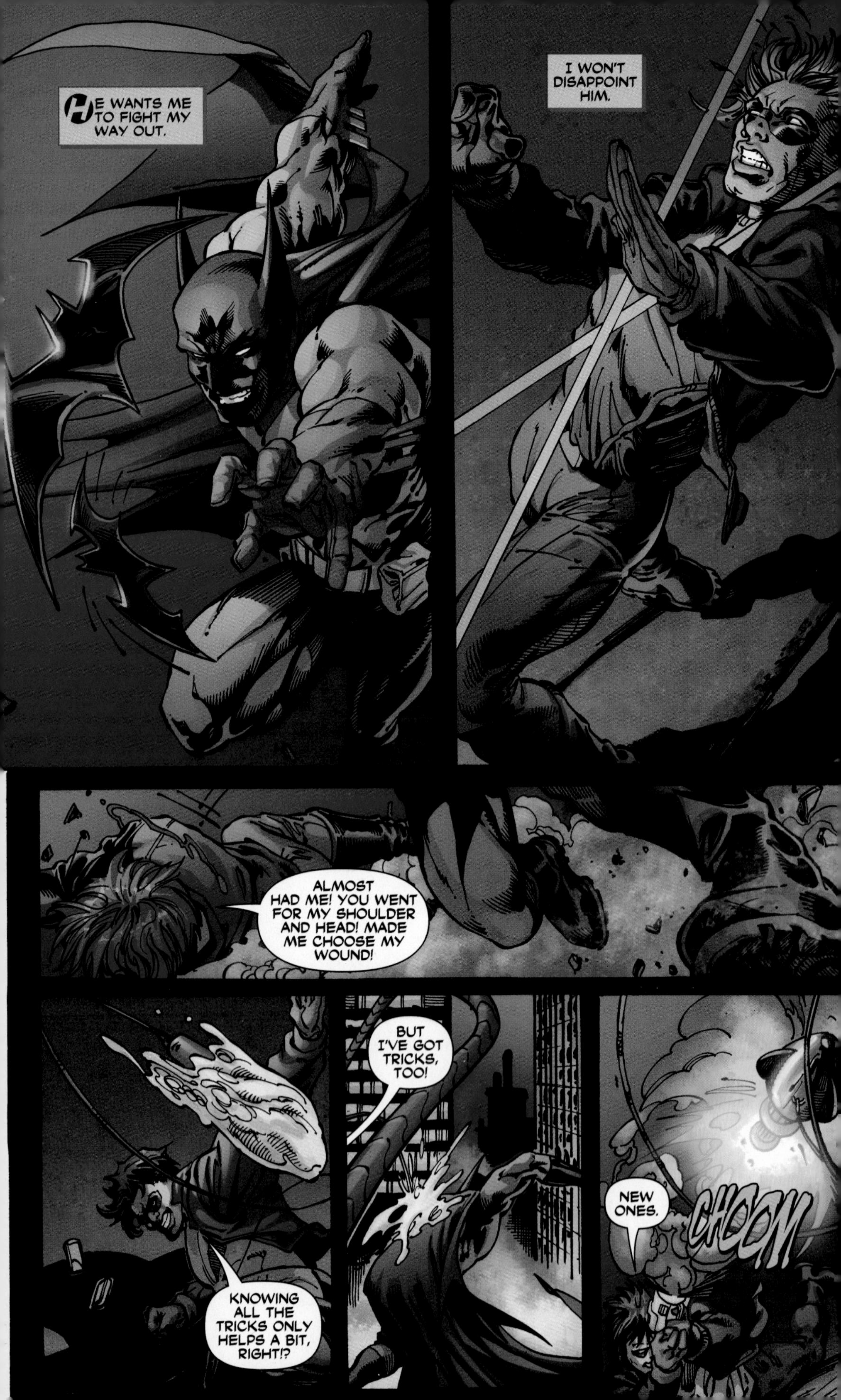
HE WANTS ME TO FIGHT MY WAY OUT.
I WON'T DISAPPOINT HIM.
ALMOST HAD ME! YOU WENT FOR MY SHOULDER AND HEAD! MADE ME CHOOSE MY WOUND!
KNOWING ALL THE TRICKS ONLY HELPS A BIT, RIGHT!?
BUT I'VE GOT TRICKS, TOO!
NEW ONES.
CHOOM

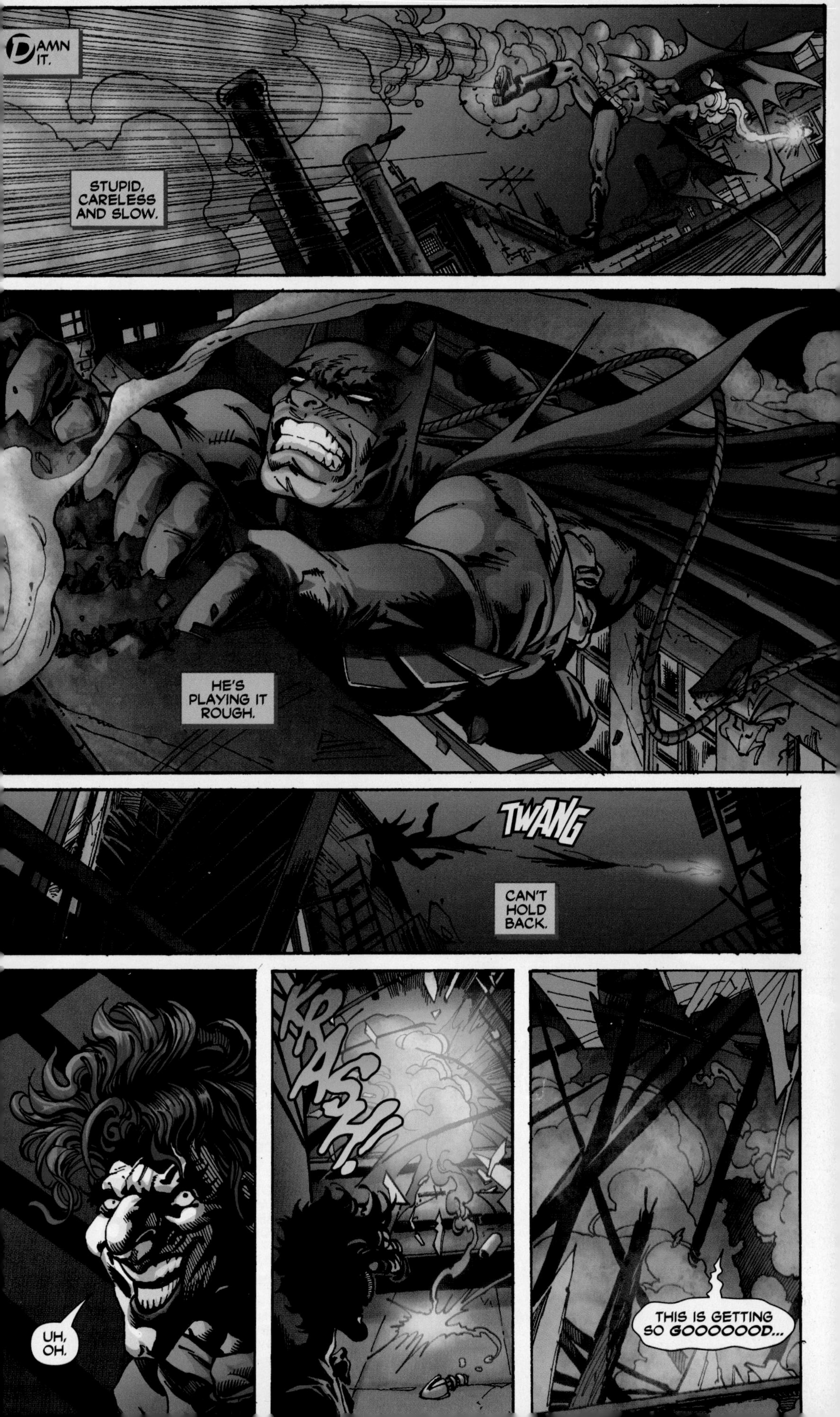
DAMN IT.
STUPID, CARELESS AND SLOW.
HE'S PLAYING IT ROUGH.
TWANG
CAN'T HOLD BACK.
UH, OH.
KRASH!!
THIS IS GETTING SO GOOOOOOD...

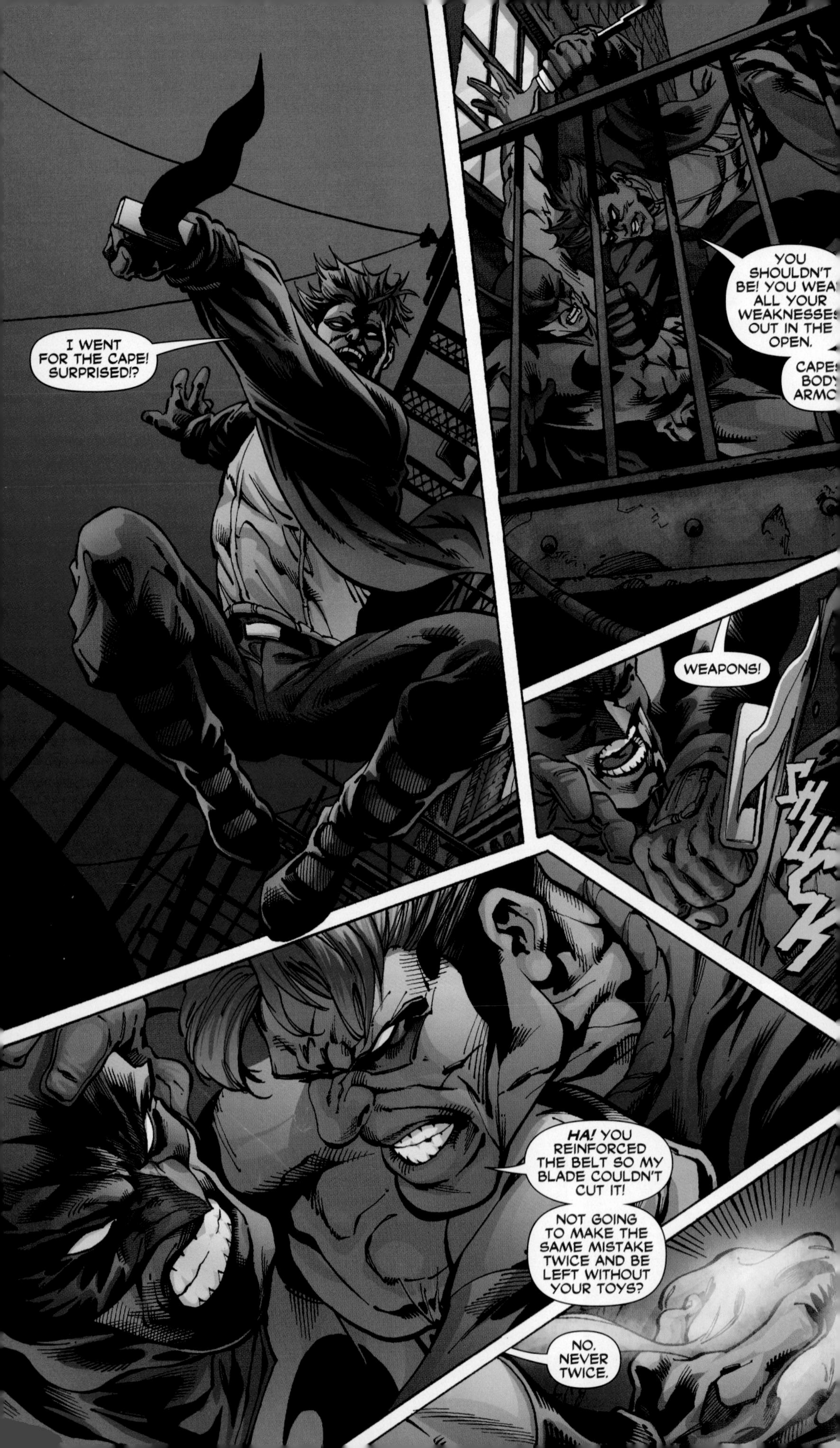
I WENT FOR THE CAPE! SURPRISED!?
YOU SHOULDN'T BE! YOU WEA ALL YOUR WEAKNESSE OUT IN THE OPEN.
CAPES BODY ARMO
WEAPONS!
HA! YOU REINFORCED THE BELT SO MY BLADE COULDN'T CUT IT!
NOT GOING TO MAKE THE SAME MISTAKE TWICE AND BE LEFT WITHOUT YOUR TOYS?
NO. NEVER TWICE.

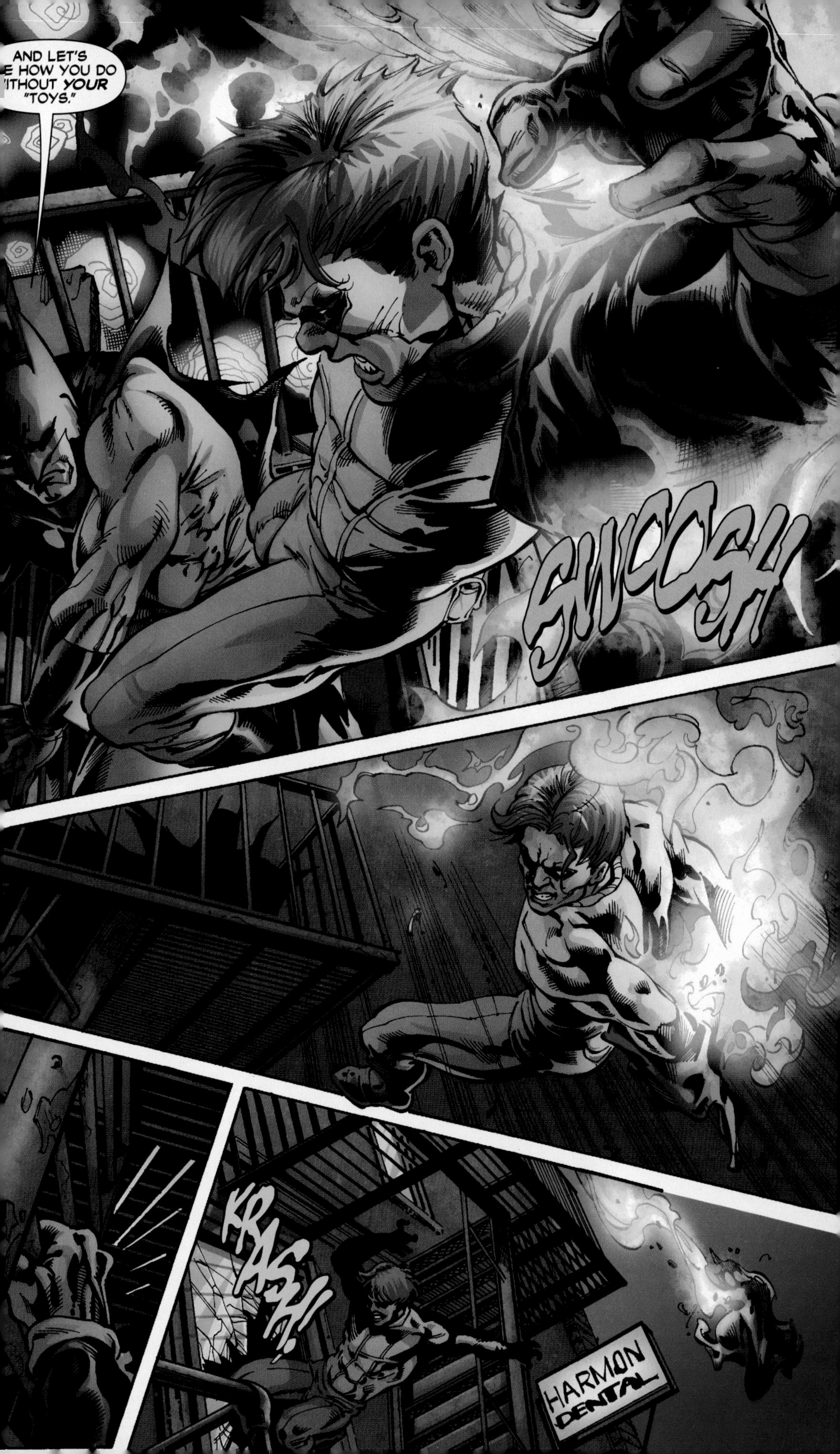
AND LET'S
E HOW YOU DO
ITHOUT YOUR
"TOYS."
SWOOSH
KRASH!
HARMON
DENTAL

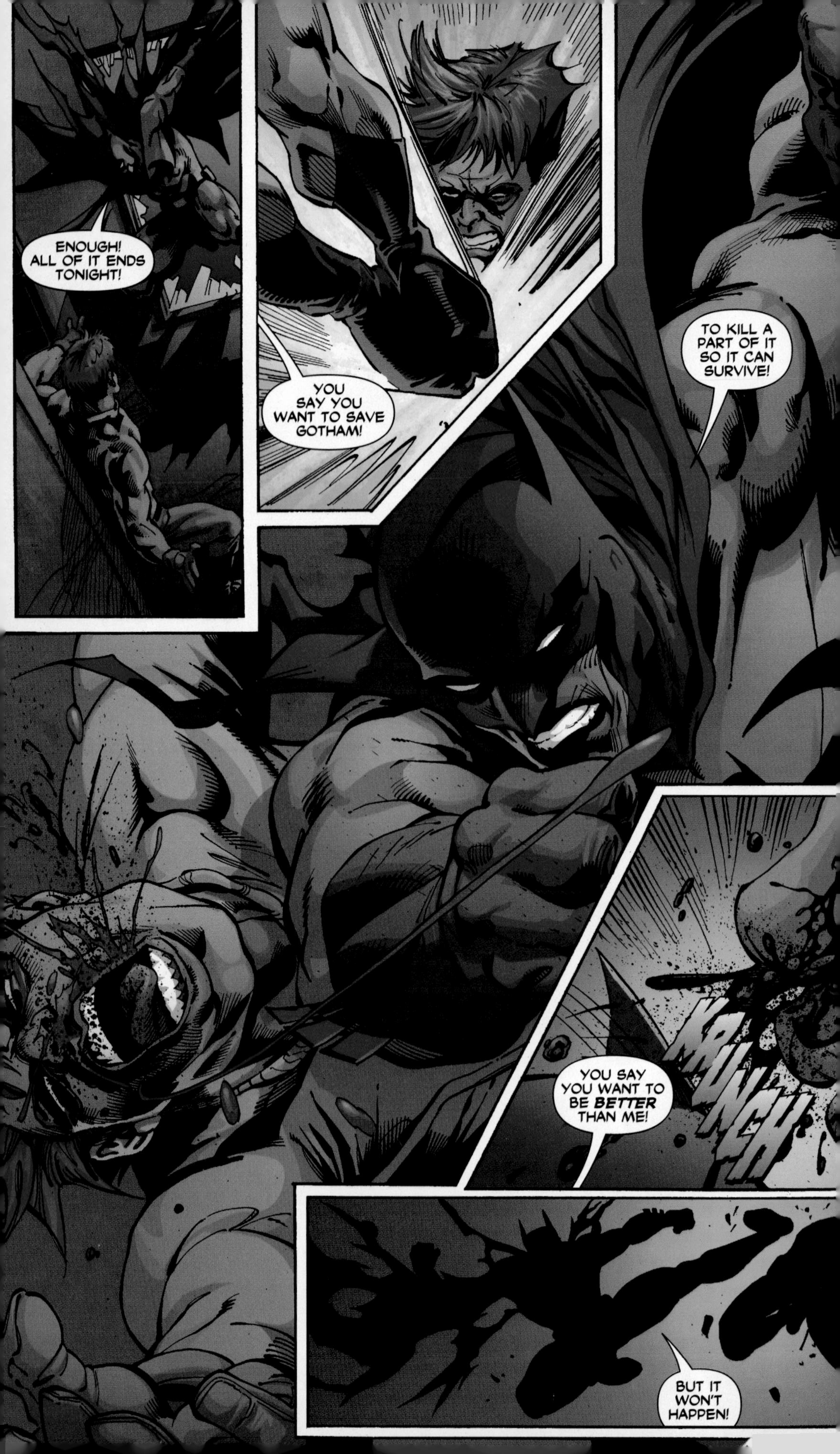
ENOUGH! ALL OF IT ENDS TONIGHT!
YOU SAY YOU WANT TO SAVE GOTHAM!
TO KILL A PART OF IT SO IT CAN SURVIVE!
YOU SAY YOU WANT TO BE *BETTER* THAN ME!
KRUNCH
BUT IT WON'T HAPPEN!

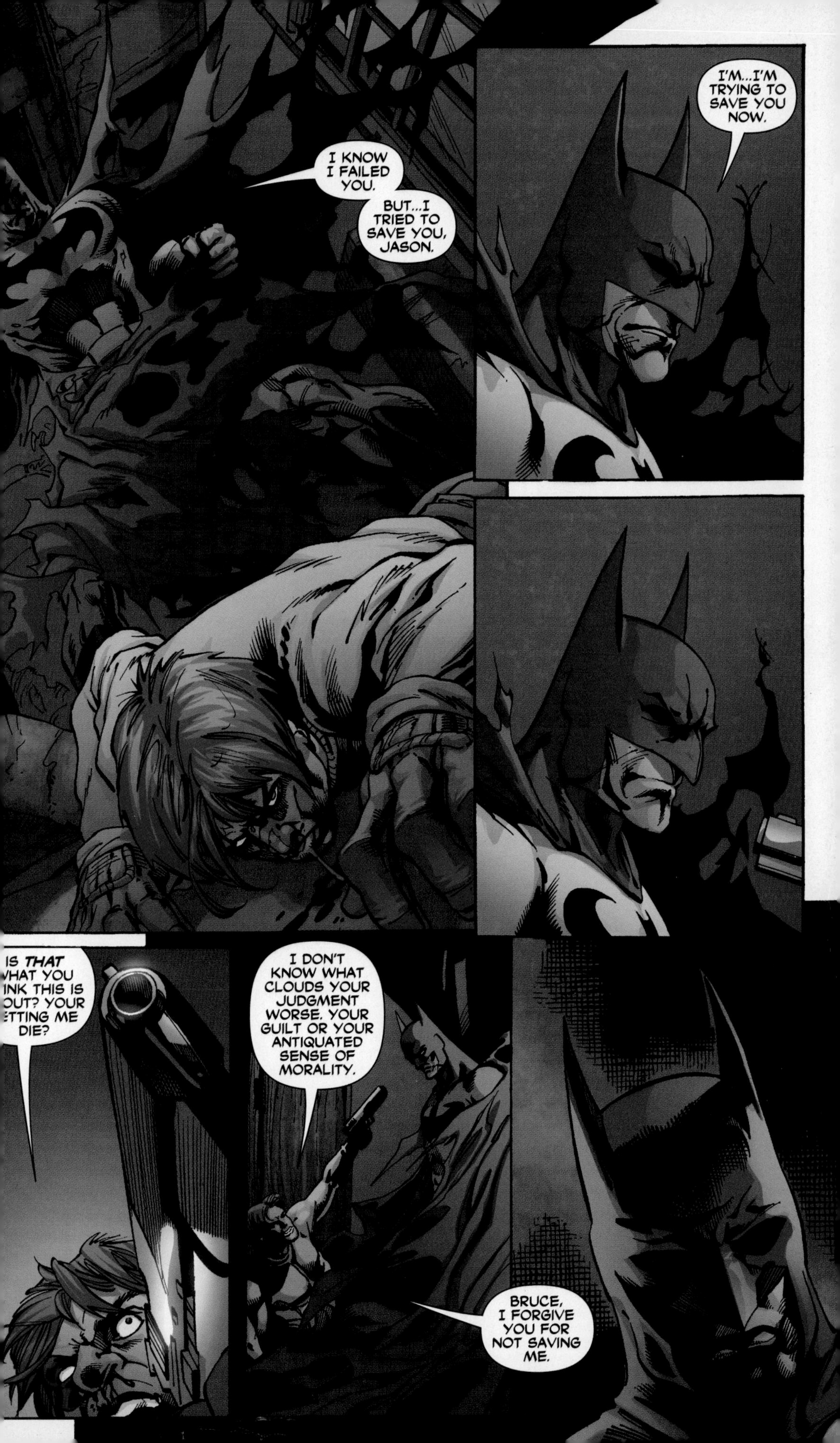
I KNOW I FAILED YOU.
BUT...I TRIED TO SAVE YOU, JASON.
I'M...I'M TRYING TO SAVE YOU NOW.
IS *THAT* WHAT YOU INK THIS IS OUT? YOUR ETTING ME DIE?
I DON'T KNOW WHAT CLOUDS YOUR JUDGMENT WORSE. YOUR GUILT OR YOUR ANTIQUATED SENSE OF MORALITY.
BRUCE, I FORGIVE YOU FOR NOT SAVING ME.

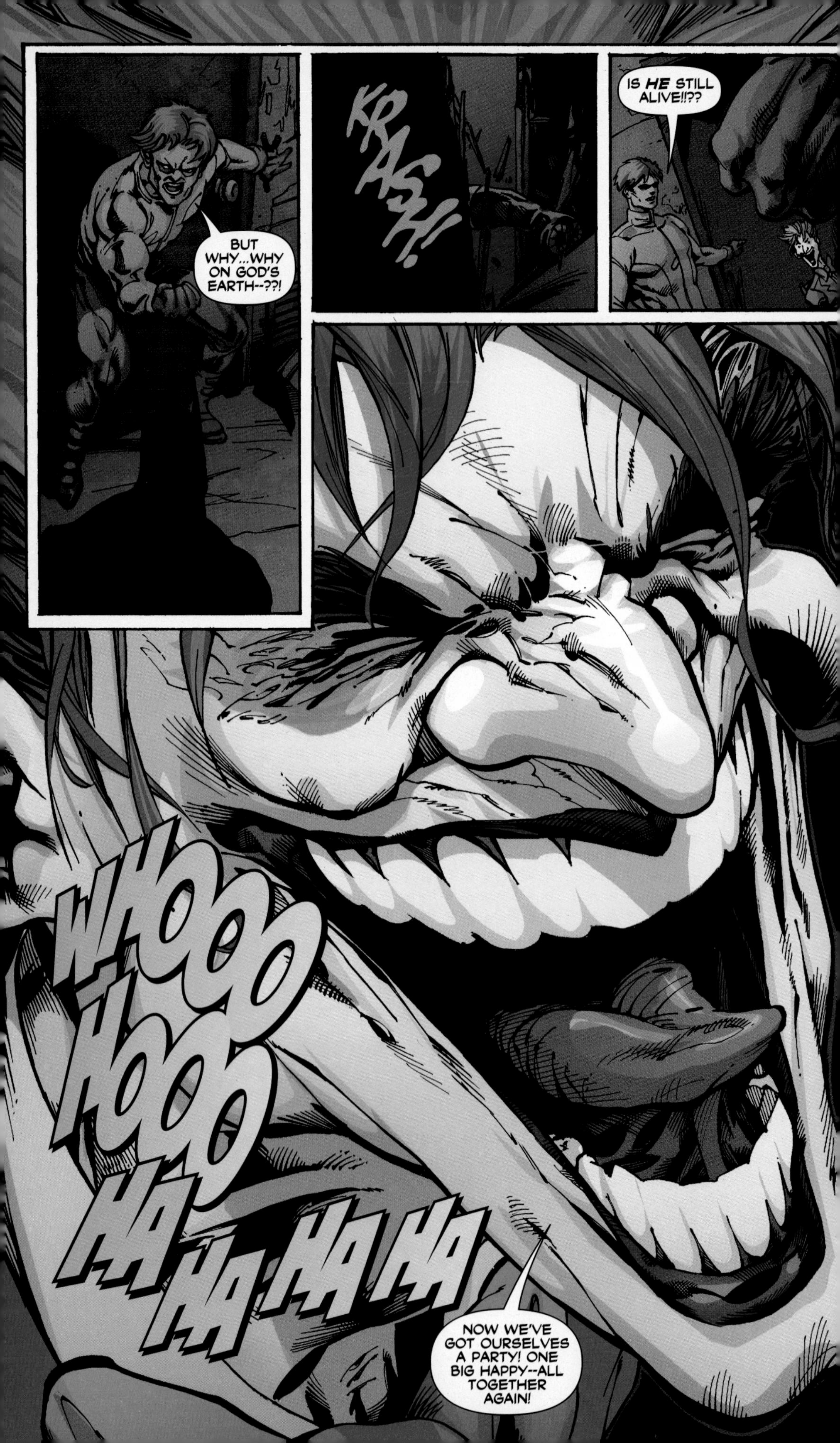
BUT WHY...WHY ON GOD'S EARTH--??!
KRASH!!
IS HE STILL ALIVE!!??
WHOOO HOOO HA HA HA HA
NOW WE'VE GOT OURSELVES A PARTY! ONE BIG HAPPY--ALL TOGETHER AGAIN!

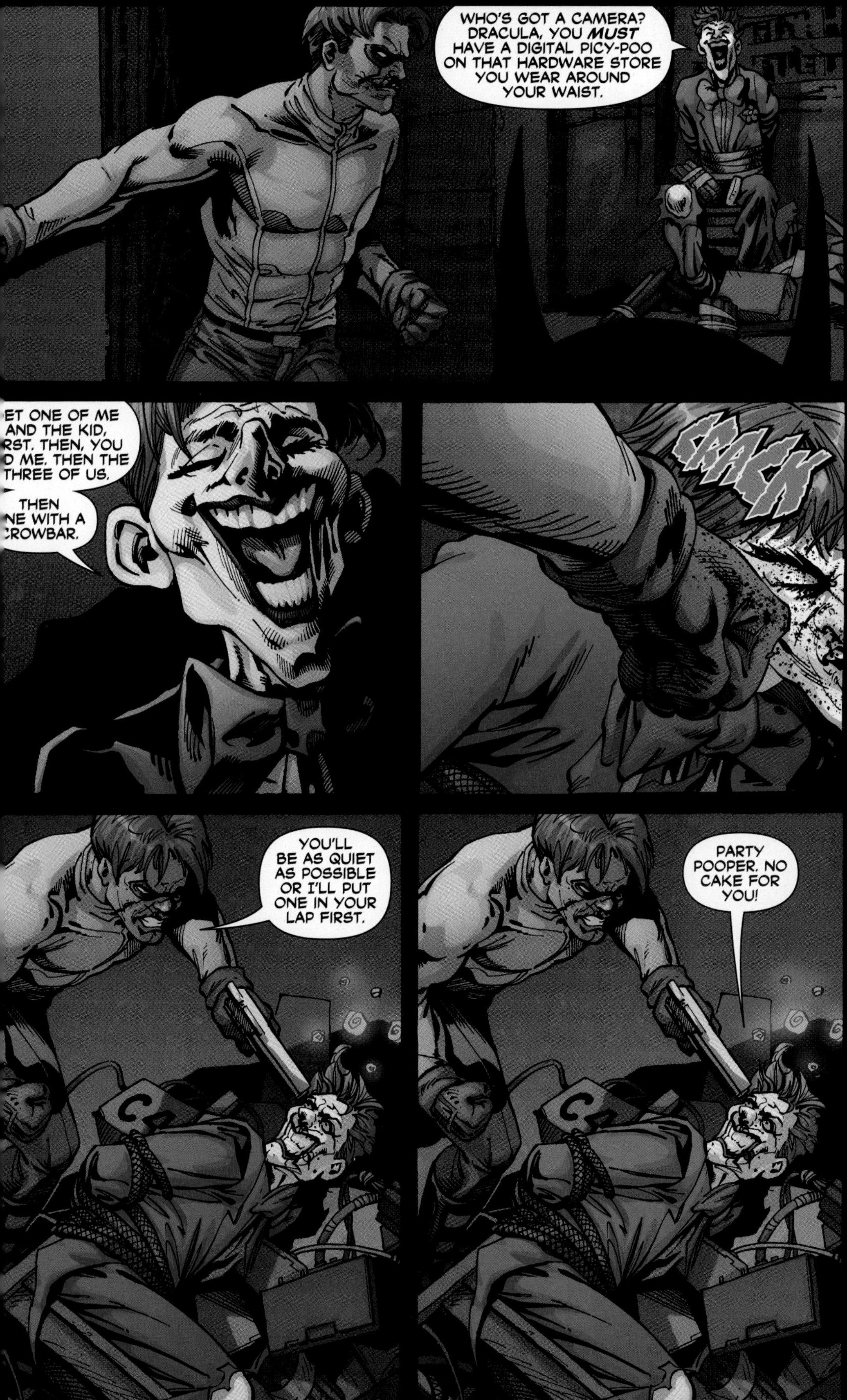
WHO'S GOT A CAMERA? DRACULA, YOU *MUST* HAVE A DIGITAL PICY-POO ON THAT HARDWARE STORE YOU WEAR AROUND YOUR WAIST.
ET ONE OF ME AND THE KID, RST. THEN, YOU D ME. THEN THE THREE OF US.
THEN NE WITH A CROWBAR.
CRACK
YOU'LL BE AS QUIET AS POSSIBLE OR I'LL PUT ONE IN YOUR LAP FIRST.
PARTY POOPER. NO CAKE FOR YOU!

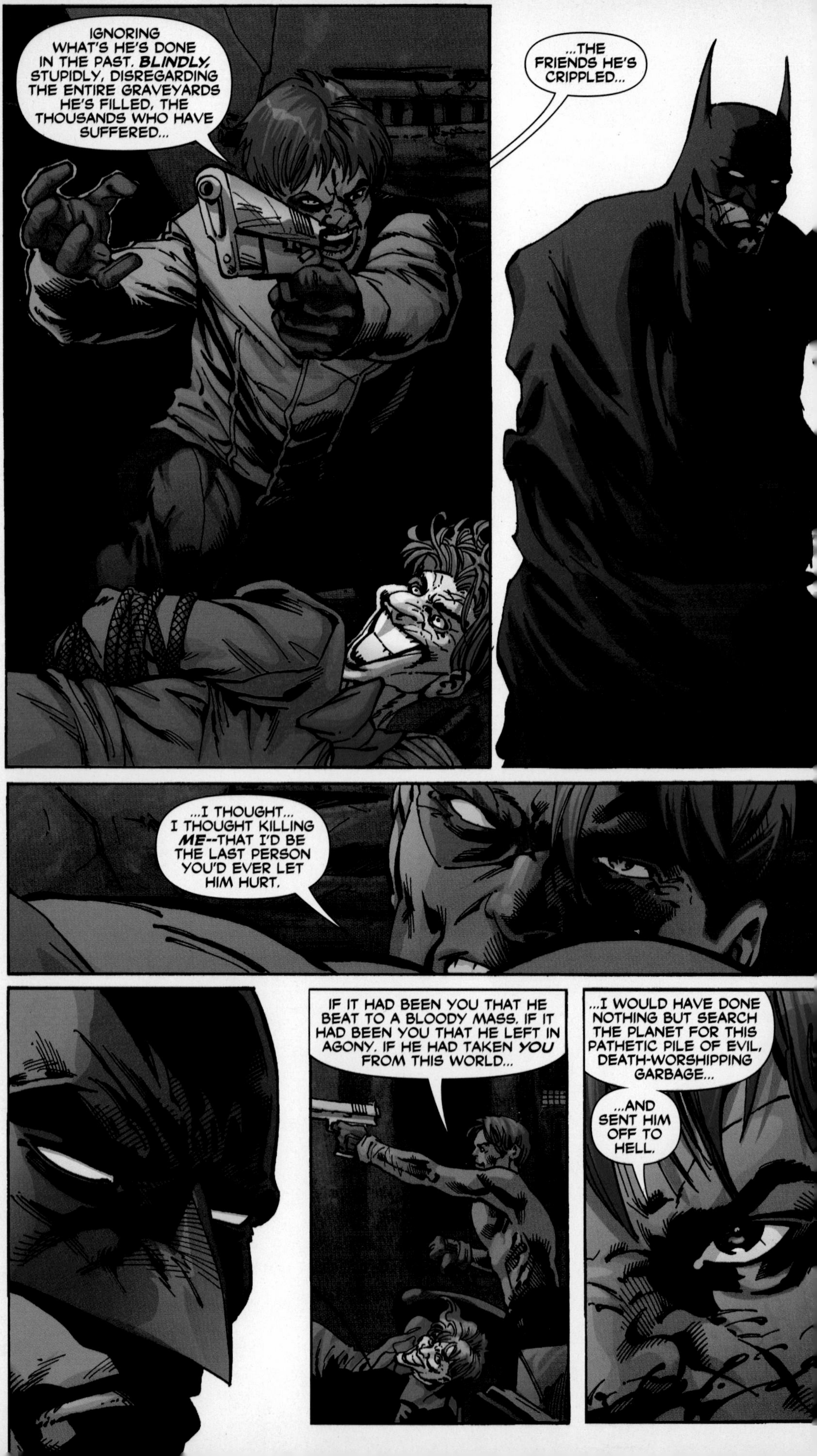
IGNORING WHAT'S HE'S DONE IN THE PAST. BLINDLY, STUPIDLY, DISREGARDING THE ENTIRE GRAVEYARDS HE'S FILLED, THE THOUSANDS WHO HAVE SUFFERED...
...THE FRIENDS HE'S CRIPPLED...
...I THOUGHT... I THOUGHT KILLING ME--THAT I'D BE THE LAST PERSON YOU'D EVER LET HIM HURT.
IF IT HAD BEEN YOU THAT HE BEAT TO A BLOODY MASS, IF IT HAD BEEN YOU THAT HE LEFT IN AGONY, IF HE HAD TAKEN YOU FROM THIS WORLD...
...I WOULD HAVE DONE NOTHING BUT SEARCH THE PLANET FOR THIS PATHETIC PILE OF EVIL, DEATH-WORSHIPPING GARBAGE...
...AND SENT HIM OFF TO HELL.

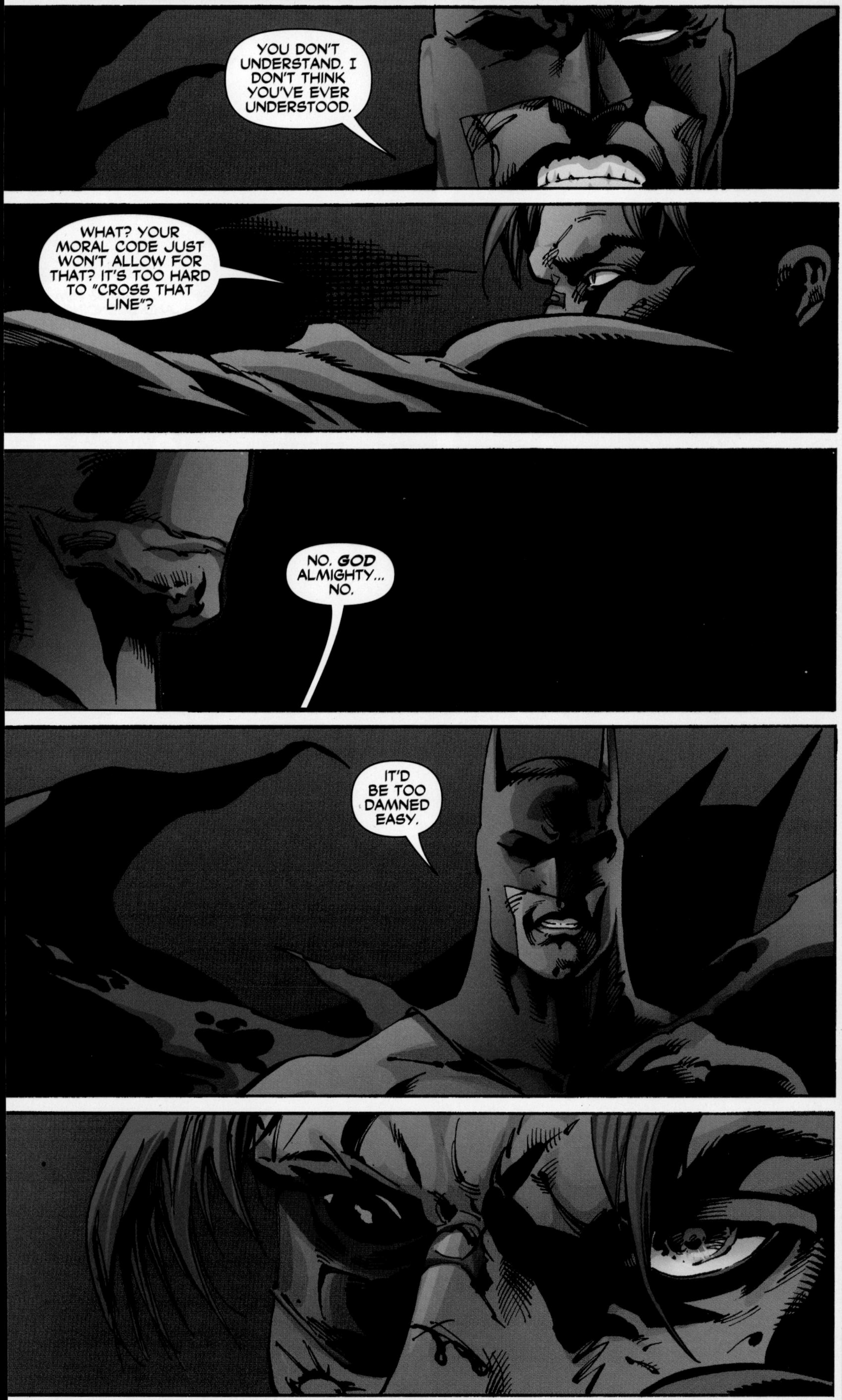
YOU DON'T UNDERSTAND. I DON'T THINK YOU'VE EVER UNDERSTOOD.
WHAT? YOUR MORAL CODE JUST WON'T ALLOW FOR THAT? IT'S TOO HARD TO "CROSS THAT LINE"?
NO. **GOD** ALMIGHTY... NO.
IT'D BE TOO DAMNED EASY.

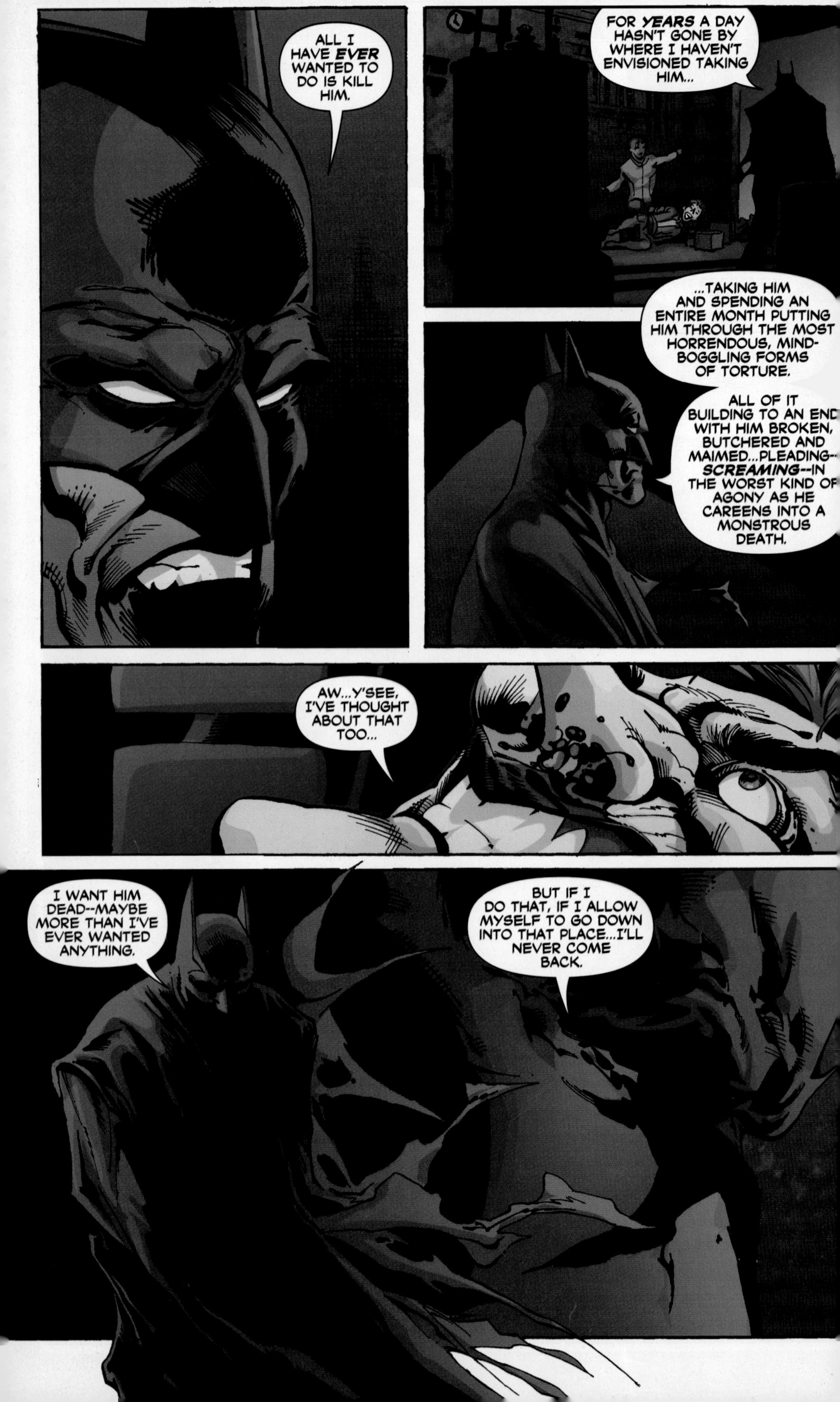
ALL I HAVE EVER WANTED TO DO IS KILL HIM.
FOR YEARS A DAY HASN'T GONE BY WHERE I HAVEN'T ENVISIONED TAKING HIM...
...TAKING HIM AND SPENDING AN ENTIRE MONTH PUTTING HIM THROUGH THE MOST HORRENDOUS, MIND-BOGGLING FORMS OF TORTURE.
ALL OF IT BUILDING TO AN END WITH HIM BROKEN, BUTCHERED AND MAIMED...PLEADING--SCREAMING--IN THE WORST KIND OF AGONY AS HE CAREENS INTO A MONSTROUS DEATH.
AW...Y'SEE, I'VE THOUGHT ABOUT THAT TOO...
I WANT HIM DEAD--MAYBE MORE THAN I'VE EVER WANTED ANYTHING.
BUT IF I DO THAT, IF I ALLOW MYSELF TO GO DOWN INTO THAT PLACE...I'LL NEVER COME BACK.

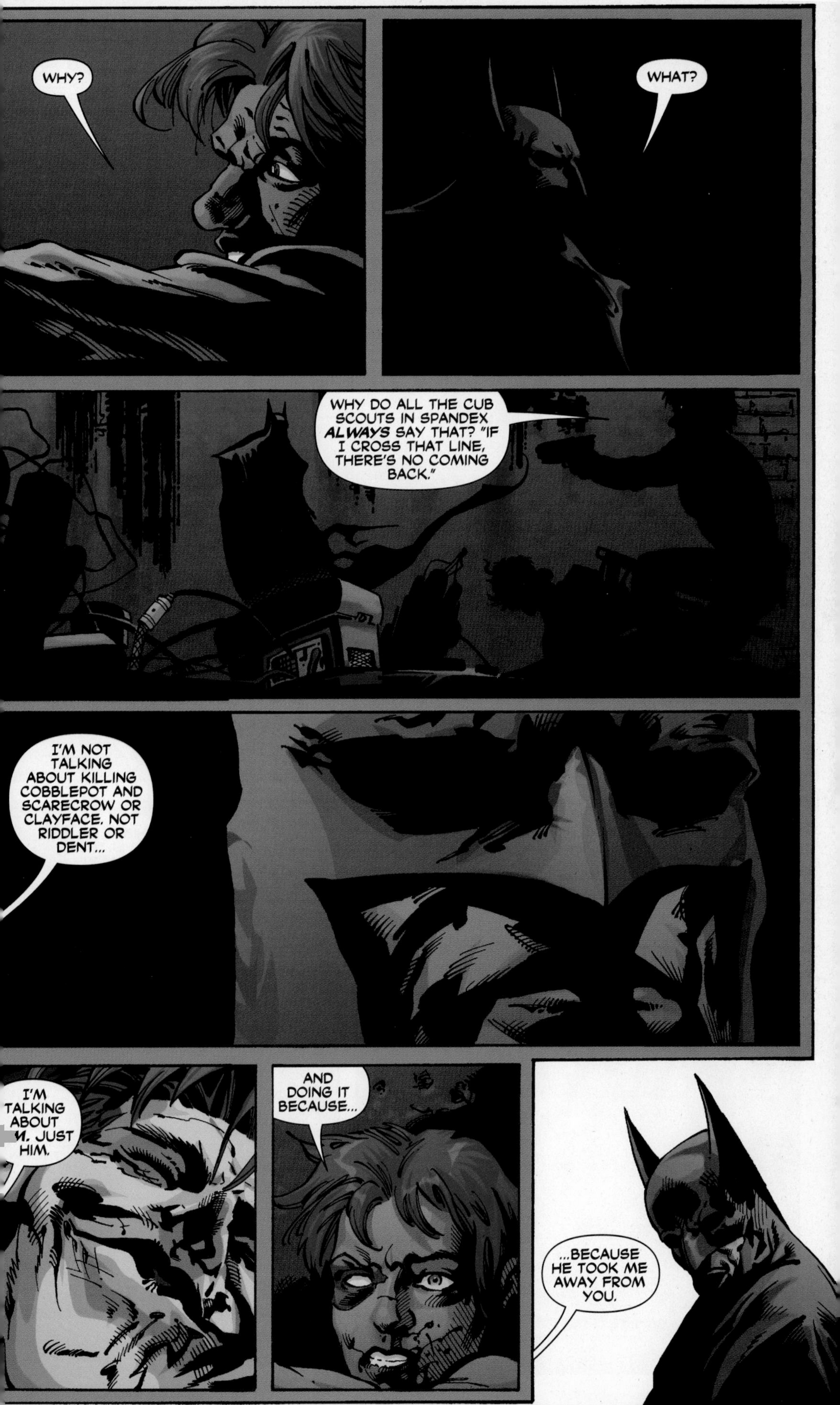
WHY?
WHAT?
WHY DO ALL THE CUB SCOUTS IN SPANDEX *ALWAYS* SAY THAT? "IF I CROSS THAT LINE, THERE'S NO COMING BACK."
I'M NOT TALKING ABOUT KILLING COBBLEPOT AND SCARECROW OR CLAYFACE. NOT RIDDLER OR DENT...
I'M TALKING ABOUT
JUST HIM.
AND DOING IT BECAUSE...
...BECAUSE HE TOOK ME AWAY FROM YOU.

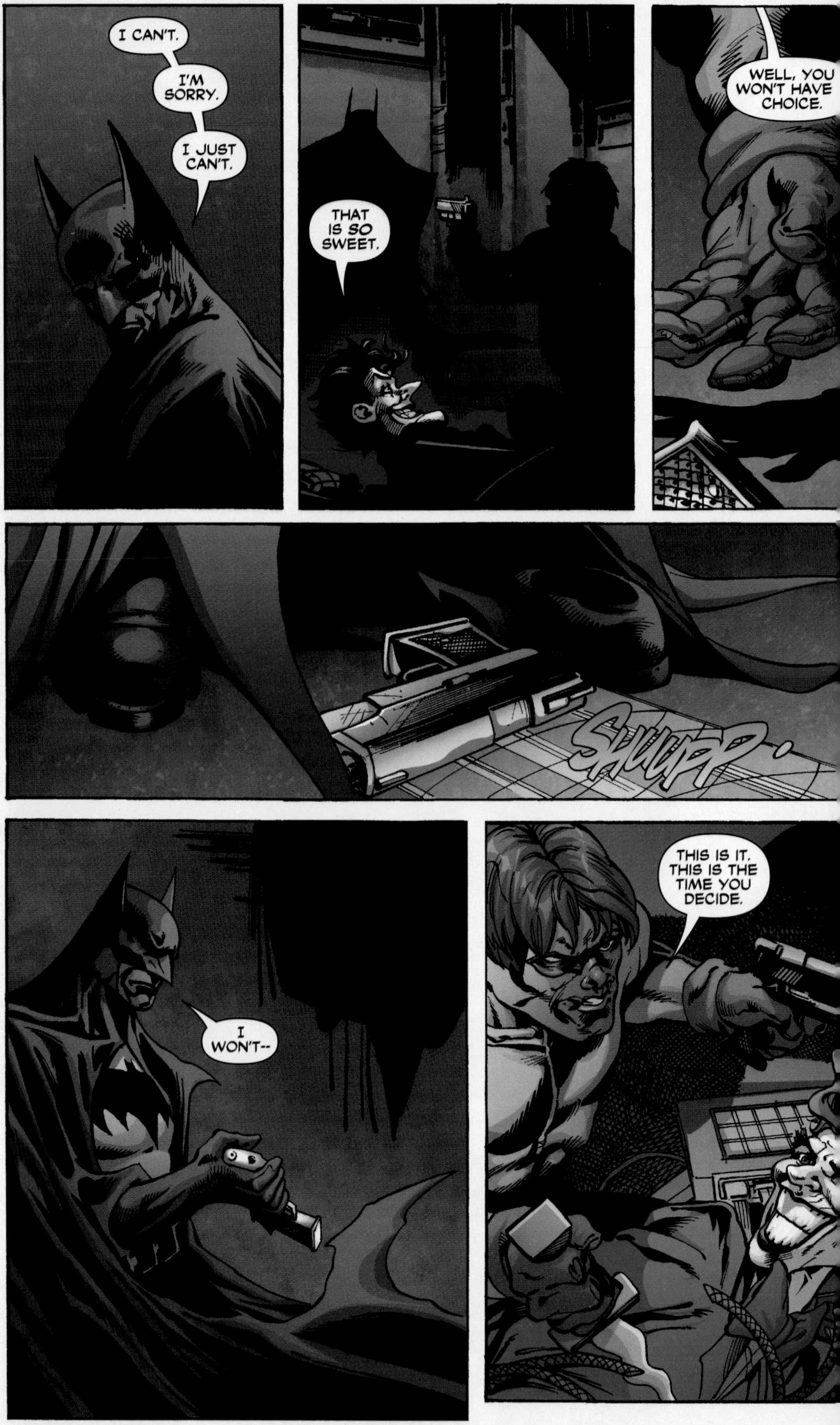
I CAN'T.
I'M SORRY.
I JUST CAN'T.
THAT IS SO SWEET.
WELL, YOU WON'T HAVE CHOICE.
SHUUPP
I WON'T--
THIS IS IT. THIS IS THE TIME YOU DECIDE.

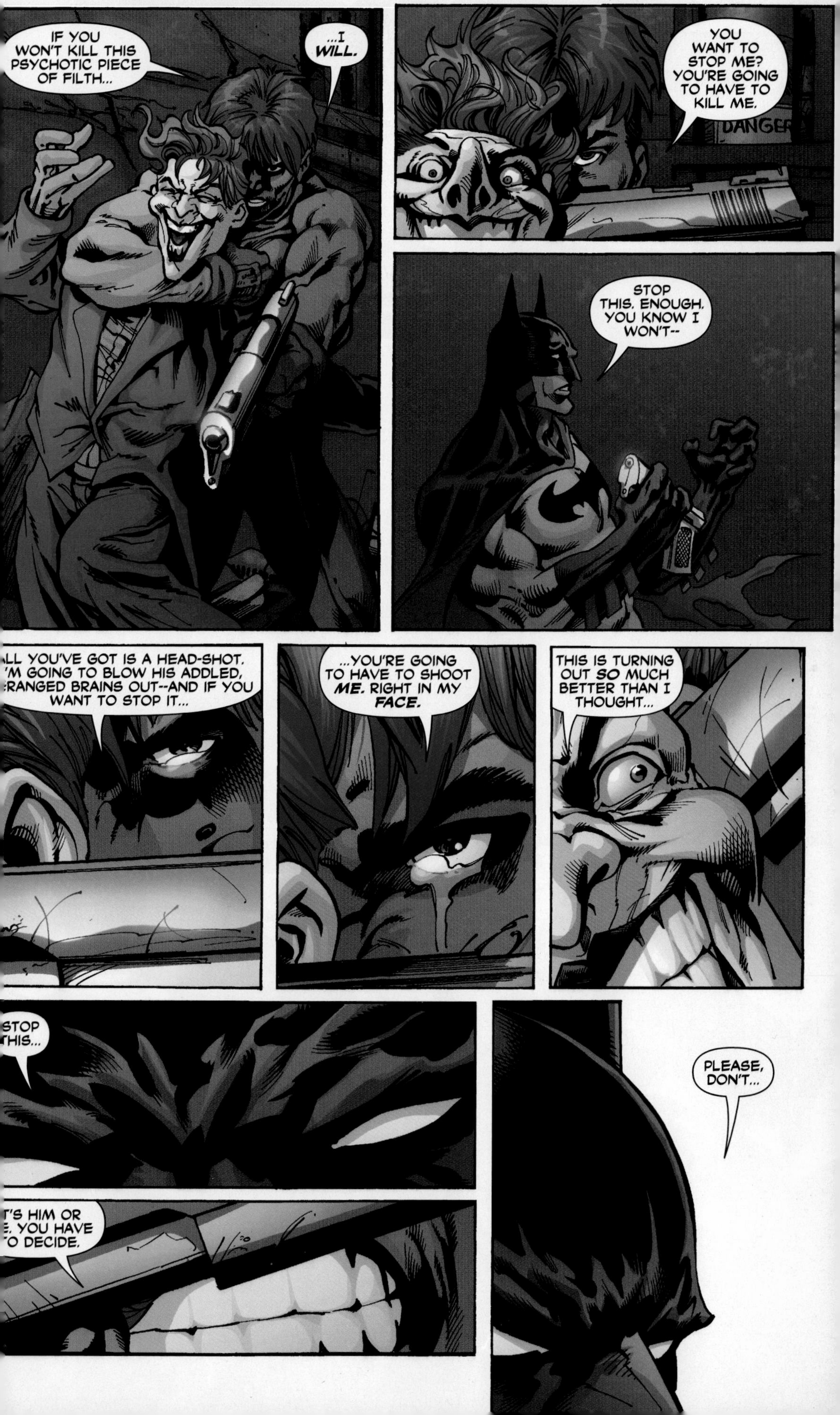
IF YOU WON'T KILL THIS PSYCHOTIC PIECE OF FILTH...
...I *WILL.*
YOU WANT TO STOP ME? YOU'RE GOING TO HAVE TO KILL ME.
DANGER
STOP THIS. ENOUGH. YOU KNOW I WON'T--
LL YOU'VE GOT IS A HEAD-SHOT. 'M GOING TO BLOW HIS ADDLED, ERANGED BRAINS OUT--AND IF YOU WANT TO STOP IT...
...YOU'RE GOING TO HAVE TO SHOOT *ME.* RIGHT IN MY *FACE.*
THIS IS TURNING OUT *SO* MUCH BETTER THAN I THOUGHT...
STOP THIS...
T'S HIM OR E. YOU HAVE O DECIDE.
PLEASE, DON'T...

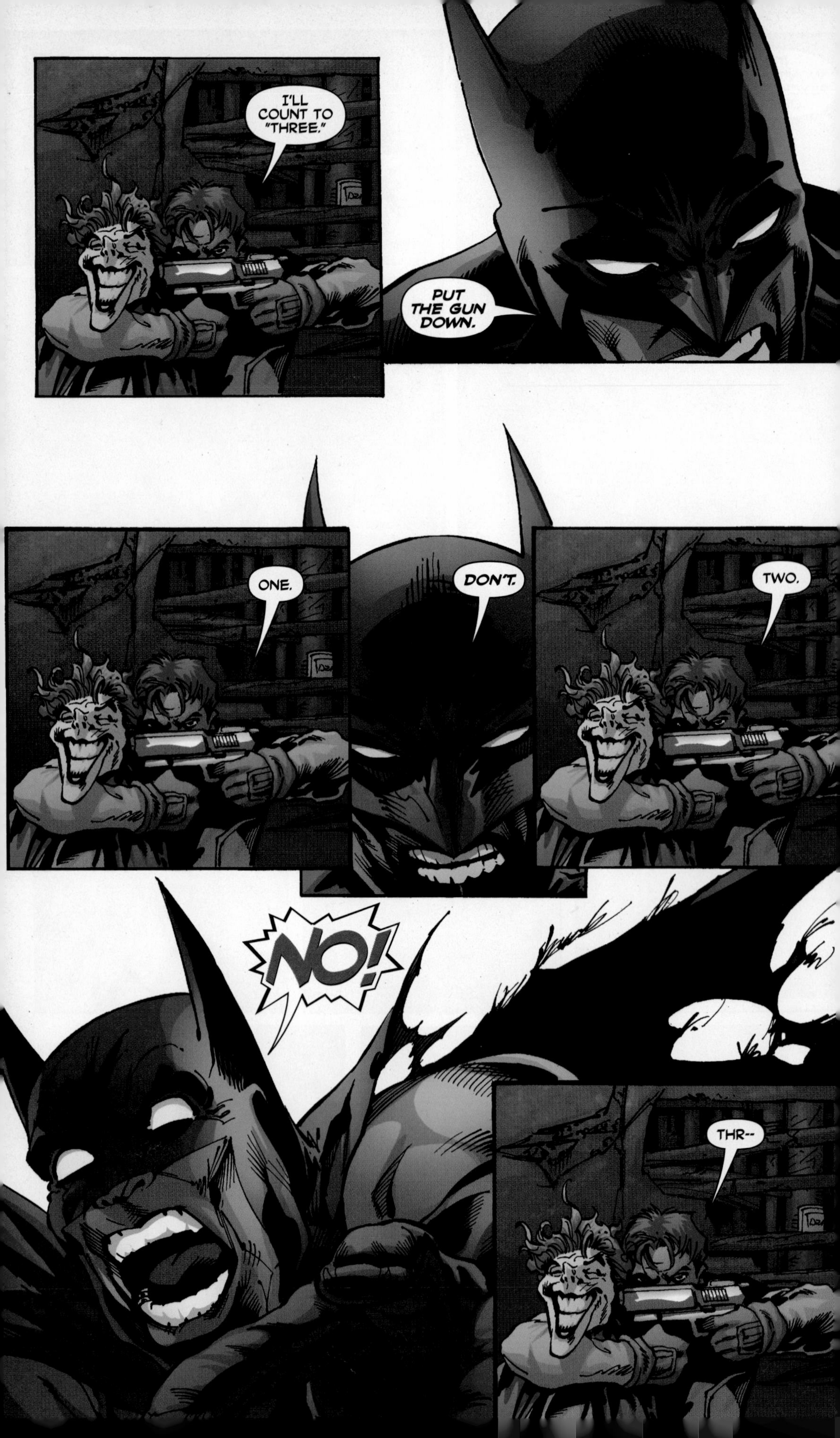
I'LL COUNT TO "THREE."
PUT THE GUN DOWN.
ONE.
DON'T.
TWO.
NO!
THR--

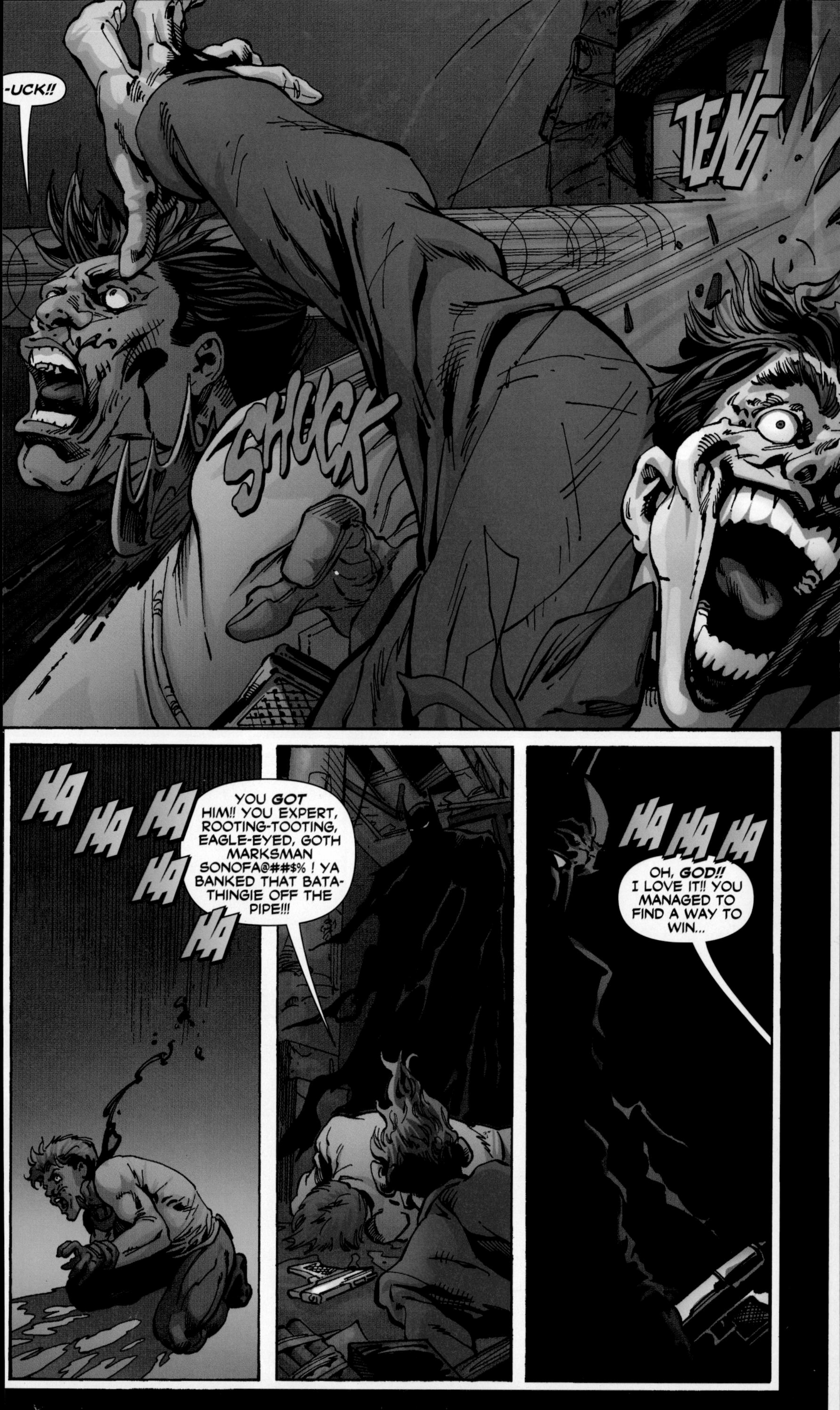
-UCK!!
TENG
SHUCK
HA HA HA HA HA
YOU GOT HIM!! YOU EXPERT, ROOTING-TOOTING, EAGLE-EYED, GOTH MARKSMAN SONOFA@##$% ! YA BANKED THAT BATA-THINGIE OFF THE PIPE!!!
HA HA HA
OH, GOD!! I LOVE IT!! YOU MANAGED TO FIND A WAY TO WIN...

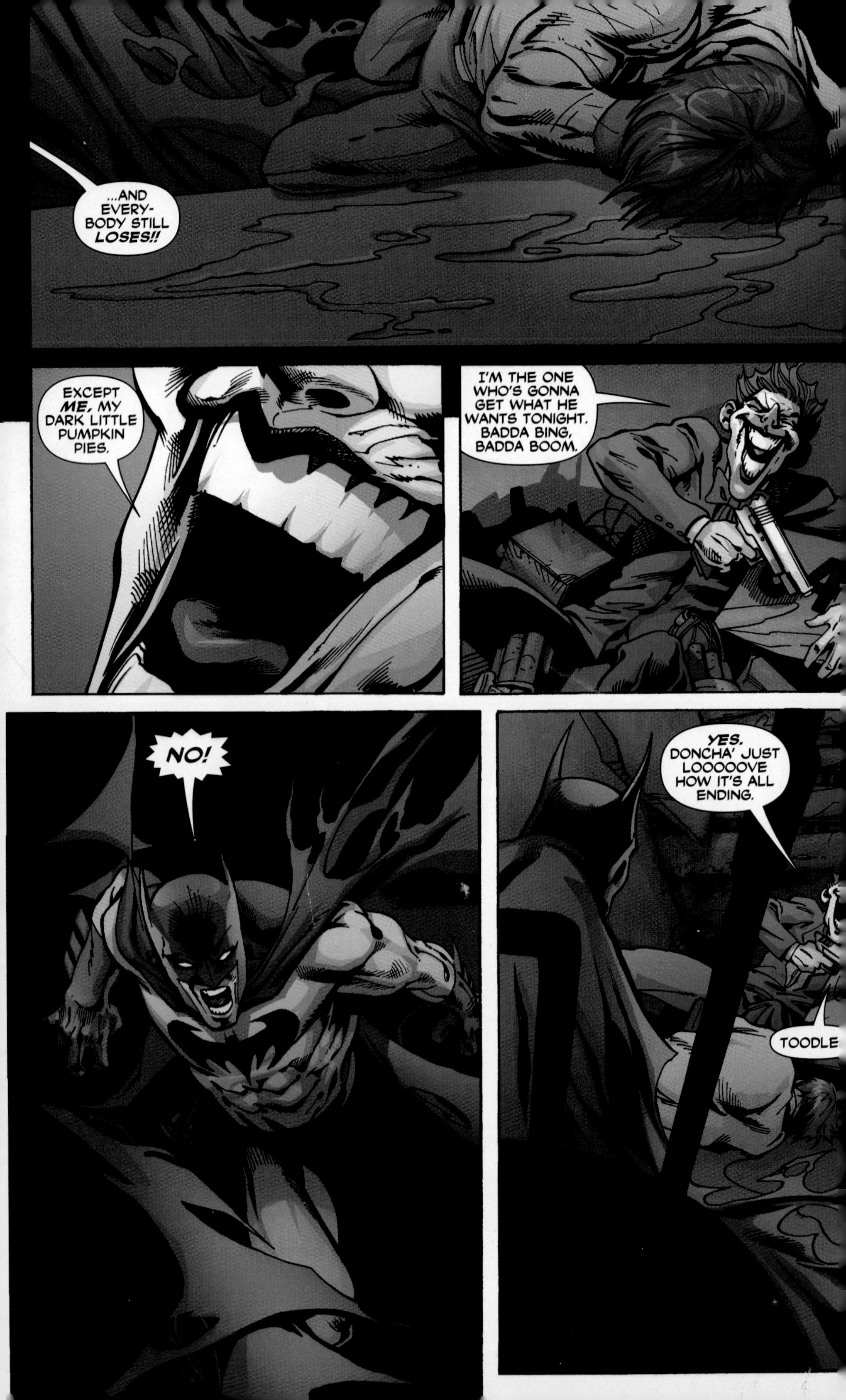
...AND EVERY-BODY STILL LOSES!!
EXCEPT ME, MY DARK LITTLE PUMPKIN PIES.
I'M THE ONE WHO'S GONNA GET WHAT HE WANTS TONIGHT. BADDA BING, BADDA BOOM.
NO!
YES. DONCHA' JUST LOOOOOVE HOW IT'S ALL ENDING.
TOODLE

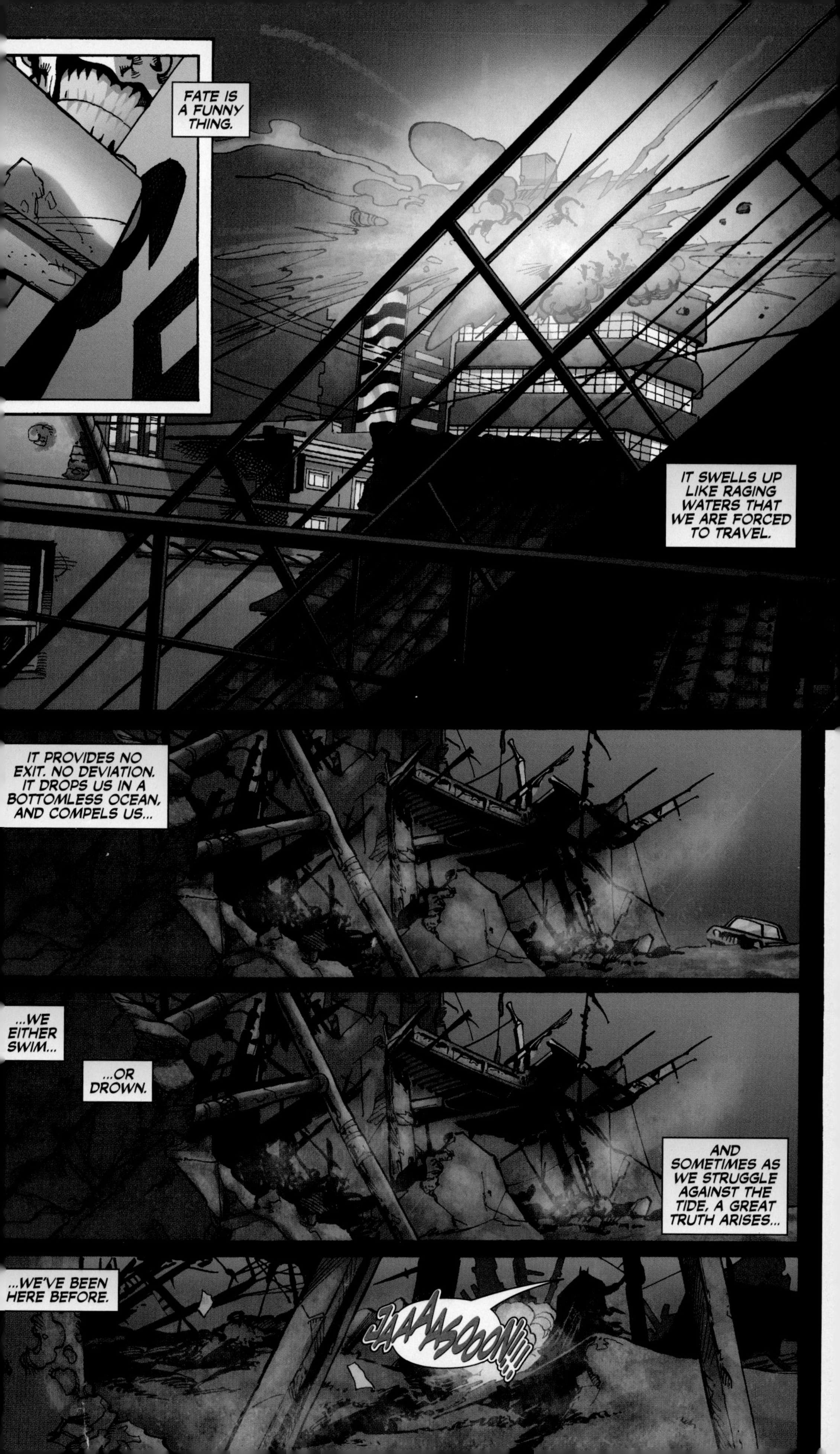
FATE IS A FUNNY THING.
IT SWELLS UP LIKE RAGING WATERS THAT WE ARE FORCED TO TRAVEL.
IT PROVIDES NO EXIT. NO DEVIATION. IT DROPS US IN A BOTTOMLESS OCEAN, AND COMPELS US...
...WE EITHER SWIM...
...OR DROWN.
AND SOMETIMES AS WE STRUGGLE AGAINST THE TIDE, A GREAT TRUTH ARISES...
...WE'VE BEEN HERE BEFORE.
JAAAASOOON!!!

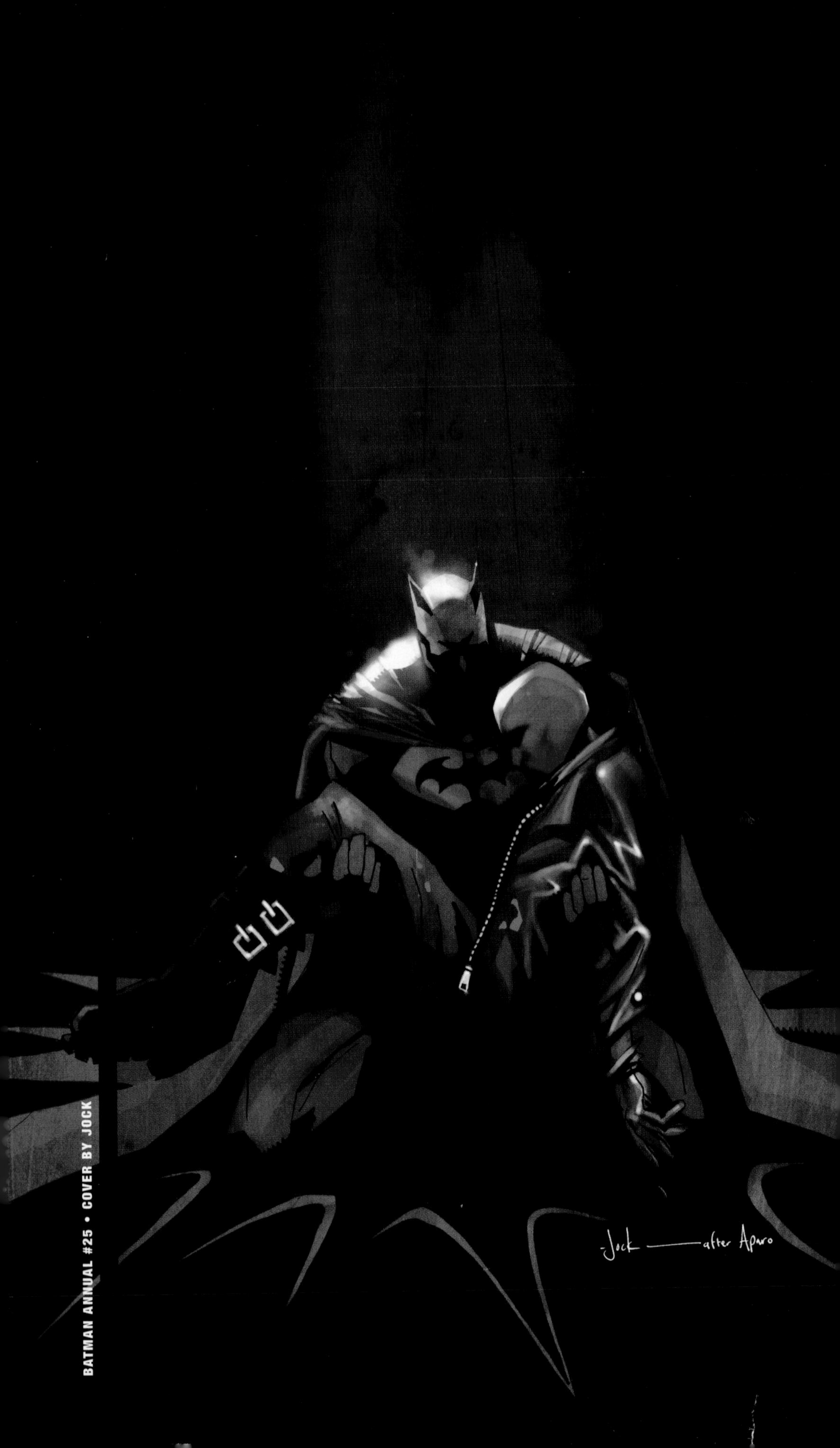
Jock — after Aparo
BATMAN ANNUAL #25 • COVER BY JOCK

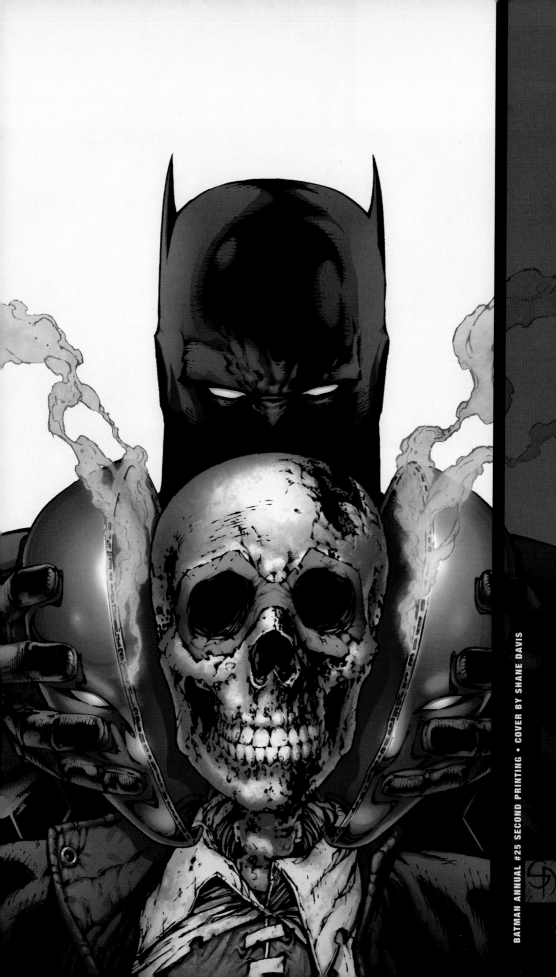

BATMAN ANNUAL #25 SECOND PRINTING • COVER BY SHANE DAVIS

DAEDALUS AND ICARUS

THE RETURN OF JASON TODD

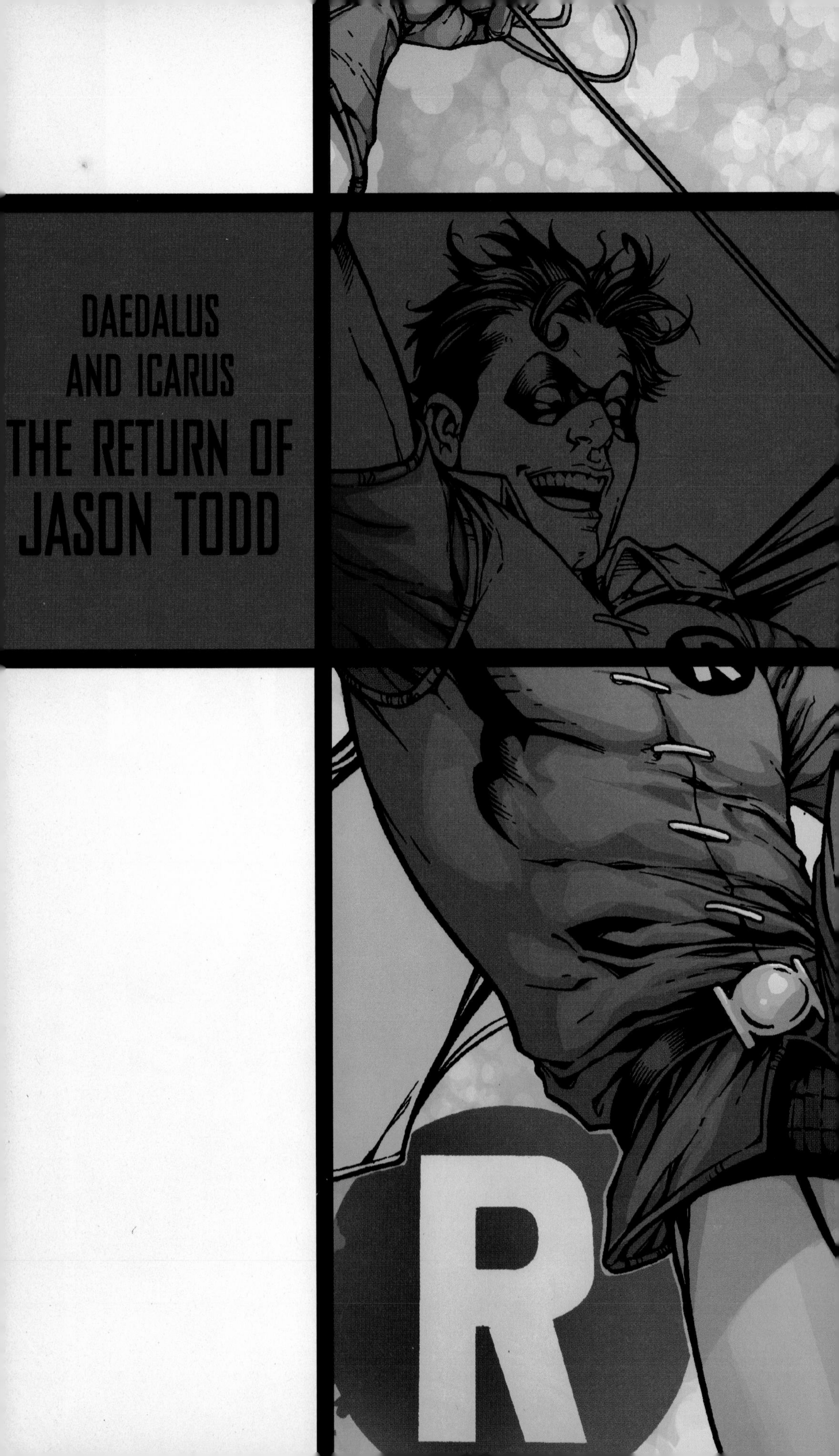

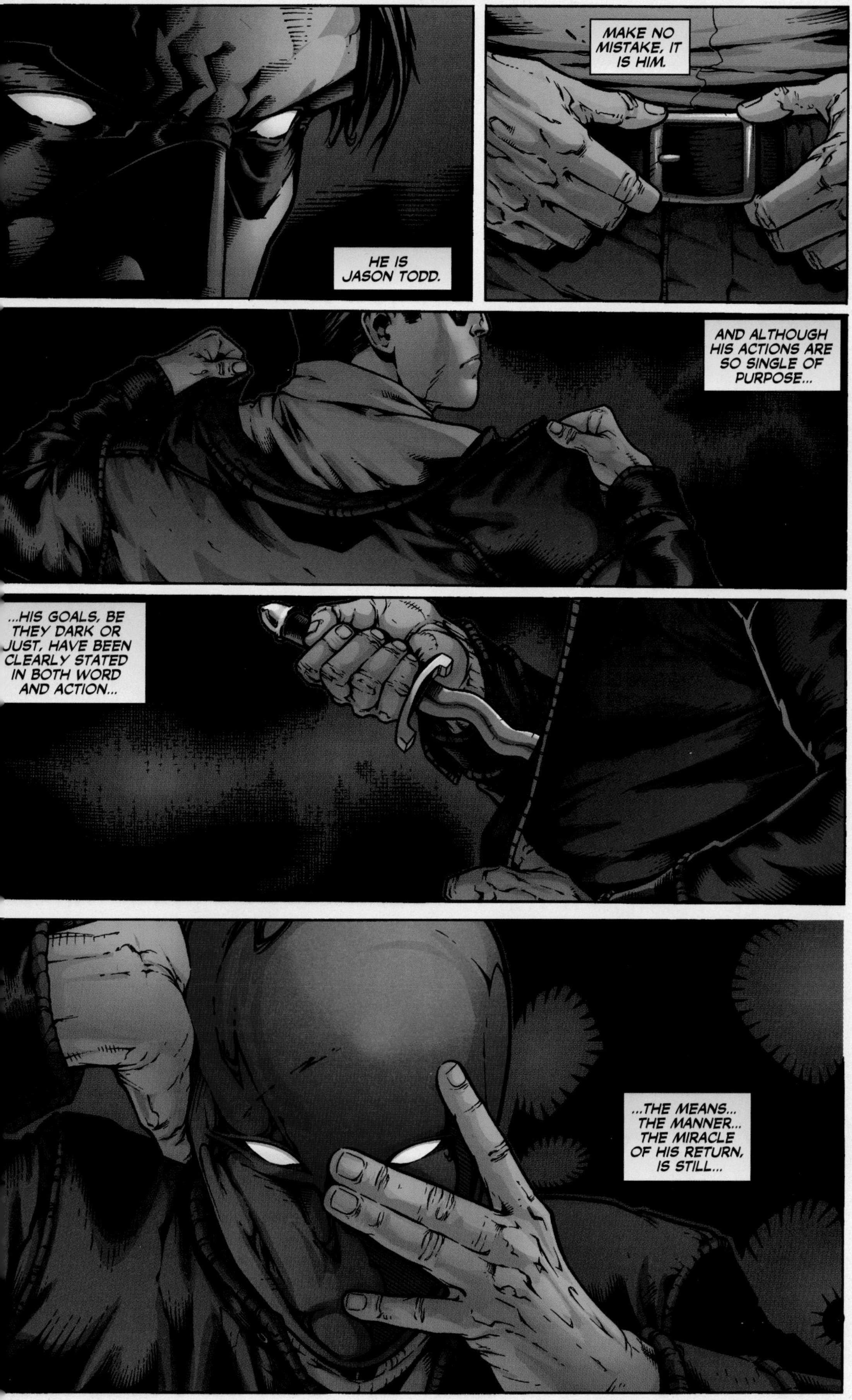
HE IS
JASON TODD.
MAKE NO
MISTAKE, IT
IS HIM.
AND ALTHOUGH
HIS ACTIONS ARE
SO SINGLE OF
PURPOSE...
...HIS GOALS, BE
THEY DARK OR
JUST, HAVE BEEN
CLEARLY STATED
IN BOTH WORD
AND ACTION...
...THE MEANS...
THE MANNER...
THE MIRACLE
OF HIS RETURN,
IS STILL...

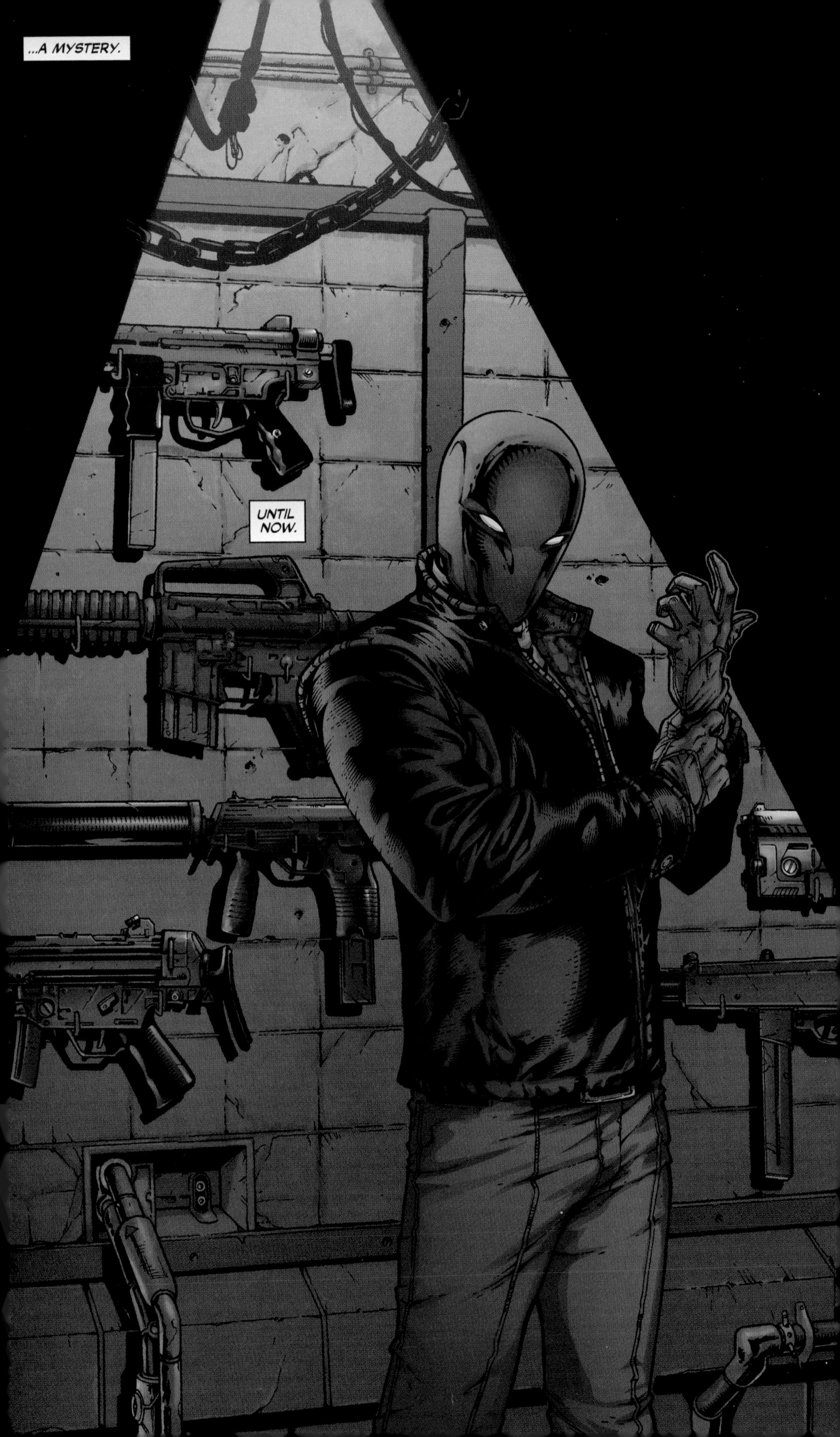
...A MYSTERY.
UNTIL NOW.

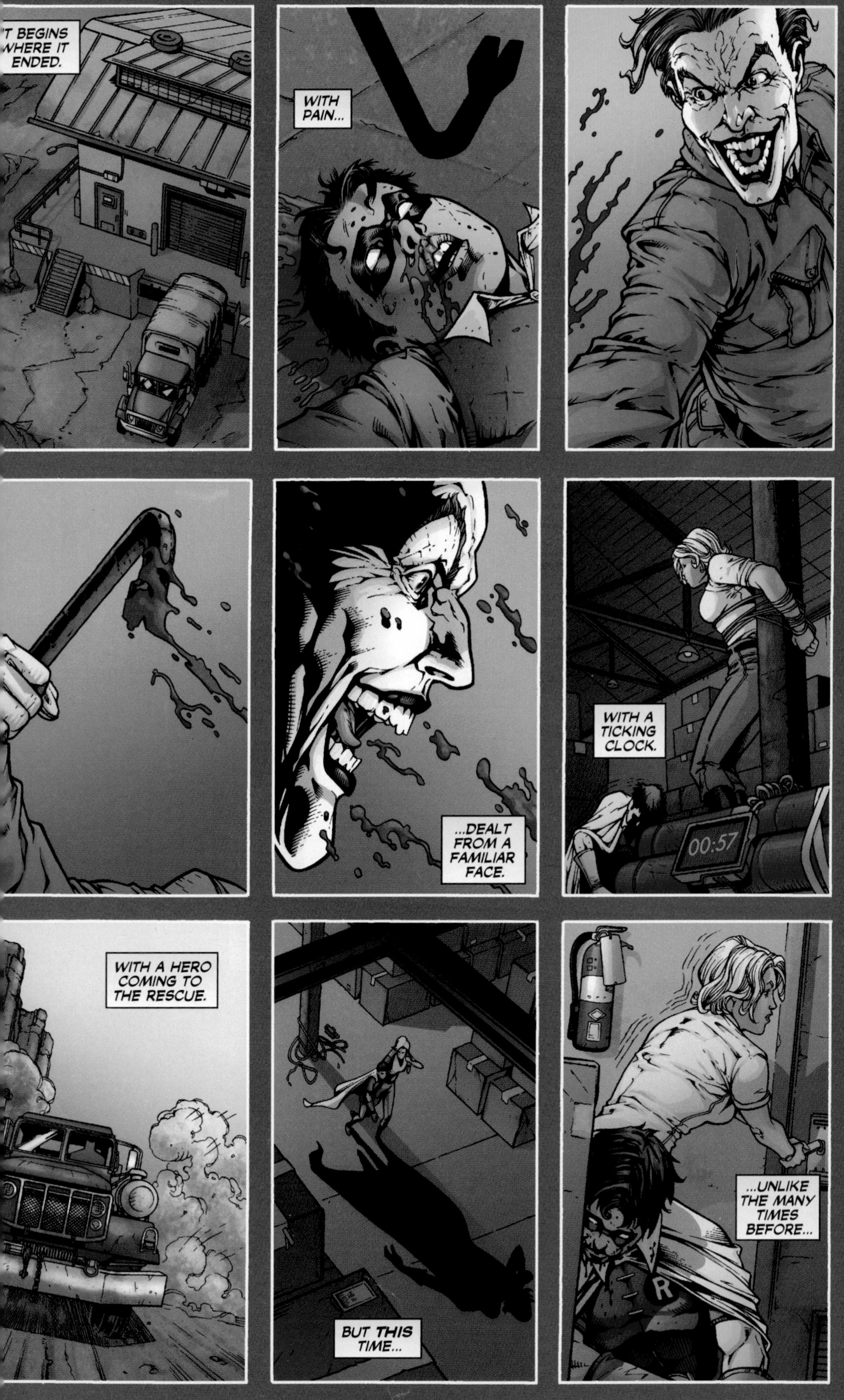
'T BEGINS WHERE IT ENDED.
WITH PAIN...
...DEALT FROM A FAMILIAR FACE.
WITH A TICKING CLOCK.
00:57
WITH A HERO COMING TO THE RESCUE.
BUT THIS TIME...
...UNLIKE THE MANY TIMES BEFORE...

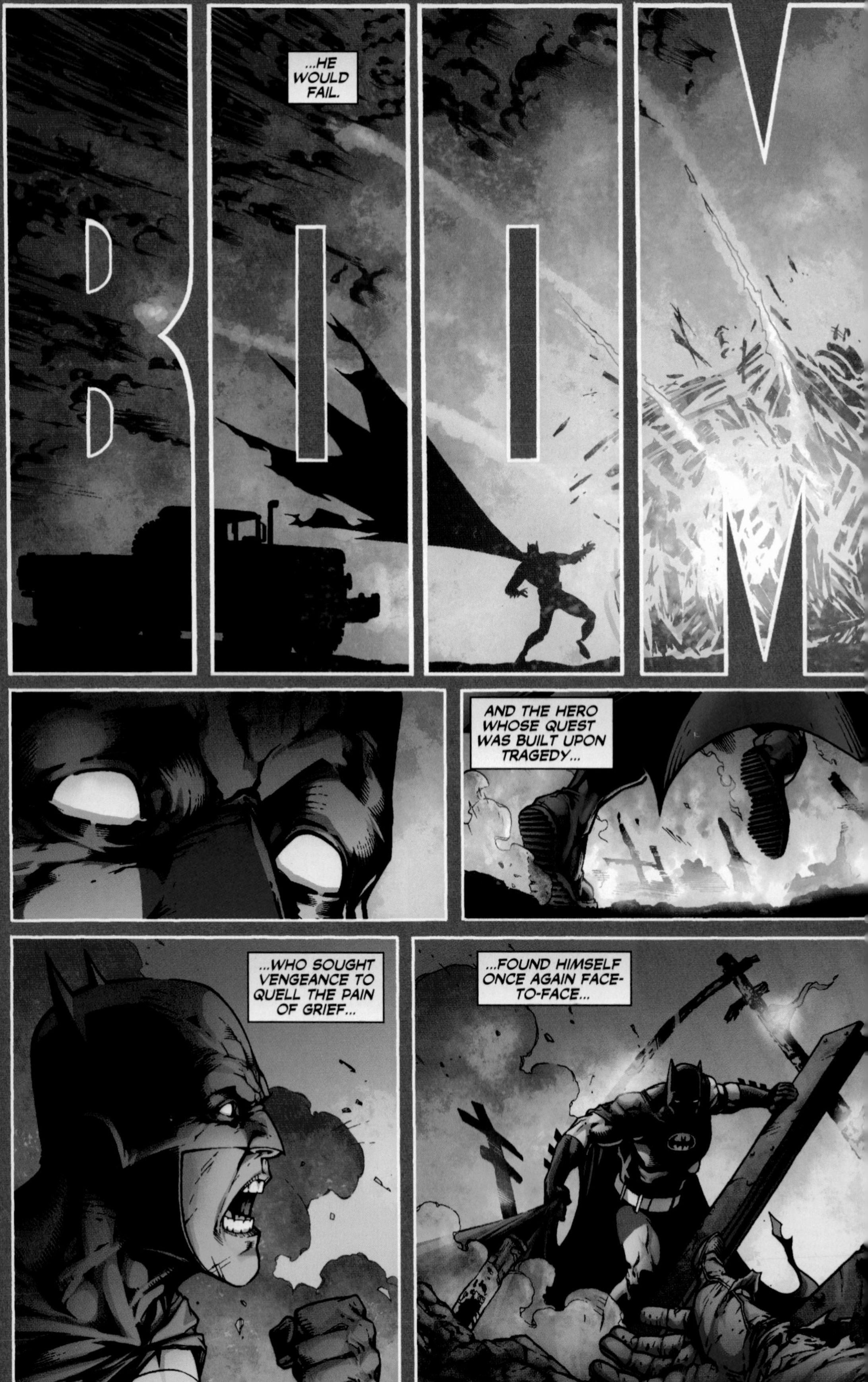
...HE WOULD FAIL.
AND THE HERO WHOSE QUEST WAS BUILT UPON TRAGEDY...
...WHO SOUGHT VENGEANCE TO QUELL THE PAIN OF GRIEF...
...FOUND HIMSELF ONCE AGAIN FACE-TO-FACE...

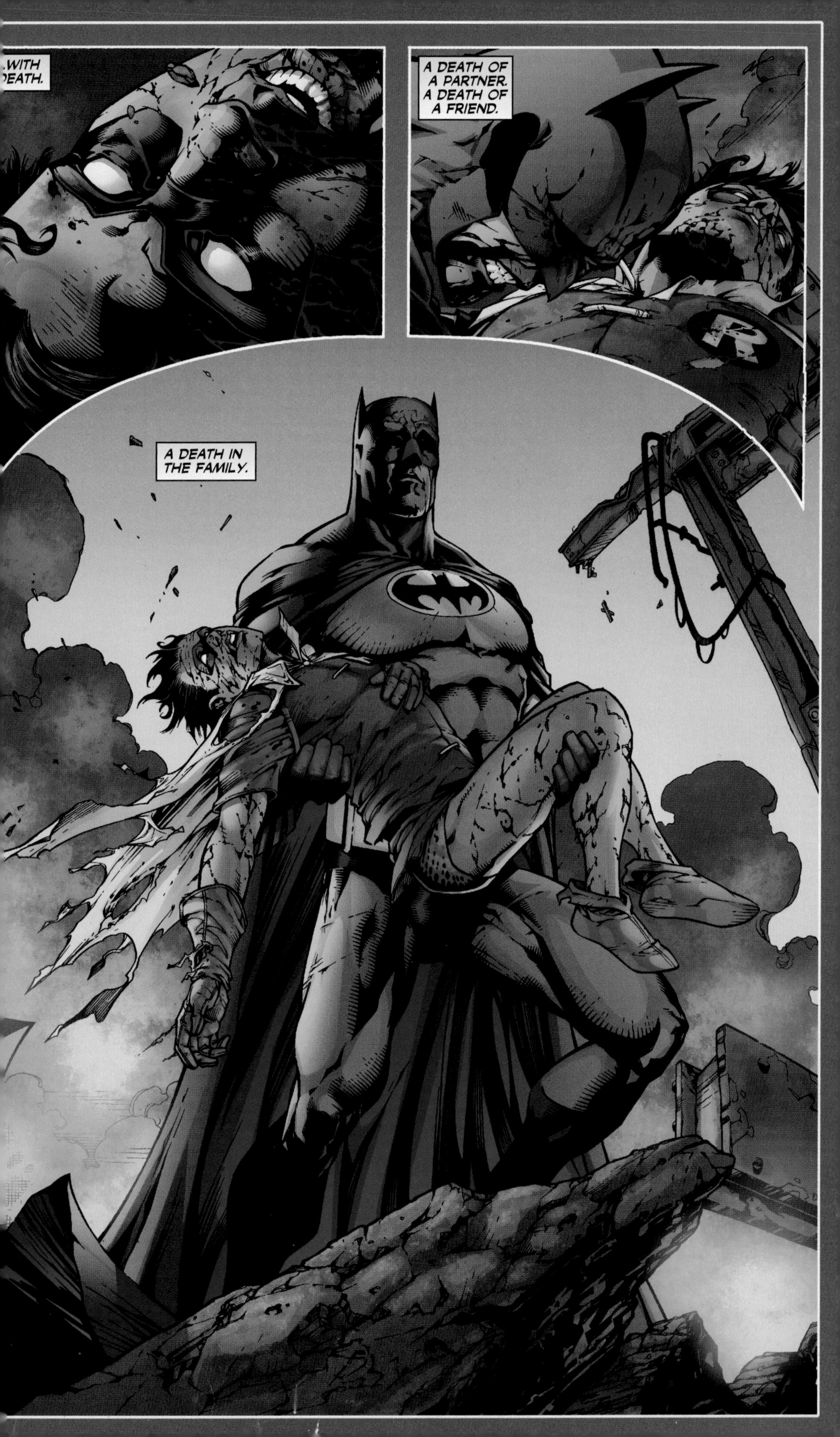
...WITH DEATH.
A DEATH OF A PARTNER. A DEATH OF A FRIEND.
A DEATH IN THE FAMILY.

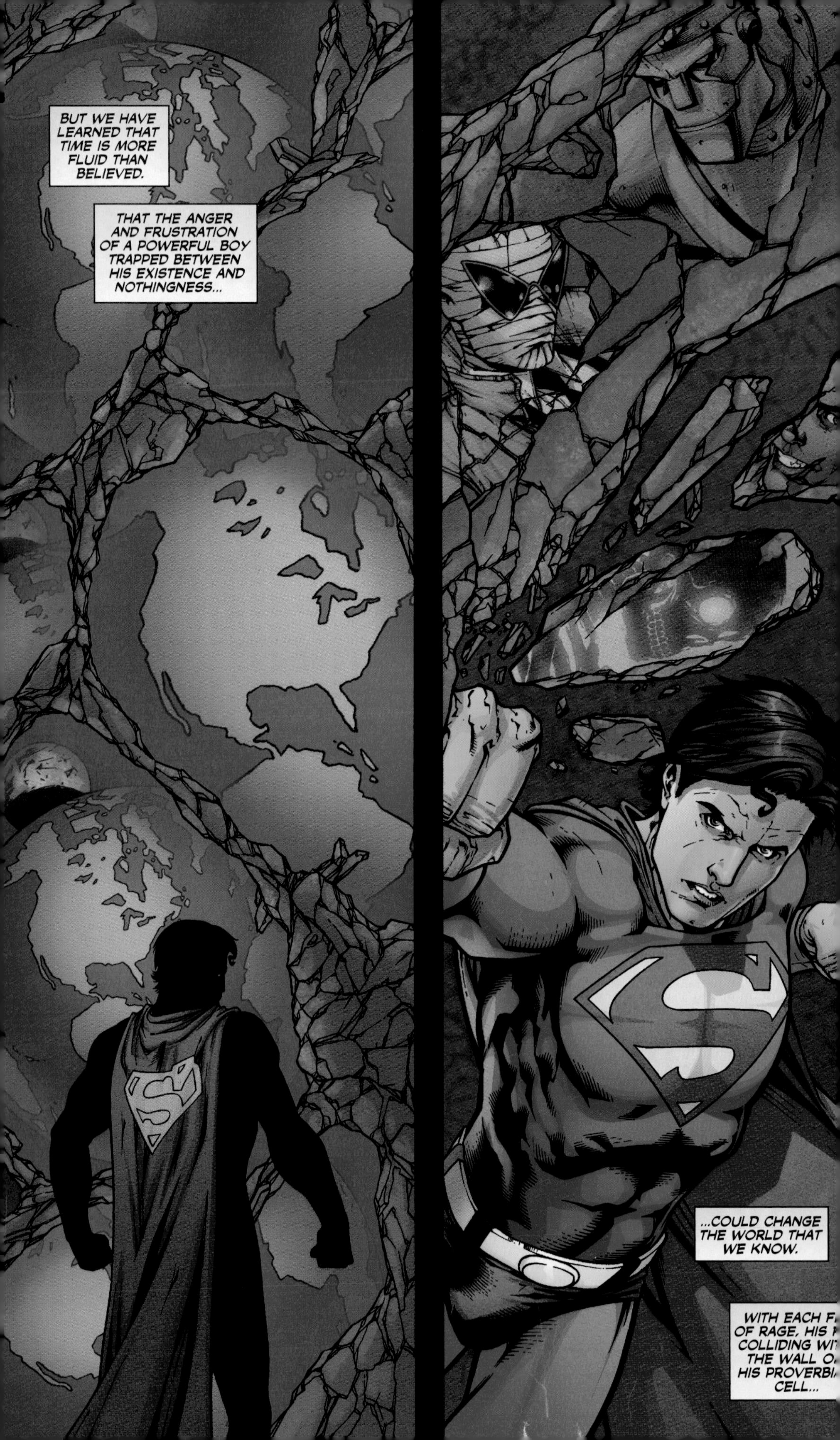
BUT WE HAVE LEARNED THAT TIME IS MORE FLUID THAN BELIEVED.
THAT THE ANGER AND FRUSTRATION OF A POWERFUL BOY TRAPPED BETWEEN HIS EXISTENCE AND NOTHINGNESS...
...COULD CHANGE THE WORLD THAT WE KNOW.
WITH EACH F
OF RAGE, HIS
COLLIDING WIT
THE WALL O
HIS PROVERBI
CELL...

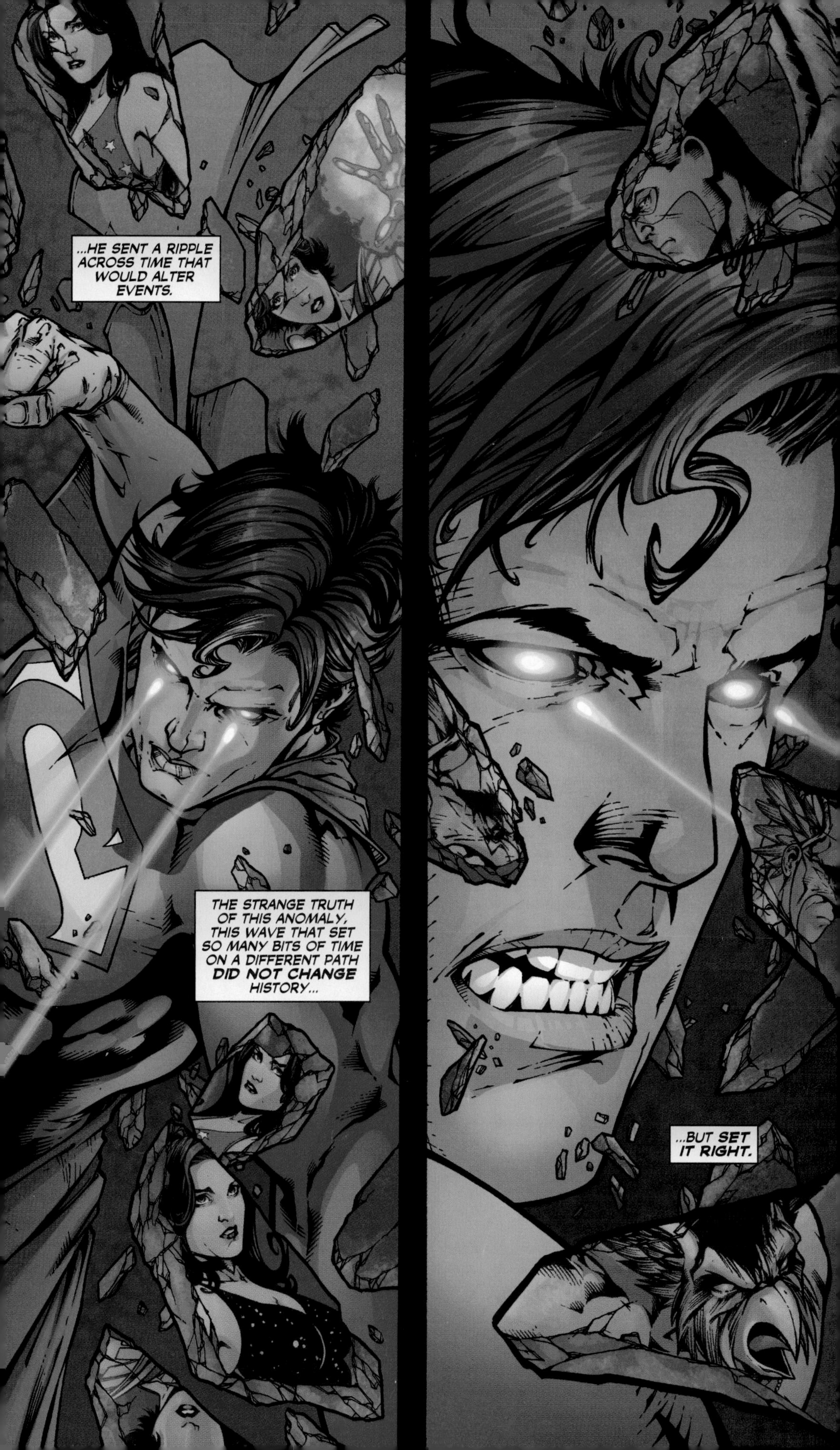
...HE SENT A RIPPLE ACROSS TIME THAT WOULD ALTER EVENTS.
THE STRANGE TRUTH OF THIS ANOMALY, THIS WAVE THAT SET SO MANY BITS OF TIME ON A DIFFERENT PATH **DID NOT CHANGE** HISTORY...
...BUT **SET IT RIGHT.**

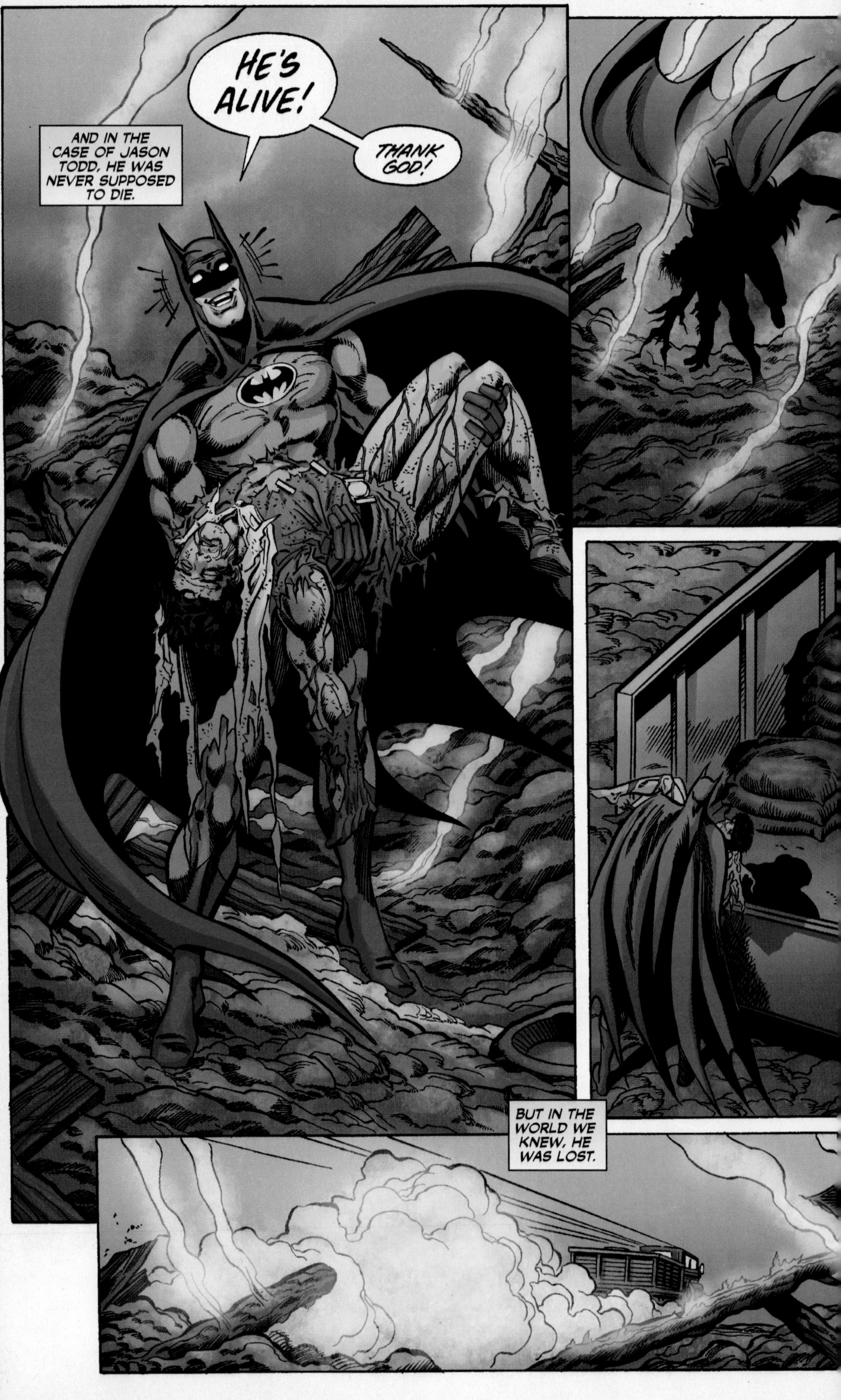
AND IN THE CASE OF JASON TODD, HE WAS NEVER SUPPOSED TO DIE.
HE'S ALIVE!
THANK GOD!
BUT IN THE WORLD WE KNEW, HE WAS LOST.

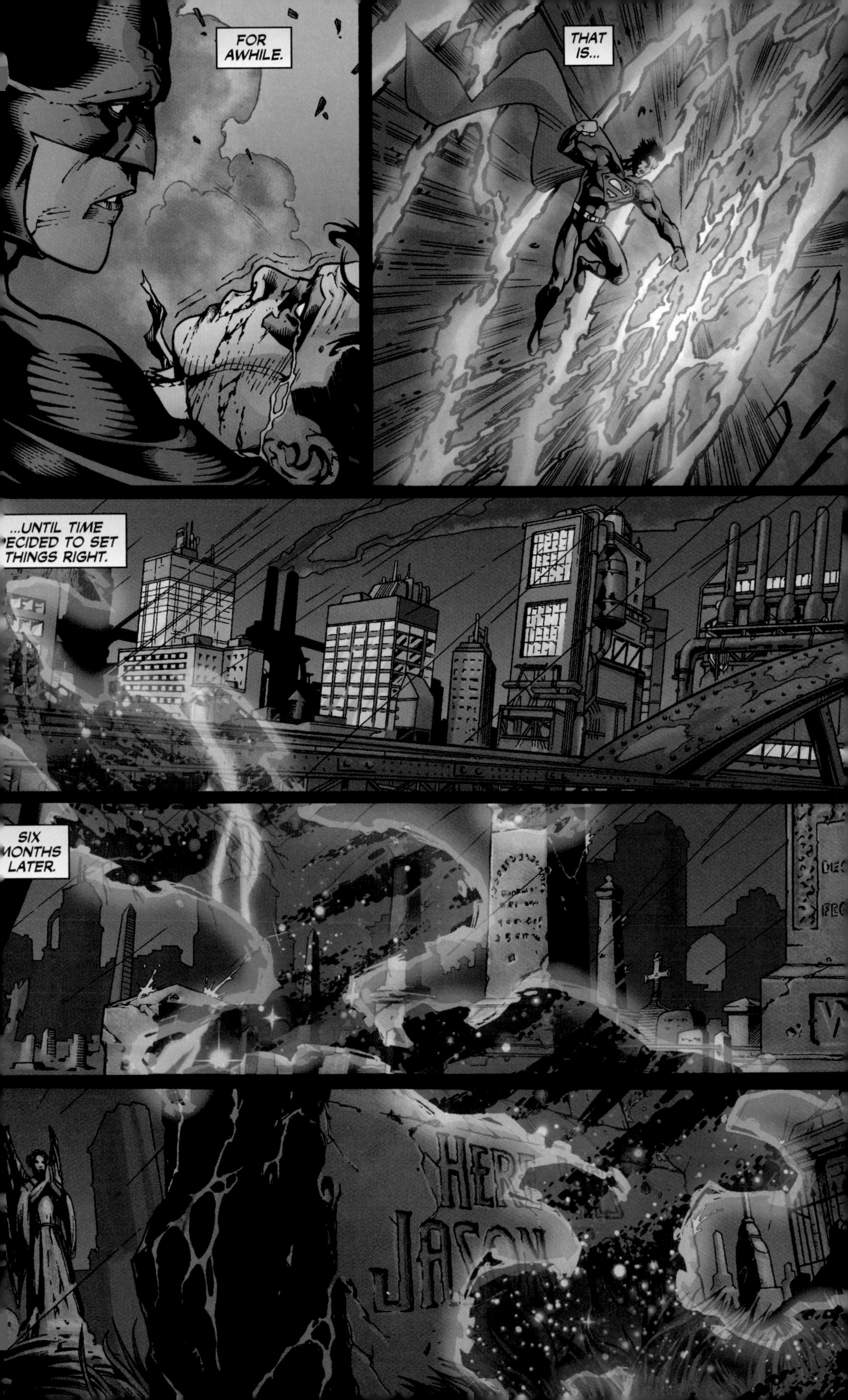
FOR AWHILE.
THAT IS...
...UNTIL TIME ECIDED TO SET THINGS RIGHT.
SIX MONTHS LATER.
HERE
JASON

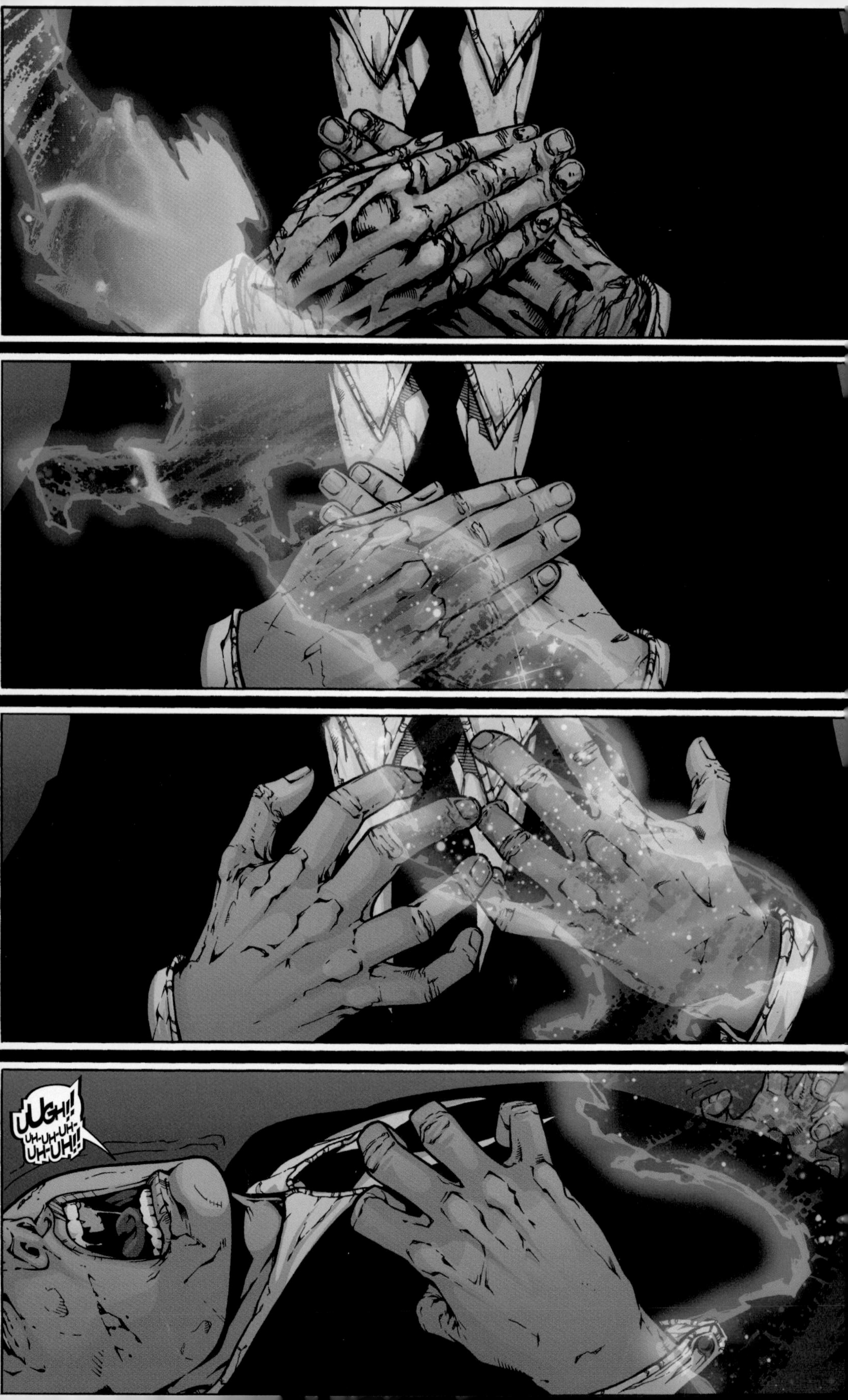
UGH!! UH-UH-UH-UH-UH!!

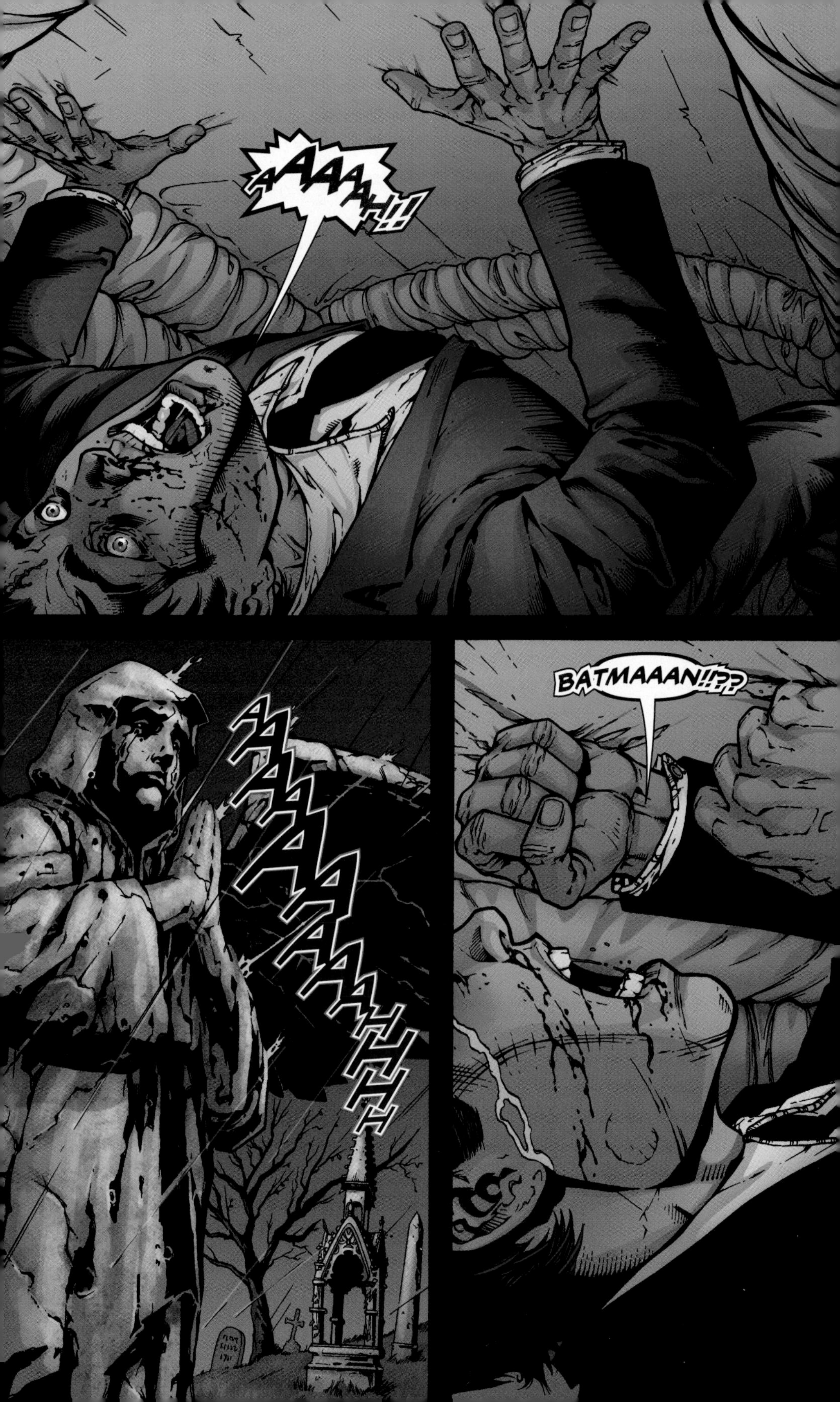
AAAAAH!!
AAAAAAAAAHHHH
BATMAAAN!!??

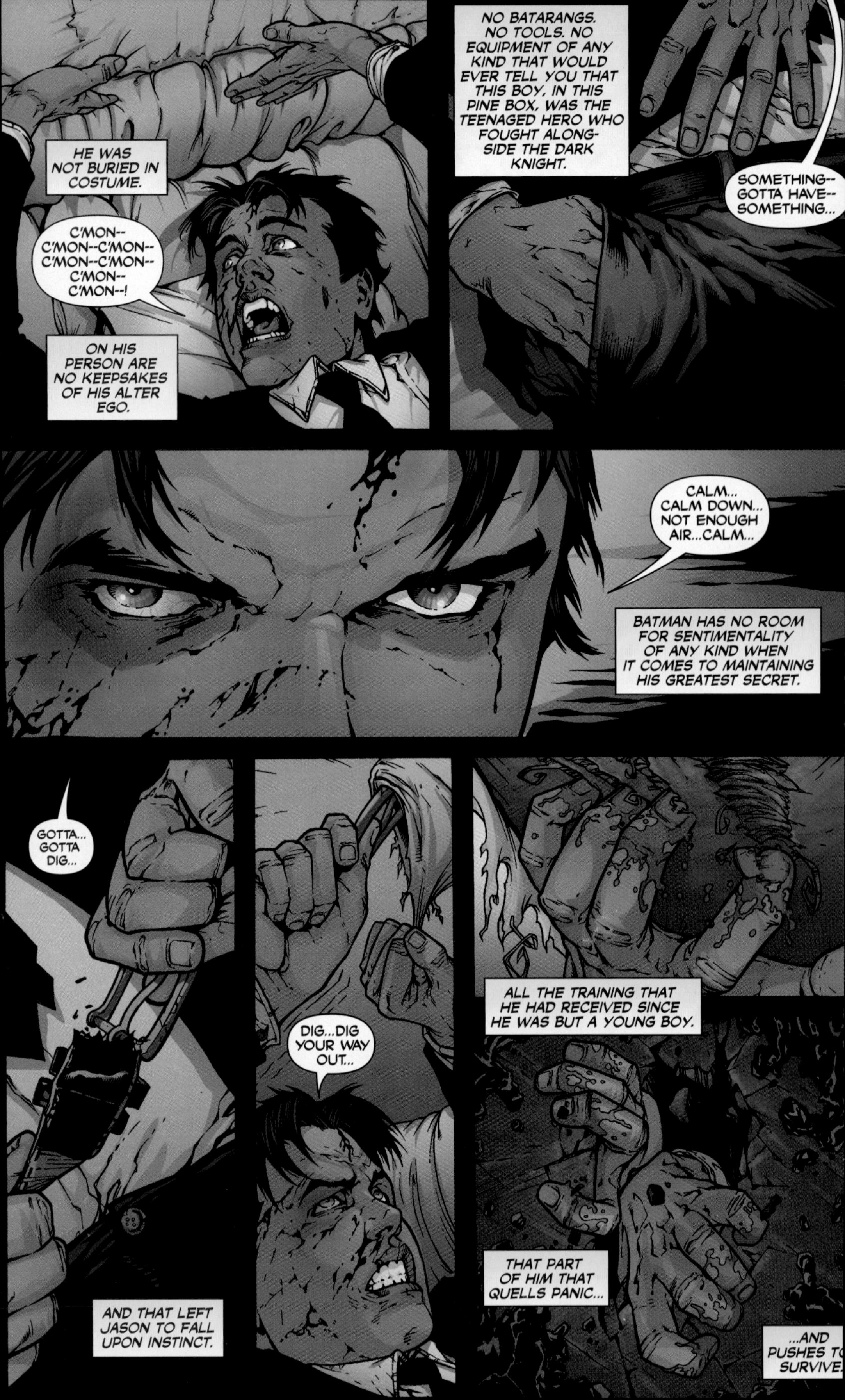

HE WAS NOT BURIED IN COSTUME.
C'MON-- C'MON--C'MON-- C'MON--C'MON-- C'MON-- C'MON--!
ON HIS PERSON ARE NO KEEPSAKES OF HIS ALTER EGO.
NO BATARANGS. NO TOOLS. NO EQUIPMENT OF ANY KIND THAT WOULD EVER TELL YOU THAT THIS BOY, IN THIS PINE BOX, WAS THE TEENAGED HERO WHO FOUGHT ALONG-SIDE THE DARK KNIGHT.
SOMETHING-- GOTTA HAVE-- SOMETHING...
CALM... CALM DOWN... NOT ENOUGH AIR...CALM...
BATMAN HAS NO ROOM FOR SENTIMENTALITY OF ANY KIND WHEN IT COMES TO MAINTAINING HIS GREATEST SECRET.
GOTTA... GOTTA DIG...
AND THAT LEFT JASON TO FALL UPON INSTINCT.
DIG...DIG YOUR WAY OUT...
ALL THE TRAINING THAT HE HAD RECEIVED SINCE HE WAS BUT A YOUNG BOY.
THAT PART OF HIM THAT QUELLS PANIC...
...AND PUSHES TO SURVIVE.

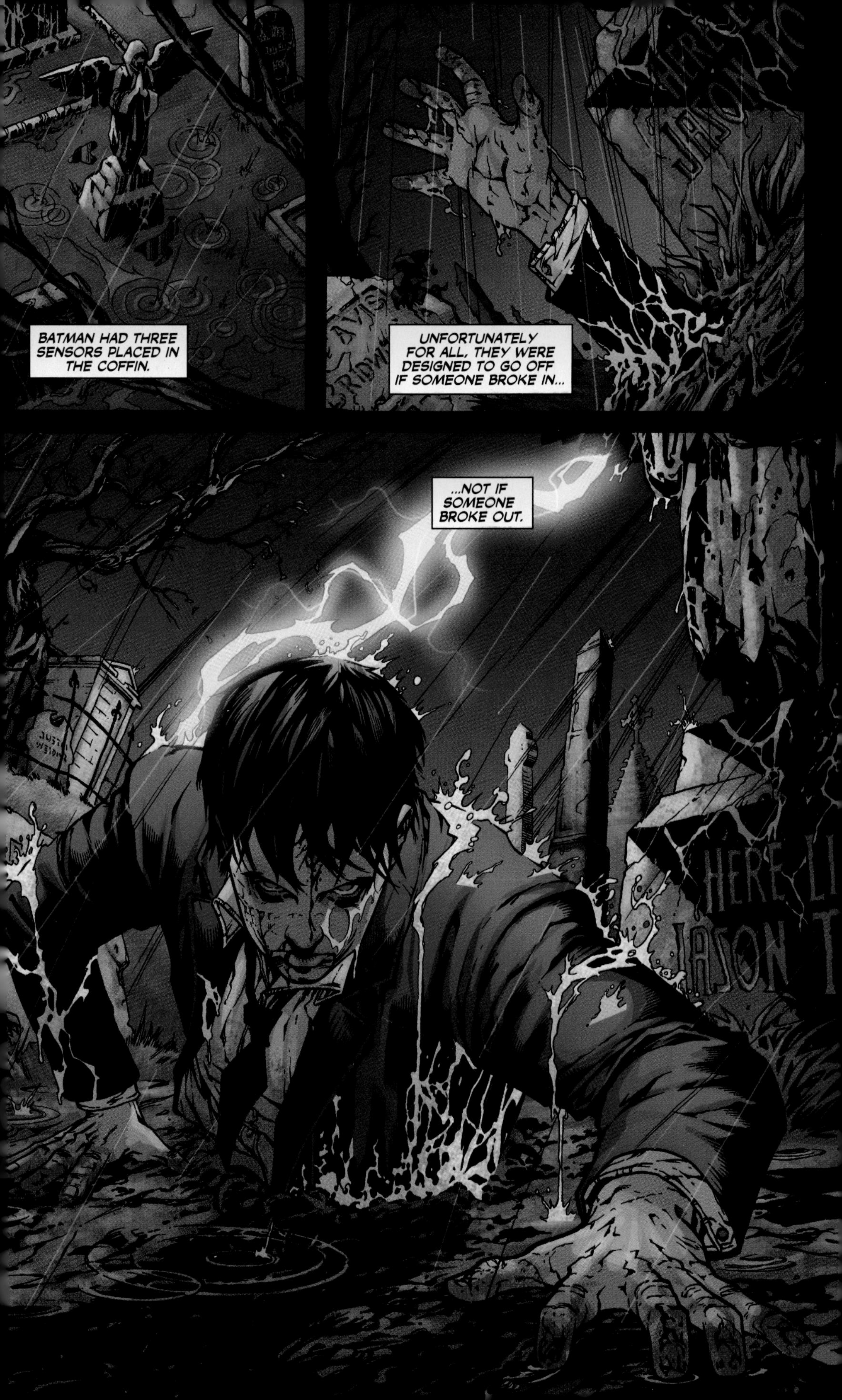
BATMAN HAD THREE SENSORS PLACED IN THE COFFIN.
UNFORTUNATELY FOR ALL, THEY WERE DESIGNED TO GO OFF IF SOMEONE BROKE IN...
...NOT IF SOMEONE BROKE OUT.

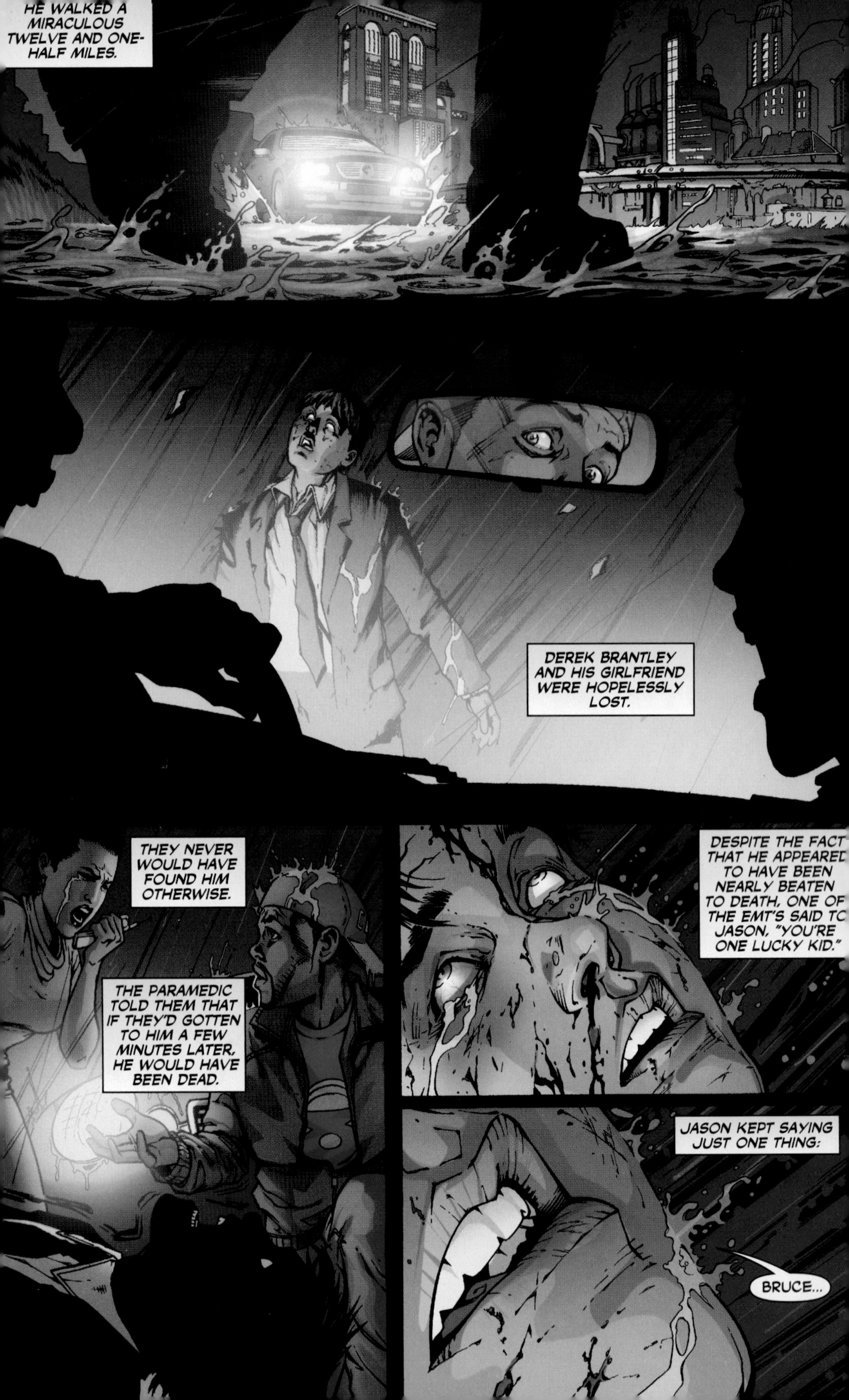
HE WALKED A MIRACULOUS TWELVE AND ONE-HALF MILES.
DEREK BRANTLEY AND HIS GIRLFRIEND WERE HOPELESSLY LOST.
THEY NEVER WOULD HAVE FOUND HIM OTHERWISE.
THE PARAMEDIC TOLD THEM THAT IF THEY'D GOTTEN TO HIM A FEW MINUTES LATER, HE WOULD HAVE BEEN DEAD.
DESPITE THE FACT THAT HE APPEARED TO HAVE BEEN NEARLY BEATEN TO DEATH, ONE OF THE EMT'S SAID TO JASON, "YOU'RE ONE LUCKY KID."
JASON KEPT SAYING JUST ONE THING:
BRUCE...

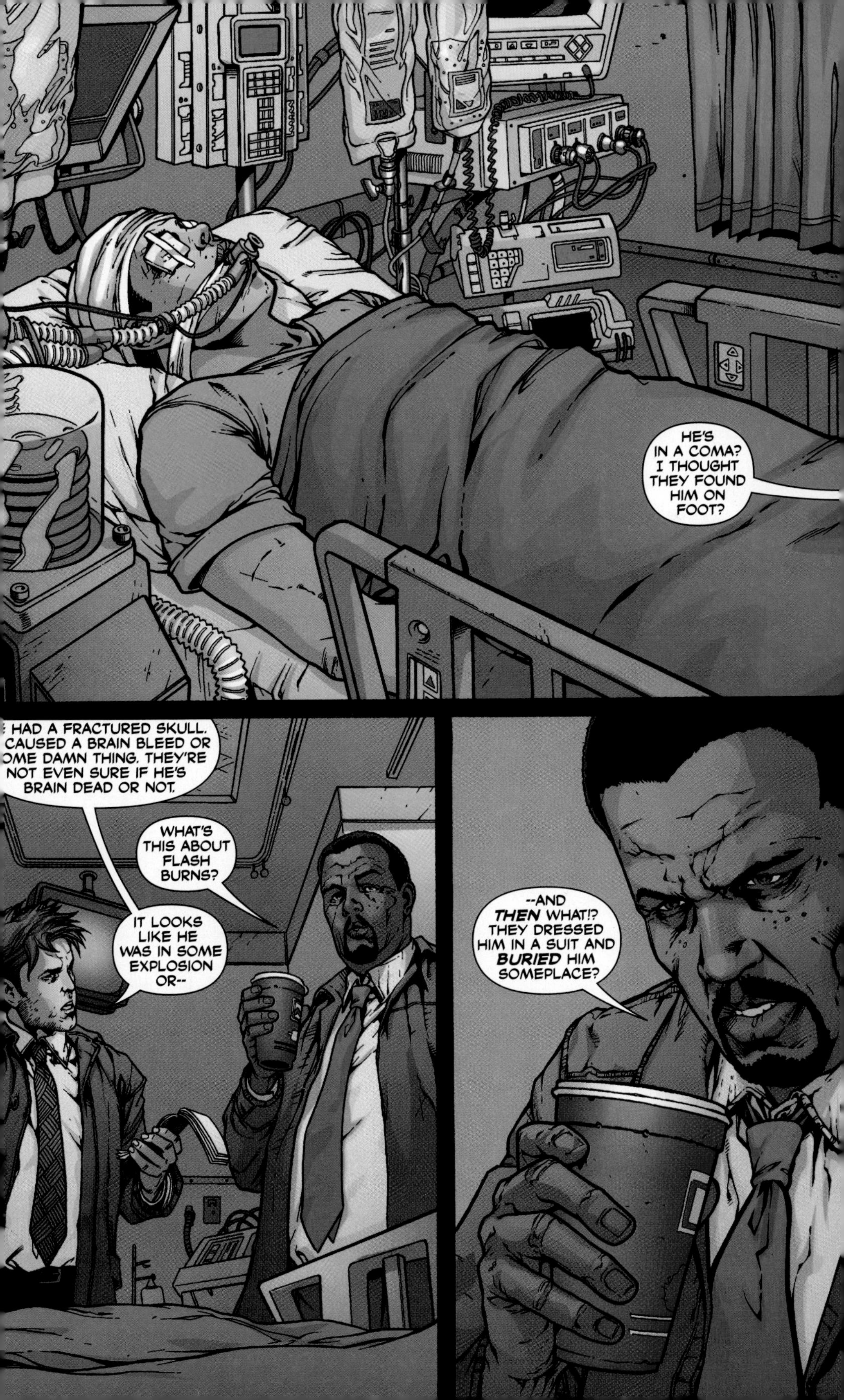
HE'S IN A COMA? I THOUGHT THEY FOUND HIM ON FOOT?
HAD A FRACTURED SKULL. CAUSED A BRAIN BLEED OR OME DAMN THING. THEY'RE NOT EVEN SURE IF HE'S BRAIN DEAD OR NOT.
WHAT'S THIS ABOUT FLASH BURNS?
IT LOOKS LIKE HE WAS IN SOME EXPLOSION OR--
--AND THEN WHAT!? THEY DRESSED HIM IN A SUIT AND BURIED HIM SOMEPLACE?

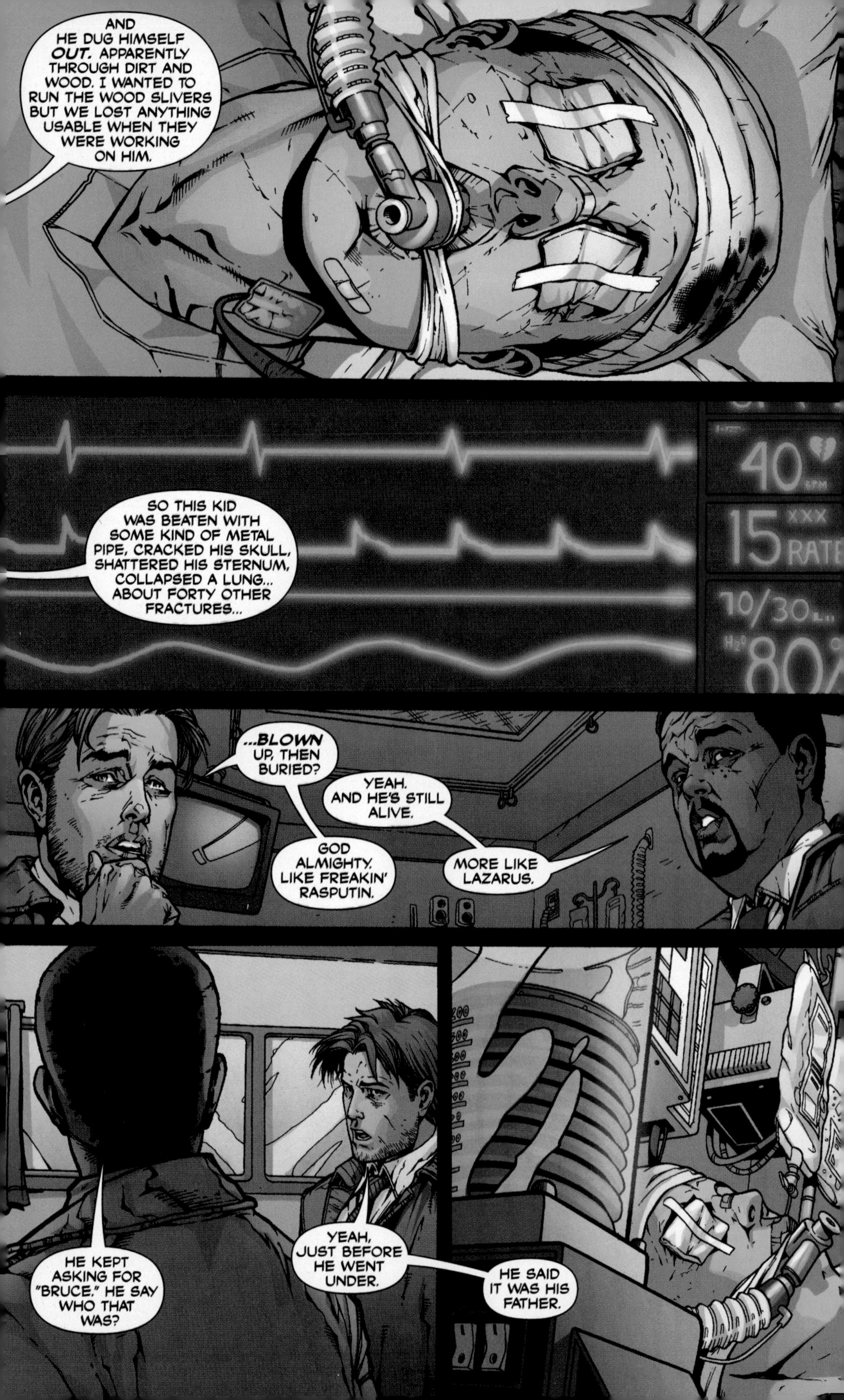
AND HE DUG HIMSELF OUT. APPARENTLY THROUGH DIRT AND WOOD. I WANTED TO RUN THE WOOD SLIVERS BUT WE LOST ANYTHING USABLE WHEN THEY WERE WORKING ON HIM.
40
15 RATE
70/30
H_2O 80
SO THIS KID WAS BEATEN WITH SOME KIND OF METAL PIPE, CRACKED HIS SKULL, SHATTERED HIS STERNUM, COLLAPSED A LUNG... ABOUT FORTY OTHER FRACTURES...
...BLOWN UP, THEN BURIED?
YEAH. AND HE'S STILL ALIVE.
GOD ALMIGHTY. LIKE FREAKIN' RASPUTIN.
MORE LIKE LAZARUS.
HE KEPT ASKING FOR "BRUCE." HE SAY WHO THAT WAS?
YEAH, JUST BEFORE HE WENT UNDER.
HE SAID IT WAS HIS FATHER.

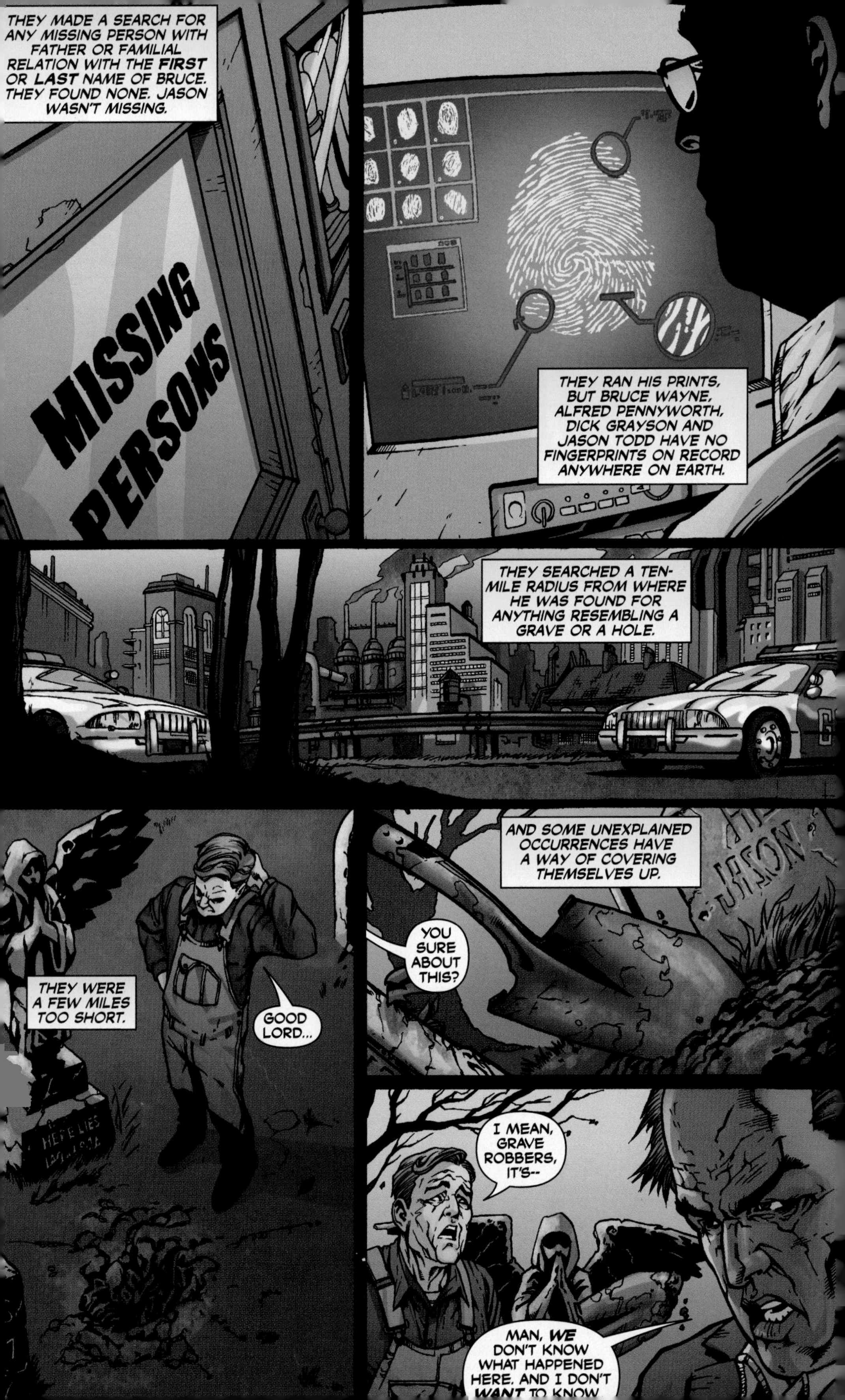
THEY MADE A SEARCH FOR ANY MISSING PERSON WITH FATHER OR FAMILIAL RELATION WITH THE FIRST OR LAST NAME OF BRUCE. THEY FOUND NONE. JASON WASN'T MISSING.
MISSING PERSONS
THEY RAN HIS PRINTS, BUT BRUCE WAYNE, ALFRED PENNYWORTH, DICK GRAYSON AND JASON TODD HAVE NO FINGERPRINTS ON RECORD ANYWHERE ON EARTH.
THEY SEARCHED A TEN-MILE RADIUS FROM WHERE HE WAS FOUND FOR ANYTHING RESEMBLING A GRAVE OR A HOLE.
THEY WERE A FEW MILES TOO SHORT.
GOOD LORD...
AND SOME UNEXPLAINED OCCURRENCES HAVE A WAY OF COVERING THEMSELVES UP.
JASON
YOU SURE ABOUT THIS?
I MEAN, GRAVE ROBBERS, IT'S--
MAN, WE DON'T KNOW WHAT HAPPENED HERE. AND I DON'T WANT TO KNOW.

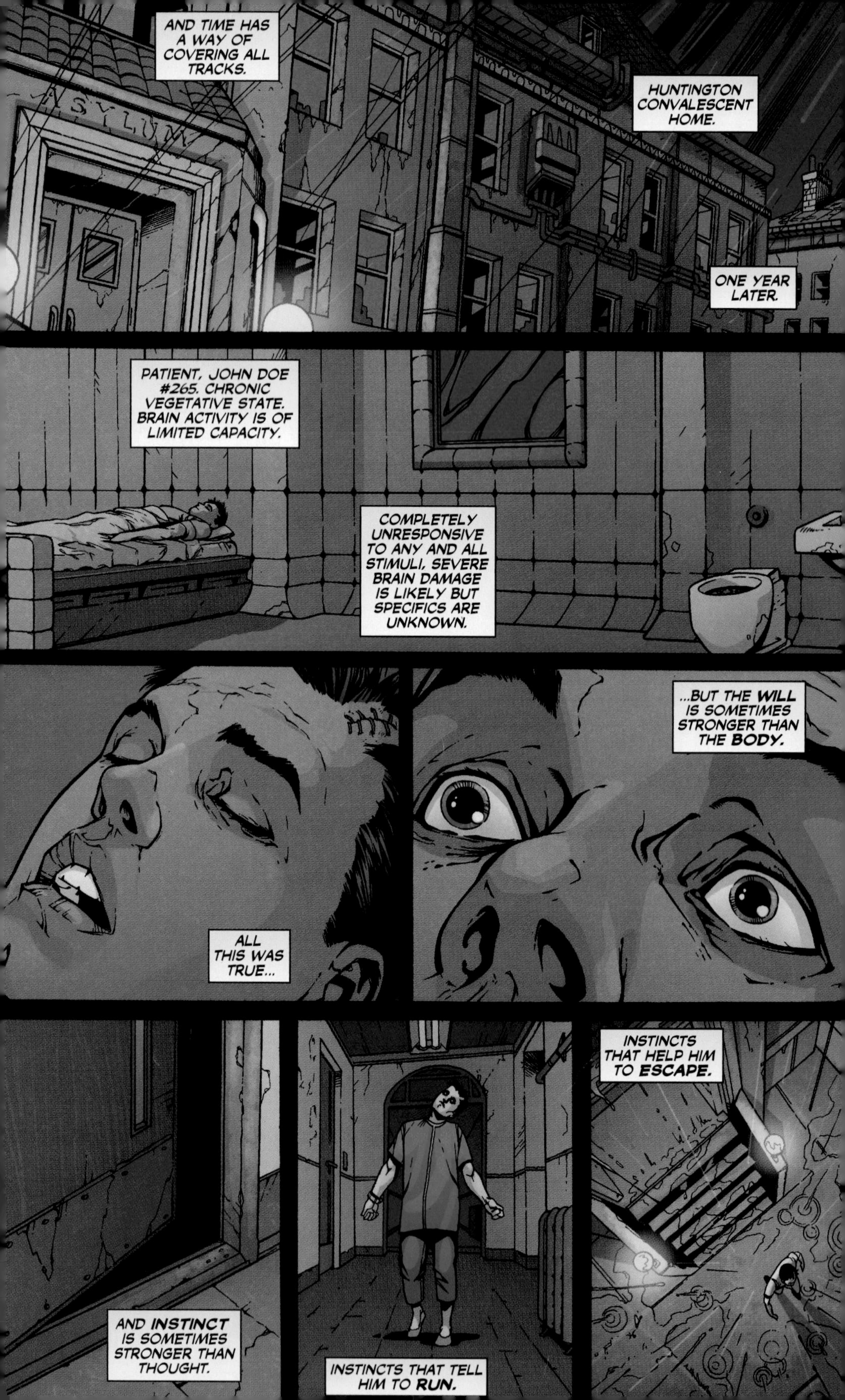
AND TIME HAS A WAY OF COVERING ALL TRACKS.
HUNTINGTON CONVALESCENT HOME.
ONE YEAR LATER.
PATIENT, JOHN DOE #265. CHRONIC VEGETATIVE STATE. BRAIN ACTIVITY IS OF LIMITED CAPACITY.
COMPLETELY UNRESPONSIVE TO ANY AND ALL STIMULI, SEVERE BRAIN DAMAGE IS LIKELY BUT SPECIFICS ARE UNKNOWN.
ALL THIS WAS TRUE...
...BUT THE WILL IS SOMETIMES STRONGER THAN THE BODY.
AND INSTINCT IS SOMETIMES STRONGER THAN THOUGHT.
INSTINCTS THAT TELL HIM TO RUN.
INSTINCTS THAT HELP HIM TO ESCAPE.

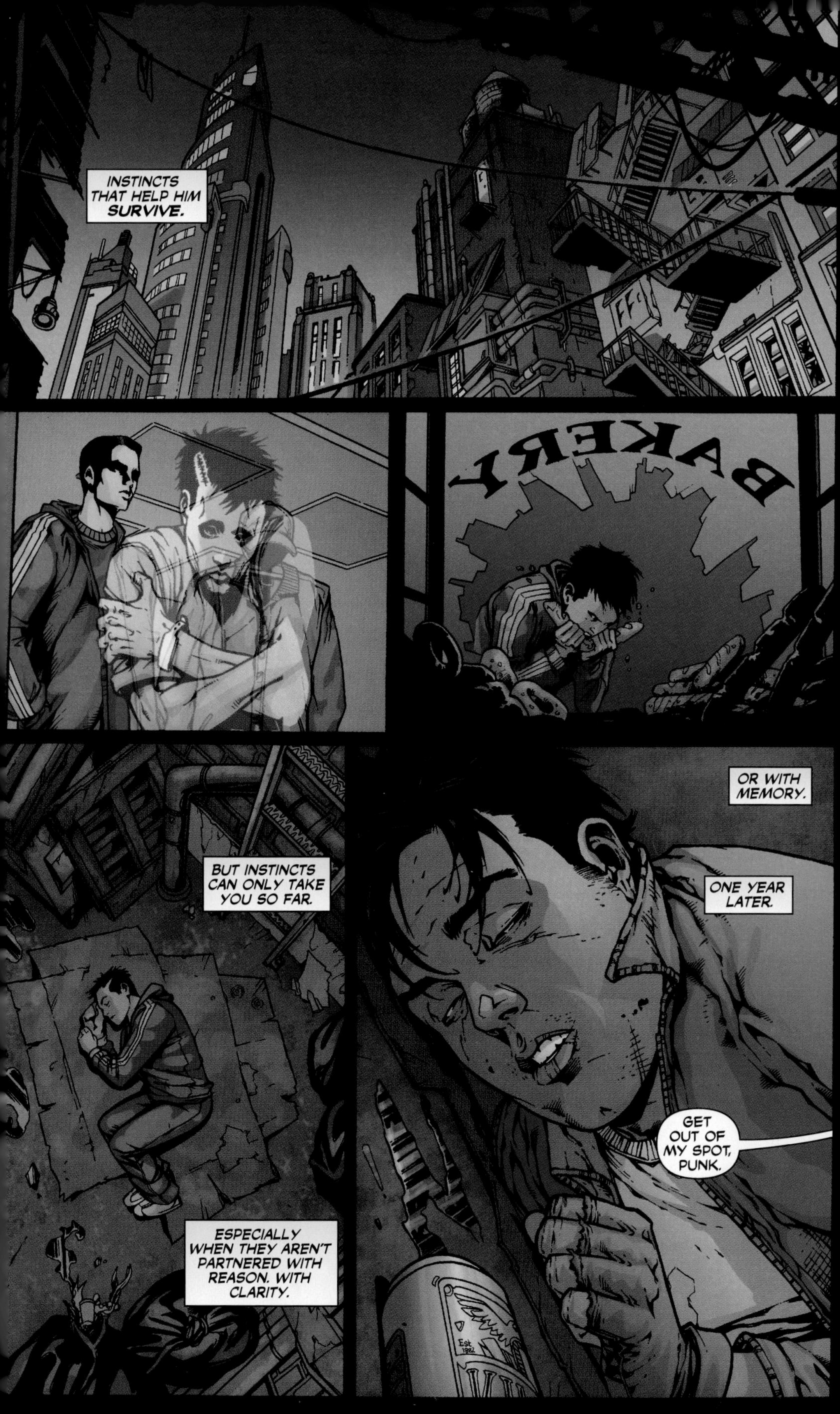
INSTINCTS THAT HELP HIM **SURVIVE.**
BAKERY
BUT INSTINCTS CAN ONLY TAKE YOU SO FAR.
ESPECIALLY WHEN THEY AREN'T PARTNERED WITH REASON. WITH CLARITY.
OR WITH MEMORY.
ONE YEAR LATER.
GET OUT OF MY SPOT, PUNK.

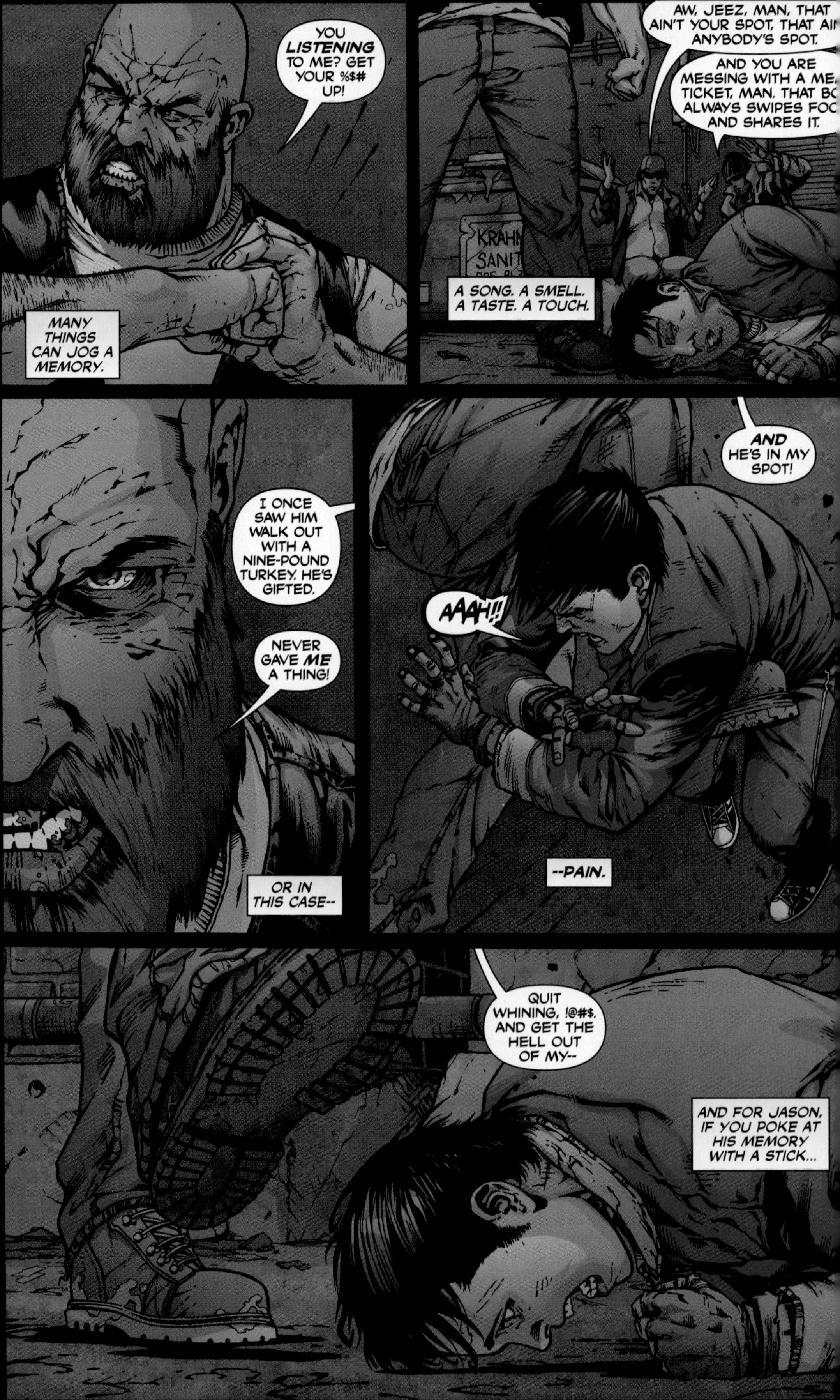
YOU LISTENING TO ME? GET YOUR %$# UP!
MANY THINGS CAN JOG A MEMORY.
AW, JEEZ, MAN, THAT AIN'T YOUR SPOT, THAT AI ANYBODY'S SPOT.
AND YOU ARE MESSING WITH A ME TICKET, MAN. THAT BO ALWAYS SWIPES FOO AND SHARES IT.
KRAHN SANIT
A SONG. A SMELL. A TASTE. A TOUCH.
I ONCE SAW HIM WALK OUT WITH A NINE-POUND TURKEY. HE'S GIFTED.
NEVER GAVE ME A THING!
OR IN THIS CASE--
AND HE'S IN MY SPOT!
AAAH!!
--PAIN.
QUIT WHINING, !@#$. AND GET THE HELL OUT OF MY--
AND FOR JASON, IF YOU POKE AT HIS MEMORY WITH A STICK...

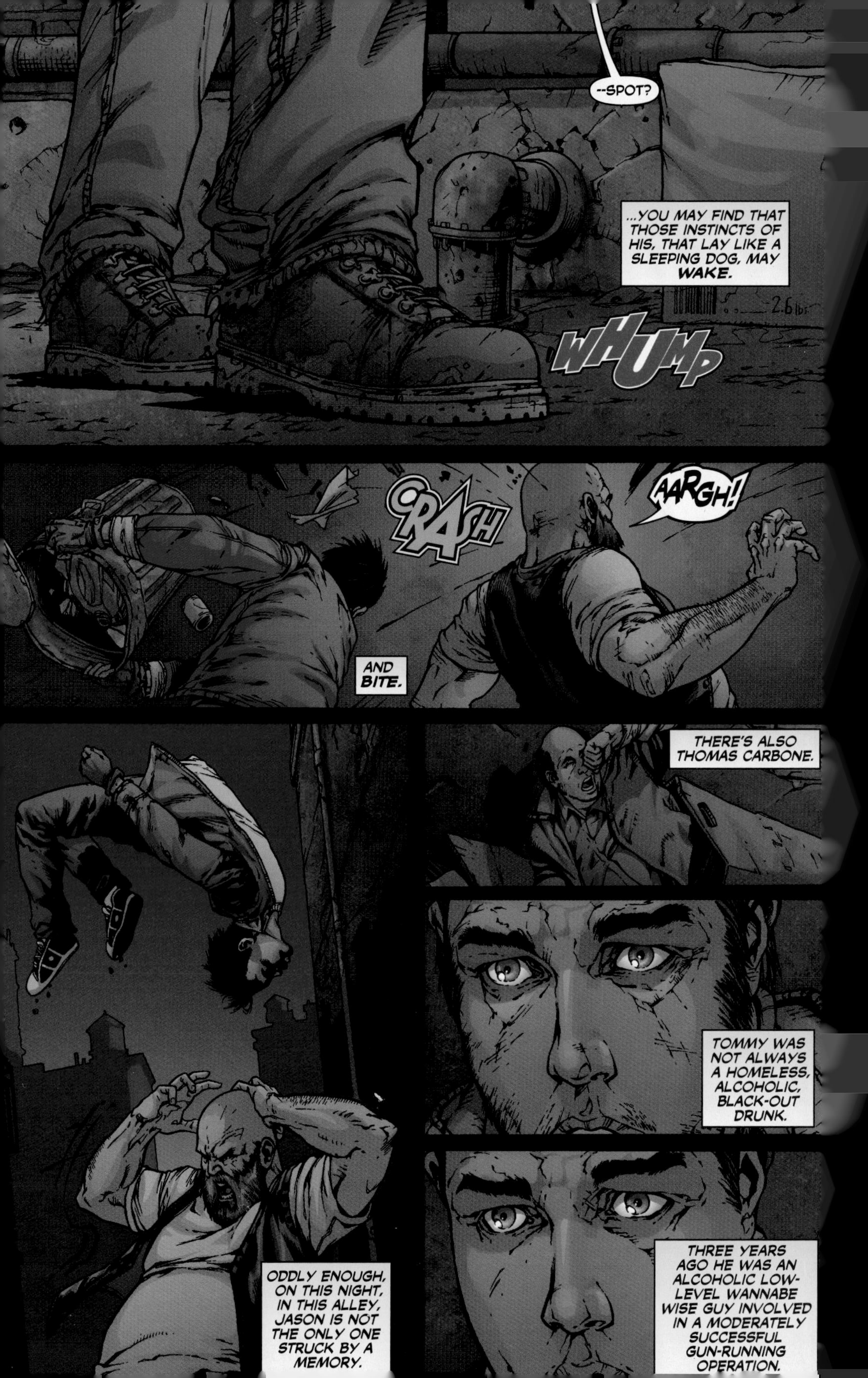
--SPOT?
...YOU MAY FIND THAT THOSE INSTINCTS OF HIS, THAT LAY LIKE A SLEEPING DOG, MAY WAKE.
2.6 lbs.
WHUMP
CRASH
AARGH!
AND BITE.
THERE'S ALSO THOMAS CARBONE.
TOMMY WAS NOT ALWAYS A HOMELESS, ALCOHOLIC, BLACK-OUT DRUNK.
ODDLY ENOUGH, ON THIS NIGHT, IN THIS ALLEY, JASON IS NOT THE ONLY ONE STRUCK BY A MEMORY.
THREE YEARS AGO HE WAS AN ALCOHOLIC LOW-LEVEL WANNABE WISE GUY INVOLVED IN A MODERATELY SUCCESSFUL GUN-RUNNING OPERATION.

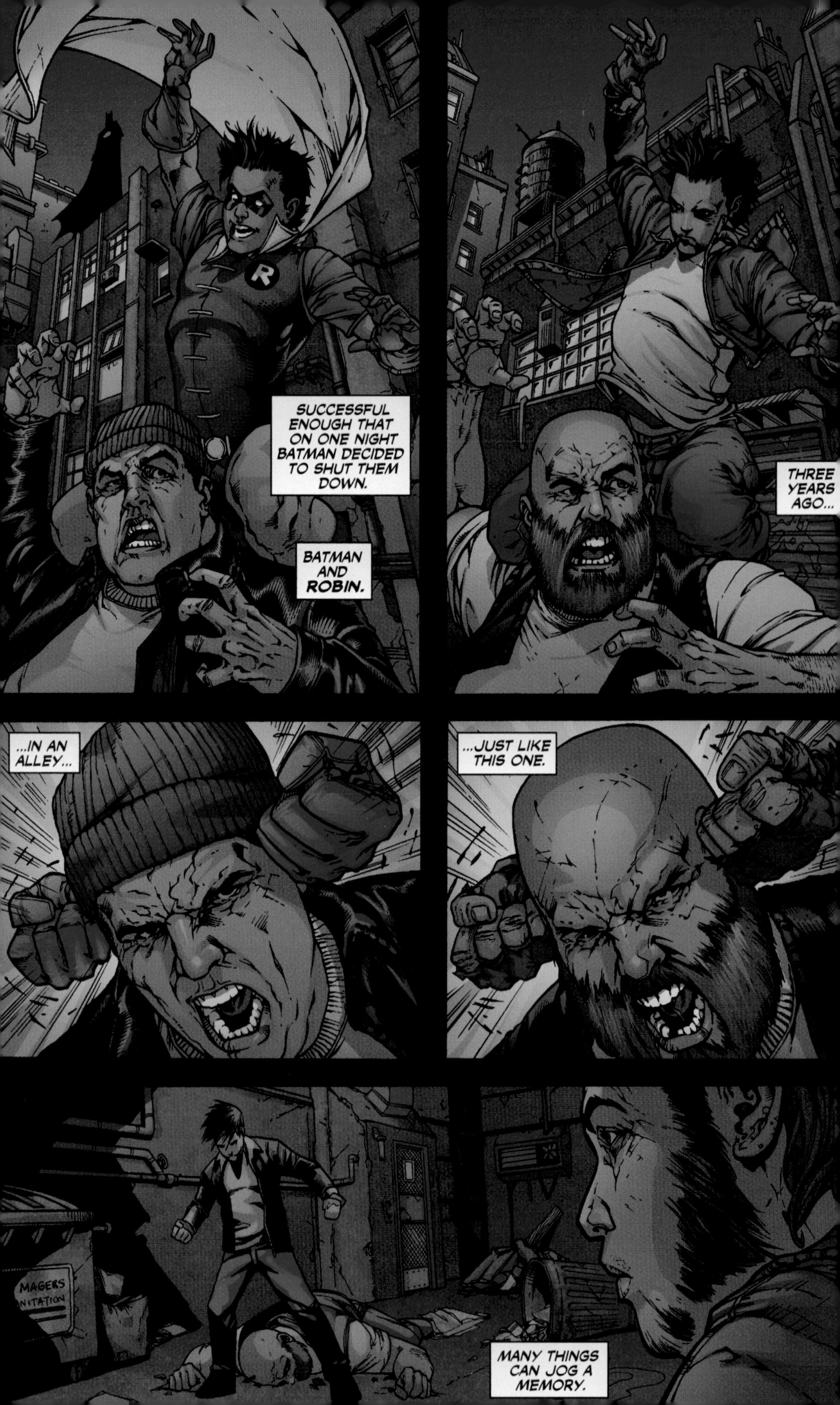
SUCCESSFUL ENOUGH THAT ON ONE NIGHT BATMAN DECIDED TO SHUT THEM DOWN.
BATMAN AND ROBIN.
THREE YEARS AGO...
...IN AN ALLEY...
...JUST LIKE THIS ONE.
MAGERS
NITATION
MANY THINGS CAN JOG A MEMORY.

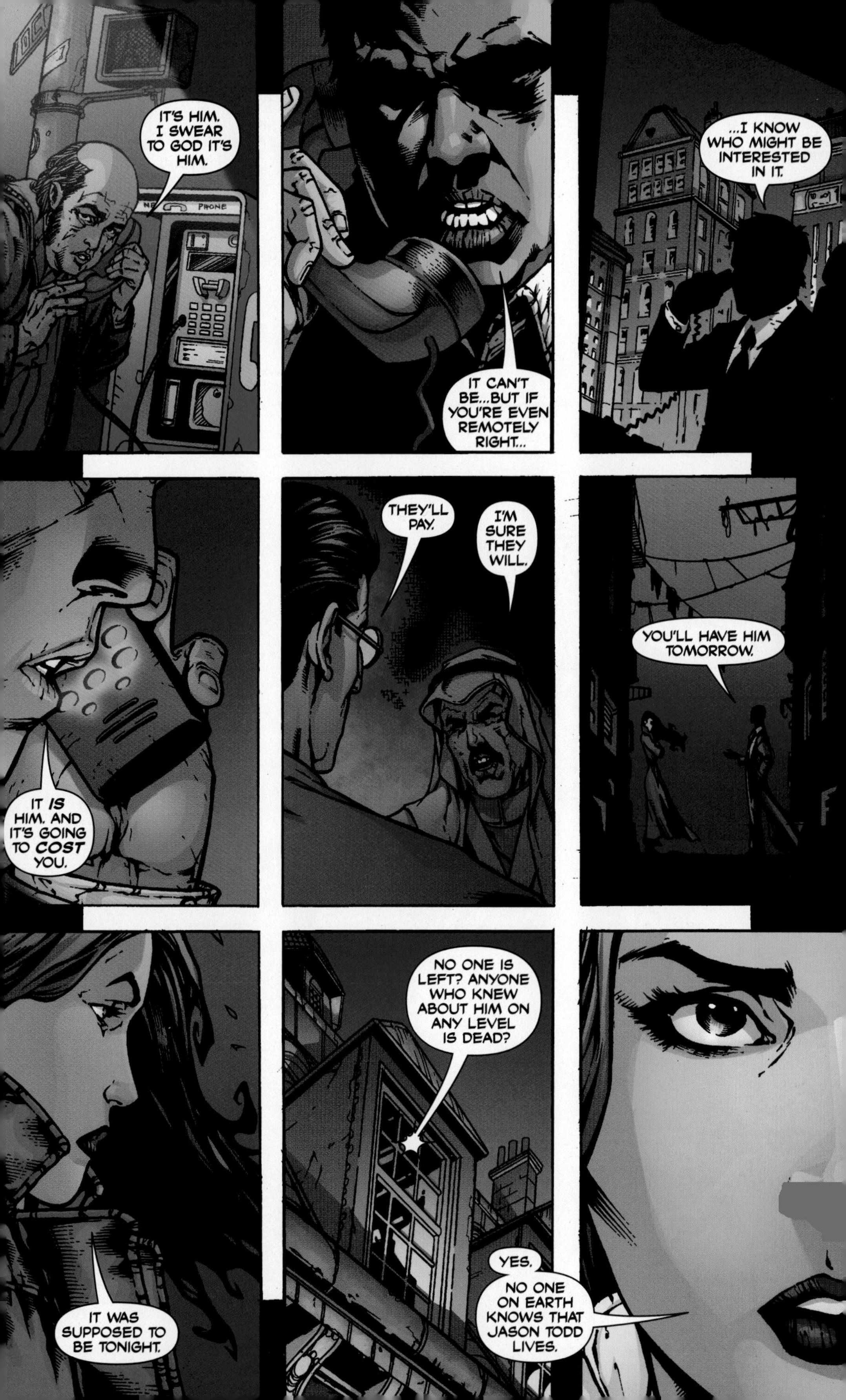
IT'S HIM. I SWEAR TO GOD IT'S HIM.
IT CAN'T BE...BUT IF YOU'RE EVEN REMOTELY RIGHT...
...I KNOW WHO MIGHT BE INTERESTED IN IT.
IT IS HIM. AND IT'S GOING TO COST YOU.
THEY'LL PAY.
I'M SURE THEY WILL.
YOU'LL HAVE HIM TOMORROW.
IT WAS SUPPOSED TO BE TONIGHT.
NO ONE IS LEFT? ANYONE WHO KNEW ABOUT HIM ON ANY LEVEL IS DEAD?
YES.
NO ONE ON EARTH KNOWS THAT JASON TODD LIVES.

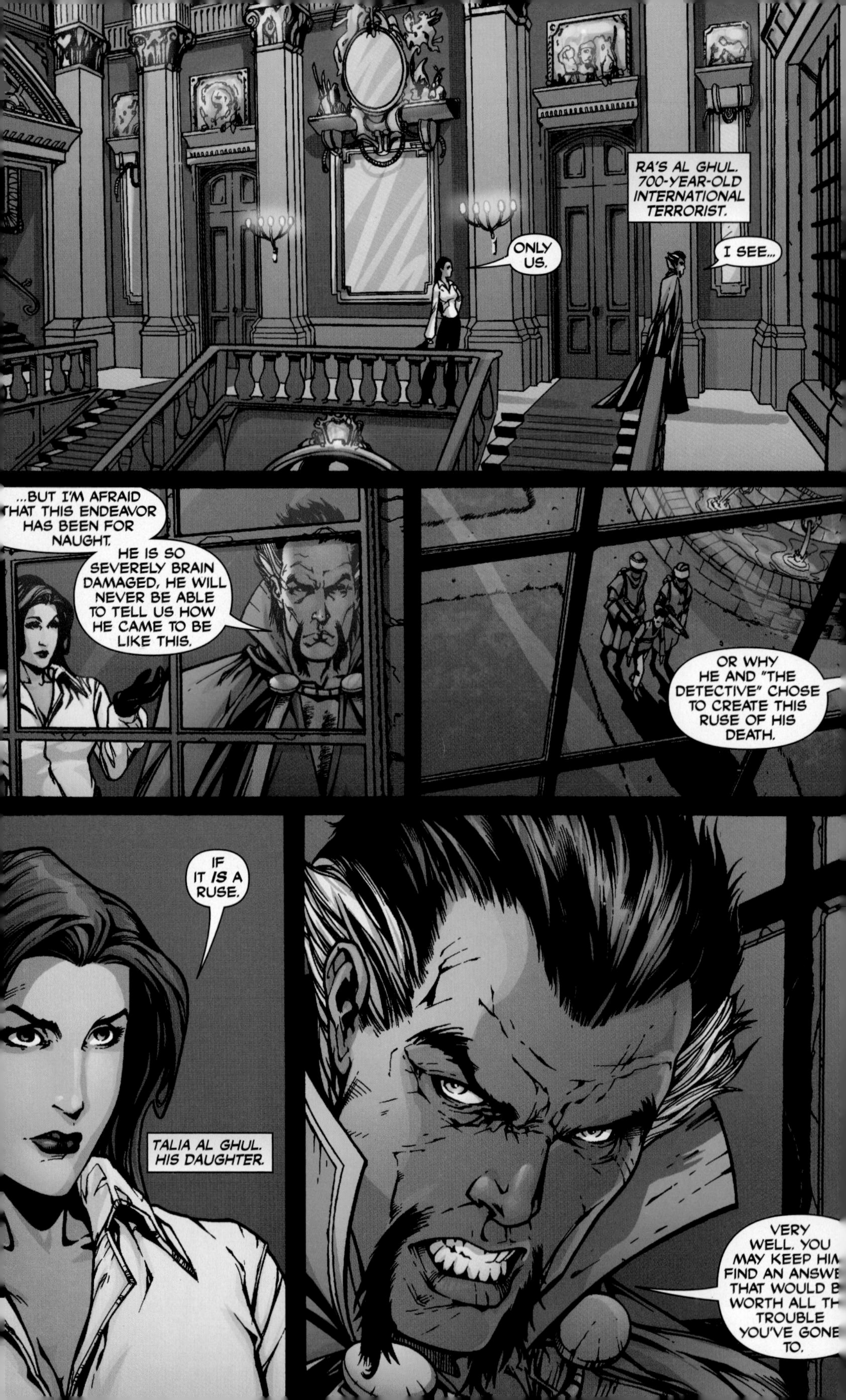
RA'S AL GHUL. 700-YEAR-OLD INTERNATIONAL TERRORIST.
ONLY US.
I SEE...
...BUT I'M AFRAID THAT THIS ENDEAVOR HAS BEEN FOR NAUGHT.
HE IS SO SEVERELY BRAIN DAMAGED, HE WILL NEVER BE ABLE TO TELL US HOW HE CAME TO BE LIKE THIS.
OR WHY HE AND "THE DETECTIVE" CHOSE TO CREATE THIS RUSE OF HIS DEATH.
IF IT *IS* A RUSE.
TALIA AL GHUL. HIS DAUGHTER.
VERY WELL. YOU MAY KEEP HIM
FIND AN ANSWE
THAT WOULD B
WORTH ALL TH
TROUBLE
YOU'VE GONE
TO.

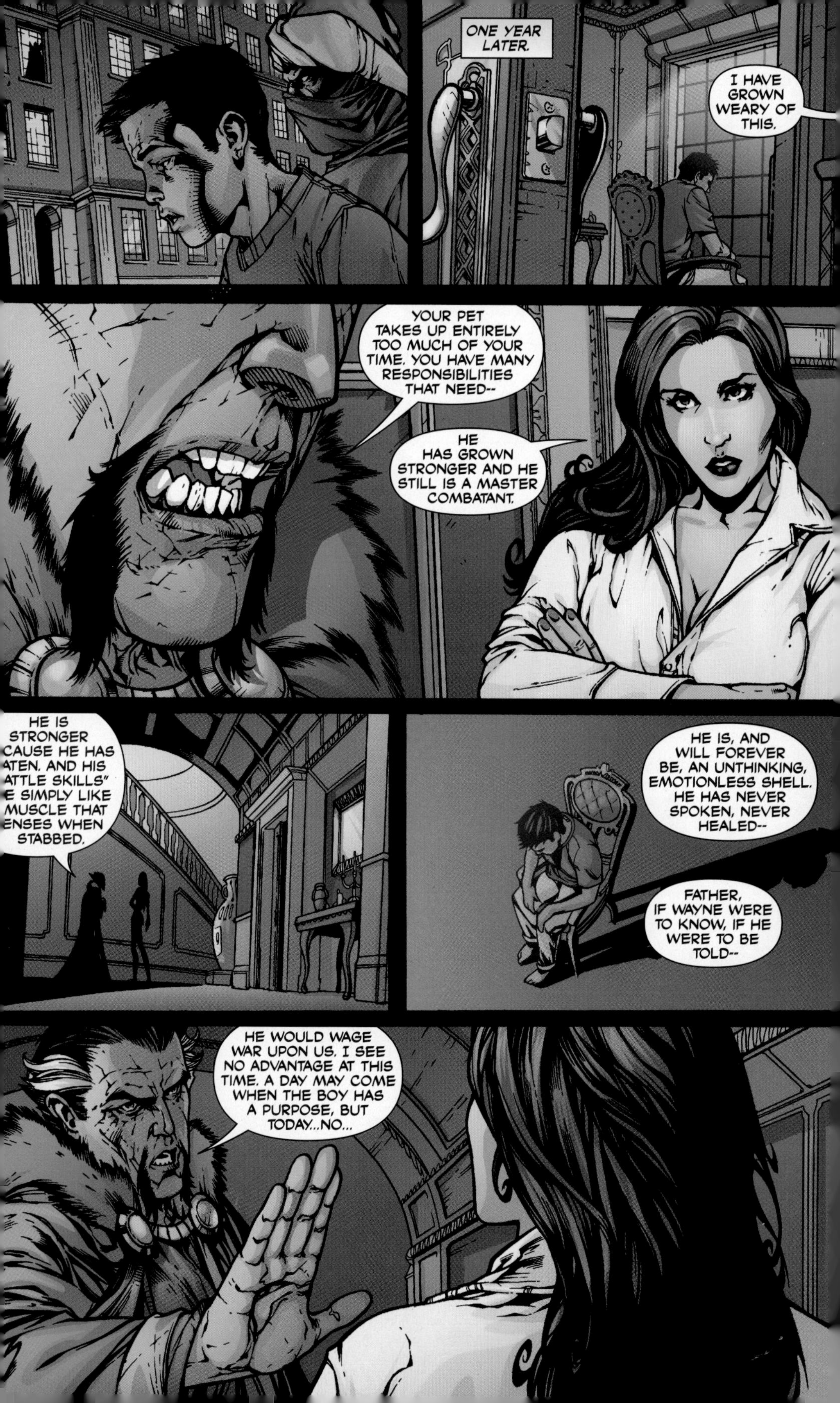

ONE YEAR LATER.
I HAVE GROWN WEARY OF THIS.
YOUR PET TAKES UP ENTIRELY TOO MUCH OF YOUR TIME. YOU HAVE MANY RESPONSIBILITIES THAT NEED--
HE HAS GROWN STRONGER AND HE STILL IS A MASTER COMBATANT.
HE IS STRONGER CAUSE HE HAS ATEN, AND HIS ATTLE SKILLS" E SIMPLY LIKE MUSCLE THAT ENSES WHEN STABBED.
HE IS, AND WILL FOREVER BE, AN UNTHINKING, EMOTIONLESS SHELL. HE HAS NEVER SPOKEN, NEVER HEALED--
FATHER, IF WAYNE WERE TO KNOW, IF HE WERE TO BE TOLD--
HE WOULD WAGE WAR UPON US. I SEE NO ADVANTAGE AT THIS TIME. A DAY MAY COME WHEN THE BOY HAS A PURPOSE, BUT TODAY...NO...

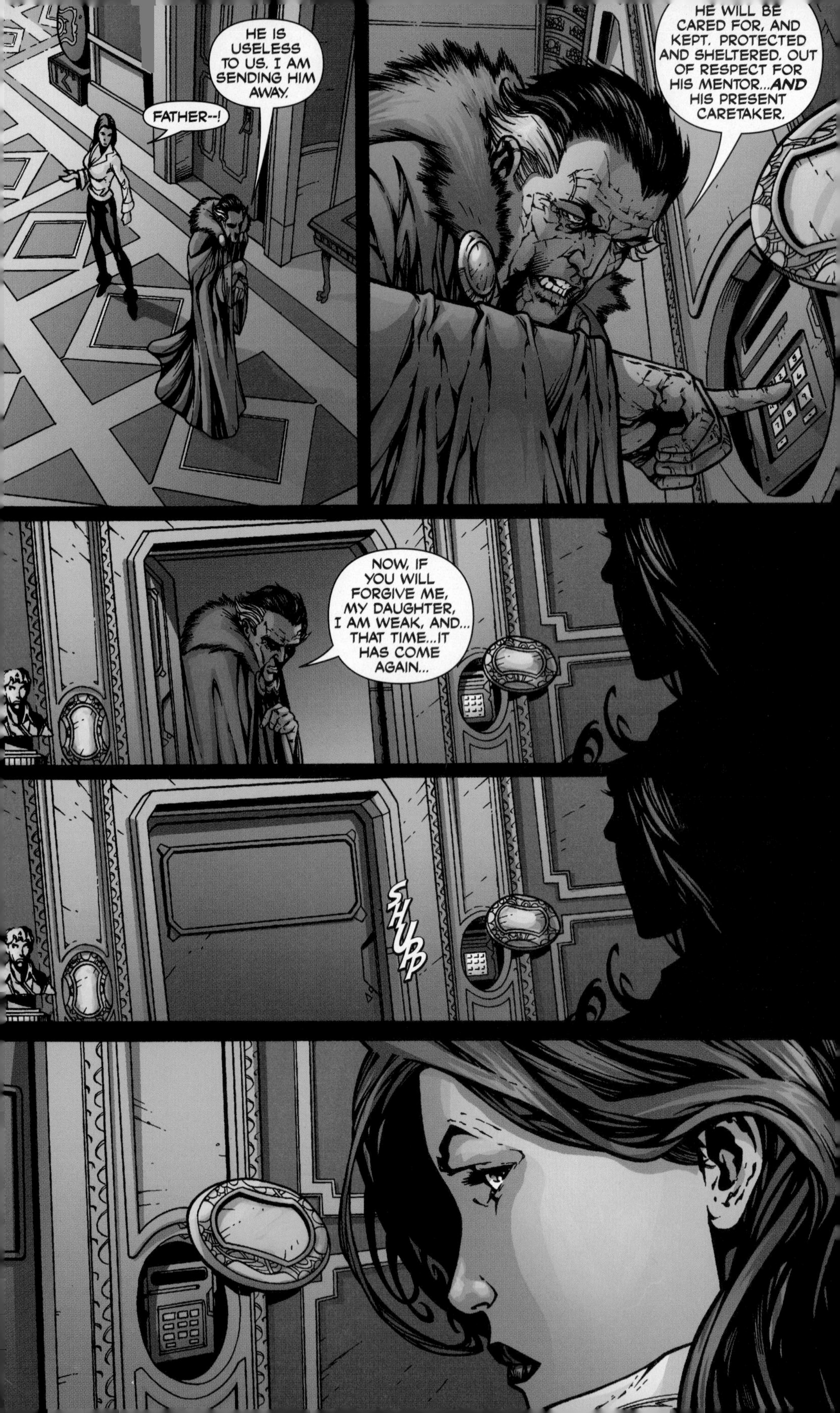
FATHER--!
HE IS USELESS TO US. I AM SENDING HIM AWAY.
HE WILL BE CARED FOR, AND KEPT. PROTECTED AND SHELTERED. OUT OF RESPECT FOR HIS MENTOR...AND HIS PRESENT CARETAKER.
NOW, IF YOU WILL FORGIVE ME, MY DAUGHTER, I AM WEAK, AND... THAT TIME...IT HAS COME AGAIN...
SHUPP

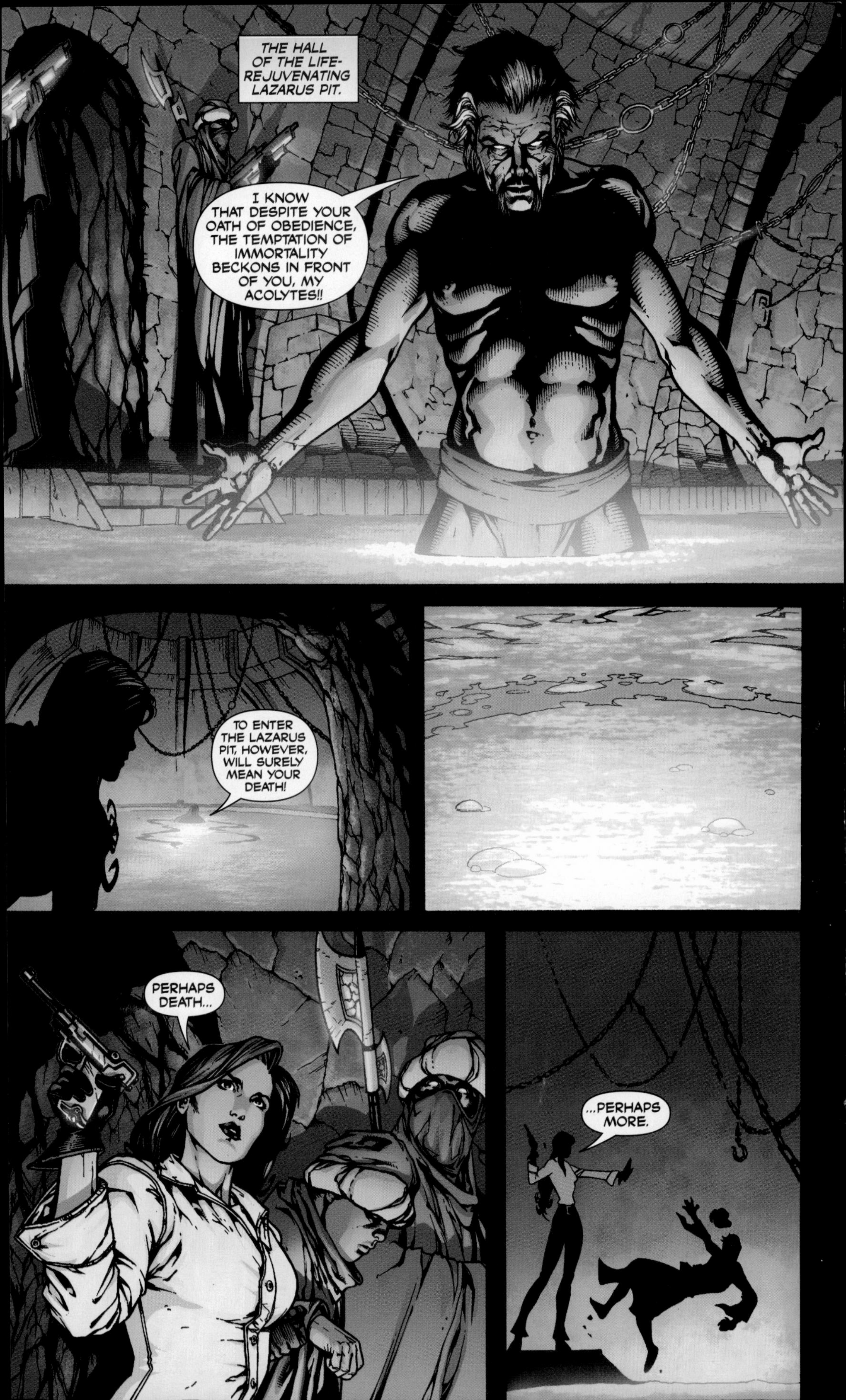
THE HALL OF THE LIFE-REJUVENATING LAZARUS PIT.
I KNOW THAT DESPITE YOUR OATH OF OBEDIENCE, THE TEMPTATION OF IMMORTALITY BECKONS IN FRONT OF YOU, MY ACOLYTES!!
TO ENTER THE LAZARUS PIT, HOWEVER, WILL SURELY MEAN YOUR DEATH!
PERHAPS DEATH...
...PERHAPS MORE.

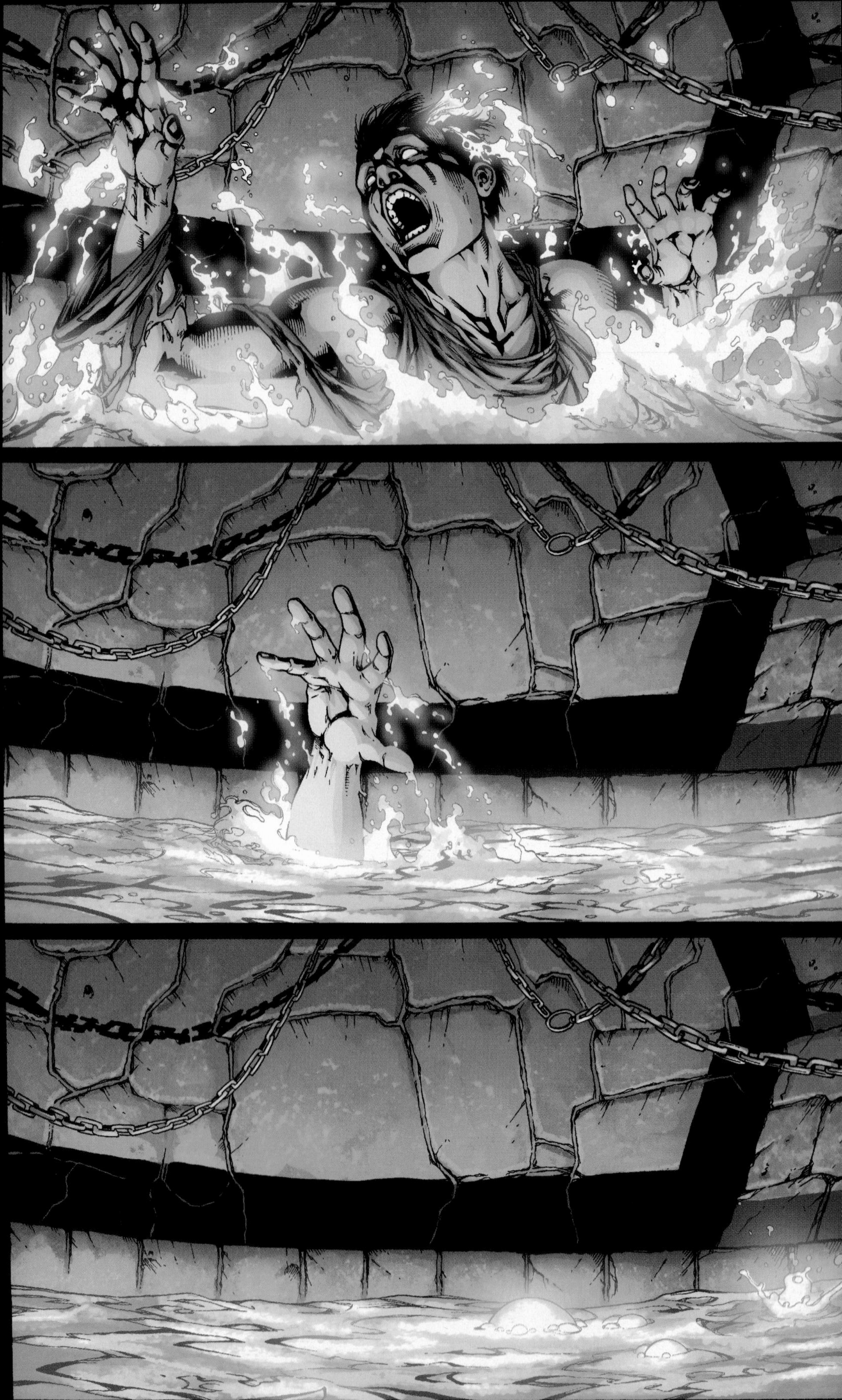

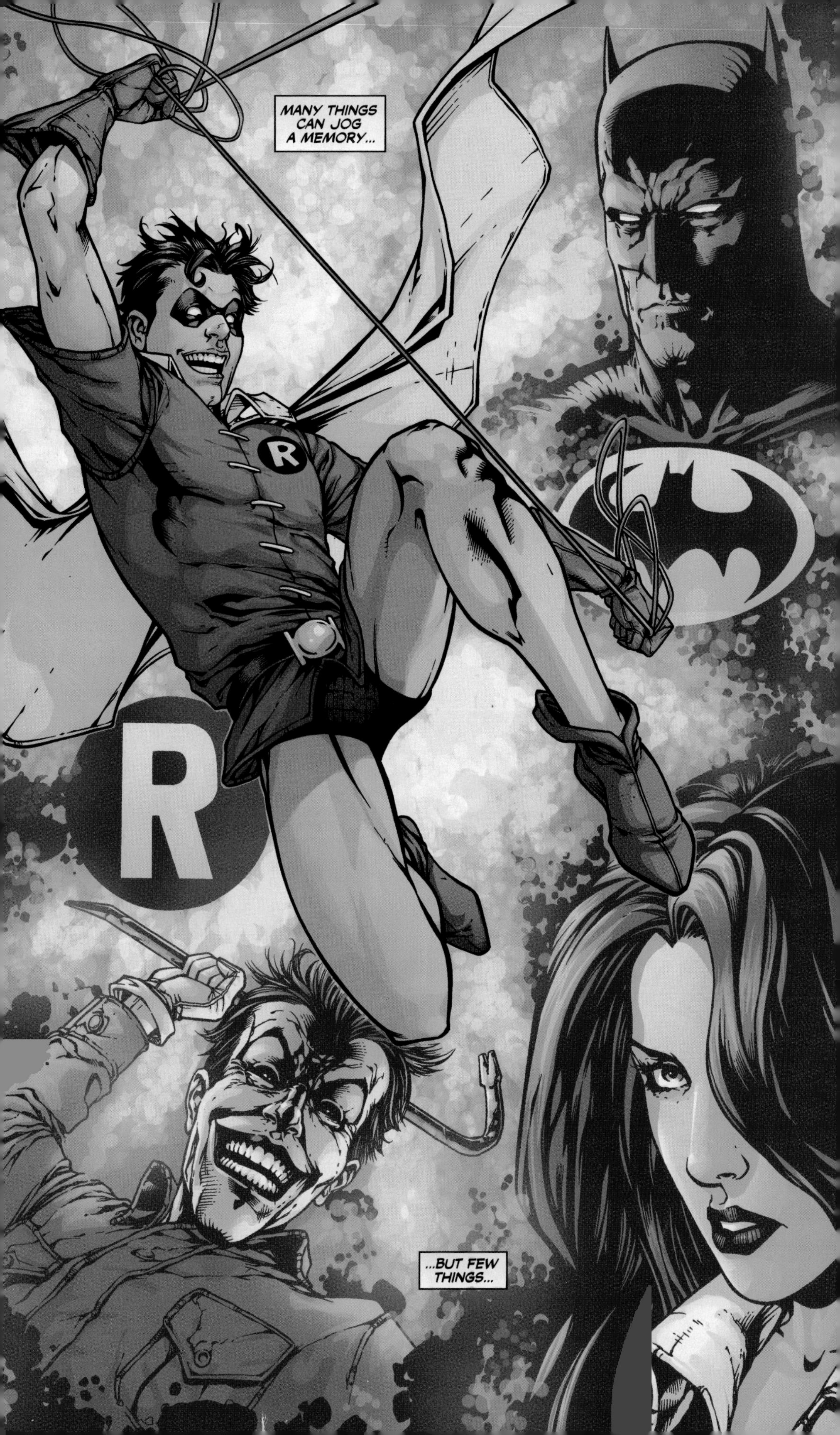
MANY THINGS CAN JOG A MEMORY...
...BUT FEW THINGS...

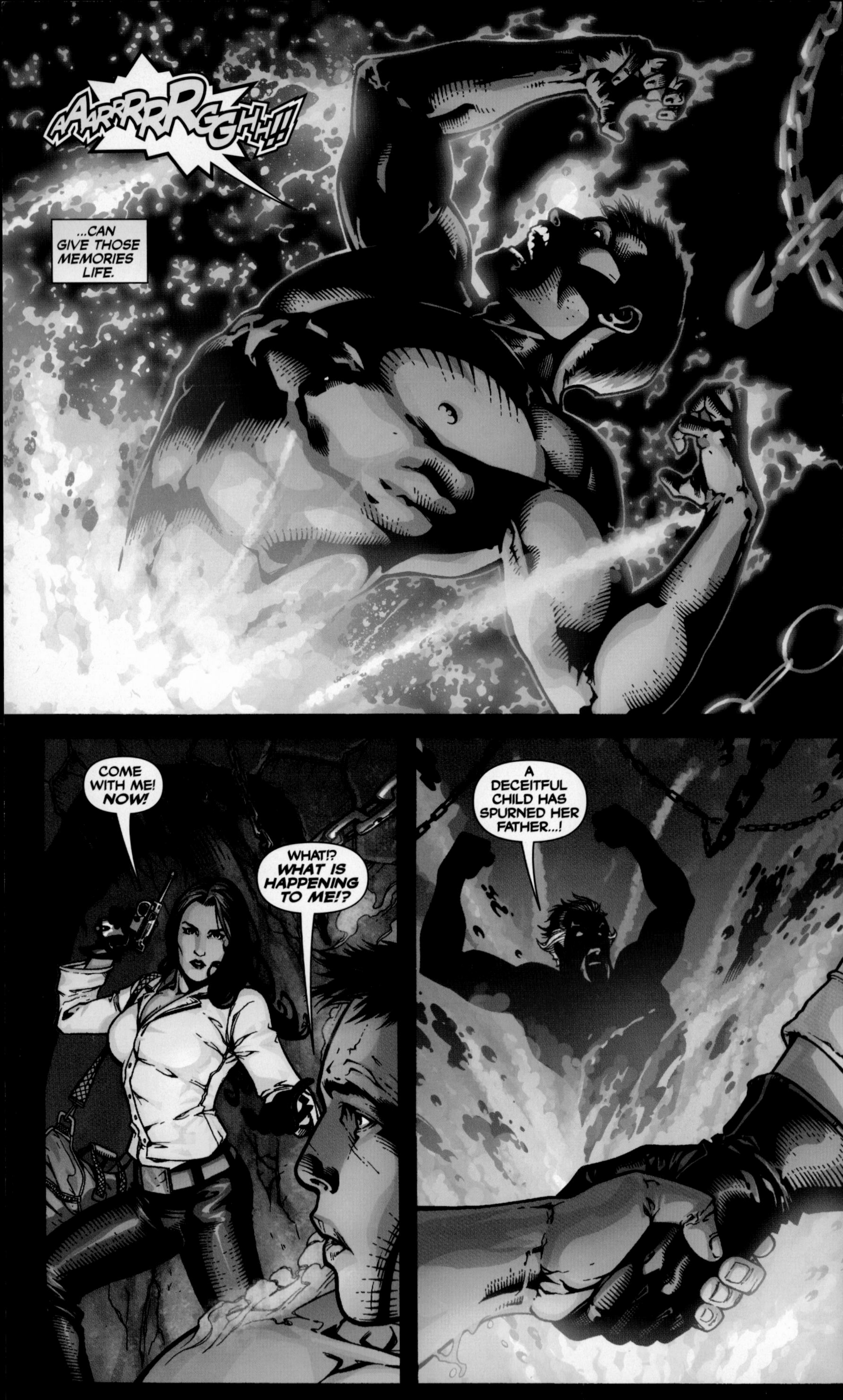
AAARRRRRGGHH!!!
...CAN GIVE THOSE MEMORIES LIFE.
COME WITH ME! NOW!
WHAT!? WHAT IS HAPPENING TO ME!?
A DECEITFUL CHILD HAS SPURNED HER FATHER...!

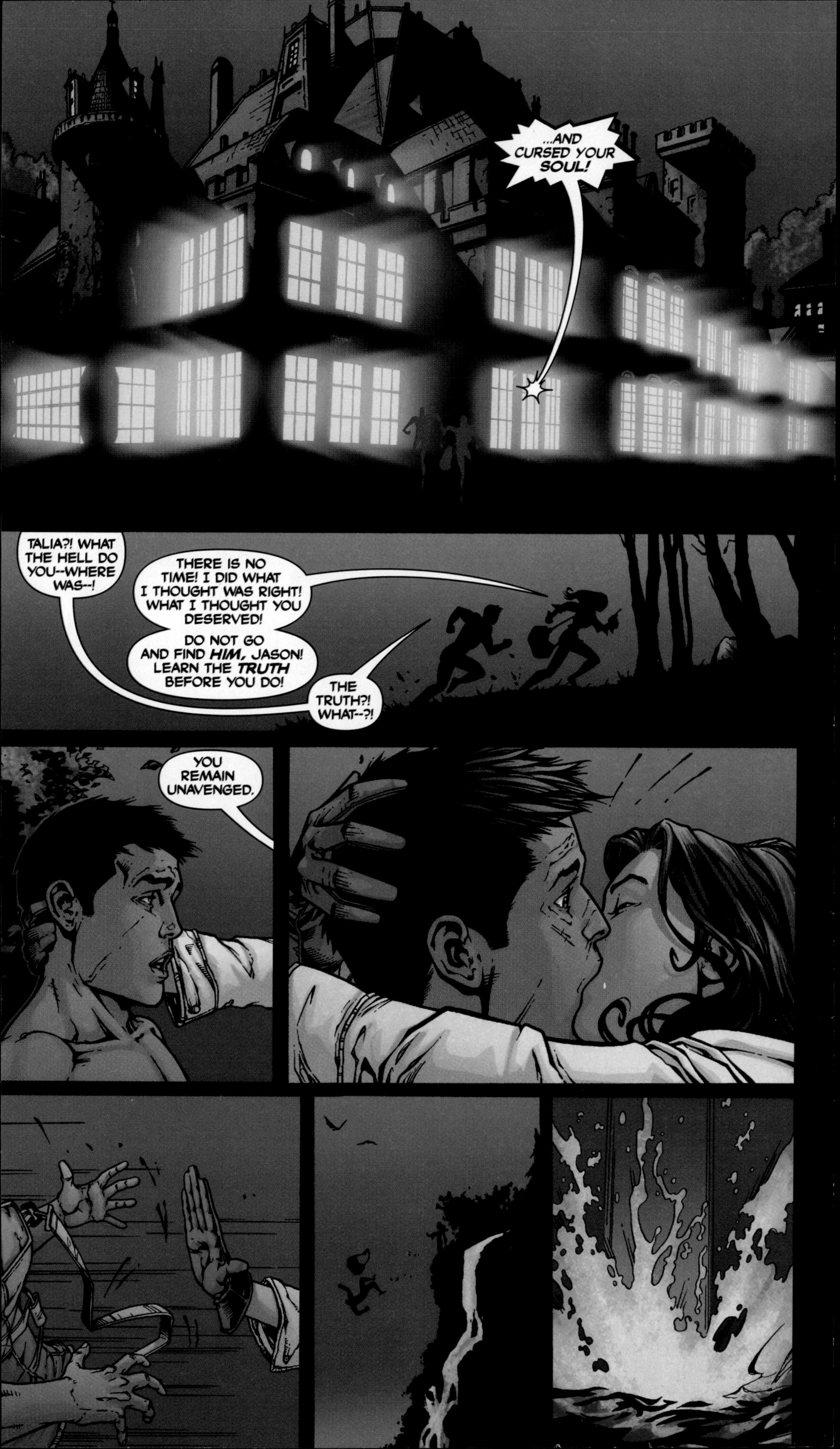
...AND CURSED YOUR SOUL!
TALIA?! WHAT THE HELL DO YOU--WHERE WAS--!
THERE IS NO TIME! I DID WHAT I THOUGHT WAS RIGHT! WHAT I THOUGHT YOU DESERVED!
DO NOT GO AND FIND HIM, JASON! LEARN THE TRUTH BEFORE YOU DO!
THE TRUTH?! WHAT--?!
YOU REMAIN UNAVENGED.

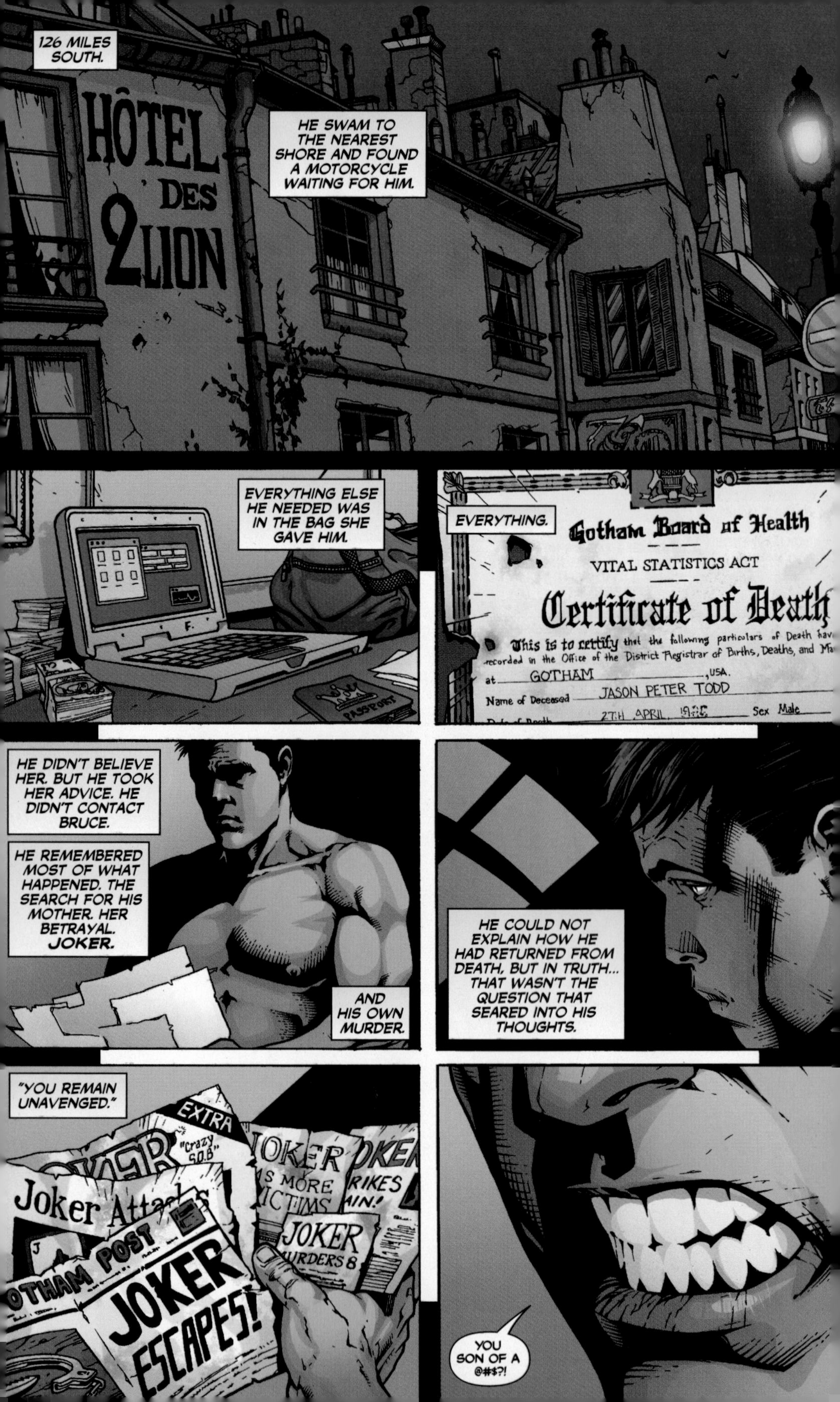
126 MILES SOUTH.
HÔTEL DES 2 LION
HE SWAM TO THE NEAREST SHORE AND FOUND A MOTORCYCLE WAITING FOR HIM.
EVERYTHING ELSE HE NEEDED WAS IN THE BAG SHE GAVE HIM.
PASSPORT
EVERYTHING.
Gotham Board of Health
VITAL STATISTICS ACT
Certificate of Death
This is to certify that the following particulars of Death hav
recorded in the Office of the District Registrar of Births, Deaths, and Ma
at GOTHAM , USA.
Name of Deceased JASON PETER TODD
Sex Male
HE DIDN'T BELIEVE HER. BUT HE TOOK HER ADVICE. HE DIDN'T CONTACT BRUCE.
HE REMEMBERED MOST OF WHAT HAPPENED. THE SEARCH FOR HIS MOTHER. HER BETRAYAL. **JOKER.**
AND HIS OWN MURDER.
HE COULD NOT EXPLAIN HOW HE HAD RETURNED FROM DEATH, BUT IN TRUTH... THAT WASN'T THE QUESTION THAT SEARED INTO HIS THOUGHTS.
"YOU REMAIN UNAVENGED."
EXTRA
"Crazy S.O.B"
Joker Attac
JOKER
S MORE
CTIMS
JOKER
RIKES
AIN!
JOKER
URDERS 8
OTHAM POST
JOKER ESCAPES!
YOU SON OF A @#$?!

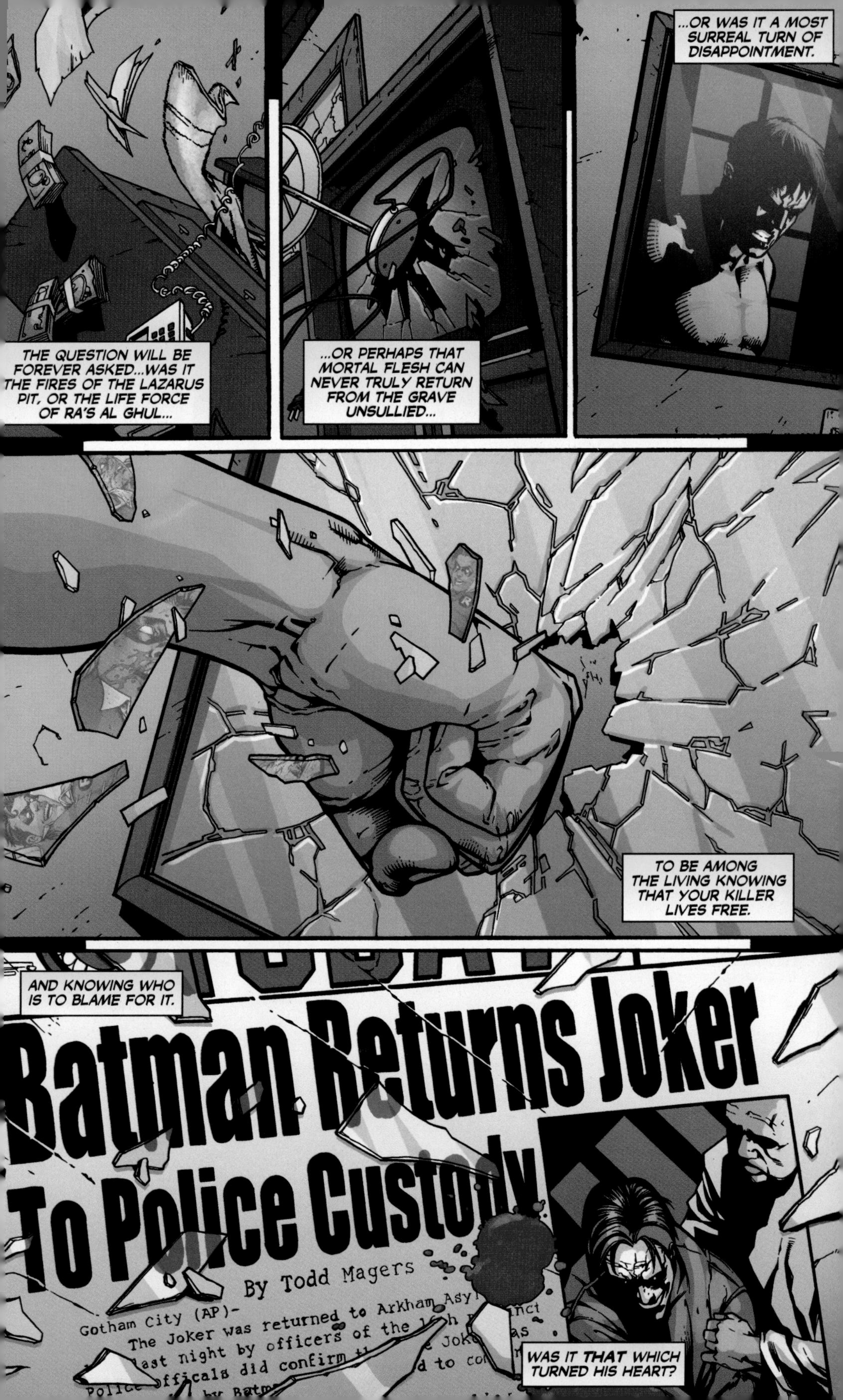
THE QUESTION WILL BE FOREVER ASKED...WAS IT THE FIRES OF THE LAZARUS PIT, OR THE LIFE FORCE OF RA'S AL GHUL...
...OR PERHAPS THAT MORTAL FLESH CAN NEVER TRULY RETURN FROM THE GRAVE UNSULLIED...
...OR WAS IT A MOST SURREAL TURN OF DISAPPOINTMENT.
TO BE AMONG THE LIVING KNOWING THAT YOUR KILLER LIVES FREE.
AND KNOWING WHO IS TO BLAME FOR IT.
Batman Returns Joker
To Police Custody
By Todd Magers
Gotham City (AP)-
WAS IT THAT WHICH TURNED HIS HEART?

THE REST WAS SIMPLE. TAKING IT STEP BY STEP.

LEARN WHAT *HE* LEARNED, BUT MAKING SURE NOT TO WALK IN *HIS* FOOTSTEPS.

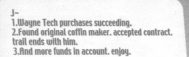

J–
1. Wayne Tech purchases succeeding.
2. Found original coffin maker. accepted contract. trail ends with him.
3. And more funds in account. enjoy.

-T

PS– New business. He is calling himself Hush. You should meet.

AND COVERING HIS TRACKS.

TAKING HELP WHERE IT WOULD COME.

I HEAR YOU'RE "WORKING" BATMAN.

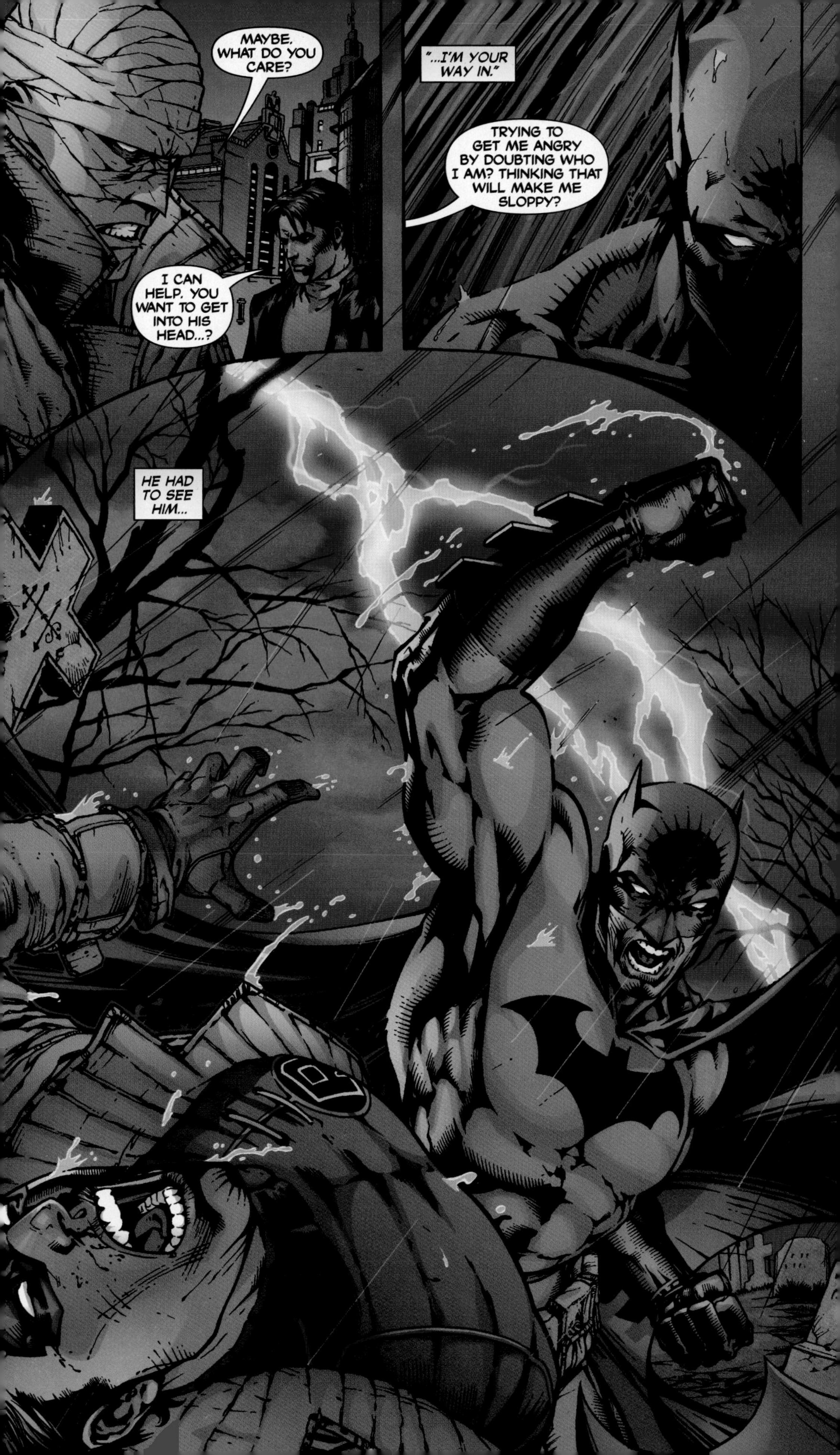
MAYBE. WHAT DO YOU CARE?
I CAN HELP. YOU WANT TO GET INTO HIS HEAD...?
"...I'M YOUR WAY IN."
TRYING TO GET ME ANGRY BY DOUBTING WHO I AM? THINKING THAT WILL MAKE ME SLOPPY?
HE HAD TO SEE HIM...

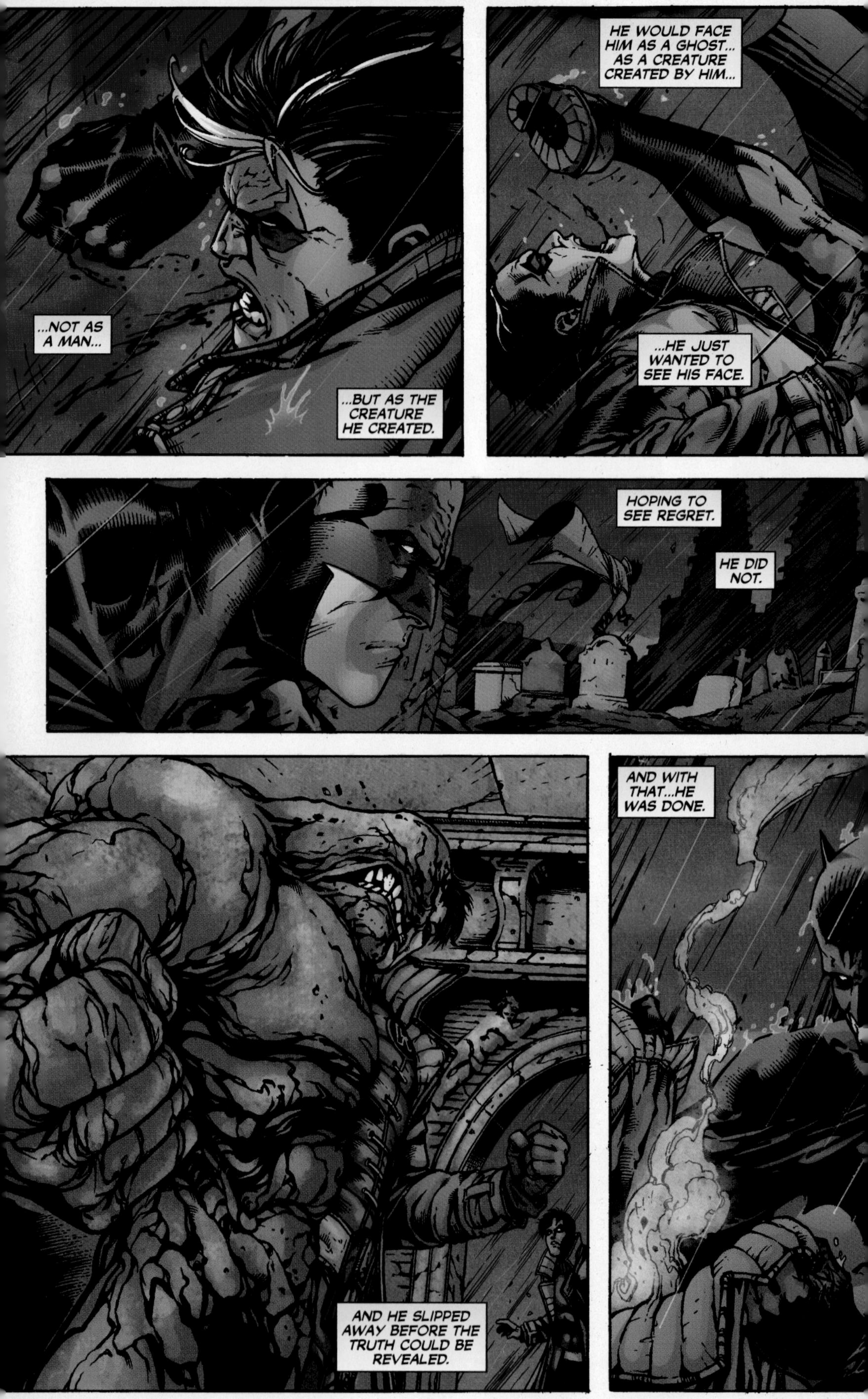
...NOT AS A MAN...
...BUT AS THE CREATURE HE CREATED.
HE WOULD FACE HIM AS A GHOST... AS A CREATURE CREATED BY HIM...
...HE JUST WANTED TO SEE HIS FACE.
HOPING TO SEE REGRET.
HE DID NOT.
AND HE SLIPPED AWAY BEFORE THE TRUTH COULD BE REVEALED.
AND WITH THAT...HE WAS DONE.

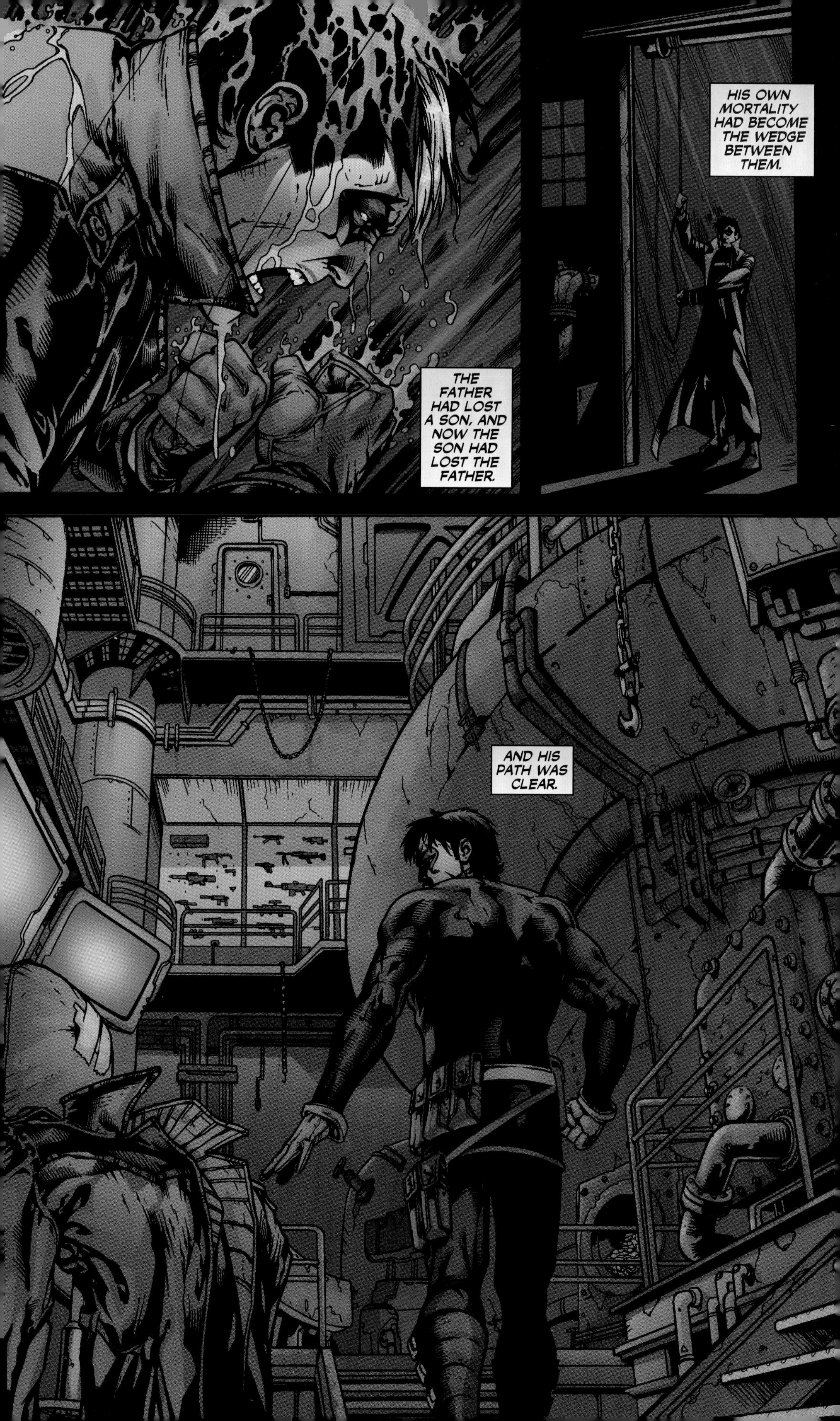
THE FATHER HAD LOST A SON, AND NOW THE SON HAD LOST THE FATHER.
HIS OWN MORTALITY HAD BECOME THE WEDGE BETWEEN THEM.
AND HIS PATH WAS CLEAR.

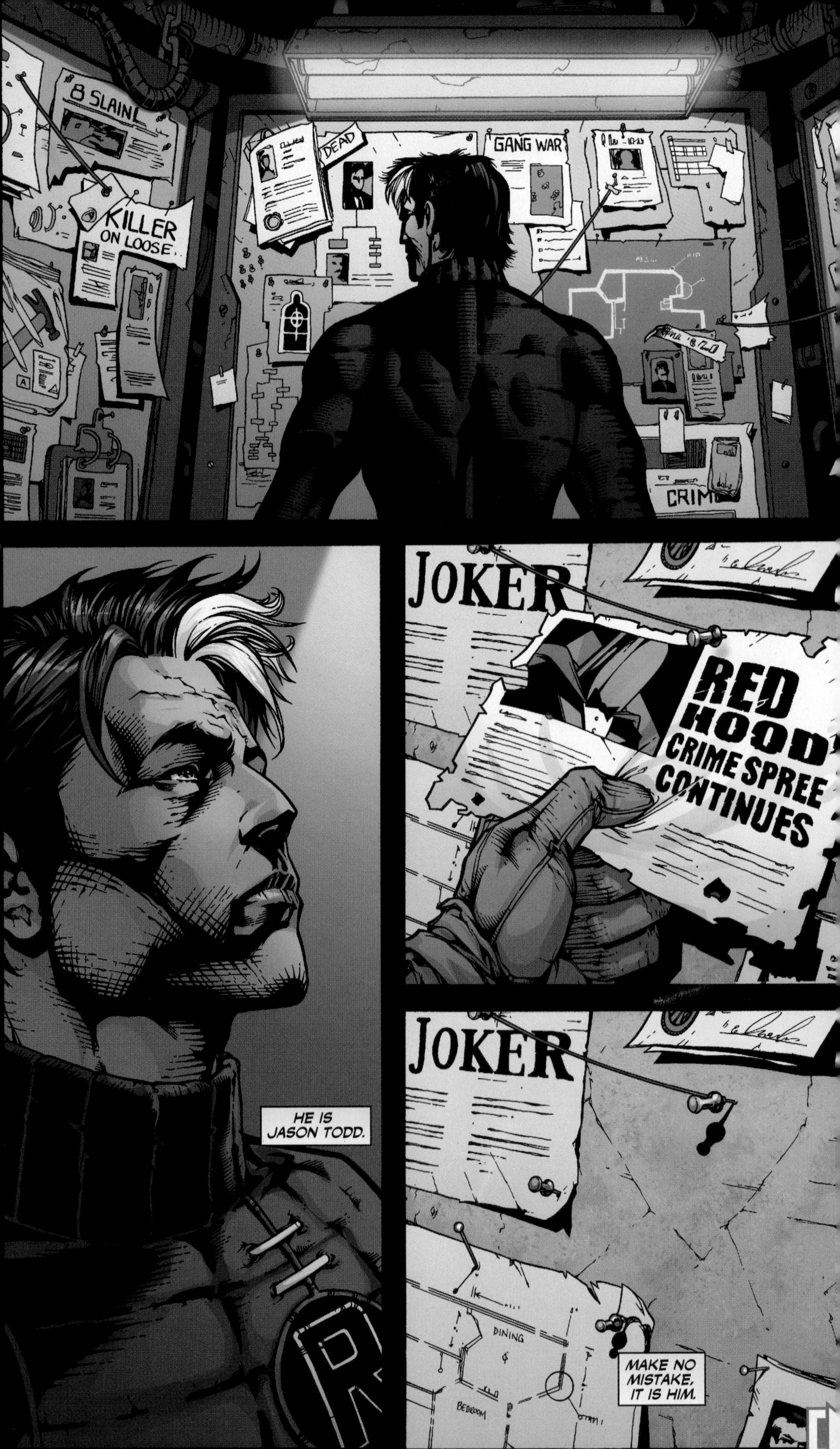
8 SLAIN
KILLER ON LOOSE
DEAD
GANG WAR
CRIM
JOKER
RED HOOD CRIME SPREE CONTINUES
HE IS JASON TODD.
JOKER
DINING
BEDROOM
MAKE NO MISTAKE, IT IS HIM.

...ATMAN:
...USH
...OLUME 1

...h Loeb, Jim Lee and
...ott Williams tell an epic
... of friendship, trust
...d betrayal, in the first
...ume of a tale that
...ns a lifetime of
... Dark Knight.

...NE ACTION IS EXCITING AND THE DETAIL
... METICULOUS."
...CRITIQUES ON INFINITE EARTHS

BATMAN:
...E DARK KNIGHT RETURNS

BATMAN:
THE LONG HALLOWEEN

BATMAN:
YEAR ONE

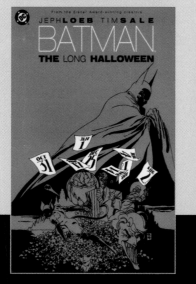

FRANK MILLER

JEPH LOEB

FRANK MILLER

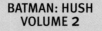